CULTIVATED FRUITS OF BRITAIN

F. A. ROACH

CULTIVATED FRUITS OF BRITAIN
THEIR ORIGIN AND HISTORY

Basil Blackwell

© F. A. Roach, 1985

First published 1985

Basil Blackwell Publisher Ltd
108 Cowley Road, Oxford OX4 1JF, UK

Basil Blackwell Inc.
432 Park Avenue South, Suite 1505,
New York, NY 10016, USA

British Library Cataloguing in Publication Data

Roach, F. A.
   Cultivated fruits of Britain: their origin
   and history.
   1. Fruit-culture—Great Britain—History
   I. Title
   634'.0941   SB354.6.G7
   ISBN 0-631-13969-9

Library of Congress Cataloging in Publication Data

Roach, F. A., 1909—
   Cultivated fruits of Britain.
   Bibliography: p.
   Includes index.
   1. Fruit-culture—Great Britain—History.
2. Fruit—Great Britain—History. 3. Fruit—Great
Britain—Origin. 4. Fruit—History. 5. Fruit—Origin.
I. Title.
SB354.6.G7R63   1985   634'.0941   84-24282
ISBN 0-631-13969-9

Typeset by Pioneer, East Sussex
Printed in Great Britain by
Bell & Bain Ltd., Glasgow

CONTENTS

LIST OF ILLUSTRATIONS

Frontispiece: from Le Régime du corps, French mid-thirteenth century: copyright British Museum, MS Sloane 2435 Addition 19720 305

Mural from Pompeii: copyright Museo Nazionale, Naples

Monastery garden Christchurch, Canterbury: copyright Trinity College Cambridge

Boy stealing apples: copyright British Museum, MS RD 7952877

Cleft grafting fruit trees: copyright British Museum

Girl selling strawberries: copyright Radio Times Library

Covent Garden in the eighteenth century: copyright Tate Gallery

Eighteenth-century instructional sketches, Batty Langley: copyright National Fruit Trials

Street market near Charing Cross: copyright Radio Times Library

Third-century Roman mosaics: copyright National Museum, Paris

Cider or cheese press: copyright British Museum, MS Roy 10 EIV

Monastery cellarer, copyright British Museum, MS Sloane 2435

Pounding apples to make verjuice, copyright British Museum, MS Sloane 2435

Saxon vine dresser, copyright British Museum, MS Cotton Tiberius

Keens' Imperial strawberry: copyright Royal Horticultural Society

Keens' Seedling strawberry: copyright Royal Horticultural Society

Illustrations of varieties of apple, pear, plum, cherry, peach, medlar, quince, strawberry, gooseberry and currants from Batty Langley, 1729: copyright National Fruit Trials

ACKNOWLEDGEMENTS

I wish to thank the Loeb Classical Library (Harvard University Press: William Heinemann) for permission to quote extracts from the Greek and Roman writers. My thanks also go to East Malling Research Station, Long Ashton Research Station and the National Fruit Trials for help in preparing many of the illustrations.

ORIGIN AND EARLY HISTORY

All the fruits cultivated in gardens or used for commercial production have originated from selection, mutation or breeding from species of wild fruits or by hybridization between species. Several genera of fruits are indigenous to Great Britain and their seeds, or other remains, have been found during excavation of sites dating back to the inter-glacial and post-glacial periods. Seeds of the wood strawberry (*Fragaria vesca*), the raspberry (*Rubus idaeus*) and the blackberry (*Rubus fruticosus*) from these periods have been discovered in Scotland and other parts of the British Isles. Of the tree fruits, stones of the sloe (*Prunus spinosa*), the wild cherry (*Prunus avium*) and seeds of the crab apple (*Malus silvestris*) dating from the post-glacial age have also been found.

INFLUENCE OF THE CLIMATE

The occurrence of different wild fruits and their distribution throughout Europe have varied with changes in the climate. In the post-glacial warm period, the forest belts in Europe spread northwards to higher latitudes than they now occupy and there have been fluctuations in the climate, varying from warmer to colder weather than today, which have affected not only the growth of our native plants but also the successful cultivation, during the time of recorded history, of fruits such as the grape vine.

During the Roman occupation of Britain, temperatures seem to have been rather higher but rainfall greater than today, to be followed by several centuries of colder winters and then a warmer period, during and after the Norman Conquest, continuing, with variations, throughout most of the fourteenth century. Throughout this milder period vineyards flourished in

Britain, but at the beginning of the fifteenth century the weather became much colder. During the first half of the century, devastatingly severe winters destroyed many vineyards in Europe, while the production of grapes for wine in Britain, which was already declining as a result of foreign competition, virtually disappeared. There was a temporary return to a warmer climate in Europe from about 1500 to 1540 and then, once again, a long period of lower average temperatures known as the Little Ice Age, with a gradual deterioration in the weather, followed by a slow improvement until fairly recent times.

EARLY USE OF FRUITS FOR FOOD

Excavation of sites of prehistoric dwellings has revealed that many wild fruits were collected for food long before any attempt was made to bring them into cultivation and long before man began to cultivate cereals or other crops. There is evidence that at all periods in man's history fruit has formed an important part of his diet, the collection and storing of berries of many kinds being especially common.

The first cultivators of a few fruits, including the wood strawberry which is indigenous to a wide area of Europe, made use of wild plants collected from the woods and planted in their gardens: this practice continuing over several centuries. With most of the tree fruits, such as apples, pears and cherries, the widely scattered indigenous species, however, are markedly inferior to most cultivated varieties and the distribution of improved and new forms took place gradually over several thousand years.

The origin of most of our temperate tree fruits and vines, and the source from which they spread to other countries, is thought to have been in the Caucasus, Turkestan and adjoining areas. On the northern slopes of the Caucasus, in the foothills and the mountain zone, from Novorossiysk on the Black Sea to the south and south-east, there are entire woods consisting of trees of wild pear (*Pyrus communis*), apples (*Malus silvestris* and *Malus pumila*) and cherry plum (*Prunus cerasifera*). Until fairly recently, fruits of the cherry plum were picked by the natives of Transcaucasia to be cooked and dried and then made into a meal with wheat or barley flour. In other areas, farmers converted pears into a meal to be mixed with barley flour.

In eastern Transcaucasia, in the forests of Azerbaijan, there are vast numbers of wild quince (*Cydonia oblonga*) and, in the same region, especially in Armenia and the adjoining area of Asia Minor in Syria, wild apricots (*Prunus armeniaca*) are found. The cherry plum (*Prunus cerasifera*), the sweet cherry (*Prunus avium*), the medlar (*Mespilus germanica*) and the grape vine (*Vitis vinifera*), although believed to have their origin in Transcaucasia, are found growing wild over a much wider area.

In the forests of Transcaucasia the wild vines twine around the trees of the wild quinces and pears, so that in autumn, when the fruits are ripening, as a Russian scientist Vavilov has said, one might think oneself in the Garden of Paradise. Both black and white forms of grapes occur wild. Their berries are often sour but white types with sweet fruits, sometimes almost identical to cultivated varieties, are found in mid-Asia. This natural habit of grapes to climb round the trunks of trees doubtless influenced Greek and Roman cultivators to use this method as one system of training the plants in their vineyards.

In the foothills of the mountain areas of mid-Asia in Turkestan, there are also forests of fruit trees. In some regions walnuts (*Juglans regia*), as well as apples, form the entire woods, and wild almond trees (*Amygdalus* spp.) constitute large groves in mountain gorges. The area of wild apples is extensive. In the Caucasus the fruits of the wild apple are fairly small, but those of Turkestan are comparatively large. Individual trees there bear fruit which is not inferior in quality to that of cultivated forms. Some are of astonishingly large size and the trees are exceptionally productive. The whole spectrum of transition from the typically small, sour apple to the cultivated, perfectly edible type is found. Among wild apples, *Malus pumila*, with purple—red colouring of the flesh, occurs. Here, the whole process of development from wild apples to acceptable forms, by hybridization between the species accompanied by mutation, took place without the intervention of man.

While *M. pumila* and *M. silvestris* are found in Turkestan, the Siberian forests are full of wild trees of *Malus baccata*, striking for its winter hardiness. The hybridization of *M. baccata*, the Siberian crab, with cultivated varieties has resulted in new apples resistant to low temperatures in the dormant season.

INTRODUCTION OF WILD FORMS INTO CULTIVATION

When clearing forests of fruit trees for the cultivation of cereals, the inhabitants of the Caucasus and Turkestan are known to have spared the trees with the highest quality apples and pears and to have introduced them into their orchards by grafting scions from them onto wild, seedling rootstocks. The very action of selecting the best wild fruits for consumption increases the chances of new seedlings of value arising around the homesteads. In this way a vast reservoir of potential fruits was built up awaiting their distribution to the developing civilized world.

Recorded history shows that the so-called Fertile Crescent, extending from the hills of Persia and south of the Caspian Sea to Turkey and through Palestine to Egypt, was the area where civilization, with its essential basis in agriculture, was first developed. Here, the climate 5000 years ago and earlier was at its best, with sufficient rain to permit the lush growth of many crops and to support an increasing population. Even Egypt had enough rainfall, coupled with the early development of the waters of the Nile for irrigation, to allow the growth of agriculture on a vast scale.

It was into this Fertile Crescent that the warring tribes of the adjoining countries spread. These tribes included those from southern Russia, the people of Caucasia who, by 4000 BC had occupied Persia and extended into parts of Europe. These tribes, used to gathering the wild fruits from their own forests, doubtless took with them dried fruits and seeds into the newly developing region and found that many fruits would grow freely in the favourable conditions existing in Persia and other parts of the Near East. In this way, the best of the apples, pears, cherries and grapes, selected in the forests of Caucasia and elsewhere in the Middle East, gradually spread throughout the Fertile Crescent. The cultivation of many fruits was thus established in this area, and vines were distributed to countries as far distant as Egypt, where the production of wine goes back 5000 or 6000 years.

Although the peach has often been associated by its name, *Prunus persica*, with Persia, it was not in fact indigenous to that country but is known to have existed in a wild state in north China and cultivated there about 2000 BC. It is thought to have been introduced to Persia and Kashmir by travellers carrying fruits or seeds over the mountains along the ancient silk route. It is likely that during one of the expeditions of Alexander the Great, the peach and other fruits were collected and taken back to Greece, so that Theophrastus, the Greek botanist, referred to it in 332 BC, as a Persian fruit.

In view of its position within the Fertile Crescent, it is not surprising that Palestine, the promised land flowing with milk and honey, should have been an important area where fruits were cultivated from early times. The Bible makes frequent reference to figs, vines, pomegranates and other fruits. There was a settlement and village in Jericho by 9000 BC, and the existence of great water tanks, dating from 6000 BC, suggests the use of water for irrigation. Grape seeds from the Early Bronze and Iron Ages have been found in excavations at Jericho, and the fig and grape were mentioned in inscriptions and documents going back to between 4000 and 5000 years ago.

Ancient Greek poets and historians, and later Roman writers, give us written evidence of early fruit production up to the time of the Roman invasion of Britain. Homer provided one of the first accounts of a fruit orchard in his description of the Palace of Alcinous in *The Odyssey*, written during the period 900−800 BC:

> Outside the courtyard, but stretching close up to the gates, and with
> a hedge running down on either side, lies a large orchard of four

acres, where trees hang their greenery on high, the pear and the pomegranate, the apple with its glossy burden, the sweet fig and luxuriant olive. Their fruit never fails nor runs short, winter and summer alike. It comes at all seasons of the year and there is never a time when the West Wind's breath is not assisting, here the bud and here the ripening fruit; so that pear after pear, apple after apple, cluster on cluster of grapes, and fig upon fig are always coming to perfection. In the same enclosure there is a fruitful vineyard, in one part of which is a warm patch of level ground, where some of the grapes are drying in the sun, while others are being gathered or being trodden. The garden is served by two springs, one led in rills to all parts of the enclosure.

In the *Homeric Hymns* of Hesiod, a Greek poet believed to have lived in the eighth century BC, he wrote of vines:

The swallow appears when spring is just beginning. Before she comes, prune the vines for it is best. . . . When Orion and Sirius are come into mid-heaven [September] then cut off all the grape clusters and bring them home. Show them to the sun ten days and ten nights; then cover them over for five, and, on the sixth day, draw off into vessels the gifts of joyful Dionysus.

Dionysus, the son of the god Zeus in Greek mythology, was believed to have introduced the vine. According to the Greek historian, Diodorus Siculus (80–20 BC) 'He made the discovery of wine and taught mankind to cultivate the vine.' Diodorus also said that the Egyptians claimed the same for their god, Osiris (2200 BC), the first of the Pharaohs.

Herodotus, the Greek historian (484–430 BC), wrote extensively of the different countries of the world as he knew it, bounded by the countries of the Mediterranean, the Middle East and parts of India. Writing of the southern Russian region he said, 'Many and all manner of nations dwell in the Caucasus and most of them live on fruits of the wild wood.' And of the people inhabiting the country bordering the eastern side of the Caspian Sea, he wrote, 'In winter they live on fruit they get from trees and store when it is ripe, for food.' This is an area where, for many centuries, plums have been used both in their fresh state and dried, being sold in large quantities by the merchants of Bokkara.

Diodorus described the fertility of the Italian coastal plains bordering the Tyrrhenian Sea:

The land the Tyrrhenians inhabit bears every crop, and from intensive cultivation of it they enjoy no lack of fruits, not only sufficient for their subsistence, but contributing to abundant enjoyment and luxury. For example, twice a day they spread costly tables and upon them everything that is appropriate to excessive luxury, providing gay coloured couches and having ready at hand, a multitude of silver drinking cups of every description and servants in waiting in no small numbers. . . . Not the least of the things which have contributed to their luxury is the fertility of the land; for since it bears every product of the soil and is altogether fertile, the Tyrrhenians lay up great store of every kind of fruit.

This love of fruits by both Greeks and Romans is evident from the writings of a number of their authors at this time. The Greek writer, Theophrastus, wrote of cultivated and wild forms of figs, olives, pears, apples and vines. The Roman, Cato (234—149 BC), wrote extensively of vines, including selection of the site for the vineyard, its planting and the propagation of grapes. Varro (116—27 BC) also wrote of vineyards and wine production, the propagation of pears and apples and the cultivation of mulberries and figs.

The Greeks and Romans were adept in the art of grafting and budding, making use of the best selected varieties which were worked onto rootstocks usually grown from cuttings. The latter were also used, without being grafted, in the propagation of some of their fruits, including grapes. Varro described the storage of apples and the construction of an apple store:

It is thought that all apples keep well in a dry and cool place, laid on straw. For this reason, those who build fruit-houses, are careful to let them have windows facing north and open to the wind; but they have shutters to keep the fruit from shrivelling after losing its juice, when the wind blows steadily. And it is for this reason too — to make it cooler — that they coat the ceilings, walls and floors with marble cement. Some people even spread a dining table in it to dine there; and in fact, luxury allows people to do this in a picture gallery, where the scene is set by nature, in a charming arrangement of fruit. Provided always that you do not follow the example set by some, of buying fruit in Rome and carrying it to the country to pile it up in the fruit-gallery for a dinner party.

Fruits featured in many of the murals which adorned the walls of the villas in Pompeii where recent excavations have shown the existence of vineyards and orchards which supplied fruits to local shops. Evidence of the quality of some of these fruits is seen in a mural illustrating a glass bowl of apples, pears, grapes and pomegranates. These fruits appear as attractive as any we have today. The vineyards on the slopes of Vesuvius were famous for the quality of their wines, some of which were exported to England, before the eruption of the volcano, to supply the Roman forces. This was shown by the discovery of an amphora in the cellar of the military stores depot at

Mural from the walls of the ruins of Pompeii showing a glass bowl containing apples, pears and grapes. The fruits would have been grown in local orchards for sale in Pompeii.

Richborough in Kent which bore a mark indicating that the wine had come from Mount Vesuvius.

Two noted authorities, Pliny and Columella, both of whom lived in Italy in the first century AD, devoted considerable space in their writings to the culture and use of many fruits, some of which had not been given much attention until their time. These included plums and peaches. They also wrote about grapes, quinces, medlars, pomegranates, apples, pears, figs, mulberries, cherries, almonds and walnuts. By this time named varieties of most of these fruits were available. Much of their advice is very sound and could be applied today with little modification.

The Roman love of fruit had made fruit cultivation for market a highly profitable undertaking, provided, as Pliny said, the orchards were growing near to a town where the fruit could be sold. He described the apple as having the highest value among fruits, and said their cultivation in the villages near Rome yielded more profit to the growers than any other form of farming. As he said, 'In the matter of fruit-trees no less marvellous are many of those in the districts surrounding the city, the produce of which in every year is knocked down to bids of 2000 sestences per tree, a single tree yielding a larger return than farms used to do in the old days.'

This practice of auctioning the fruit on the trees is still carried out in some of the Kent orchards, especially with cherries.

ROME AND EUROPE

The Greek geographer, Strabo (64 BC — 25 AD), included much information in his books of the many countries of the Mediterranean area, giving details both of the countries and their crops and exports. Southern Spain was of particular importance for its production of olives, grapes and figs, and Spanish wine was regarded by the Romans as equal to some of the best in Italy. So important was the trade between Spain and Rome that great merchant ships sailed regularly to and from Ostia, the port of Rome.

Strabo also wrote of trade connections with the other countries of Europe, including Britain before the Roman invasion. He described how vessels, even of fairly large size, could be navigated inland up the Rhône and connected with traffic on its tributary the Saône and thence with the Doubs. From this river, the traffic was taken by land as far as the Seine and so to the English Channel. Strabo described four passages regularly used across to Britain, from the mouths of the principal rivers, the Rhine, the Seine, the Loire and the Gironde. However, travellers crossing from the Rhine did not put to sea from the river mouth but from the coast of the Marini near Itium (Calais).

From the Celtic coast, Strabo said, you could put to sea on the ebb tide at nightfall and land upon the coast of Britain at about the eighth hour of the following day — rather like the present-day service from Le Havre to Southampton. This relatively easy communication between the Continent and Great Britain is important when considering the possibilities of the importation of new fruits and plants to Britain. Already there was considerable trade in tin mined in Cornwall which Diodorus described, saying that the tin was traded with merchants who came from Gaul to Ictis (St Michael's Mount), was carried on foot through Gaul for some 30 days and then taken on horseback to the mouth of the Rhone.

Strabo gives the following description of Britain:

> *Most of the island is flat and overgrown with forests, although many of its districts are hilly. It bears grain, cattle, gold, silver and iron. These things accordingly, are exported from the island, as also hides, and slaves, and dogs that are by nature suited to the purpose of the chase.*
>
> *Their habits are simple and barbaric, so much so that, on account of their inexperience, some of them, although well supplied with milk, make no cheese; and they have no experience in gardening or other agricultural pursuits.*

Although Strabo was disparaging about the level of British agriculture, his statement concerning the production and export of grain is supported by the evidence of a fairly extensive Celtic field system in use in pre-Roman Britain, showing that agriculture was well developed, especially in the lowland areas and coastal regions of Kent and Essex where the Belgic tribes from the Continent had settled. Strabo said that the Britons had no knowledge of gardening; it is possible that some attempt to grow fruits near their homesteads was made by the wealthier landowners, but there is no evidence of this.

One of the articles imported by those Britons who could afford it was wine, the usual drinks being beer and mead. Wine was also an important part of the trade between Rome and Gaul, as at this time the cultivation of vines was limited to the warmer parts of the countries bordering the Mediterranean and other countries to its east. Diodorus described this trade:

> *Since Gaul suffers from excessive cold, the land produces neither wine nor oil, and, as a consequence, those Gauls who are deprived of these fruits make a drink out of barley which they call zythos or beer, and they also drink water with which they cleanse their honeycombs. The Gauls are exceedingly addicted to the use of wine which is brought into their country by merchants. Many of the Italian traders, induced by the love of money which characterizes them, believe that the love of wine by these Gauls is their own Godsend. For these transport the wine on navigable rivers by means of boats and through the level plain on waggons, and receive for it an incredible price; for in exchange for a jar of wine, they receive a slave, getting a servant in return for the drink!*

Many slaves were also sent to Rome from Britain, even before the Roman invasion — perhaps in exchange for wine?

As in other countries of Europe, there is evidence from excavation of sites of prehistoric and later dwellings in Britain that the fruits of a number of indigenous wild plants were collected for food. Seeds of the wild raspberry (*Rubus idaeus*), dating from the Early Bronze Age, were found near Stonehenge and also at Shippea Hill, in Cambridgeshire, dating from an even earlier settlement. Blackberry seeds (*Rubus fruticosus*) were found at a Neolithic settlement, at Westward Ho! in Devon, at a Late Bronze Age site at Minnis Bay in Kent and at Iron Age lake village settlements at Glastonbury, Somerset and other sites, indicating a widespread distribution of this fruit.

Seeds of the wood strawberry (*Fragaria vesca*) have been found at a number of ancient sites, while there are numerous records of the discovery of fruits of the sloe (*Prunus spinosa*) on sites dating from the Neolithic, Bronze and Iron Ages. Even seeds of the plum (*Prunus domestica*) have been found at the Late Iron Age site at Maiden Castle in Dorset, where charcoal remains believed to be of the sweet cherry (*Prunus avium*) were also discovered.

Sour cherry remains from the Neolithic and Middle Bronze Ages were found at Notgrove Long Barrow, Gloucestershire and at Haugh Head, Northumberland. Impressions of crab apple pips (*Malus silvestris*) from the Neolithic period have been found on shards excavated at Windmill Hill in Wiltshire, while there is evidence from Europe that apples were dried and stored for food by prehistoric people.

This evidence shows that the fruits of wild plants were collected for food, but there is no indication that any attempt was made to cultivate them at this period. However, increasing trade with the Continent must have brought many people into contact with the cultivation of fruits there and encouraged their culture in Britain, especially following the invasion by Rome.

ROMAN BRITAIN

After the initial resistance and unrest had been overcome, the period of the Roman occupation of Britain, though disturbed by border wars, was a period of increasing prosperity. The British ruling classes often cooperated with the occupying forces, as Tacitus said in his *Agricola*, written in AD 97—98 sometime after his visit to Britain:

> *Agricola [the Roman governor] educated the sons of the chiefs in the liberal arts, and expressed a preference for British ability as compared with the trained skills of the Gauls. The result was that, instead of loathing the Latin language, they became eager to speak it effectively. In the same way, our national dress came into favour and the toga was everywhere to be seen. And so the population was gradually led into demoralizing temptations of arcades, baths, and sumptuous banquets. The unsuspecting Britons spoke of such novelties as 'civilization', when in fact they were only a feature of their enslavement.*

With the growth of an efficient system of roads, farmsteads and settlements were established over most of the country. Large quantities of cereals were grown for the occupying forces, and the wealthier Britons, especially during the third and fourth centuries, adopted the Roman way of building villas and doubtless furnished their gardens with some of the fruits imported from Rome or the other countries of Europe.

The Romans had a policy of establishing colonies of army veterans on special settlements, and two were started at Colchester and Gloucester. The veterans were given an area of land as a smallholding, on which they could grow some of the fruits and vegetables they had been used to having during their service days; records show that fruits formed a regular part of the military diet.

The palace at Fishbourne, built during the first century AD, had a large garden laid out in typical Roman style, and the sites of other villas have yielded a variety of seeds of fruits doubtless grown in their gardens. The account by Tacitus gives us the only recorded evidence of the range of fruits that must have been grown in Britain during his time, including those with which the Romans were familiar in their own country:

> *The climate is wretched, with its frequent rains and mists, but there is no extreme cold. Their day is longer than in our part of the world. . . . The soil will produce good crops, except olives, vines and other plants which usually grow in warmer lands. They are slow to*

ripen, though they shoot up quickly, both facts being due to the same cause, the extreme moistness of the soil and atmosphere.

If fruits such as plums, apples and pears, so popular in Rome, had not been grown in Britain, Tacitus would surely have noted this since he especially picked out vines and olives for mention. There is the account of Diodorus, writing about a hundred years earlier, that vines were not grown in Gaul. The remark of Tacitus, that the weather was mild but excessively wet, is supported by research which has shown that during the time of the Roman occupation the levels of peat increased progressively as a result of high rainfall.

CULTIVATION OF VINES AND TREE FRUITS

There is evidence from the discovery of grape seeds at a number of sites, including Silchester, Gloucester, York, Doncaster and London, that vines were probably planted in villa gardens. However, it is unlikely that vineyards were planted to any extent during the early years of the Roman occupation for several reasons including the unsuitability of the climate in Britain and northern Europe, remarked upon by Tacitus and Diodorus.

The other major factor affecting the planting of vineyards was the edict of the Emperor Domitian (81 – 96 AD) forbidding the planting of new vineyards in Italy and reducing the acreage of those in the Provinces at least by half if not completely. The Roman writer Suetonius (born 64 AD), in his book *The Twelve Caesars*, said that when a bumper vintage in Europe followed a poor grain harvest the Emperor concluded that the cornlands were being neglected in favour of the vineyards. However, Suetonius added that Domitian took no steps to implement his edict. Two hundred years later, in 280 AD, the Emperor Probus issued an edict permitting the cultivation of grapes in Gaul, Spain and Britain; in fact, he seemed to be encouraging their cultivation.

Following the edict of Probus, there is some evidence that an experimental vineyard was planted at North Thoresby in Lincolnshire but this seems to have been short lived. However, even though there may have been no widespread planting of vines in Britain, it is likely that some of the early settlers, used to growing their own grapes in Italy, would have tried growing vines in their villa gardens. Whether grapes were grown or not, the Romans and the wealthier Britons still relied on imported wines to satisfy their own needs and those of the Roman forces who were given an allocation of wine in their rations.

The seeds of the apple, *Malus silvestris*, found on Roman sites, could have come from wild fruits collected locally but, in view of the great popularity of apples among the Romans in their own country, it seems likely that some of their numerous varieties must have been tried by Roman gardeners in Britain, and perhaps grown commercially on farms. The discovery of pruning hooks at Darenth and Hartlip in Kent suggests that they were used for pruning fruit trees, and it is likely that the first of the famous Kent orchards was planted during the Roman occupation. Kent, with its ready access to the Continent by boat from Dover to the French coast and the development of a road system linking the port with the rest of the country, was favourably situated for such developments.

According to Pliny, cherries had been imported into Britain in 46 AD, and seeds of both the sweet cherry (*Prunus avium*) and the acid cherry (*P. cerasus*) have been found during excavation of Roman sites, though it is impossible to say if these were of cultivated varieties. Seeds of various other *Prunus* species, the sloe (*P. spinosa*), the bullace (*P. institia*) and the domestic plum (*P. domestica*), found at Silchester could have been from indigenous plants or, in the case of the domestic plum, from imported varieties.

The mulberry seeds (*Morus nigra*), found at Silchester, must have come from imported plants as this fruit is not indigenous in Britain but was commonly grown in Italy at this time as was the medlar (*Mespilus germanica*). It is likely that the sweet chestnut and the walnut were also imported.

SOFT FRUITS

There is no evidence that any of the soft fruits were ever cultivated by the Romans in Italy before the invasion of Britain, although there is some reference to wild blackberries, strawberries and raspberries in the books and poems of the classical writers. The blackberry was mentioned by the Greek writer Theophrastus in 370 BC, and this berry, together with wild cherries and strawberries, was described by Ovid as being collected for food in his account of the Golden Age. Pliny made several references to the blackberry from which, he said, men learnt the method of layering plants, while he wrote of the medicinal value of the berries for treating inflamed tonsils and gums. Blackberries and their juice were recommended for infections of the mouth and eyes by herbalists as late as the sixteenth century.

The wood strawberry (*Fragaria vesca*) was known to both the ancient Greeks and Romans but was not cultivated by them, though there is evidence from Virgil, Ovid and Pliny that the berries were sometimes collected for food.

The wild raspberry (*Rubus idaeus*) was also known to the Greeks and Romans but was not apparently used for food, although Pliny recommended using the blossoms, mixed with honey, for making an ointment for sore eyes and erysipelas, a practice also advised by herbalists in Tudor times. The Roman author, Palladius, writing in the fourth century, mentioned the raspberry as being cultivated at that time, but there is no other evidence of their cultivation then or until many centuries later.

Red, white and black currants and gooseberries seem to have been unknown to Greek and Roman writers. The fact that these species of *Ribes* were native to more northern regions and that the fruits of the wild plants were small and unattractive meant that they would not be likely to attract the attention of the Romans who saw them growing in other countries. For many centuries the black currant was thoroughly disliked on account of its strong smell and flavour. In any case, the Greeks and Romans had so many exotic fruits, including peaches, grapes, apples and pears, freely available. However, there is evidence that during the Roman occupation of Britain both wild strawberries and blackberries were collected as food by them. Seeds of *Fragaria vesca* and *Rubus fruticosus* have been excavated from the Roman site at Silchester and from the Roman fort at Newstead, near Melrose, while blackberry seeds have been found at the fort at Caerws in Wales. A number of other Roman sites on the south coast and in London have also yielded blackberry seeds.

Even before the end of the Roman occupation of Britain, the country suffered from increasing invasions by tribes from the north and, following the withdrawal of the Roman legions in 410 AD, there were major attacks by the Jutes, Saxons and, later, the Danes. Many of the earlier battles were fought in Kent so that it is likely that any orchards which may have been established in that area quickly suffered devastation. The ensuing unrest and warfare was not conducive to the further development of fruit growing in Kent or in many other parts of the country.

Little is known of the state of the country at the beginning of the Dark Ages, but by 450 AD civilized life in most towns had probably disappeared. The Venerable Bede in his *History of the English Nation Church and People* wrote, in AD 731, that the island formerly had 28 noble cities which had been destroyed. The breakdown in organized life meant that people became destitute, short of food and resorted to living in the woods and hunting wild animals. Under these conditions, it is unlikely that most people had any fruit except that picked from wild plants, though trees and seedlings from some of the fruits imported during the Roman occupation probably existed in abandoned gardens and the adjoining countryside.

INFLUENCE OF THE MONASTERIES

Christianity had reached Britain not later than AD 200 and became the official religion of the Roman Empire in the fourth century but, following the withdrawal of the Romans, Britain was taken over by pagans, and only remnants of Christian communities were left in isolated pockets in the west and north. The arrival of St Augustine in Kent in AD 597 not only brought back the Christian religion but also restored contact with civilization in southern Europe which had lapsed during the troubled times of the fifth and sixth centuries.

Augustine built the first monastery at Canterbury in AD 602 and, by 674, monasteries existed in other parts of the country, including Scotland. It was the establishment of the monasteries which, during the following centuries and especially after the Norman Conquest, greatly influenced the development of horticulture and fruit growing in Britain. The early monasteries established in the seventh century included men and women and their families. An example of such a monastery was that founded by Bishop Wilfrid at Selsey in AD 681 on 87 hides of land given to them by King Ethelwalh. These communities endeavoured to be self-sufficient. The priests and monks often became keen gardeners and though their gardens at first probably contained mainly herbs, their contacts with the monasteries on the Continent would enable them to exchange ideas and bring over plants being grown there.

When Bede wrote in AD 731, it was obvious that agriculture and horticulture in Britain had made considerable recovery:

> *Britain excels for grain and trees, and is well adapted for feeding cattle and beasts of burden. It also produces vines in some places . . . Ireland, in breadth, and for wholesomeness and serenity of climate, far surpasses Britain; for the snow scarcely ever lies there above three days . . . the island abounds in milk and honey, nor is there any want of vines, fish or fowl.*

The fact that Bede specifically mentions vines, which require a certain amount of expertise in their cultivation, shows that knowledge of horticulture and fruit growing must have made considerable advances in Britain as it had also on the Continent by the time of Charlemagne, the ruler of the Frankish kingdom who was crowned as the first Holy Roman Emperor in AD 800. Charlemagne showed interest in growing grapes for wine and brought stocks of these from Spain, Italy, Burgundy, Lorraine and Hungary for planting vineyards at his palace at Ingleheim in Germany.

About, or soon after, his crowning as Emperor, a list of plants appeared in one of the laws he introduced, the *Capitulare de Villis,* relating to the management of towns, which laid down that the crown lands in every city of the Empire should have a garden planted with herbs and fruits. The list of fruits included apples, pears, plums, peaches, quince, figs, cherries, medlars, service tree berries, chestnuts, hazel nuts, walnuts and almonds.

Charlemagne's list of plants is evidence of the interest which was being taken in the cultivation of fruits over a large part of Europe — his empire extended throughout France, Belgium, Holland, Switzerland, parts of Germany and Austria, half of Italy and part of Spain. It is worth speculating whether these developments in Europe had any influence in Britain, where at this time Egbert was King of Wessex. Egbert had been a refugee at the court of Charlemagne from 787 to 802 when he returned to England to become King of Wessex and, by 827, after a series of campaigns, king of much of the country from Devon and Cornwall to Kent, East Anglia, Wales and Northumbria. Egbert had become a friend of Charlemagne and had learnt statesmanship from him; for much of his reign there was relative peace in his kingdom. This would have favoured the extension of the planting of vineyards and perhaps other fruits which Egbert would have seen during his travels on the Continent.

That vineyards must have been relatively common during the ninth century is shown by one of the laws of Alfred the Great (AD 849−99), who was a grandson of Egbert. This law decreed that anyone who damaged the vineyard or field of another should pay compensation. Alfred, like his grandfather, had travelled extensively in Europe and stayed at the Frankish court. His stepmother was a Frank and had a major influence on the education of her stepson. She, like Alfred and his grandfather, would have been aware of the horticultural developments in Europe at this time.

THE VINEYARDS AT ELY

Many of the monasteries established in the seventh and eighth centuries suffered severely during repeated attacks by invaders, especially the Danes. By the 880s, when Alfred had restored peace to the country, nearly all the monasteries in England had either been destroyed or reduced to small communities of a few monks or secular priests. However, although the number of monks and nuns was pathetically small, the monasteries still had their lands and some of their buildings and were able to develop later on this basis.

After his successful campaigns, Alfred and his followers formed a close alliance with the church, and his grandson, Edmund (940−6), did much to help reconstruct the monasteries. Dunstan was restored by 943 and the Benedictine monks re-established Glastonbury. Within 50 years the monasteries in Britain had been brought back to full life.

Further Viking expeditions towards the end of the tenth century, before the establishment of Canute as king, led to the destruction of a number of monasteries but the majority continued to flourish and by the mid-eleventh century, on the eve of the Norman Conquest, England had about 50 monasteries and 12 nunneries in possession of one-sixth of the land of the country.

One of the earliest references to the cultivation of fruits before the Conquest was to those in the gardens attached to the monastery at Ely which was later to become famous for its vineyards. This house of monks and nuns had been founded about 679 by Etheldreda, who became the first abbess. The monastery was one of those devastated by the Danes but was refounded by St Aethelwold in 972 when Brithnot, the first Abbot of Ely, was responsible for establishing orchards and a nursery of various fruits. By 1108, when the estates of the abbey were divided up to endow the newly formed bishopric, the monastic vineyard which lay on the east-facing slopes was retained by the cathedral priory, which had succeeded the abbey, and a new vineyard was made for the bishops. Later references showed that the vineyards were still in existence in 1251, but soon after this time they seem to have been replaced by orchards.

St Aethelwold also built a church at Thorney in Cambridgeshire which was surrounded by trees of various kinds. It was later described as being encircled by apple trees and vines, some of the latter trailing on the ground and others supported on poles, the whole area resembling Paradise.

King Edwy, a great-grandson of Alfred (955—9) granted the vineyard at Pathensburgh to the monks at the newly restored Glastonbury Abbey. This abbey was, for many centuries, associated with fruit growing.

FRUIT GROWING AFTER THE NORMAN CONQUEST

Although at the time of the Norman Conquest in 1066, Britain already had one of the most civilized and successful societies in Europe, the arrival of William the Conqueror resulted in considerable changes, not only in the government of the country but also in the life of the rural communities, affecting both agriculture and fruit production.

William's followers became the new ruling class in Britain — the earls, barons and knights who were given land by the king and who ruled the country, first from their wooden and earth castles and later from ones made of stone. The king retained the ultimate ownership of all lands held by the manors and also held large royal estates. One of his most significant actions, however, was to replace the English bishops and abbots by Normans and Frenchmen. By 1100, the English monasteries were ruled by French-speaking foreigners.

The monasteries were responsible not only for developing their adjoining property, but also for farming the extensive lands which the kings, both before and after the Conquest, had allocated to them. In Kent in 1086 the *Domesday Book* valuation of the land owned by Christ Church and St Augustine's priories at Canterbury showed that, together, they possessed almost half the county. The monks were progressive farmers and, from 1150, the monasteries pursued a policy of bringing as much land as possible under the plough. They cleared the forests, which at this time covered much of the land, increased crops by manuring, used rotations, grew wheat instead of barley and oats and grew vegetables. Food crops were grown for sale rather than just for the use of the monasteries as in the past. Large amounts of wheat were grown for sale and the production of wool became a major industry.

After the initial unsettled period, two of the principal developments in fruit growing following the Conquest were the use of apples for making cider, together with the planting of orchards for this purpose, and an extension in the planting of vineyards for wine. As before, it was the monasteries, initially those under the Benedictine order, who were the chief innovators. Before the Conquest, the principal drink of the monks had been ale or beer, supplemented when it was available by wine. This might be either produced in their own vineyards or imported from the Continent. The earliest picture of a monastery garden, with its orchard and vineyard, is part of a plan of Christ Church, Canterbury, made about 1165. The *pomerium* included in the plan would normally consist of apples and pears for eating raw or cooking and apples for cider.

While the monasteries began by growing apples and making cider for their own use, they often sold any surplus. In 1275, the cellerar's roll for Battle Abbey in Sussex recorded the sale of cider. At this time, it seems, cider was made in areas of England where the climate would not be considered very suitable today. For example, in his accounts for 1282, the bailiff at Cowick, near Richmond in Yorkshire said he had made 60 gallons of cider from three-quarters and a half of apples. The climate at the time of the Conquest, and for about 250 years after, was rather milder than during later centuries or today.

The milder weather also favoured the planting of vineyards in Britain.

Part of the plan of the garden of Christ Church monastery, Canterbury,
from a MS circa 1165, bound up with the Great Psalter of Eadwin
in the library of Trinity College, Cambridge.

Their planting had been fairly widespread before the arrival of the Normans, and *Domesday Book* recorded 38 vineyards in counties throughout the south and west of England and as far north as the Midlands. Gloucestershire was famous for its vineyards by 1125 and, even earlier, according to the Malmesbury Chronicle, the first vineyard was planted on the southern slopes adjoining the monastery in Wiltshire by a Greek monk who joined the monastery about 1084.

Many of the new Norman lords of the manors brought with them their own workers, skilled in the art of viticulture and wine production, while the newly arrived monks often had experience of grape culture. Although the period from the Conquest to the early fourteenth century was probably the most favourable in British history for the production of wine, and the early cultivators of vineyards took full advantage of favourable sites, such as south-facing slopes, there were years when the grapes did not ripen satisfactorily and were only fit for making into verjuice and vinegar. This happened progressively as the climate deteriorated after the fourteenth century. Although home-produced wine supplemented that drunk by the Court, the ruling classes and the monks, it was rarely sufficient to provide all their needs and much reliance was still placed on wine imported from France.

In the Middle Ages, wine was also made from mulberries and various wild fruits, including blackberries and elderberries, and a wide range of herbs was used for special purposes. According to Gerald of Wales, mulberries were used for wines at Canterbury Cathedral Priory in the twelfth century; and it is recorded that in the late thirteenth century, sweet blackberry wine was added to that made from grapes at the manors of Teynham and North Fleet belonging to the Archbishop of Canterbury. East Kent had been famous for its vineyards at the time of the *Domesday* survey, and those developed by the archbishops and the clergy during the twelfth to fourteenth centuries were some of the best in the country. Apart from Gloucestershire, Worcestershire and Herefordshire, other important areas for wine production were East Anglia and the Fenlands.

NEW VARIETIES OF FRUITS

Following the Norman Conquest, new varieties of fruits were imported from the Continent and these, together with the best of the selected native varieties, were used for planting the new orchards and gardens. Two English apples, first recorded in the thirteenth century and grown extensively, were the Pearmain and the Costard. The Pearmain was one of the main varieties grown for over 500 years and was noted for its quality for eating and for making cider.

A number of thirteenth-century accounts show that scions of apples and pears and their rootstocks were bought and sold; these accounts often related to purchases for the royal estates. The wife of Henry III, Eleanor of Provence, was a keen gardener like her husband and, having been accustomed to the pears grown in France, had the French variety, Caillhou, planted in the gardens at Westminster and the Tower. The first wife of Edward I, Eleanor of Castille, developed a new garden at Kings Langley in Hertfordshire and had it planted with vines and fruit trees. In 1280, the accounts showed that she bought grafts of the Blandurel apple. Her gardener had come over from Aragon and so the apple was probably Haut-Bonte, synonymous with Reinette Grise, also called Blandulalie, which originated at Poitu and was known in 1200. In 1275 Edward I bought peach trees to be planted in the Tower gardens, the slopes of Tower Hill being terraced and planted with vines and fruit trees. These and the gardens at Westminster Palace were the most important of the royal gardens. At Westminster, nuts, quinces, peaches, cherries and gooseberries were among the fruits grown.

In addition to the royal family, many of the aristocracy and bishops who had properties in London developed gardens famed for their fruits, two of the most important being those of the Earl of Lincoln in Holborn and the Bishop of Ely in Ely Place. The Earl of Lincoln sent to the Continent for new apples and pears. He grew apples, pears, walnuts and cherries and had one of the most productive vineyards in London. His gardener sold both surplus fruits and plants. In the gardens of Westminster Abbey apples, pears, cherries, plums nuts and medlars were grown.

Cultivated varieties of cherries, which had, according to Pliny, been brought to England by the Romans, but may have disappeared in the Dark Ages, were a very popular fruit in the Middle Ages and the *ciris beam*, or cherry tree, was regularly grown in the gardens and orchards of the monasteries and manors. Wild cherries were also gathered and sold. At Norwich Priory, besides the *pomerium*, the appleyard or orchard, there was a *cherruzed* or *orto cersor*, the cherry garden. At Ely in 1302, the records of sales from the vineyard planted in the garden of the bishop show that cherry trees were also growing there: 'Of 20d from cherries in the vineyard sold'.

Confirmation that cherries were popular is given in the poem, *Piers Plowman*, by William Langland of Malvern. In this, in 1362, he wrote that the poorer classes were living chiefly on vegetables but also ate baked apples and cherries. The 'cherrytime', coming at the height of the summer, was a time for merry-making, 'the cherry feast'.

In his translation of the *Roman de la Rose* in 1372, Chaucer also spoke of cherries, together with peaches, quinces, apples, pears, plums, medlars and chestnuts, being grown in the garden. These and other references show that all the tree fruits which had been grown in Italy by the Romans at the time of their invasion of Britain were now being grown in Britain. Some of them had probably existed from the time of the occupation but many would have been re-introduced, either before or after the Conquest, in particular the improved varieties which had then become available.

Pears were much planted in medieval orchards and gardens and new varieties were often brought over from the La Rochelle area of France, noted for its pears. These pears, like those grown by the Romans, were generally hard and mostly used for cooking, the Warden variety being traditionally used for baking. Other pears were used for making jams and other preserves. Forms of wild pears, some of which were natives of Europe, were not only hard, but often had an especially unpleasant, stringent taste and so were unsuitable for any form of cooking but were made into perry, the fermented juice of pears. This was produced on a much smaller scale than cider and might be mixed with cheap ale.

Nuts of various types were sold in the markets, including hazel nuts collected in the countryside and 'great nuts' or walnuts, which were valued for their oil, used both in cooking and cosmetics. Walnut wood was also a valuable commodity.

The peach was one of the fruits which were grown more commonly in the gardens of the wealthy in the past than they are today. King John was reported in one of the chronicles of Roger of Wendover to have died in 1216 from dysentery brought on by eating a surfeit of peaches washed down with ale. These were probably unripe fruits from trees growing in the open, though in later times peach trees were usually given some protection by being grown on walls.

The quince was grown and used in the thirteenth century for making into quince marmalade, as it had been for many centuries in other countries of Europe, and also for tarts; and both cultivated and wild forms of plums were employed in medieval kitchens. For hundreds of years damsons, bullaces and sloes were collected from the countryside. Plums were often pulped, thickened with flour and breadcrumbs and made into a purée or 'murrey' with the addition of sugar, spices and colouring. One of the most popular murrey dishes was made with mulberry juice, from whose Latin name, *Morus* it got its name.

It is significant that at this time, as at the time of the Roman empire, there was practically no reference to the cultivation of any of the soft fruits. Raspberries and blackberries only existed in the wild state and their fruits could often be collected in the country throughout Britain. The only strawberry then known in Britain, as in most of Europe, was the wood strawberry (*Fragaria vesca*). This was picked by women and children and sold in country markets or hawked through the streets of London. The first evidence of the cultivation of this strawberry was in France in the fourteenth century, and later the practice of collecting plants from the woods for transplanting to gardens became established in other countries, including Britain.

An exception to the use of wild fruits was the cultivation of the gooseberry, although this seems to have been unusual in Britain during Medieval times but more common on the Continent. It was from France that the fruiterer to Edward I obtained gooseberry bushes in 1275 costing 3d, with other plants for the gardens at the Tower of London. These imported bushes must have given larger berries than the wild *Ribes grossularia* which, in their original state, give fruits of insignificant size though these were occasionally gathered for use as a substitute for verjuice in sauces and pickles.

SALE OF GARDEN PRODUCE

The century from 1225 to 1325 saw the manor farming system and agricultural production by the monks and their lay workers at its most prosperous. Existing records indicate that there was considerable planting of orchards and vineyards. Apart from the surplus fruits and cider sold by the monasteries, smallholders and gardeners took their produce for sale at the 'market cross'. In London, the gardeners of the wealthier, landowning upper classes, the aristocracy and the bishops, were allowed to sell surplus produce, while the sale of fruit and other crops became so profitable that the system of renting gardens and orchards to grow especially for market became established. Tower Hill was one of the earliest sites where this was carried on, some of the holdings being on Corporation of London property. Other gardens in the fourteenth century, mostly growing fruit, were at Billingsgate, East Cheap, Lombard Street and Bow Lane.

The produce was sold from street stalls, either by the gardeners themselves or by fruiterers who had purchased it. One of the principal market sites was opposite the church of St Austin, near St Paul's churchyard. Such sales had taken place freely for many years before 1355; as records at the time show, citizens of London were in the habit of selling 'their pulse, cherries, vegetables and other wares to their trade pertaining, on a piece of ground opposite to the church of St Austin.' However, by 1355, this market had grown to such an extent and become so crowded as to 'hinder persons passing on foot and horseback', and the 'scurrility, clamour and nuisance of the gardeners and their servants' had become so obnoxious to the people living in the houses round about, and 'such a nuisance to the priests who are singing matins and mass in the church of St Austin and to others, both clerks and laymen, in prayers and orisons there serving God', that the mayor and aldermen were petitioned to remove the market to a more suitable place. After some reluctance, the mayor agreed to a conference at which it was decided that:

All gardeners of the city, as well aliens as freemen, who sell their pulse, cherries, vegetables, and other wares aforesaid in the city, should have as their place the space between the south gate of the churchyard of St Austin's and the garden wall of the Friars Preachers at Baynards Castle, in the same city, that so they should sell their wares aforesaid in the place by the said mayor and aldermen thus appointed for them, and nowhere else.

The period of farming prosperity during the twelfth and thirteenth centuries, when corn and wool were exported on a considerable scale and forests were cleared to allow even further production, suffered a reversal in the early part of the fourteenth century. A succession of droughts and pestilence seriously devastated both crops and livestock, while the Black Death, 1348—9, probably killed about a third of the population. The result was that many rural areas were deserted and everywhere there was general unrest. Many of the monks and lay workers attached to the monasteries died so that the lands farmed by them suffered from lack of attention. In the fifteenth century, the Wars of the Roses led to further destruction in the countryside.

The depression and shortage of labour following the Black Death affected the production of fruits and vegetables, and fruit growing fell behind that on the Continent. Such was the scarcity of good quality produce in England that there was increasing dependence on the importation of fruits and vegetables from the Low Countries and France to supply the Court, the aristocracy and others who could afford the cost.

At this time also, there was a marked decline in the planting of vineyards and the production of wine. Quite apart from increasing competition from the Continent, there was a gradual deterioration in the climate, culminating in a succession of extremely severe winters in the first half of the fifteenth century. This cold weather destroyed many vineyards in northern France and must have had an equally devastating effect in Britain. The combined effect of the poorer climate and the general depression in rural areas virtually meant the end of any wide-scale wine production in Britain. Although there have been many advocates in the past 400 years suggesting that vineyards should again be planted, it is only in comparatively recent years that the establishment of vineyards has once more been undertaken in Britain.

Boy caught in the act of stealing apples, from a fourteenth-century MS of the Luttrel Psalter.

The *Holinshed Chronicles*, published c.1580, referring to this period of depression, blamed the idleness of the people for not producing at home, things which were then imported. Harrison (1534—93), Dean of Windsor, wrote this account:

> After such time as Calis was wonne from the French [1347], and that our Countriemen had learned to trade with divers countries (whereby they grew rich) they began to wax idle also, and therefore not onlie left off their former painfulnesse and frugalitie, but in like sort gave ourselves to live in excess and vanitie whereby manie goodlie commodities failed, and in short time they were not to be had amongst us.
>
> Such strangers also as dwelled here with us, perceiving our sluggishnesse, and espieing that this idleness of ours might rebound to their own great profit, forthwith imploied their endevours to bring in the supplie of such things as we lacked, continuallie from

foren countries which yet more augumented our idleness. For having all things at reasonable prices as we supposed, by such means from them, we thought it meare madness to spend either time or cost about the same here at home.

Such herbes, fruites and roots also as grow yearlie out of the ground, or from seed, have been very plentiful in this land in the time of the first Edward [1272—1307] and after his daies; but in process of time they grew also to be neglected so that, from Henrie the fourth [1399—1413] to the latter end of Henrie the seventh [1485—1509] and beginning of Henrie the eight [1509—1547] there was little or no use of them in England but they remained, either unknowne or supposed as food more meet for hogs and savage beasts to feed then mankind.

Harrison went on to describe the great improvements in his own day. All kinds of vegetables were now available, he said, to the poor as well as to the nobilitie who:

. . . make their provision yearlie for new seeds out of strange countries, from whence they have great abundance. And even as it fareth with our gardens, so doth it with our own orchards, which were never furnished with so good fruit, nor with such varieties as this present. For beside that, we have most delicate apples, plummes, peares, walnuts, filberds etc. and those of sundrie sorts, planted within fortie yeares passed, in comparison of which most of the old trees are nothing worth; so we have no lesse store of strange fruits as abricots, almonds, peaches, figges and conetrees in noble men's orchards. So that England for these commodities was never better furnished neither any nation better under their clime more plentifullie indeed with these and other blassings from the most high God.

The account given by Harrison of the scarcity of fruits and vegetables in the previous century may have been somewhat exaggerated but there is definite evidence of the decline in wine production as shown in the accounts of the Abingdon Abbey vineyard from 1369 to 1450, while the very severe frosts of the first half of the fifteenth century must have devastated all fruit crops in Britain as they did in northern France. His description of the improvement in supplies of home-grown fruits in the sixteenth century is strongly supported by the writings of others at the time and an explanation for this improvement is given in William Lambard's book, *A Perambulation of Kent*, in 1576.

THE TUDOR PERIOD

The change in horticulture followed the accession of Henry VIII. The King spent lavishly on improving his palaces and building a new one, Nonesuch at Cheam in Surrey. This had extensive garden walls, which were clothed with fruit trees, as well as fruit trees in the kitchen garden. In order to provide this and the other gardens supplying the royal household with the best varieties, in 1533 Richard Harris, fruiterer to the king, brought over grafts of numerous fruits from France and the Low Countries. According to Lambard:

> *Those plantes which our ancestors had brought hither out of Normandie, had lost their native verdour, whether you did eat their substance or drink their juice, which we call Cyder, he [Harris], about the yeare of our Lord Christ, 1533, obtained 105 acres of good ground at Tenham, then called the Brennet, which he divided into ten parcels and with great care, good choice and no small labour and cost, brought plantes from beyonde the Seas, and furnished this ground with them so beautifully, as they not onely stand in most right line, but seeme to be of one sorte, shape and fashion, as if they had been drawen therow one Mould or wrought by one and the same patterne. Our honest patriote Richard Harris planted — the sweet Cherry, the temperate Pipyn and the golden Renate. For this man, seeing that this Realme (which wanted neither the favour of the Sunne, nor the fat of the Soile meete for the making of good apples) was nevertheless served chiefly with that Fruit from forrein Regions abroad.*
>
> *This Tenham with thirty other parishes (lying on each side of this porte way and extending from Raynham to Blean Wood) bee the Cherry garden and Apple orcharde of Kent.*

Lambard's view of the flourishing state of fruit growing in Kent was supported by William Camden, who wrote in his *Britannia* in 1586 of Kent:

> *Almost the whole county abounds with meadows, pastures and corn fields, is wonderfully fruitful in apples, as also cherries, which were brought from Pontus into Italy in the year of Rome 680 and about 120 years after, into Britain. They thrive here exceedingly, and cover large tracts of ground, and the trees being planted in the quincunx, exhibit an agreeable view.*

The 'quincunx' arrangement of planting trees was the one used by the Roman fruit growers in their own country at the time of the Roman invasion of Britain.

The importance of the action of Henry VIII in instructing Richard Harris to bring over the best available varieties of apples, pears and cherries then growing on the Continent cannot be overstated. At the beginning of the sixteenth century, the orchards which had survived the years of neglect consisted of old, outdated varieties, some of which had been grown since they were introduced from Normandy at the time of the Conquest. Within a few years of the planting of the model orchard at Teynham, which might be likened in a minor way to the present-day National Fruit Trials Station at Faversham, scions of the new varieties had been distributed to other growers in the country and used in the propagation of their own trees. Orchards of these were planted by fruit growers from Rainham near Sittingbourne to Blean Wood near Canterbury.

In turn, the lead given by Kent was followed by growers in other parts of the country, and successful orchards were reported in places as far distant as Derbyshire, Lancashire, Suffolk and Gloucestershire. This impetus was continued during the reign of Elizabeth I (1558—1603). Fruit growing was increased, and Britain's dependence on imports of vegetables and fruits from the Continent was reduced by the immigration of the Walloon refugees, between 1560 and 1570, who settled at Sandwich in Kent and established their market garden industry. A few years later, some of the Dutch settlers moved to north-west Kent and Surrey to be nearer the London markets. The development of market gardens around London was later followed by the planting of apples and other fruits, including the soft fruits, which became a feature of the holdings throughout the following centuries.

The marked improvement in the fruit industry was described by the author of *The Fruiterer's Secrets* in 1604:

> *One Richard Harris, Fruiterer to King Henry VIII, fetched out of France great store of graftes, especially pippins, before which time there were no right pippins in England. He fetched also out of the Lowe Countrie, cherrie grafts and peare grafts of divers sorts. Then took a peece of ground belonging to the King in the parish of Tenham in Kent, being about the quantitie of seven score ares; whereof he made an orchard, planting therein all those foreign grafts. Which orchard is, and hath been, the chiefe Mother of all other orchards for those kindes of fruit in Kent and divers other places, and afore these said grafts were fetched out of France and the Lowe Countries, although there were some store of fruite in England, yet there wanted both rare fruites and lasting fine fruit. The Dutch and French, finding it to be so scarce, especially in these counties neere London, commonly plyed Billingsgate and divers other places with such kinde of fruite. But now (thanks to God) divers Gentlemen and others taking delight in grafting have planted*

many orchards, fetching these grafts out of that orchard which Harris planted. And by reason of the great increase that now is growing in divers parts of this Land of such fine fruit, there is no need of any foreign fruit, but we are able to serve other places.

The question of competition from imports of apples and other fruits from the Continent is one that has been raised from time to time up to the present day, and it has always been the French who have been seen as the chief rivals of the British growers. The latter owe much to the French for their knowledge of new techniques, the use of vegetatively propagated dwarfing rootstocks and the introduction of new varieties, but competition from French apple imports almost resulted in Kent growers giving up apple production altogether during the nineteenth century.

IMPORTANCE OF KENT

The cherry orchards of Kent continued to be of importance and held their position as the major production area for this fruit up till the present day. The cherries impressed Celia Fiennes when she made her journey on horseback through Kent in 1697:

> *I travelled along in sight of the Medway to Roachester. So next day I went in sight of the Thames, but from Roachester, I went that night to Gravesend which is all by the side of Cherry grounds that are of several acres of ground and run quite down to the Thames, which is convenient to convey the Cherries to London for here the great produce of that fruit is, which supplyes the town and country with Kentish Cherrys, a good sort of Femish fruite.*

The poor state of the roads at this time and for many years afterwards was a considerable hindrance to the movement of produce to market, and was one of the factors leading to the developing importance of Kent and the areas around London for the production of fruit and other crops. Gravesend became the leading port for loading barges for London. Even in 1794, Boys in a report to the Board of Agriculture, mentioned that in the Maidstone district of Kent: 'The easy water carriage to the metropolis, from the Medway up the Thames, renders the growth of fruit a very profitable article of husbandry. The sorts of apples for domestic use are sold to fruiterers who send to London by the hoys and to the north of England by the coal barges.'

Contributing to the success of Kent in agriculture and horticulture were the fertility of the soils, the favourable climate and the fact that the open field system of strip cultivation, common in other parts of the country, never dominated in Kent. After the dissolution of the monasteries in 1536, Kent was not a county of great landowners. Farmers frequently owned the land they farmed, and as this was enclosed, forming complete units, there was nothing to discourage progressive growers from planting apple or cherry orchards or those of any other fruit.

The introduction of printing at the end of the fifteenth century, and the publication in the early sixteenth century of the first printed books to mention any of the fruits, coincided with the renewal of interest in fruit growing in Britain and the importation of new varieties from the Continent.

Before this time, the main source of information on cultivating fruits was that given in the works of the ancient Greek and Roman writers, often basically sound but frequently incorporating the mythology of the ancients. Although these books would be known to the monks and workers in the monasteries and were used by many of them, the very limitation of the hand-copying of manuscripts meant they were not available to all.

The first books on the subject of plants, fruits and their culture published in Britain in the sixteenth century often repeated in detail what the Roman writers, Pliny and others, had written, with little attempt to alter any of the recommendations to suit the differences in the climate and growing conditions in Britain.

The earliest books to mention any fruits were the herbals, of which *The Grete Herball* 'translated out ye Frensshe into Englysshe' by Peter Treueris in 1526 was the first. This herbal dealt briefly with some of the fruit plants but gave more information about their medicinal uses. The language of *The Grete Herball* was picturesque, even if the information it gave was limited. For example, it said of strawberries: 'Fragaria is an herbe called strabery. It groweth in woodes and grenes / and shadowy places / is pryncypally good agaynst all evylles of the mylt [mouth]. The iuce therof dranken with hony proftyteth marvaylously.' This herbal also included filberts, crab apples, plums, walnuts, medlars, grapes and currants, but there was no mention of different varieties of these fruits.

Cleft grafting of fruit trees. Crescentius, Basle, 1548.

The second important writer was William Turner, whose earliest book was dated 1538. Turner, who was one-time Dean of Wells and chaplain to the Duke of Somerset, travelled extensively abroad, pursuing his interest in botany and collecting plants which he grew in his own garden. Some of what Turner wrote about fruits such as the raspberry was quite useful, but, like others, he copied much direct from Pliny. Turner carried on the tradition set by the monks in the monasteries, and some of the early writers on fruit growing in France, by combining his vocation with a love of plants.

One of the earliest English writers on agriculture, who also included a section on fruit growing in his *Boke of Husbandry* in 1525, was Sir Anthony Fitzherbert. He spoke of the propagation of apples, pears, cherries, damsons and plums, using crab seedlings as apple rootstocks, pears for pears, but suggested the stone fruits could be grown from their own stones or propagated from suckers. He did not mention soft fruits at all.

The *Five Hundred Pointes of Good Husbandry*, the 1580 edition of an earlier work by Thomas Tusser, a scholar and farmer from the eastern counties, written in rhymed couplets, gave hints about various crops and their management throughout the year and included a list of fruits to be planted in a garden. This is the first list in any English book which includes both tree and soft fruits:

(1)   Apple trees of all sorts

(2)   Apricocks
(3)   Barberies
(4)   Boollesse black and white [bullace]
(5)   Cherries, red and black
(6)   Chestnuts
(7)   Cornet plums
(8)   Damsons white and black
(9)   Filberdes, red and white
(10) Gooseberries
(11) Grapes, red and white
(12) Greene or graffe plums
(13) Murtell beries [myrtle]
(14) Medlars or marles
(15) Mulberie
(16) Peaches, white and red
(17) Peares of all sortes
(18) Perarephis, black and yellow
(19) Quinces
(20) Respis [raspberry]
(21) Reisons [currants]
(22) Small nuts [hazel nuts]
(23) Strawberries, red and white
(24) Service trees
(25) Walnuts
(26) Wardens, white and red [cooking pears]
(27) Wheat plums

Tusser's list shows that gardeners in the latter part of the sixteenth century now had a wide range of different fruits available for planting, including the myrtle, so beloved of the Romans, the berberries or barberry, whose berries were popular for flavouring, and the fruits of the rowan or service tree, which are still used in some northern countries. The strawberries were red and white forms of the wild wood strawberry, *Fragaria vesca*, and the 'reisons' were red currants, the black currant not yet being accepted into gardens. The raspberries were still early types selected from the wild.

Tusser gave a few practical hints on the cultivation of some fruits and the 1574 edition of Thomas Hill's, *The Profitable Arte of Gardeninge*, had something to say about grafting, but the first really practical work for the fruit grower was Leonard Mascall's, *The Booke of Arte and Maner, howe to plant and graffe all sortes of trees*, first published in 1572. Mascall was a farmer and fruit grower who owned the manor farm attached to Plumpton Place near Lewes in Sussex. Mascall is said to have imported the first Pippins from the Continent in 1525 and to have grown apples and trees for the London market. His book, like several herbals and books on horticulture published in the sixteenth and seventeenth centuries, was a translation of one originally published in France, written by a member of the Abbey of St Vincent. It also included a section on Dutch methods.

In his introduction, Mascall referred to the fact that in the past England had lacked much of the fruit grown in other countries:

> *For this I can blame nothing more than the negligence of our nation which hath had small care heretofore in planting and graffing; in some places of this realme whereas good and well disposed have graffed, the evill and malicious person hath soon after destroyed them againe; but if we woulde endevour ourselves thereunto (as other countries doe) we might flourish and have many a strange kind of fruit (which now we have often time the want thereof.)*

The reference to the destruction of fruit trees by 'malicious persons' emphasizes one of the difficulties which the intending fruit grower had to contend with in the sixteenth and seventeenth centuries, when lawlessness was a common feature of the countryside. In the time of Henry VIII, malicious barking of apple trees or other fruit trees was made a felony.

Rind grafting of established fruit trees as stocks. Mascall, 1575.

Mascall's book came out at a very opportune time, when many people were becoming interested in the new varieties imported by Harris in 1533, but lacked basic knowledge of their planting and propagation. Mascall dealt in detail with the raising of rootstocks for apples, pears and plums and the methods of grafting and budding both these and figs, quinces, medlars, apricots and peaches. He also dealt with the propagation, by cuttings, of mulberries, gooseberries and currants.

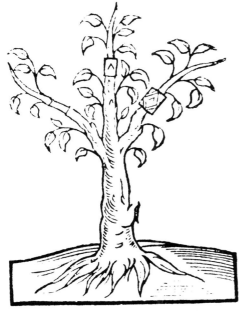

Ring budding, a form of the patch method. Mascall, 1575.

Another writer of note at the end of the sixteenth century was John Gerard, an apothecary who had his own garden in London and, in 1597, published his famous *The Herball*. This included hundreds of woodcuts, and much of the text was taken from the work of a Belgian botanist, Rembert Dodoens. In addition to an account of the plants and fruits, the book gave a description of some of the varieties then cultivated in gardens in Britain. The 1633 edition, revised by Johnson, included many more varieties of fruits, illustrating the rapidity with which new ones were being introduced.

By the time John Parkinson, another apothecary, published his, *Paradisi in Sole* in 1629, he was able to give details of large numbers of all kinds of fruits and vegetables. His book was freely illustrated and was the first written in English to provide so much information about the fruits and their culture as practised in the early seventeenth century.

Batty Langley, a landscape gardener and nurseryman, published his *Pomona or the Fruit Garden Illustrated* in 1729, copiously illustrated with woodcuts. In it he selected the varieties then considered the best, many of which are still grown today.

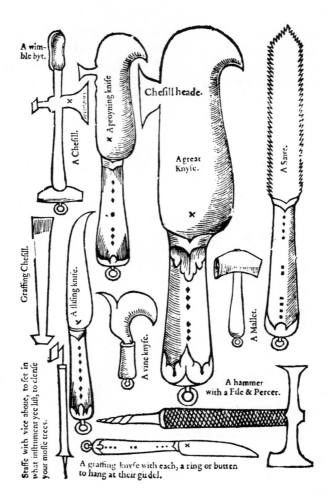

Tools used in grafting and budding. Mascall, 1575.

The books of Gerard, Parkinson and Langley were the only ones which included illustrations showing a wide range of fruit varieties grown during the sixteenth to eighteenth centuries. The famous pomonas of the nineteenth century generally covered a limited number of selected types of fruits and varieties, although they were beautifully coloured. It is the illustrations of these three authors which have been used in this book.

DEVELOPMENTS IN THE SEVENTEENTH CENTURY

7

The early years of the seventeenth century were ones of increasing interest in gardens and the planting of both tree and soft fruits in Britain, using the many new varieties which were imported from the Continent together with new home-raised seedlings. Parkinson who, in 1629, wrote about most of the important varieties then available, said the number of different apples was so great that he could not mention all of them. He did name no less than 64 pears, 61 plums, 6 quinces, 23 grapes, 3 medlars, 36 cherries, 6 apricots, 21 peaches, 2 raspberries, 5 gooseberries, 3 currants, 2 barberries and 3 figs, together with filberts and walnuts.

Some of the new varieties had been introduced in the sixteenth century but their numbers had been greatly augmented by imports, especially through the activities of John Tradescant who travelled extensively abroad collecting plants in Russia, North Africa, Virginia and many parts of Europe. He began this work while gardener at Hatfield House, using many of the new fruits he had brought from other countries. He continued to obtain new plants while working in other posts and, in 1630, was appointed Keeper of his Majesty's Garden at Oatlands, Surrey, where he stayed until his death in 1638. Tradescant was followed at Oatlands by his son, who also introduced many new plants and who remained in the service of Charles I until the king's death in 1649.

Parkinson praised Tradescant for the many new varieties of plums he had imported, and said he had 'wonderfully laboured to obtain all the rarest fruit he can hear of in any place of Christendom, Turkey, yea in the whole world'. Among the fruits which Tradescant introduced and which became popular, especially in the second half of the seventeenth century, were peaches, nectarines, apricots and figs, all of which needed some protection and so were commonly grown on the walls which were increasingly used for surrounding the gardens of the large houses and mansions which had replaced the castles of the more unsettled previous age. The new varieties were generally much superior to those of the sixteenth century, and this encouraged the planting of these rather exotic fruits so that they became more generally grown in the larger gardens than they are today. Many trees were imported from the Continent, especially from French nurseries and, in turn, English nurseries were able to supply these and numerous other varieties. For example, John Rea, in 1676, listed 35 varieties of peaches and 11 nectarines. Even apricots were so widely planted that Worlidge, in 1697, said that they were well known almost everywhere.

Workers in an orchard. Lawson, 1618.

INFLUENCE OF FRANCE

The cultivation of new varieties of apples and pears also increased considerably in the seventeenth century and, according to Parkinson, the number of pears was as great, if not greater, than that of apples. Many new, good-quality plums became available, mostly introduced from France, including the famous Green Gage. The quince was of much greater importance at this time than it is today, being especially popular for preserving.

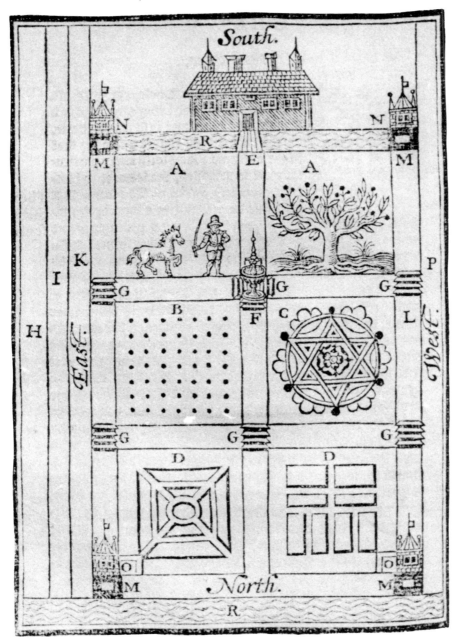

Design for a formal garden, 1618. Areas A and B were set aside for fruit trees,
the recommended planting distance being '20 yards'.

During the seventeenth century interest in growing fruit became fashionable among the ruling classes in France. The enthusiasm for pears of Le

Lectier, attorney to the King at Orléans, led to their culture becoming a craze, especially among the aristocracy, and the interest in growing fruits of all kinds reached a peak during the latter part of the century with the establishment of the royal gardens at Versailles for Louis XIV, under the direction of de la Quintinye. These gardens, with their attached nurseries, contained hundreds of varieties of all types of fruits. De la Quintinye was a friend of John Evelyn and visited England on several occasions; he doubtless had a marked influence on the culture of fruits in Britain.

Although figs were grown in some gardens in the seventeenth century, they were not common, mainly owing to the problem of obtaining satisfactory crops, the result of adverse weather. Worlidge dismissed the fig from his books as being of little use in rural areas. Dried figs were, however, imported in large quantities from Italy and Spain.

Walnuts had been fairly common in Britain in the sixteenth century but there were few distinct varieties at this time, or for several centuries, since problems with vegetative propagation meant that seedlings, giving variable progeny, were used. Spring frosts frequently limited the cropping of walnuts, but the trees were very valuable for their timber, being used for making furniture and the butts of guns.

Hazel nuts, being indigenous to Britain, were commonly collected from the wild, but improved varieties, including filberts, were introduced during the seventeenth century, and the cultivation of cob nuts became of major importance in Kent and so established an industry around Maidstone which was to persist for the next 300 years.

Although mulberry trees were grown in many of the London gardens in the Middle Ages, their fruits being used in the kitchen and their juice for making wine and providing colour for adulterating other wines and cider, it was not until the seventeenth century, at the instigation of James I, that attempts were made to grow mulberries for silk production and so save the considerable cost of imports. However, although Queen Anne was able to wear a taffeta costume made from her own silk, commercial pressure by silk importers led to the collapse of the new industry, although some of the mulberry trees planted at the time still exist today.

One of the few fruits which existed in gardens in the sixteenth and seventeenth centuries, but was little more popular then than it is today, was the medlar, only appreciated by a limited number of connoisseurs. Although writers at that time often regretted the virtual disappearance of vineyards and the decline in wine production in Britain, few of the attempts made to revive it met with any success. There was, however, interest in grape production for dessert where the vines were given some protection, especially with the increased use of glass, but vines were also used, as they had been for several centuries, for growing as arbors around garden seats.

COMMERCIAL PRODUCTION OF FRUIT

From 1649 to 1659, the time of the Commonwealth, great concern was expressed about the poor state of the countryside. Agriculture and horticulture had been neglected during the Civil War, and various proposals were now made for the improvement of the country by the planting of orchards. In 1652, Samuel Hartlib published *A Designe for Plentie by an Universal Planting of Fruit-trees*, in which he proposed a plan to make the planting of fruit trees compulsory:

> *First we do contend that it will make much for the benefit and public relief of this whole nation and for prevention of famine in time to come (through the blessing of God) if there were a law made and put into force by Authority for a general and Universal Planting of such wholesome fruits (according to proportion) for the relief of the poor, the benefit of the rich and delight of all.*
>
> *Apples, pears, walnuts and quince. Proportion ordained every five pounds (rateable value) per annum plantable land:*
>
> *5 l. 20 fruit trees — apples, pear, walnut and quince.*
> *10 l. 40 " "*
>
> *and so on.*
>
> *. . . each town to appoint two officers (called Fruiters or Woodwards or such like name) who shall have power to call out and appoint certain common days to work in dressings, pruning, molding, mossing, triming of said trees etc.*

The compulsory planting of fruit trees was also put forward by Ralph Austen, a nurseryman at Oxford, whose book *A Treatise of Fruit Trees*, first published in 1653, ran into several editions. Austen, perhaps not disinterestedly, was most anxious to encourage the planting of fruit trees. He thought that if people were compelled by law to plant their own trees they would be less likely to steal freshly planted trees or fruits from other orchards. Austen also considered that the prunings and dead fruit trees would, together with the planting of forest trees, provide valuable fuel: 'By reason of the great destruction of Wood, Fuell is growen exceeding scarce and deare; and will certainly be much more scarce hereafter if men be not more diligent in planting. The poorer sort of people in many places make lamentable complaint for want of Fuell in winter time.'

Austen was undoubtedly an authority on orcharding at this time. In a letter published in 1677 from Anthony Lawrence to the Secretary of the Royal Society, Lawrence was full of praise for Austen and his encouragement of the planting of orchards around Oxford and suggested that the same might be done for Cambridge:

> *For besides the Amenities and other Advantages of health and sweet air, where both Universities shall be invested in a Golden Grove, it will have a good influence to allure like improvement in all parts of England. What is well done for Ornament, Health, innocent Pleasure and considerable Profit (all joyned together) in the Eyes of both Universities, will doubtless more speedily be everywhere and effectually obtain a progress all over the Kingdom.*
>
> *And if Cambridge should be an Example it would without doubt, excite very great improvements towards the North and in many countries about the Heart of England. For if any Expedient can invite the Countries that are about Cambridge to Inclosure, I think Orchards, Gardens, Nurseries and Groves are most likely to do it.*

There was at this time considerable opposition to the enclosure of land, much land still being cultivated on the strip system or used for cattle grazing as unfenced commons.

At the Restoration of the Monarchy in 1660, John Evelyn, the diarist, was appointed, 'for the retrieving the calamaties of England and re-animating the spirit of his Countrymen for their planting and sowing of woods'. For many years the timber in the forests of Great Britain had been used with little attempt to replace it. This had, as Austen said, resulted not only in a shortage of fuel, but also of timber for ships for the navy. Evelyn's *Sylva*, 1664, dealing with forestry but to which was added a pomona on the planting of orchards and cider apple production, became a standard work. He also translated into English several French books, including *The Manner of Ordering Fruit Trees* by Le Gendre the Curé d'Henoville, published in Britain in 1660, and the famous de la Quintinye's *Compleat Gardiner*, in 1693. As a young man, Evelyn had spent several years travelling on the Continent and, being a keen horticulturist, not only brought back new ideas on gardens but, by translating the books he thought could be of value to fruit growers in Britain, became one of those instrumental in setting the pattern for our modern orchards.

The book by Le Gendre was of particular importance as it described the use of dwarfing and semi-dwarfing rootstocks for apples — the Paradise and Doucin, types of which we still have today — and quince stocks for pears. Up till this time most of the orchards in this country had been planted using seedlings or suckers for the rootstocks, which generally produced large trees, unsuitable for the smaller gardens or for intensively planted orchards, which were popular in France.

RECOVERY AFTER THE CIVIL WAR

During the 30 years following the disruption of the Civil War, the agricultural and horticultural industries gradually showed improvement, and new ideas about the planting and management of orchards seem to have gained favour. In 1681, Langford wrote: 'Advantages of Dwarfs. These trees have been of late much affected and coveted because they are of special advantage for Table-fruit (whether Pears, Apples, Plums or Cherries) and being of low stature, may be planted in borders or Garden walks.' This development was so important that it is of interest to see what Worlidge of Petersfield, a leading writer on horticultural and agricultural subjects, had to say in 1691. Dealing with the planting of apple orchards he wrote:

> To dispose of the trees to your best advantage . . . plant your tall Standard Trees in such places where you intend to make use of the land for Grazing, that they may be above the reach of Cattel. But, in such places where you can dispense with the Cattel and use the Land only for the Scythe or Spade, there it is best to plant dwarf on low grafted Trees for several Reasons:
>
> 1. You may plant more of them on the like quantity of Land, because the Shadow of the one Tree doth not reach the ground of the other, as that of the tall tree doth.
>
> 2. The Low Trees sooner attain to be Fruit-bearing Trees, and grow fairer than the tall.
>
> 3. The lower and broad spreading Tree is the greater bearer, by reason the blossoms in the Spring are not so obvious to the bitter blasts, nor the Fruit in the Autumn to the fierce and destructive Winds.
>
> 4. Fruits are more easily gathered from a low than a tall Tree, beating or shaking down the Fruit from such Trees, being rejected by all.
>
> 5. Any fruit on a low, well spread Tree, is better and fairer than that on a tall Tree by the same reason that the Tree is fairer.
>
> This way of planting dwarf Trees is but lately in use, deriving its original from France.

The reasons given by Worlidge for planting dwarf trees are practically identical to the arguments put forward today in favour of the smaller tree as a way of obtaining earlier and heavier crops, of better quality and more easily picked. In another book Worlidge recommended the Paradise apple as a rootstock for dwarf trees.

To what extent the planting of dwarf trees was taken up by growers towards the end of the seventeenth and early part of the eighteenth centuries is not very clear as the term 'dwarf' was also used for low-worked trees, trained as espaliers and planted along the sides of the walks in enclosed gardens. However, this method of growing apples and pears certainly seems to have been used by market growers around London as Professor Bradley, professor of botany at Cambridge University, writing in 1726, said:

> For dwarf apples I believe everyone will allow that those grafted upon Paradise stocks are best. I mean for keeping in a small compass and bearing abundance of fruit with very little pruning. Paradise stocks are raised by cuttings or suckers. They are brought originally from France but now are to be had in almost every nursery about London.
>
> I have had the opportunity of observing this year the gardens of Messieurs Warners of Rotherhith . . . they could not have a better Example for the management of Dwarf-trees of Apples and Pears in England. One of these Gentlemen, in this bad year, in one part of his Garden, not much more than half an acre, has more Fruit than any garden, among the many I have seen, can boast of in three acres, yet we may see at the same time a promising Prospect of Blossoms for the Furniture of next Summer.

APPLE GROWING IN THE WEST COUNTRY

8

While apple, pear and cherry orchards to provide fruit for market were being planted in Kent during the sixteenth and seventeenth centuries, the growing of apples and pears was well advanced in Hereford and other western counties, including Gloucestershire and Worcesteshire. Here the bulk of the apples was used for cider, and in Gloucestershire pears were often used for making perry. In 1597 Gerard wrote:

> *Kent doth abound with apples of most sorts; but I have seen in the pastures and hedge-rows, about the grounds of a worshipful gentleman dwelling two miles from Hereford, so many trees of all sortes that the servants drink for the most part no other drinke but that which is made of apples. The quantitie is such, that by the report of the gentleman himselfe, the parson hath for tithe many hogsheads of cyder.*

This emphasis on cider production was referred to in 1657 by John Beale when he wrote an article entitled, *Herefordshire Orchards — a Pattern for all England*, addressed to Samuel Hartlib. Beale wrote:

> *. . . that this County [Hereford] is reputed the Orchard of England. From the greatest Persons to the Poorest Cottages, all Habitations are encompased with Orchards and Gardens; and in most Places our Hedges are enriched with rows of Fruit-Trees, Pears or Apples, Gennet- Moyles or Crab trees. I need not tell you how all our Villages, and generally all our Highways (all our Vales being thick set with Rows of Villages) are in the Springtime sweetened and beautify'd with the bloomed Trees which continue their changeable*

Varieties of Ornament, till (in the end of Autumn) they fill our Garners with pleasant Fruit, and our Cellars with rich and winy Liquors. I conceive that if other Countrys [counties] would submit to the same Patience and Industry, as is usual amongst us, they might partake of a great measure (at least) of the same Blessings. As wee see in our Borderers of Shropshire, Worcestershire and Gloucestershire and also in Somersetshire, and much more in Kent and Essex . . . Worcestershire is more proper for Pears and Cherries than Herefordshire and Herefordshire more proper for apples.

One reason why Fruit do so abound in this Country, is for that no Man hath of late years built him a House, but with special regard to the proximity of some Ground fit for an Orchard. And many times, Servants when they betake to Marriage, seek out an Acre or two of Ground which they find fit for Orchards; for thus they give a Fine, or double value for years or Lives; and thereon they build a Cottage, and plant an Orchard, which is all the Wealth they have for themselves and their Posterity.

For Gardens, we have little encouragement to design more than is for the necessary use of our own Families, except our River Wye may be made navigable for transportation. And by defect of transportation, our Store of Cyder is become a Snare to many who turn God's Blessings into wantonness and drunkenness.

This reference to lack of transport pin-points the main reason for the type of orchard being developed in Herefordshire. At this time, and even as late as the end of the eighteenth century, transport by road was often extremely difficult, especially during the winter, and only areas adjacent to towns or having the benefit of water transport were able to send their fruits to market. From Kent much produce was sent by barge from Gravesend to London, or by returning coal barges to Newcastle. But Herefordshire and other countries of the west had no such facilities, and so surplus apples were usually made into cider and surplus pears into perry.

The widespread building of canals during the latter part of the eighteenth century and early part of the nineteenth, though mainly intended for the transport of heavy goods and the carrying of manufactured goods from the rapidly developing industrial areas, also helped the west country growers. By the end of the eighteenth century, it was estimated that some 10,000 hogsheads (110 gallons each) of cider were being sent by barge each year from Worcestershire to be sold in other parts of the country. Unlike Herefordshire, where apples predominated in the orchards, the orchards of Worcestershire included other fruits, with plums and cherries being important for sale in Midland markets.

Although for many hundreds of years, cider production was of importance in most counties of the west and south-west, including Somerset, Devon and Jersey in the Channel Isles, where it had been important from about the middle of the fifteenth century, having replaced mead as the common drink, Herefordshire was the leading county, especially for quality cider. Celia Fiennes, reporting her journeys on horseback throughout England in 1685, wrote of Somerset:

> *In most parts of Sommersetshire it is very fruitful for orchards, plenty of apples and peares, but they are not curious in the planting the best sorts of fruite which is a great pitty, being so soon produced and such quantityes; they are likewise as careless when they make cider, they press all sorts of apples together, else they might have as good as the Herefordshire.*

In 1696 she likened Herefordshire to a county of gardens and orchards as it was so fully planted, even in the cornfields and hedges, with apple, pear and other fruit trees.

The planting of cider apples trees in and around the fields where cattle were grazed in Herefordshire was extolled in the seventeenth century as providing earlier grass and shade for the cattle, a practice continued for hundreds of years. And the planting of apple varieties specifically for making cider in the west country, compared with the more general-purpose varieties such as Kentish Codlings grown in Kent, set a pattern which persists to the present day. In Kent and other counties within reach of London, although cider had been produced in the monasteries in the centuries following the Norman Conquest it was now only made when the crop of apples was particularly heavy and market prices were too low to make their sale profitable, such was the increasing demand for fresh produce for the London market.

Although the fruits of wild strawberries, blackberries and raspberries were collected as food from the earliest times, there is little evidence that any of the soft fruits were cultivated in gardens in Britain before the Norman Conquest. The main reason for this was probably that most of these berries, even when cultivated, showed little improvement over the wild types.

One of the first fruits to be brought into gardens was the strawberry, plants of *Fragaria vesca* being collected from the woods for planting in the garden where they were fruited for one or two years before being renewed. This practice, which was first recorded in France in the fourteenth century, was continued for several hundred years, with virtually no change or improvement in the plants used over those of the woodland, though both red- and white-fruited types were known.

While *Fragaria vesca* was still the main species grown in gardens, a variation, *F.vesca semperflorens,* the Alpine strawberry, was introduced during the second half of the eighteenth century. This had been known to occur wild in the mountains of Switzerland early in the sixteenth century and, like the wood strawberry, had been collected for food for many years before its value as a garden plant was appreciated.

The Hautbois, *Fragaria elatior*, was another species cultivated in gardens from the seventeenth century, but it was the introduction of the Virginian strawberry, *Fragaria virginiana*, in the seventeenth century, followed by the Chilean strawberry, *Fragaria chiloensis*, brought to France by Captain Frézier in 1712, which, by their hybridization, eventually led to the development of the present day, large-fruited varieties.

There is no evidence that the fruits of the wild gooseberry, *Ribes grossularia*, were collected for food, as seeds of this fruit have not been found during excavations of prehistoric or Roman sites. The first record of

Strawberry girl crying her wares, about 1800.

gooseberries being cultivated in England is an item in the accounts of the
fruiterer to Edward I, dated 1275, which was for the cost of gooseberry

bushes imported from France for the royal gardens, although no specific varieties are named. In 1509, there was another royal account for Henry VIII for bushes of the 'pale' gooseberry, brought over from Flanders.

Turner, in 1548, wrote that he had seen the gooseberry growing wild in fields in Germany, but he had only seen it growing in gardens in England, so it seems that, unlike the wood strawberry, blackberry and raspberry, the gooseberry was not indigenous to Britain. However, the British quickly took to the gooseberry and, by the end of the sixteenth century, Gerard included a number of different varieties and said that gooseberries were grown in great abundance in London gardens and elsewhere. Within a few years, the number of varieties had increased considerably, augmented by further importation of a good-quality variety from Holland. As with other soft fruits, especially red and white currants, Holland was an important source of many of the better new varieties.

The gooseberry became increasingly popular during the seventeenth and eighteenth centuries, culminating in the setting up of the gooseberry clubs in Lancashire and adjoining counties, where members vied with each other to produce the heaviest single berry. This had the effect of multiplying the number of varieties still further as the club members bred their own plants from seed, and justified the opinion of many that the gooseberry was 'the English fruit'.

No seeds of currants have been excavated from any prehistoric sites in Britain, although there is evidence of the use of currants, with other wild fruits, at a Mesolithic site in Denmark. The first records of black currants being used in Britain and France were for adding colour and flavour to wines in Medieval times. Red currants also have a long history of use in wine making, but the Common Red was probably grown in gardens in France, Germany and Holland before being taken up in England.

The early herbals referred to currants for their health-giving properties, as appetizers or for adding piquancy to dishes or for making into verjuice. In 1548, Turner mentioned that he had seen *Ribes* growing wild in Somerset at Clouer, which seems to have been only a short distance away from Glastonbury where blackberry seeds from an Iron Age lake settlement were found.

Red currants and, to a lesser extent, white currants were extensively planted during the seventeenth century, especially after the introduction of the greatly improved Great Red Dutch variety from Holland in 1611 by John Tradescant. These currants were very popular eaten fresh as dessert, for making jellies and for wine production, and continued to be one of the most widely planted soft fruits until well into the nineteenth century when, to some extent, they gave place to the new, large-fruited strawberries and improved raspberries.

While red and white currants were so acclaimed, the opposite is true of the black currant. The 1633 edition of Gerard gave this account of the black currant: 'fruit as big againe as the ordinary red but of a stinking and somewhat loathing savour, the leaves also are not without the stinking smell'. These currants had been imported from Holland by John Tradescant in 1611, as the account for the bushes supplied for the garden of the newly built Hatfield House, owned by the Earl of Salisbury, Tradescant's patron, included the item 'for on dussin of greate blacke currants, 1 s'. This hostility to black currants was repeated by Parkinson in 1629, though he did admit that some people liked the fruit and were not 'offended by the taste or smell' although many 'misliked it'.

The raspberry (*Rubus idaeus*) was mentioned by the herbalist Turner and included in Tusser's list of fruits to be grown in the garden, and in the early seventeenth century was liked both as fresh fruit and for making wine. This was a time when the other soft fruits were often used for producing wine.

Compared with the gooseberry and the red currant, the development of new raspberry varieties was relatively slow, and the same limited number was grown until towards the end of the eighteenth century, when the introduction of a new variety from overseas brought in new characteristics which resulted in the breeding in England of many larger-fruited red and yellow types. The important new variety was of Hungarian origin, brought over from Antwerp and named Golden Antwerp.

The berries of the blackberry (*Rubus fruticosus*) were collected as food by prehistoric man and by successive generations for about 2000 years, but the blackberry was always regarded as a wild, unruly type of plant which was better used for hedges to keep out marauders than brought into the garden. It was not until the nineteenth century that much attention was paid to this fruit and the various naturally occurring types were selected from the wild for growing in gardens.

Another plant cultivated in gardens until the first half of the nineteenth century, was the barberry, *Berberis vulgaris*. There were several varieties: the Red without stones, the White, Black Sweet, the Common Red with stones, normally used as an ornamental shrub, and the Purple fruited. The barberry was known to Pliny who said that the berries, raw, dried or boiled in wine, were used medicinally, while the ancient Egyptians macerated the fruits in about twelve times their quantity of water, let them stand for about 24 hours, added a little fennel seed and gave the product to those suffering from fever. Gerard said the young leaves were used as a salad and to season meat dishes, while the berries were preserved and pickled and used for garnishing both meat and fruit dishes until the early nineteenth century. The berries were also candied with sugar and used as a sweetmeat. The yellow inner bark of the bushes, treated with alum, produces a bright yellow dye which was used in France for dyeing both silk and cotton, for staining wood and, in Poland, for colouring leather. It was also used, in Gerard's time, for dyeing the hair. Today, in Britain, the *Berberis* is commonly confined to use as a garden shrub.

FRUIT GROWING IN THE EIGHTEENTH CENTURY

The late seventeenth century marked the beginning of a period of renewed interest in gardens, not only those laid out for the royal palaces and the many large private houses built at this time but also the gardens attached to the more humble dwellings of country people.

The walls around the gardens of the houses of the rich were clothed with trained trees of apples, pears, plums, cherries, peaches and other tree fruits, while trees trained as espaliers or in bush form, the apples often being on dwarfing rootstocks, were planted alongside the paths and walks. Soft fruit bushes, especially red and white currants and gooseberries, were planted out in beds and strawberries were generally planted in beds adjoining walls. Peaches, nectarines, apricots and figs, like other fruits such as May cherries and soft fruits required for early use, were frequently given the protection of glass frames, built up in front of the garden walls. Various other systems of protecting these fruits from frost damage were also employed, including straw mats and net coverings.

The highly developed art of producing out-of-season fruits by forcing, using large quantities of fermenting manure or hot-air flues, is indicated by a note in a book by Professor Bradley, in 1726, when, writing of the produce on sale in Covent Garden market in April 1721, he said, 'Among other Rarities, some Cherries have been brought to Town near a month ago, having had the benefit of Forcing frames.' In March of the following year, he reported, 'I have heard that there were ripe Cherries at Mr. Millet's of North End about the beginning of this Month; and also large green Abricots.'

The fruit-growing orchards of Kent were extended for the London markets, and the latter were increasingly supplied with both tree and soft fruits from the expanding market gardens around London. In the west of the country, there was much planting of cider apples in Herefordshire, Gloucestershire,

*Harvesting apples for store in the Palace Gardens at Versailles
at the end of the seventeenth century.*

Somerset and Devon and of perry pears, especially in Gloucestershire. In Worcestershire, the cultivation of tree fruits, including plums for market, was encouraged by the development of the canals but, in more remote parts of the country, if apples and other fruits were wanted, they had to be grown either in the garden or farm orchards.

Cider was a very popular drink at this time, and apart from the farms in the west country, where the workers received a daily allocation of cider as part of their wages, cider was also made from apples grown in small farm orchards well away from the traditional areas. Large quantities of cider were supplied to the ships in Bristol harbour, and cider was sent by sea from the ports of Devon to London, where it was often adulterated and sold as imported wine. Wines made from the soft fruits, gooseberries, red currants and raspberries, were also popular and often passed off as French products.

During the late seventeenth and early eighteenth centuries, the raising of new varieties of tree fruits and some soft fruits continued in Britain, while such was the demand for trees for planting that great quantities were imported. In Europe the raising of new pears was centred on Belgium, where Hardenpont was one of the first breeders to select his parent plants with care, and his work was followed by that of Van Mons of Louvain. Together, they introduced many pear varieties of merit.

Most of the tree fruits were supplied by nurseries near London, one of the most important being Brompton Park started in 1681. Outside London, John

Frontispiece.

*An early eighteenth-century garden showing the use of protection
for wall trained trees, cloches and bell jars for strawberries.*

Covent Garden in the eighteenth century.

Rea (1605—81) had a nursery at Kinlet in Shropshire, and those of John Telford at York and John Prefect at Pontefract were both started in the seventeenth century. They supplied both fruit and ornamental trees and shrubs and were the forerunners of other leading Yorkshire nurseries.

Two important nurseries in the early eighteenth century were those of Batty Langley and Robert Furber. Batty Langley was one of the leading garden designers and wrote several books on this subject in addition to his *Pomona*. Robert Furber was a nurseryman at Kensington who, with Thomas Fairchild, Philip Miller and other leading nurserymen, were members of the Society of Gardeners. In 1730, this society published the first part of a catalogue of trees and shrubs for sale in gardens near London, illustrated by a Dutch artist, Jacob van Huysum. If successful, it had been intended to follow this publication with others dealing with exotic plants, flowers and fruits. Unfortunately these never appeared but, in 1732, Robert Furber issued his *Twelve Months of Fruits*, a catalogue, including twelve hand-coloured prints, of 364 varieties of fruits available from his nursery. These illustrations, like those of Batty Langley, are most valuable in showing the vast range of fruit varieties then available for planting in the rapidly expanding gardens around London and further afield.

Unfortunately, nurseries were frequently unreliable and did not provide plants true to name. One of the reasons was their practice of selling trees brought over from Continental suppliers. As Philip Miller, writing of peaches in 1731, said:

> *I shall now proceed to mention the several sorts of good Peaches and though perhaps a greater Number of Sorts may be found in some Catalogues of Fruits, yet I doubt whether many of them are not the same Kind call'd by different Names.*
>
> *The present Confusion of Names of Fruits have been many times owing to the bringing over Trees from France; for the Persons who are generally employ'd to bring over those Trees for Sale, are intirely ignorant of their Various Sorts and do themselves take 'em upon Trust from the Persons, who make it their Business to propagate great quantities to supply Markets of France, whither they are brought in Waggons and sold out in Parcels to those Persons who bring them to England.*
>
> *It also happens many times, that if they are received by right Names, that these, in Length of Time, are lost, or the Trees come into Possession of other Persons, who not knowing the true name of the fruit, do often give them New names, whereby there is such confusion in the Names of Fruit, as it is impossible to rectify.*
>
> *And hence some Persons have suppos'd much greater variety of Peaches, than there is in reality; tho' as the greatest part of them have been obtained from Seeds, so their Varieties may be multiply'd annually until there is no End of Sorts.*

Miller went on to list 27 varieties of peaches which he said were those best known in England, together with 27 kinds of pears, saying that there were many others still existing in old gardens. He also included 32 of the best plums and numerous varieties of apples.

There was keen rivalry among the wealthy landowners at this time to have the best garden and most comprehensive collection of different fruits. The owners of large gardens often preferred to raise their own rootstocks which they budded or grafted themselves with scions of their own selected seedlings or established varieties of repute, or with scions obtained from others. This practice had been referred to by Parkinson early in the seventeenth century when he wrote: 'Many Gentlemen and others are much delighted to bestowe their paines in grafting themselves, and esteeme their owne labours and handie worke farre above other mens.'

DECLINE IN ORCHARDS

Although the planting of apples, both in farm orchards and market gardens, had flourished in the early part of the eighteenth century, towards the end of the century there was general concern in most of the country about the declining health and vigour of the trees. Canker, caused by *Nectria galligena*, was rife and fruit quality and crop yields were very poor.

At this time, a number of societies, including the Society for the Encouragement of the Arts, Manufacturers and Commerce, offered prizes for suggestions for the improvement of orchards. One of the prizes was awarded to T. S. Bucknall MP for his work in showing how an orchard at Sittingbourne had been improved by pruning and general management. In his report of 1797, Bucknall said: 'It is necessary to admit that several species of fruit trees have for some years declined and that, rapidly in some situations where they formerly used to thrive. I . . . am disposed to ascribe

Eighteenth-century instructional sketches of grafting and budding, including a splice graft, T and shield budding and a short ladder for use when grafting tall trees.

the most material cause to neglect.' When pruning and cutting out cankers, Bucknall advised painting the wounds with a medicated tar, 'composed of half an ounce of corrosive sublimate [mercuric chloride] reduced to a fine powder and then put into a three pint earthen pipkin, with about a glass full of gin or other spirit, stirred well together, and the sublimate thus dissolved. The pipkin then filled by degrees with vegetable or common tar.' The use of a mercury paint in this way is interesting in view of the introduction during the present century of canker paints based on the same material.

There was also much concern about the poor condition of many of the orchards in the west of the country, especially in Herefordshire. One of the reasons for their decline was the increased demand for more essential foodstuffs; it became more profitable for farmers to produce corn and cattle than cider apples. Orchards received less care and attention, and there was a general decline in both the standard of health and productivity of the trees. Less care was paid to the choice of the best apple varieties and the poorer quality of the cider proved a drag on the market.

The decline of apple orchards in Herefordshire was also of concern to the celebrated Thomas Andrew Knight, who in 1811, became President of the recently formed Horticultural Society. Knight was firmly of the opinion that individual varieties of fruits had a life limited to that of the original tree, and that, after a period of continued propagation by grafting, they lost their inherent vigour and became useless. He described how grafts of the old varieties grew well for two to three years, after which they became cankered and failed to make any headway. In his efforts to improve fruit growing, Knight began an intensive programme of breeding new varieties of many fruits, including apples, pears, cherries, nectarines, damsons and straw-berries. In this work, he was the first to employ scientific methods of breeding by controlled cross-pollination. Although he was wrong in his conclusions concerning the limited life of varieties, by focusing attention on the problems of fruit growers, Knight initiated valuable work which was continued by the Horticultural Society.

Away from the west country, the poor state of English orchards was emphasized by William Salisbury who said in 1816:

> I must say that the bad state of our apple trees at this time is the general theme; for if we travel in a stage coach or mix with company at an inn, or call at a farm house, the conversation is generally found to turn to this point and mostly ends with the prediction that there is no chance again of seeing a general hit of fruit or that cider will ever again be made in this country as it used to be; farmers declared that the land would be more valuable if all thus occupied was turned to another mode of culture for that apple trees in their present state are little more than an incumberance.

Records of the time show that during the last phase of the Little Ice Age, which lasted until about 1850, average winter temperatures were lower than today.

Another trouble which was widespread in many nurseries and orchards at the beginning of the nineteenth century, and was doubtless a contributing cause of canker, was 'American blight' or woolly aphid. Bliss, in 1825, said that this had first appeared in a nursery at Chelsea and had been brought to this country on dwarf apple trees, worked on Paradise rootstocks, growing in pots and imported from France. The pest quickly spread to other nurseries, including one at Knightsbridge. The nurseries near London were, for many years, the chief source of fruit trees for most parts of the country, and not only did the woolly aphids do much damage to trees in the nurseries, but was also spread on them to orchards in many parts of the country. In 1809, Knight warned apple growers against buying trees from London nurseries and not to trust their assertions that they could supply trees of Golden Pippin, or any other kind of apple, that would not canker.

Reports of the difficulty of gapping up old orchards in Herefordshire with young trees also indicated problems with apples due to replant disease. As early as 1697 Worlidge had fully appreciated the problems which could arise from trying to plant up fruit trees of the same kind on land where old orchards had been pulled out.

At the end of the eighteenth century, the newly formed Board of Agriculture, as one of its first activities, arranged for surveys of the state of farming to be carried out in every county. These reports, like others, showed the poor condition of many farm orchards, especially in Herefordshire.

In addition to the declining condition of their orchards, apple growers in the nineteenth century had to face increasing competition from imported fruit. During the Napoleonic Wars the home market was protected from foreign competition, which had previously come particularly from Flanders and France. After the defeat of Napoleon in 1815, fruit imports were revived and this resulted in a brief period of depression for the English growers until the government imposed a tariff of 4s a bushel (40 lb.) on imported apples, a large sum for those days. The result of this protection was a great expansion, during the 1820s and 1830s, in the planting of new orchards, mainly in Kent. The need for good-quality apples to replace foreign imports was emphasized by Bliss in 1825, who said that apples from old, diseased trees would not keep and so all through the spring, at a time when prices were high, Covent Garden market was supplied with thousands of pounds' worth of French apples.

After some recovery, the fruit industry again faced a crisis in 1837, as a result of the tariff alteration to 5 per cent *ad valorem*, equivalent to 3—7d a bushel. By 1842, it was reported in the *Maidstone Gazette* that fruit growers were having great difficulty in selling their apples, and Lord Torrington gave the opinion that the sooner Kent was without an apple tree the better. When Kent apple tree growers could not find a market for their fruit, they frequently made it into cider which was given to workers in place of their normal daily allowance of beer. The cider, made from cooking apples, was generally of poor quality so that the workers protested at the change.

The national scarcity of sugar from 1832 to 1842 caused a rapid rise in its price and meant that jams and preserves became a luxury, resulting in a further decline in apple consumption and other fruits used in jam making. Although tariffs on sugar were progressively reduced, foreign imports of

Street market near Charing Cross.

apples continued and there was further grubbing of orchards, including ot old derelict cider orchards. Imported French apples continued to sell better than English fruit, especially after Christmas. Robinson, in 1869, said that he had seen French apples sold in Covent Garden and in Regent Street marked 2s and 3s each!

It was not until after 1870 that major changes occurred and apple growing, and that of most other fruits, again became profitable. During the rest of the century there was an enormous increase in the orchard acreage. The reasons for this change are to be found in the rapid rise in the *per capita* income, following the industrialization of much of the country, and the development of the railways, resulting in a marked fall in transport costs. The jam industry now developed a substantial export trade, based on the cheapest sugar in the world, and this led to an increased demand for home-grown fruits. Although at this time there was general agricultural depression, fruit farming remained profitable and many general farmers turned to apple production. Even with the increased production, the demand was such that large quantities of apples were imported from America.

CULTIVATION OF SOFT FRUITS

While there was a decline by the beginning of the nineteenth century in the health and production of apple orchards, this was a time when the cultivation of soft fruits received an impetus following the introduction of new varieties. Many growers, nurserymen and private gardeners were now trying to raise new soft fruits from seed. For several centuries, seeds of the tree fruits had been sown for raising rootstocks and their grafting delayed to see if the fruits they bore were worth growing on their own account. In this way, a number of valuable varieties were bred, especially of cider apples. During the eighteenth century, the keen competition between members of the gooseberry clubs resulted in the introduction of hundreds of new gooseberry varieties. Now the interest spread to other soft fruits, in particular to strawberries.

The most successful of those growing strawberries was a market gardener, Michael Keens of Isleworth, who raised his plants from seed. Using the seed of the large-fruited Chilean strawberry, *Fragaria chiloensis*, which had been cross-pollinated by *Fragaria virginian*, he bred Keens' Imperial. From this variety, which itself created a sensation, he bred Keens' Seedling which showed a much-improved flavour as well as having large fruits of good colour. These two varieties were used as parents in raising many improved strawberries in England, France and the United States which transformed the strawberry industries of these countries.

The scientific approach to breeding of Thomas Andrew Knight was of prime importance in the introduction both of tree fruits and strawberries and also some currants, as was his work as a founder member of the Horticultural Society in 1804. The setting up of the Society's experimental garden at Kensington in 1818, followed by its transfer to Chiswick in 1822, was another major step forward. Here all the known varieties of temperate tree and soft fruits, both from Britain and overseas, were planted and a start made in sorting out the many hundreds of varieties then available. In 1826, the Society published a catalogue of 3825 varieties of fruits of all kinds then grown in the trials, but many of these proved to be synonyms. On the other hand, of the 360 varieties of gooseberries listed in 1831 nearly all proved to be true to type, a fact attributed to the keenness of the gooseberry club members in breeding and seeking out those with the largest berries.

During the nineteenth century the black currant became generally accepted in gardens, mainly on account of its considered medicinal value, and the various types of blackberries and American hybrid berries were introduced. There was also considerable interest in the breeding of improved raspberries. Phillips, writing in 1827, said that raspberries were much cultivated in the neighbourhood of Isleworth and Brentford, whence they were sent in swing carts to London distilleries for making brandy and vinegar and to confectioners and pastry cooks. Fruits intended for dessert were taken to Covent Garden on the heads of market women, in round baskets holding 12 gallons each. Although the distance from Isleworth to the market was ten miles, these women regularly covered the journey, for which they were paid 3s 6d, in two hours. From the Hammersmith gardens, the women took three loads a day to Covent Garden, for which they were paid 8d a load. These women porters came to London for the season each year from Wiltshire, Shropshire and Wales and seldom walked at less than five miles an hour.

Among the nurserymen who bred new soft fruits, the most noteworthy was Thomas Laxton of Bedford who, during the second half of the nineteenth century, raised many valuable varieties of strawberries, currants and other soft and tree fruits. Laxton did more than anyone else to improve the quality and productivity of many of these, and his name and that of his successors is remembered in such varieties as Royal Sovereign strawberry, Laxton No. 1 red currant and Laxton Giant black currant.

EXTENSION IN FRUIT GROWING

At the time that British apple growers were facing keen competition from the French, some British producers of soft fruit were finding it difficult to sell their red currants at a profit against the lower prices of imports from Holland. As in the previous two centuries, red currants were very much more popular than they are today, and in England and Holland they were grown on a large scale for market. In 1839, John Wilmot, a market gardener from Isleworth, gave evidence to the House of Commons inquiry into the fruit trade about currant growing. Wilmot was a neighbour of Michael Keens and, like the latter, raised several outstanding varieties of strawberries. His Black Prince, bred from seed of Keens' Imperial, was popular for over a hundred years. Wilmot told the Committee that, the previous year, the Dutch had began sending red currants to the English markets, a thing he never expected. They were sold for not more than double what it cost him for picking. He paid 6d a sieve for picking and sold for double that. Never had they had so many imported currants on the London markets.

However, with the improvement in the prosperity of the fruit industry during the last quarter of the nineteenth century, there was a very marked increase in the acreage of soft fruits as there was of orchards. In the early years after planting new orchards, soft fruits were frequently used as an interplant and grown until the trees needed extra space. A typical pattern used in Kent orchards was of dessert apples on semi-dwarfing rootstocks planted 12 ft apart with an underplant of gooseberries or currants. Alternatively, standard trees on seedling rootstocks were interplanted with other apples on less vigorous stocks, the whole plant filled in with soft fruits or nuts. It was also common practice to plant apple or cherry trees in hop gardens two or three years before the hops were due to be grubbed. As cherry trees were always very widely spaced, plums or apples were generally grown as an intercrop, to be removed when the orchards were grassed down and sheep used for grazing.

Young orchards of fruits for market were kept clean cultivated in contrast to farm orchards of standard trees of culinary or cider apples which, like cherry orchards, were usually laid down to grass, in the Hereford area, to be grazed by cattle. In the Wisbech region, however, the tradition was, and still is to some extent, to grow gooseberries underneath the Bramley trees. In fact, these systems of planting were very similar to those advised by Austen in 1657, when he suggested that orchards of widely spaced apple or pear trees should have soft fruits, roses, flowers or vegetables used as an interplant in the early years. In the Evesham area, the cultivation of plums became of special importance in the market gardens, where vegetables, including asparagus, were usually grown between the rows of plums. Around Cambridge, the high-quality Cambridge Gage became one of the major crops.

IMPORTANCE OF SOFT FRUIT PRODUCTION

The demand for jam during the latter years of the nineteenth century and the increasing demand for fresh fruits, especially strawberries, led to an enormous extension in the acreage devoted to this crop in Kent. Here around the St Mary Cray and Swanley areas, within easy reach of the London markets, the extent of strawberry cultivation reached a peak never seen since. One grower alone, in the 1880s, had 2,000 acres of strawberries.

Considerable acreages of woodland were grubbed and planted with soft fruits. The availability of plentiful supplies of horse manure collected from London stables, and transported by rail to the Kent farms, greatly increased soft fruit yields. The gangs of workers picking strawberries for market started at 3 a.m. so that the fruit could be sent off to Covent Garden and other markets in time for morning sales. One firm of growers, who also made jams, claimed that their strawberries were picked, made into jam and the jam was delivered to London for sale by grocers and stores by mid-day. Several growers who started making jams on their own farms later developed large commercial jam factories, a prominent example being in the Cambridge area.

Many growers had their own horse-waggons to transport their fruit to market or to the nearest station. The rail companies cooperated by providing special vans equipped with shelving for the punnets and baskets of strawberries and, in addition, there were special fruit trains to take the berries to the northern markets of Manchester, Liverpool and Birmingham.

At the same time that soft fruit growing was extending in Kent, the early production areas of the Tamar Valley, bordering Devon and Cornwall, the Cheddar area of Somerset and the Swanley district of Hampshire were concentrating on fresh strawberries for the early market. The extensive acreages of strawberries in the Wisbech region were grown almost entirely for the processing trade. In Scotland, strawberries were grown for market in the Clyde Valley to follow the earlier crops of the south, while the cultivation of raspberries, specially suited to the cooler, moister climate of Blairgowrie, became a major industry, especially for processing.

The Board of Agriculture figures show how the acreage of soft fruits increased:

Total United Kingdom acreage of soft fruits:	1888	36,700
	1890	46,200
	1891	58,700

By 1907, the total acreage had extended to 82,175 consisting of:

	Acres
Strawberries	27,827
Raspberries	8,878
Currants and gooseberries	25,590
Other fruits	19,880

Kent was still the leading county with 23,019 acres of soft fruits.

CULTIVATION OF FRUITS IN PRIVATE GARDENS

Though there were fluctuations in the prosperity of commercial fruit growers during the nineteenth century, the cultivation of fruits in gardens showed a marked and steady increase. In this the Royal Horticultural Society played a very important part and provided help and information to gardeners which had never been available before. This came at a time when there were major developments in the breeding and introduction of new varieties of soft and orchard fruits, both those bred in Great Britain and those brought from abroad. Numerous new varieties of strawberries, currants, raspberries and other fruits filled the pages of nursery catalogues, offering gardeners a far wider range than they had ever been offered before or since.

The RHS, with its extensive fruit trials, helped to sort out the many varieties and their synonyms, while the great nursery firms of Laxtons, Rivers, Bunyards and Pynes were responsible for introducing many new varieties of value. This was the time when these nurseries were very active in breeding new fruits.

Encouragement to gardeners was not only given by the RHS, but also by numerous local societies, which held regular shows, and the publication of many books on the subject; 1841 saw the publication of the first *Gardeners' Chronicle.*

In 1854, a new society, the British Pomological Society, was started with the object of 'promoting fruit culture in British dominions, especially to direct attention to the production of new varieties of fruits, examining and reporting on their merits and endeavouring to classify the fruits of Great Britain, the European Continent and America'. The president was Sir Joseph Paxton, the secretary Robert Hogg, remembered for his *Herefordshire Pomona*, and two members of the Council, the nurserymen, Thomas Rivers and James Veitch. Although this society had a limited existence of about ten years, it played an important part in giving publicity to the merits of the recently released Cox's Orange Pippin apple.

During the nineteenth century, great armies of gardeners worked in the gardens of the increasing numbers of the wealthy, who had profited from the industrial success of Britain, and produced an unsurpassed range and quality of fruit, while the owners of the smaller gardens took considerable interest in growing their own produce. The enthusiasm which was given to the growing of apples was demonstrated by the success of the Great Apple Show organized by the RHS in 1883. Of the 183 exhibitors of dessert apples, 123 showed Cox's Orange Pippin, and a poll taken among the exhibitors showed that 98 considered King of the Pippins to be their best dessert apple but 89 put Cox first.

THE SCIENTIFIC APPROACH TO FRUIT GROWING

In the nineteenth century, there was a new scientific approach to many aspects of agriculture and horticulture. The establishment of the Horticultural Society engendered more interest in the study of the various factors affecting the growth of plants, and the papers submitted to the Society and published in its *Transactions* show a very high degree of knowledge about all fruits, quite up to and often surpassing that of the present day. However, apart from the gardens of the RHS, it was many years before the first centre devoted to fruit experiments was started. This was the Woburn Experimental

Fruit Farm, a private undertaking founded in 1894 by the Duke of Bedford and Spencer Pickering. Although this farm only had a fairly limited existence and some of its conclusions — for example the adverse effects of grass on apple trees, attributed to an exudate from the grass roots and not to competition for nitrogen and water — were erroneous, useful work was done on such subjects as the time of planting fruit trees, planting strawberries, manuring and pest control.

It was not until 1903 that the first fruit research station was established at Long Ashton, Bristol, initially as the Cider Institute. This was followed, in 1913, by East Malling Research Station.

In the early years of the twentieth century, the planting of new orchards and the extension of the production of soft fruits, characteristic of the last quarter of the nineteenth century, continued. The peak for both classes of fruit was reached in the period 1906—10 when the total orchard area amounted to 250,000 acres and that of soft fruits to 84,000. The orchard area was maintained at about this level for 20 years and then started to rise again in the mid-30s to reach a new peak of 273,000 acres from 1951 to 1955, since when there has been a steady but drastic reduction to about the level of a hundred years ago. Soft fruit acreages have also been cut to about half their peak level.

To meet the growing demand for apples at the beginning of the century there was increased planting, especially of cooking apples of which Bramley's Seedling was the principal variety. This was widely planted in Kent, the Wisbech area and in parts of the west country. Cox's Orange Pippin was one of several dessert apples planted by commercial growers but, though popular with consumers, it still presented a number of cultural problems, including its susceptibility to apple scab.

The years of the Great War, 1914—18, resulted in a lack of sufficient attention being paid to many orchards, especially to farm orchards in the west country, and by 1919—20 many of the old unproductive cider apple trees were removed without replacement, though planting in Kent of apples for market was continued. The importation of dessert apples from America, which had become of importance during the latter part of the nineteenth century, continued, with a break during the war, until the start of the Second World War in 1939. The American apples mainly met the winter demand for red varieties, and Jonathan and Baldwin were especially popular in the industrialized cities of the north. Golden Russet from Nova Scotia and Newtowns from Oregon sold readily in other parts of the country.

During these years, the only way in which apples and pears could have their season extended was by being put into refrigerated stores. However, the discovery by Kidd and West in 1926 of the value of controlling the store atmosphere greatly prolonged the marketing period and has proved of outstanding importance to fruit growers throughout the world. The first commercial gas store was installed near Canterbury in 1928.

EARLY RESULTS OF RESEARCH

Apart from the valuable work on fruit storage carried out at Ditton Laboratory, fruit growers in the 1920s benefited from the investigations of the research stations at Long Ashton and East Malling. Long Ashton work proved of great value to the cider apple growers and the cider industry for which purpose the station was begun in 1903. As a result of the research of Professor Wallace, much information became available on the nutrition of fruit crops, prominence being given to the importance of potassium, which had previously been neglected.

At East Malling, Hatton's work on fruit tree rootstocks was of worldwide influence. Increasing information on pest and disease control and developments in spraying machinery, especially the use of high volumes applied at greater pressures, resulted in improved production of cleaner fruit. However, some diseases such as apple scab, *Venturia inequalis*, became more widespread and some varieties such as Bramley's Seedling, once considered resistant to scab, showed considerable infection. The same applied to the breakdown of the resistance of Conference pears to pear scab. Better knowledge of its nutrition, disease control and general management led to increased planting of Cox's Orange Pippin. New orchards of this variety, with suitable pollinators, gradually replaced the dominance of Bramley's Seedling and other culinary apples in the orchards planted in the 1930s.

In the 1920s and 1930s various types of planting plans were recommended for apples: for example, for arable orchards, standard trees of Bramley's Seedling and Newton Wonder on the vigorous Malling 12 or 13 rootstocks planted 40 ft square, interplanted with bush trees of Allington Pippin and Worcester Pearmain on M 2 stocks at 20 ft, the whole area being interplanted with blackcurrants and gooseberries, the latter to be grubbed first, followed by the bush trees. For orchards of permanent bush trees of dessert varieties, including Cox's Orange Pippin, on M 2 rootstocks, a planting distance of 14 ft square was suggested, or 18 ft for trees on M 1, again with an interplant of gooseberries, currants, raspberries or strawberries. These ideas were practically identical to those suggested at the end of the nineteenth century, with the exception that the rootstocks were more reliable. For intensive plantations, dwarf bush trees on M 9 stocks with no interplant were used and the cultivation of cordons, planted 3 ft by 5 ft, was considered suitable for the production of high-quality dessert varieties of apples.

Where apple trees were growing without an interplant, orchards of dessert varieties were usually laid down to grass once the trees were well established, as this was found to encourage cropping by checking their vigour and also to improve fruit colour. The grass was cut several times during the summer. Orchards of culinary varieties of apples, plums and pears were kept clean cultivated. Orchards of sweet cherries, grown as standard widely spaced trees, were also clean cultivated in their early years but later grassed down and, in Kent, traditionally grazed by sheep. The cherries were grown either on F 12/1, the vegetatively propagated rootstocks selected at East Malling, or wild 'geans', seedlings of *Prunus avium* found growing in woodlands. The latter rootstocks had been used for cherries for many hundreds of years.

The use of seedling pear rootstocks for pears had been practically given up by the 1930s and the Malling Quince A used for the plantations of Conference and Doyenné du Comice. A number of different rootstocks were used for plums but, of these, a Malling selection of St Julien, 'St Julien A', was becoming popular.

BREEDING NEW FRUIT VARIETIES

In the first half of this century, the breeding of new varieties of fruits by commercial nurserymen, who had been responsible for so many outstanding varieties in the nineteenth century, was largely given up and the first results of breeding by the research stations were seen. Of these, the black currant, Wellington XXX from East Malling was quickly accepted as of commercial importance. During the next 20 years, Malling introduced raspberries bred by Norman Grubb, of which Malling Promise and Malling Jewel became leading varieties, to be followed by new apple rootstocks bred in cooperation with John Innes Horticultural Institute. The latter was responsible for a number of first-quality sweet cherries, several new apples and pears and also new strawberries. A number of new strawberries of outstanding merit were bred by Robert Reid at Auchincruive, later to become part of the Scottish Horticultural Research Institute. Spinks at Long Ashton introduced several new dessert apples and black currants.

EFFECTS OF THE SECOND WORLD WAR

In Britain during the war period, 1939—45, the planting of new orchards was strictly controlled but there was concentration on trying to improve the production of existing orchards by better pest and disease control. The War Agricultural Executive Committees provided help by carrying out routine spraying of farm orchards and gave permits for the supply of the limited quantities of potash fertilizers to fruit growers. Encouragement was given to the cultivation of black currants to be used for making a purée or juice to be given to schoolchildren as a source of vitamin C.

Just as major changes occurred in the fruit industry after the Great War, so there were even greater changes following the Second World War. The destruction of orchards in Europe, and the need to replace apple imports from America to conserve dollars, resulted in extensive planting of new orchards of apples in Italy, France, Holland and, to a lesser extent, in other countries of Europe. In Italy there was also much planting of pears, in particular of the variety, Passe Crassane. In Europe the main apple used for the new orchards was Golden Delicious, valued for its heavy and precocious cropping and for the way in which its fruit can be stored and marketed over a long period. There was also a renewal of planting orchards in England which had been held up during the war years.

A primary influence in the type of planting and tree training system to be used for the new orchards was the high cost of planting and the increasing cost of labour involved in their routine maintenance and in the harvesting of the crop. This led to the use of intensive and semi-intensive systems of planting which, with suitable rootstocks and light pruning, result in early cropping, while the trees can be managed and the fruit picked from ground level.

Throughout the fruit-growing countries of the world, there has been a move to plant trees relatively closely in the rows, with wider spacing between rows, the trees being trained with a central leader. Such planting systems have been simplified by the use of herbicides to control grass and weeds in the tree rows, or herbicides can be used for all-over weed control. The introduction in the 1950s of the first soil-applied herbicides which control weed seedlings without cultivation has revolutionized the management of many fruit crops, in particular the soft fruits. All of these can now be grown from time of planting without any need for cultivations, and the use of herbicides to control weeds around young trees has a marked effect on improving their growth.

With soft fruits, there has been a considerable extension in the planting of black currants for juice production, the crop being harvested mechanically. The first use of mechanical harvesting was developed in the USA where bush shakers were used for harvesting blueberries and tree shakers used for acid cherries. Since then, in the early 1960s, mechanical harvesting has been used for raspberries, gooseberries and plums, especially for processing. There has only been limited success in harvesting strawberries mechanically.

The breeding of special types of plants suited to mechanical harvesting has involved cooperation between the plant breeders and engineers.

Although machines are widely used for harvesting soft fruits and some tree fruits, the degree of damage suffered by the fruits has proved a considerable problem, and hand-picking is still preferred for fresh fruits for market. The high cost of picking soft fruits has led to a great extension in the 'pick-your-own' method of sale, especially for strawberries, raspberries, gooseberries and currants, and to a more limited extent the same system is used for selling tree fruits.

MODERN BREEDING

Many new varieties of tree and soft fruits have been bred during recent years. No longer is their breeding a rather haphazard method of crossing existing varieties of merit and hoping that the offspring will prove of value. The plant breeder now selects the characteristics he wishes to introduce, such as disease resistance, heavy cropping capacity, quality and good flavour, and endeavours to combine these. Modern breeding often involves the hybridization of many species not used in the past in order to introduce new desirable characteristics and offers the possibility of new fruits unknown to fruit growers in the past. These growers often had a high appreciation of flavour and quality in their fruits and might not find that modern-day varieties, with their emphasis on good size and marketing properties, to their liking, but they would marvel at some of the modern methods of production of new seedlings and at the methods of producing healthy planting material from virus-infected parents.

With modern techniques of heat therapy and micropropagation, using tissue cultures, it is possible to rid existing varieties of fruits of virus infection which may have been impairing both their vigour and cropping capacity. Clonal stocks of both these, and new varieties, are maintained in a healthy state so that the nursery industry and growers can be regularly supplied with the best planting material. By routine renewal of the parent stock held by propagators, and by growing this in isolation away from infected plants, growers are provided with plants of soft and tree fruits which have greatly improved yields and quality of the fruit.

In the testing of new varieties, both those imported and those bred in Britain, which are distributed by the Nuclear Stock Association, there is close cooperation with the National Fruit Trials station of the Ministry of Agriculture at Faversham, where trials of all new varieties of fruits are carried out, comparing these with standard existing ones. Here also, the examination of varieties entered for Plant Variety Rights is made.

Another major development in growing fruit has been the use of growth-controlling chemicals which can be used to set a crop following frost damage to the blossoms of some pears and apples, to hasten the ripening and colouring of apples or to check unwanted growth of trees. The use of chemicals in the nursery to induce the production of 'feathers', or lateral shoots in young trees in their first year of growth, came at a time when well-feathered trees were vitally important in ensuring early cropping of intensively planted trees. Suitable chemicals can also aid the initiation of fruit buds or thin out the young fruits where there has been too heavy a set of apples. Nevertheless, the cropping and general quality of the fruits are still subject to the over-riding influence of the climate.

APPLES

13

The many and diverse types of apples grown today have all derived from species of the genus *Malus*. The two which have had the major influence in the past are considered to be *M. silvestris*. which has glabrous shoots and leaves, and *M. pumila*, in which the young shoots and undersurfaces of the leaves are covered with down. Both these species are now widely distributed in western Europe and western Asia, *M. silvestris* being the common crab apple which is found throughout the British Isles.

M. pumila is a dwarfer growing apple which is more limited in its distribution but is found, with *M. silvestris*, growing wild in the forests of the Caucasus and Turkestan. It is believed that the original 'Paradise' rootstocks were forms of *M. pumila*, found growing in the high lands of Armenia where the site of the Garden of Eden and Paradise was placed by some in the seventeenth century. The Greek, Theophrastus, mentioned a low-growing apple among those sent back to Greece following the conquests of Alexander the Great and this could well have been *M. pumila*.

A third species, which has been used in more recent years in the breeding of new varieties of apples, is *M. baccata*, the Siberian crab, a native of Russia. This species is particularly winter hardy and is able to withstand low winter temperatures which would kill other species of *Malus* or varieties developed from them. It has also proved of value in breeding apples showing resistance to the disease apple scab, caused by *Venturia inequalis.*

The genetic make-up of the apples cultivated today is very complex. The freedom with which hybridization between the species has occurred naturally in the past, and the thousands of years during which man has selected and bred new varieties, has further complicated their genetic composition so that the seedlings arising from the fruits on any one tree give rise to many varied types, the vast majority of which will prove of little value.

APPLES IN ANTIQUITY

There is evidence that the fruits of wild apples were collected as food by prehistoric man. Carbonized fruits dating from 6,500 BC were found at Catal Huyuk in Anatolia and, during excavations of prehistoric lake dwellings in Switzerland, remains of both sour crab apples and a larger form, which may have been cultivated, were discovered. These fruits seem to have been cut into two pieces and dried. Drying was a common method of preserving both apples and plums used by the inhabitants of the areas adjoining the fruit tree forests in Caucasia and was also used by the ancient Romans. In England, impressions of apple pips were found on six shards found at Windmill Hill in Wiltshire, suggesting that their fruits had been used for food in the Neolithic period.

The improved forms of apples, along with other fruits selected from the forests of Asia Minor, the Caucasus and adjoining areas, were spread through the Fertile Crescent and reached the Holy Land about 2,000 BC. Apples feature in the Bible in Solomon's *Song of Songs*:

> *As the apple tree among the trees of the wood, so is my beloved among the sons. Stay me with flagons, comfort me with apples; for I am sick of love.*

From Palestine, apples were taken to Egypt. The Third Papyrus of Anastasi of the reign of Rameses II (1298−1235 BC) mentions plantations in the Nile Delta, 'most pleasant and full of all things good, and not least, apples'. The Harris Papyrus of Rameses III's time (1198−1166 BC) states that 848 baskets of apples were brought to the Temple of Ra in Heliopolis every day as offerings. The Fourth Anastasi Papyrus, also from the reign of Rameses II, mentions a gift of apples from Kharu to the Pharaoh.

That apples were grown and were of importance in the time of the ancient Greeks and Romans is shown by the frequent references to them in Greek and Roman literature. The earliest references to apples occur in *The Odyssey* of Homer, written between 900 and 800 BC, in the description of the orchard at the Palace of Alcinous, which included apple trees. Later, Theophrastus spoke of the difficulty of propagating apples from cuttings, the use of budding and grafting being the generally accepted methods.

The Roman writers, Columella, Varro, Cato, Virgil and Pliny, all dealt with various aspects of apple culture. Columella, writing on propagation, said that the 'ancients' had handed down two kinds of grafting, the cleft and rind forms carried out in the spring, and budding done in the summer. He gave a full description of grafting in the orthodox ways and then continued:

> *A third kind of grafting is our own invention; being a very delicate*

operation, it is not suited to every kind of tree . . . You should look
out for a bud which has a good appearance. Make a mark round it
enclosing two square inches, so that the bud is in the middle, and
then make an incision all round it with a sharp knife and remove the
bark carefully so as not to damage the bud. Also choose the healthiest
branch of the other tree, which you are going to innoculate, and cut
out a part of the bark of the same dimensions as before and strip the
bark off the firm wood. Then fit the scutcheon, which you have
prepared, to the part which you have barked, so that it exactly
corresponds to the one on the other tree from which the bark has
been stripped. Having done this, bind the bud well all round and be
careful not to damage the sprout itself. Then daub the joints of the
wound and ties round them, with mud, leaving a space, so that the
bud may be free and not be constricted by the binding. Cut away the
shoot and upper branches of the tree into which you have inserted
the bud, so that there may be nothing to which the sap can be drawn
off or benefit from the sap to another part rather than the graft.
After the twenty-first day unbind the scutcheon.

These instructions are practically identical to those given in any modern account of patch budding which has come into general use again in recent years. Pliny, describing the same technique, suggested using a hollow punch, such as used by shoemakers, to obtain a close fit between bud and rootstock.

All the Roman writers included the names of a number of apple varieties. Columella recommended the Scaudian, the Matiam, the Globe-apple, the Cestine, the Pelusian, the Amerian, the Syrian and the Honey-apple. Pliny listed 23 varieties and pointed out that they were usually named after those who had introduced them or after some famous person as Matius, Castius, Mallius and Scaudius, although the Sceptian apple had been named after the freed slave who had discovered it. Pliny said that Cato had also mentioned the Quirinian and the Scantian which he said was stored in casks, but the apple most recently introduced was a small one of good flavour named the Persian. Some apples were the colour of blood but wild apples were usually of little value and some had such acid juice that it would blunt the edge of a sword. The Flour apple, although the earliest to be picked, was a very poor variety, just as our present-day very early kinds are mostly of poor quality.

PRESERVING APPLES

The prehistoric lake dwellers of Switzerland stored dried apples and this method was also used by the Romans. Columella described how in August or early autumn, apples and pears of the sweetest flavour were picked when moderately ripe, cut into two or three pieces with a reed or a bone knife, and placed in the sun to dry. He added that if there were a quantity of them these fruits could provide country folk with not the least part of their food during the winter, for they served instead of a relish, as did dried figs.

An interesting observation about dried apples was made by Suetonius (born AD 69) in his *The Twelve Caesars*. He wrote that Augustus was an abstemious drinker, seldom touching wine but instead he moistened his throat with a morsel of bread dunked in cold water or ate a slice of cucumber, the heart of a young lettuce or a sour apple, fresh or dried. In Wales, in this century, coal miners were still in the habit of taking sour cider apples with them down the pits as they found these refreshed them better than anything else during the course of their arduous work.

The apple was one of the favourite fruits of the Romans and featured in several of the murals on the walls of the ruins of Pompeii. Roman mosaics, illustrating the seasons, at St Romain-en-Gal, Vienne in France, dating from the third century, showed the grafting of trees and the harvesting of apples. The popularity of apples with the Romans, and the fact that they were grown in Roman-occupied France, encourages the belief that they must have grown apples during their occupation of Britain.

APPLES IN ROMAN BRITAIN

There is little doubt that the Romans found apples growing in Britain for the crab apple is indigenous, but it is not known if there was any cultivation of the apple or any other fruit in Britain before the invasion. That apples were known in this country from the earliest times is shown by the fact that in Celtic the apple is 'abhall' and in Cornish 'avall'. Ancient Glastonbury was called Yrys Avallac or Avallon by the Britons, which indicates an apple orchard and from which the Roman, Avallonia was derived.

Evidence of the consumption of apples and other fruits during the Roman occupation has recently been provided by excavations on known Roman sites. In Bermondsey, in Tooley Street, a section of the Thames alluvium yielded a collection of seeds, assumed to be household refuse, including apple pips. At Frenchgate, Doncaster, among other seeds found in a pit, were numerous apple seeds representing 150—300 apples. These may have been the remains of apples used for food or for the production of an alcoholic drink. A second-century building in St Thomas Street, Southwark, stood on a site where excavations disclosed 14 rectangular pits. In one were found organic remains including those of apples, cherries, figs, plums and grapes. However, to what extent apples were cultivated during the Roman occupation must still remain a matter for debate.

*A Roman mosaic from St Romain-en-Gal, Vienne, France, showing
fruit picking, third century.*

EARLIEST EVIDENCE OF CULTIVATION

Following the Roman occupation of Britain, during the period of the Dark
Ages, there is little direct evidence of the cultivation of apples, although the
record of fruit production in the Isle of Ely in the tenth century suggests that
apples were being grown there. But in spite of a lack of direct evidence,
corroboration from the language and the fact that apples were being grown
in the neighbouring countries of Europe, as shown by Charlemagne's list of
fruits, supports the idea that apples and other tree fruits were being
cultivated, as were vines, in Britain before the Norman Conquest.

After the Conquest, there are many records of apple culture in Britain. These followed the developments introduced by the monasteries, the importation of new varieties of fruits from France and the use of apples for cider. Among the apples grown by the monks and nobles in the thirteenth century, the Pearmain, also known as the Old English Pearmain, was the first to be recorded by name in a deed of 1204, relating to the Lordship of Runham in Norfolk. The manor was required to pay the Exchequer each year, on the feast of St Michael, 200 Pearmains and four hogsheads of cider made from Pearmains. It probably had its origin in England as both German and French synonyms referred to it as the English Pearmain. It was illustrated by Parkinson in 1629 and it is thought it may be the Pearmain still included in the National Fruit Trials at Faversham. It was prized both for dessert and for making good-quality cider.

Roman mosaics from St Romain-en-Gal, Vienne, France, left, preparing a tree for grafting and, right, inserting a scion using cleft graft, third century.

The Costard is another of the old English varieties which is recorded as being sold in Oxford in 1296 for 1s for 100 fruits, and in 1325 the price of 29 Costard apple trees was 3s. It was a cooking apple popular for making pies until after Shakespeare's time, but was fast disappearing by the end of the seventeenth century. This apple was also known as the English Costard on the Continent. Its name is preserved today in 'costermonger', originally a seller of Costard apples.

EARLY LITERATURE ON APPLE GROWING

Apart from the references to apples and orchards in various Rolls and in other accounts of the court, monasteries and estates in the Middle Ages, one of the earliest recorded references to the cultivation of apples in England was in a poem, 'The Feate of Gardeninge by Mayster Jon Gardener' (1440—50). This was obviously written by an experienced gardener as the poem gives practical instructions for the cultivation of fruits, vegetables and flowers. The dialect of the language used in the poem shows that the author was from Kent or the south-east counties. Kent was already of importance in the supply of produce to the London markets:

> *Off Settyng' and Reryng of Treys*
>
> *Yn the calenders of Januar'*
> *Thu schalt treys both set and rere*
> *To graffy then yn appyl and pere*
> *And what treys ys kynd hem to bere*
> *Appul and A-appul-tre*
> *For ther ys kynd ys most to be*
> *Of pere y mynde zonne*
> *To graffe hym a-pon a haw-thorne.*
>
> *Of Graffyng' of Treys*
>
> *Thus myzt graffe appul and pere*
> *Fro the moneth of september to averer [April]*
> *Wyth a saw thou schalt the tre kytte*
> *Klene A-tweyne the stok of the tre*
> *Where-yn that they graffe schall be*
> *Make thy Kyttyng' of thy graffe*
> *By-twyne the newe and old staffe*
> *So that hit be made to lyfe*
> *As the bake and egge of a knyfe.*

There was reference to the medicinal use of apples in *The Grete Herball* by Peter Treueris, published in 1526:

De Macianis pomis. Wood crabbes or wyldynges

Ala maciana ben wylde apples and ben colde and drye and have power to staunche.

Those that be somewhat colde of savour ben best to eate and they that have fevers ought to eate them cawe and rosted after meate. But rosted be best.

For them that have had sickeness lately and have yil dygestyan / caused of colde in the stomake / use them thus. Cleve them in two and take out the kynalles / and y harde skynnes that lye in and fylle the holownesse with powdre of nutmygges / cloves and cocle sede / and sometyme is onely put powdre of cynamone / gynger / and peper and so rosted in the fyre / and it wyll conforte gretely.

William Turner in his herbal, which was first published in 1551, wrote of apples and their uses:

Apples ben of divers kindes. The apples specyally / conforteth the herte with his sweet odour. And they be good for the that hath the passy ptysys.

Apples eaten raw doothe moe dysseases tha any other fruytes / for they causeth ye humpurs through all the membyes.

There be swete apples and they ben warme dry of nature. Some ben watery / soure / and eygre of taste / and colde of complexyon. The iuce of those dyvers apples may not be kept / but alone the iuce of quynces / and it confyet with hony and sugre / and with other good spyces it endureth the longer. This is all about the apple.

Recently, the 'family tree', which has several varieties grafted on to it, has become popular for planting in small gardens. This idea, however, is by no means new as it was described by Mascall in 1575: 'To graffe many sortes of Apples on one Tree. Yℇ may graffe on one Apple tree at once, many kinde of Apples, as on every braunch a contrary fruite, and of peares the lyke: but see as nighe as ye can, that all your Cions be of lyke springing, for else the one wyll out growe and shaddowe the other.'

The early writers also emphasized the need for care when harvesting apples. Thomas Tusser, in his *Five Hundred Pointes of Good Husbandrie*, wrote in 1580:

Forget it not fruit bruised will rot.
Light ladder and long doth the tree least wrong.
Go gather with skill, a bad gather that will
Fruit gather too timely, will taste of the wood,
wil shrink and be bitter, and seldome proove good.
So fruit that is shaken, or beat off a tree
with bruising in falling some faultie wil bee.

In 1604 the author of the *Fruiterer's Secrets*, also had some interesting points to make about harvesting and handling fruits. As he said, great pains are taken in grafting, planting and pruning the trees and good ground is taken up in growing them, all of which effort can be wasted if care is not exercised when harvesting. He gave details of a gathering apron to be used when picking apples, which had a loose end fastened under the girdle so that by bending down to one side the fruits could be carefully released into a 'prickett' or basket in such a way that their stalks would not damage other apples nor be damaged themselves. This is still sound advice today when picking bags, which undo at the bottom, are commonly used but considerable damage is still done by careless handling.

Where the apples were gathered fairly close to the storage place, the author advised emptying the picking aprons into 1- or 2-bushel baskets or prickets, equipped with two ears or handles so that they could be held by two men or the basket could be carried on a cross-staff. However, where the harvested fruits were to be carried some distance by cart or water, they should be taken in larger baskets or 'Maunds'. Where delicate fruits such as summer pears were to be carried, the Maunds should be lined with green fern, placed with the stalks sticking outwards to avoid pricking the fruits. The Maunds should also be covered with fern.

In the seventeenth century, the roads of Britain were in such a poor condition that many of them were impassable in winter, and so wherever the rivers were navigable or passage by sea was possible, this method was used for sending fruit to market. As the author of the *Fruiterer's Secrets* said, although short-lived summer varieties were not worth sending any distance, good-quality storing varieties, when sent by water, were best laid carefully by hand in dry hogsheads or barrels as this would ensure close packing, whereas when fruits were poured into the barrels, hollows could be left resulting in the jogging and tossing of the fruits in transit, causing severe bruising.

Small quantities of fruits could be taken to market in dossiers or panniers, hung on either side of a horse, the containers for cherries and pears being lined with green fern but those for apples simply having pads of sweet straw at the top and bottom. This advice, given in 1604, shows that there was as much concern at that time as there is today to ensure that fruits were carefully handled from the time of their picking to the time of their sale at the market.

Apple Varieties in the Sixteenth and Seventeenth Centuries

In the National Fruit Trials at Faversham the oldest apple variety, Decio, is thought to date from the time of Attila c.AD 450, and is said to have been brought by a Roman general, Ezio, from Latium. Apart from this, several varieties from the thirteenth century still exist, but it is from the sixteenth century onwards that the bulk of the old varieties, still preserved today, date. This was the time when the new varieties from the Continent were imported for Henry VIII by Harris, and when other growers such as Mascall were bringing over new kinds. It is significant that a number of these old varieties originated in France and bore the name Caville. Two in the Fruit Trials are Caville Blanc d'Hiver, 1598, and Caville Rouge d'Hiver, 1600.

The introduction of the new varieties in the sixteenth century was accompanied by a revival of interest in growing apples and many new orchards were planted. The rootstocks generally used were apple seedlings, and Mascall advised delaying their budding or grafting until after they had fruited in order to see if any should bear apples of good quality. In 1618, William Lawson reiterated this advice, saying that if the apple seedlings grew well, having broad, greenish yellow leaves, this indicated the possibility of their producing large, pleasantly flavoured fruit. In this way, the number of new varieties was considerably increased.

This increase was commented on by Gerard in 1597. He included illustrations of several apples in his *Herbal*, saying they grew in his garden in Holborn. They were, the Pome Water, the Baker Ditch, the King of Apples, the Summer Pearmain, the Winter Pearmain and the Quining or Queen of Apples. He said the infinite kinds of apples varied in size, taste and skin colour and were also affected by the soil and climate — shrewd observation.

Parkinson in 1629 said the different sorts of apples were so many that it was impossible to give the names of all the varieties then grown. He did describe 54 covering a long season of use, starting with the Summer Pearmain. He gave the Golding or Golden Pippin as the greatest and best. The Great Pearmain differed little in taste or keeping qualities, and it was regarded as the second best. Among other apples of good quality, he mentioned the French Pippin, the Russeting, the Broading, Pomewater, Flower of Kent, Gilliflower, Margilo, Harvey Apple, the Queen, Leathercote, Spicing, Catshead, Kentish Codlin and Geneting. Three good apples from France were Rambures, Carpendu and Calval.

Both Gerard and Parkinson wrote of the various uses of apples. In the sixteenth century and earlier, the fruits were often used for making cosmetics which Gerard said were used to soften the skin and fade freckles: 'There is an ointment made with the pulp of apples and swine's grease and rosewater, which is used to beautify the face, and to take away the roughness of the skin, called in shops pomatum, of the apples whereof it is made.' Parkinson, who, like Gerard, was an apothecary, had more to say of the uses of apples:

The best sorts of Apples serve at the last course for the table, in most mens houses of account; where, if there grow any rare or excellent fruit, it is then set forth to be seene and tasted.

Divers other sorts serve to bake, either for the Master Table or the meynes sustenance, either in pyes or pans, or else stewed in dishes with Rosewater and Sugar and Cinamon or Ginger cast upon.

Some kinds are fittest to roast in the winter time, to warme a cup of wine, ale or beere, or to be eaten alone, for the nature of some fruit is never so good or worth the eating, as when roasted.

Some sorts are fitted to scald for codlins and are taken to coole the stomache, as well as to please the taste, having Rosewater and Sugar put to them.

The juice of Apples, likewise as of pippins and pearmains, is of very good use in Melancholic diseases, helping to produce mirth and to expel heaviness. The distilled water of the same apples is of like effect.

1 *Malus Carbonaria.*
The Pome Water tree.

One of the sixteenth-century apples used for the production of the cosmetic pomatum, used to soften the skin and take away freckles.

3 *Malum regale.*
The King of Apples.

4 *Malum reginale.*
The Quining, or Queene of Apples.

5 *Platomela siue Pyra æstiua.*
The sommer Pearemaine.

6 *Platarchapia siue Pyra hyemalia.*
The winter Pearemaine.

Winter Pearmain, also known as Old English Pearmain was the first apple recorded in England in 1204. It was valued for high quality cider and dessert use.

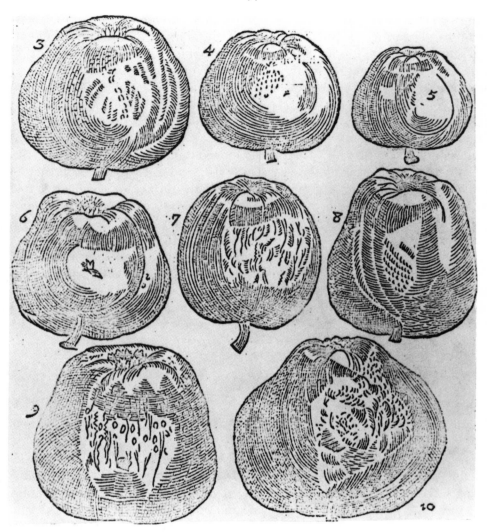

Important early seventeenth-century apples: 3. Pomewater 4. Golden Pippin
5. The Pearmain 6. The Queene apple 7. Genneting 8. Pound Roy
9. Kentish Codlin 10. Bardfield Quining.

CONTINUED APPLE PLANTING

The impetus given to the planting of new orchards in the latter part of the
sixteenth century continued throughout the next century, encouraged by a
number of nurserymen who regularly brought over new varieties from the
Continent. Austen of Oxford was one of the leading nurserymen at this time
and, in 1657, published a list of what he considered the best varieties of

apples. These were the Summer and Winter Pearmains, both for their quality and bearing, the Small Spice apple, the Harvey, the Queen, the Great Russetting, Kerton Pippin and Holland Pippin. Golden Pippin he gave special merit like all other writers. In 1697, Worlidge considered that there were nearly 500 varieties of apple in Great Britain, including table and cider ones.

An interesting sidelight on the enmity which existed between Britain and France in the eighteenth century is given by Switzer when, writing from Somerset in 1724, he said: 'The French indeed (who would faith be the first in every thing) will scarce allow us here in England to have any Fruit that is valuable but what comes from them.' Still, he did acknowledge that the Nonpareil, which still exists today, had come from France and first brought to the Ashtons in Oxfordshire and planted by a Jesuit in Queen Mary's or Queen Elizabeth's time. However, in addition to their importation, the raising of new apples from seed in Britain continued unabated throughout the early part of the eighteenth century, so that in 1739 Bradley said that to list the names of all the varieties would be almost impossible seeing how many new ones were raised from seed every year in almost every county in England. For dwarf trees grown as espaliers, he suggested Codlin, Nonpareil, Golden Pippin, Kerton Pippin and Holland Pippin.

APPLE ROOTSTOCKS

The ancient Greeks and Romans used grafting and budding to perpetuate their choice varieties of fruits. Knowledge of the propagation of fruit trees was spread through Europe and the technique probably reached Britain during the Roman occupation. After the Norman Conquest there was increased interest in planting the improved varieties of apples then available, and there is definite evidence of the sale and purchase of both rootstocks and scions or grafts in the thirteenth century; for example in 1265 at Rimpton in Somerset of grafts of apples and pears and their rootstocks. Other records exist of the purchase of grafts at Wellingborough and of apple trees in Oxford for planting at Cuxham in Oxfordshire.

The Romans generally used rootstocks raised from cuttings or suckers taken from existing trees, but the earliest books on fruit growing in England advised ones raised from seed. In the mid-fifteenth century, Mayster Jon Gardener simply said the trees to be grafted should be planted out in January, without specifying their source, but in 1525 Fitzherbert recommended the crab stock as best.

In 1575, Mascall, the fruit grower at Plumpton in Sussex, who raised his own trees as well as growing apples and making cider, described how to raise rootstocks from cider apple pomace, the remains of the apples,

D

containing the seeds, left after the juice has been extracted. The use of pomace has been one of the main sources of seed for rootstocks up till the present century, but one drawback about its use has been the variability in vigour of the rootstocks and trees worked on them. For this reason, seedlings of crab apples, *Malus silvestris*, have often been preferred. Austen used crab seedlings and Lawson, in 1618, advised sowing groups of apple seeds *in situ* in the orchard and later selecting one of the seedlings to be grafted without transplanting.

The Greek, Theophrastus, spoke of a low-growing apple, probably *Malus pumila* or a derivative, but it was not until the sixteenth and seventeenth centuries that mention was made of apple rootstocks used to dwarf their growth in comparison with the vigour imparted by the commonly used seedling stocks. The name 'Paradise' was first recorded by Ruellius in his book *De Natura Stirpium Tres*, published in 1536. In 1597, Gerard referred to this type: 'We have in our London gardens a dwarffe kinde of sweete Apple, called Chamaemalue, the dwarffe Apple tree or Paradice Apple, which beareth Apples very timely without grafting.' Parkinson, in 1629, described the Paradise apple as growing:

> . . . *not much higher than a man may reach* . . . *the fruit is a faire yellow apple and reasonably great but very light and spongy or loose and a bitterish taste and nothing pleasant* . . . *it* [*the tree*] *will have many bunches or tuberous swellings in many places* . . . *the roots sendeth forth many shoots and suckers whereby it may be much increased.*
>
> . . . *being a dwarfe Tree, whatsoever fruit shall be grafted on it, will keep the graft low, like unto itselfe and yet beare fruit reasonably well. And this is a pretty way to have Pippins, Pomewaters or any other sorte of Apple (as I have had myself and also seen with others) growing low, that if they will, they will make a hedge row of these low fruits, planted in an orchard all along by a walke side.*

This French Paradise, Pommier du Paradis, which was also known as *Malus paradisiaca*, was no doubt one of the dwarf-growing apples of Armenia, probably forms of *M. pumila* or hybrids between this and *M. silvestris*. Armenia was an ancient apple-growing region where various forms of apple trees, including dwarf kinds, flourished. *M. pumila*, and other types used as rootstocks, produce suckers freely and root readily, which encourages easy propagation. As Parkinson said, the tuberous swellings or burr knots readily form roots which make these types of rootstocks relatively easy to grow from cuttings or by layering. Some cultivated varieties of apples such as the Codlin, grown for many years in the Middle Ages and later, also root easily from cuttings and layers, and were widely used as rootstocks for dwarf trees.

Dwarf trees were not mentioned again in the fruit-growing literature of the seventeenth century until 1660 when Evelyn's translation of the Curé d'Henoville's *The Manner of Ordering Fruit Trees* appeared in Britain. The Curé described at length the methods of growing apples and pears on dwarf trees, a practice well established in France. For apple trees trained on walls as espaliers or in hedges and for dwarf bush trees, he advised the use of Paradise stocks which he said were a type of Codling apple. These could be propagated from cuttings. The Sweeting or Doulcain (Doucin) apple could also be used as a rootstock but grew more vigorously and could not be kept as a low, dwarf-growing tree. The Curé said that trees on seedling or 'Free' stocks grew vigorously and were slow to crop, while the more the trees were pruned the more strongly they grew. He suggested planting apples on Paradise stocks 9 ft apart on the square or 6 ft apart in a single row, compared with 18–24 ft apart for trees on seedlings — very similar to spacings used today.

Worlidge in 1691 and Bradley in 1726 both wrote enthusiastically about dwarf apple trees and both said that the first Paradise rootstocks had been brought over from France but, as Bradley added, almost every nursery around London could by then supply this stock.

Dwarf Trees for Gardens

In 1731 Miller wrote that although Paradise rootstocks had been much used recently, the trees were short-lived unless they were planted so deeply that the scion variety became rooted. He said that although these stocks were much used in France they were not so popular in England. However, not many people agreed with Miller. Gibson in 1768 said that Miller had persuaded people to plant espalier-trained apple trees worked on seedling rootstocks in their gardens, but these had often grown too vigorously and proved indifferent bearers whereas, when worked on Paradise stocks, the trees were easy to train, required little pruning and cropped well. Gibson wrote that many people who had only small gardens could still have room for one or more dwarf trees of apples on Paradise or pears on quince rootstocks. Such trees were especially suitable for city gardens, requiring little room, a minimum of pruning and soon coming into fruit. In large gardens more vigorous trees on seedling rootstocks, trained as the owner pleased, could be used.

The arguments on the relative values of trees on dwarfing or more vigorous rootstocks have continued right up to the present day, with the same points put forward by the proponents as were offered by writers in the seventeenth and eighteenth centuries. It was his interest in growing smaller trees which led the English nurseryman, Rivers, to look at new seedlings of his own raising, in particular at two of a batch bred from the pips of Golden Pippin, Golden Reinette, Ribston and other good varieties, which could be readily propagated from cuttings. One of these was a vigorous grower and had very broad leaves, which he called the Broad-leaved English Paradise (later M 1). The second was equally vigorous but trees worked on it had a greater tendency to form fruit spurs; this he called the Nonesuch Paradise (M 6). At this time, in 1865, Rivers thought that the new rootstocks might revolutionize apple culture and, in fact, the Broad-leaved English Paradise did maintain considerable popularity for about 100 years as a rootstock for large bush trees, but neither could be considered to induce dwarfing.

NAMES OF ROOTSTOCKS

Several types of Paradise rootstocks were grown during the sixteenth to eighteenth centuries, and from the descriptions given by Parkinson, the Curé and others, and the subsequent trials, one of these was the same as, or very similar to, the very dwarfing M 8 of the Malling classification, also known as Clark's Dwarf in the United States. The dwarfing rootstock most widely used during this century, Jaune de Metz, was introduced by a French nurseryman, M. Dieudonne of Metz, in 1828. The 'Doulcain' of the Curé d'Henoville was probably the Doucin, M 2, also known as the 'Dutch Creeper' or Dutch Paradise.

During the nineteenth century there was increasing confusion about the naming and performance of the many rootstocks then being used by nurserymen, both on the Continent and in Britain. There was particularly confusion over the trueness to type of the dwarfing Paradise stocks. Rivers himself seems to have added to the confusion by calling his two vigorous rootstocks Paradise types. As Hatton said, in a report on rootstock research in 1920, 'the original distinction between true Paradise or dwarfing Apple Stock and the true Crab or free growing Stock, had imperceptibly changed to a distinction in method of propagation, all those Apple Stocks which were raised vegetatively being known as "Paradise", and those raised from seed, known as "Crab."'

In 1871, in order to try to sort out some of the apple rootstocks, A. Barron, superintendent of the RHS experimental gardens at Chiswick, collected 18 different rootstocks from nurserymen in Britain, France and Germany. He grew these both unworked and grafted with scion varieties for comparison. Among these rootstocks were crab, Dutch Paradise, Rivers' Nonsuch, English Paradise, Scotts Paradise, the Doucin and several French Paradise. One of the latter, Barron considered to be the true French Paradise, producing a dwarf, early-cropping tree. Other French Paradise stocks and Paradise apples supplied by nurserymen were found to be quite different from, and inferior to, the true type. The Doucin came second in precocity. The editor of the *Gardeners' Chronicle* in 1874 hoped that, 'this trial at Chiswick may draw the attention of our nurserymen to this particular variety [the true French Paradise] and that they will take means to propagate it and experiment with it'.

In spite of the hopes expressed in the *Gardeners' Chronicle*, the confusion in the naming of rootstocks continued, and it was not until work on the sorting out and classification of the many rootstocks then available was begun at East Malling, which resulted in the valuable reports of Hatton, that the confusion was finally cleared up and rootstocks true to type became available to propagators and fruit growers. By 1917, at least nine varieties of 'Paradise' and 'Doucin' were in commercial circulation and many more about to be introduced. These varied from the very dwarf French Paradise, M8, to the intermediate types such as the Doucin, M2, and the more vigorous forms of Paradise including M10, 13 and 16.

The rootstocks selected for further trial were the very dwarf French Paradise, M8, the dwarf Jaune de Metz, M9, intermediate Doucin, M2, and Improved Doucin, M5, vigorous Broad-Leaved English, M1, and Nonsuch, M6, and the very vigorous M10, 13 and 16.

LATE EIGHTEENTH- AND NINETEENTH-CENTURY APPLE VARIETIES

In the eighteenth century, apple growing in gardens was widespread throughout most parts of the country. Owing to the difficulties in distribution of produce, if apples were desired in the more remote parts they had to be grown in the garden or farm orchards. In 1768, in a book dealing with fruit growing in Scotland, John Gibson mentioned Golden Pippin, Golden Rennet, Coville and Nonpareil as some of the best varieties, the same ones esteemed by growers in England at that time. The Scottish author also said that many varieties had vague and fanciful names and were not worth growing. He described most pippins as generally small, several like crab apples; Golden Pippin as charming and with a pleasant juice; the Rennets as coming from France, and the russets as probably having been raised in England.

At the end of the eighteenth century, a series of reports on the state of agriculture in the different counties of Britain, prepared for the newly established Board of Agriculture, gave an account of the condition of the orchards and useful information on the varieties of apples being grown. In the report for Kent in 1794 by John Boys, the following were listed as apple varieties grown for domestic use: 'Lemon Pippin or Quince apple, Farley Pippin, Royal Russet, Ribstone Pippin, Holland Pippin, Pigsnout, Walling, Loand Pearmain, Nonpareil, Golden Pippin, French Pippin, Kentish Pippin and Golden Nob'. Bucknall, writing in 1797, stated that the ancient orchards

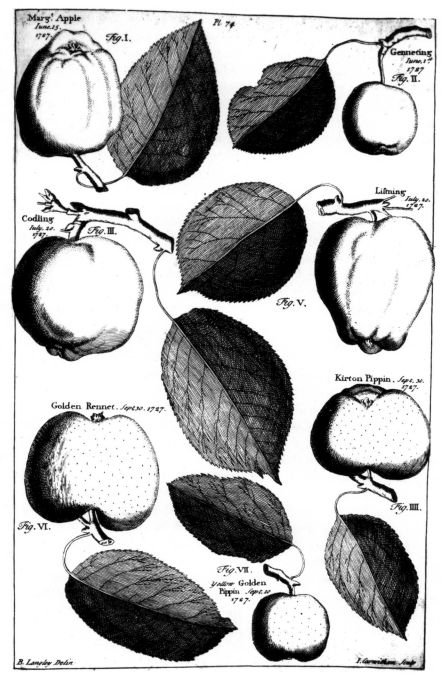

Important early eighteenth-century apples: Golden Pippin, popular for dessert and cider; Golden Reinette, a high quality dessert apple, popular for several hundred years both in Britain and Europe.

of Kent, which had mostly been grubbed 50 years before, produced 'Kentish Pippin, Lemon Pippin, Russet, Cat's-head and other varieties, but as the age refined in luxury the more delicate apples were introduced'. One variety introduced in the eighteenth century was Ribston Pippin, raised from seeds brought from Rouen and sown at Ribston Hall, Knaresborough about 1707. By 1875, Hogg said that no other apple was grown so widely as Ribston. It is still popular today.

Two other important apple varieties bred in the eighteenth century were Ashmead's Kernel, raised about 1700 by Dr Ashmead, an eminent physician of Gloucester, and Blenheim Orange, discovered about 1740 at Woodstock in Oxfordshire but not distributed until 1818.

The problems affecting apple orchards during the latrter part of the eighteenth century led to more attention being given to possible remedies. The work of Thomas Andrew Knight in breeding new fruits was accompanied by the efforts at the gardens of the Royal Horticultural Society to sort out the many hundreds of varieties of apples and other fruits which had become available in increasing numbers following the revival of fruit growing in the sixteenth century. In 1826, 1,205 varieties of apple were planted at Chiswick and this was increased to 1,400 by 1831.

In the first half of the nineteenth century, dessert varieties recommended included Ribston, Court of Wyck Pippin, Duchess of Oldenburgh, Old and Scarlet Nonpareil, Golden Pippin, Golden Reinette, King of the Pippins and Wellington. For cooking, Beauty of Kent, Kentish Codlin, Keswick Codlin, Lemon Pippin and Blenheim Orange were suggested. Of these apples, Golden Pippin, which had been popular for about 200 years, was gradually giving way to the newer varieties, although in 1827 Phillips said that this variety, in spite of reports of its decline, was still being sent to Covent Garden in large quantities and that excellent quality fruit of Golden Pippin was being imported to this country from several parts of America.

During the nineteenth century, many of the apple varieties grown today were introduced, these often having originated as chance seedlings. Bramley's Seedling, Cox's Orange Pippin, Lord Derby and Worcester Pearmain are examples of notable introductions.

Bramley's Seedling was raised at Southwell, Nottinghamshire, between 1809 and 1813 by Mary Ann Brailsford, but was not introduced into commerce until 1876 by the nurseryman, Merryweather of Nottingham. Its values as a cooking apple were quickly appreciated and, in 1883, it was awarded a First Class Certificate by the RHS. Towards the end of the nineteenth century and the first quarter of the twentieth, there was extensive planting of Bramley's Seedling as standard trees in Kent, Wisbech and elsewhere. These orchards often had Worcester Pearmain as pollinator. This is said to have been a seedling from Devonshire Quarrenden raised by a Mr Hale of Swan Pool, near Worcester and introduced in 1874. It was awarded a First Class Certificate by the RHS in the following year, illustrating the way in which the society quickly recognized varieties of merit.

Cox's Orange Pippin was raised by Richard Cox, a keen gardener and brewer who retired early, at the age of 45, to live at Colnbrook Lawn, Slough. Here he lived with his wife and a staff of six, including three labourers, and devoted himself to his hobby. He had a garden and small paddock extending to nearly two acres. In 1825 or thereabouts, Cox took the pips from a Ribston, one of the most popular apples at the time, and sowed two in a flower pot. The two seedlings so raised were planted out in his garden and later became Cox's Orange Pippin and another dessert apple, Cox's Pomona. When the trees fruited, Richard Cox realized he had, by great good fortune, raised two most promising sorts and, in 1836, he supplied grafts of both varieties to Messrs Smale and Sons, nurserymen at Colnbrook who sold the first trees in 1840.

Among those who were interested in the new varieties was Thomas Ingram, head gardener to Queen Victoria at Windsor. Ingram entered the royal service at Frogmore in 1816, and in 1833 was appointed by William IV superintendent of the whole royal gardens, a post he held until 1868. He was

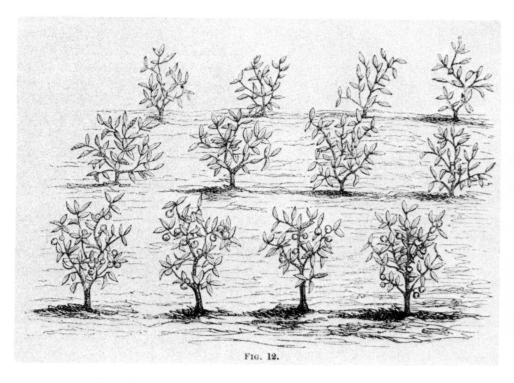

Fig. 12.

*Part of an early plantation of Cox's Orange Pippin apples
on dwarfing rootstocks, 1865.*

a founder member of the short-lived British Pomological Society and, in December 1856, sent specimens of Cox's Orange Pippin and Cox's Pomona to a meeting of their committee. The minutes of the meeting record, 'Mr Ingram sent specimens of two varieties he found little known excepting in the locality of Frogmore, and which he considered worthy of being more extensively grown. Cox's Orange Pippin considered one of their best table sorts. It was found to be sweet, aromatic and very tender, a fair sized and handsome fruit, altogether highly commended.'

This early appreciation of the value of the new variety led to it being taken up by Thomas Rivers, also a member of the Pomological Society and one of the country's leading nurserymen. Cox's Orange soon became popular with gardeners and growers so that, by the time of the RHS great apple exhibition of 1883, it was already one of the principal apples in the country. This position, established by Cox's Orange Pippin in the nineteenth century, has been maintained until the present day, and the high opinion of it formed over a hundred years ago has been fully justified. The RHS awarded it a First Class Certificate in 1862.

By the end of the century, the dessert varieties considered suitable for planting included Mr Gladstone, Allington Pippin, Worcester Pearmain, Duchess of Oldenburgh, Cox's Orange Pippin, King of the Pippins and Scarlet Nonpareil. For cooking, Potts Seedling, Ecklinville, Lane's Prince Albert, Warner's King, Bramley's Seedling and Newton Wonder were popular. Of the really old varieties, Red Juneating and Devonshire Quarrenden were still grown for dessert and orchards still contained many varieties which were a legacy from the past.

TWENTIETH-CENTURY APPLE VARIETIES

During the early years of this century, the firm of Laxton Brothers of Bedford added to the long list of fruits bred by their founders by introducing a number of new apples. These apples were all the result of controlled hybridization and not chance seedlings as so many new varieties have been. In their apple breeding, Laxtons made use, as parents, of well-established good-quality varieties, in particular Cox's Orange Pippin crossed with other sorts such as Wyken Pippin. Of the new apples, three, Laxton's Fortune, Laxton's Superb and Lord Lambourne, were fairly widely planted. Fortune, a cross between Cox's Orange and Wealthy, was raised in 1904 and introduced in 1931. Laxton's Superb, Cox's Orange crossed with Wyken Pippin was bred in 1897 and introduced in 1922; and Lord Lambourne, having James Grieve and Worcester Pearmain as parents, was introduced in 1921. Laxton's Superb proved valuable for its late keeping but is much subject to biennial cropping.

Another new variety having Cox's Orange as one parent was Ellison's Orange, the other parent being the old French variety, Caville Blanche. Raised in 1904 and introduced in 1911 by Messrs Pennel of Lincoln, this is one of the most aromatic apples.

By the 1920s and 1930s the varieties recommended for dessert were Beauty of Bath, Worcester Pearmain, Allington Pippin, James Grieve, Ellison's Orange, Laxton's Superb and Cox's Orange Pippin. For culinary use, Early Victoria, Grenadier, Lord Derby, Newton Wonder, Bramley's Seedling, Annie Elizabeth and Lane's Prince Albert were planted.

The research stations of Long Ashton and East Malling and the John Innes Horticultural Institution have all introduced new apples. Spinks at Long Ashton bred several varieties including Exeter Cross, but none of them achieved much prominence. Merton Worcester, bred by M. B. Crane at John Innes in 1914 and named in 1947, was one of a number of varieties raised by this worker, nearly all of which had Cox's Orange as one parent.

At East Malling, Tyderman is remembered for his Tyderman's Early Worcester, McIntosh crossed with Worcester Pearmain, raised in 1929 and introduced in 1945, and Late Orange, Laxton's Superb crossed with Cox's Orange, raised in 1930 and introduced in 1949. Early Worcester has proved popular as an early dessert apple to be marketed before Red Delicious in Washington State where it is known as Tyderman's Red.

During more recent years, East Malling has played the most prominent part in the breeding of new apples in Britain. Here, under the initial guidance of Knight, the aim has been to breed heavy and regular cropping varieties of good quality, including ones which will have good storage properties. Two of the first varieties released were Greensleeves, a cross between James Grieve and Golden Delicious, introduced in 1977, and Suntan, Cox's Orange Pippin crossed with Court Pendue Plat in 1975. Greensleeves is one of the many new apples, bred in several countries, which have Golden Delicious as one parent. This American variety has been very widely planted in most of the apple-producing countries of Europe, especially in France. Its advantages are early and heavy cropping and easy management as a spindlebush type of tree.

Several varieties imported from abroad have been planted in commercial orchards in England. Of these, Katja or Katie, bred from the two English varieties, James Grieve and Worcester Pearmain, came from Sweden, Jonagold from the New York State Agricultural Experiment Station, and Spartan, a cross between McIntosh and Newtown Pippin, from Summerland Dominion Experiment Station in British Columbia.

Another important aspect of the breeding at East Malling has been the production, in cooperation with John Innes, of new apple rootstocks. These have included the extreme dwarfing M27, the semi-dwarfing M26 and the more vigorous MM106 and MM111. The use of these rootstocks has replaced the old M2, the Doucin, and most of the other apple rootstocks with the exception of the dwarfing M9 which is more popular than ever.

Although many new varieties of apples have been tested and grown in the orchards of Britain during this century, the two outstanding varieties raised in the previous century, Cox's Orange Pippin and Bramley's Seedling, still predominate, being valued for the quality of their fruits for dessert and culinary use.

CIDER APPLES AND CIDER MAKING

14

Although remains of wild or crab apples, *Malus silvestris*, have been found on sites of Neolithic settlements and their seeds have been excavated from Late Iron and Bronze Age sites in Britain, there is no evidence that at that time the fruits were used other than for food. It is believed that the Druids planted apple trees in the vicinity of their sacred groves of oak trees but it is likely that the apple trees served as hosts for mistletoe, of great importance to the Druids.

According to the Greek historian Strabo, some 2,300 years ago, a Greek sea captain and astronomer, Pytheas of Marseilles, sailed from the Mediterranean on a voyage which took him round Britain, and reported that the inhabitants brewed a drink made from corn and honey and, for many centuries, the usual drink of most people was home-brewed ale or mead made from honey collected from wild bees. Beer was also the common drink in Gaul as Diodorus, another Greek historian, wrote, 'Since Gaul suffers from excessive cold, the land produces neither wine nor oil, and, as a consequence, those Gauls who are deprived of these fruits, make a drink of barley which they call zythos or beer, and they also drink water with which they cleanse their honey-combs.' Pliny said, during the first century, that pears were used to make wine, and Palladius, in the fourth century, wrote that the Romans preferred wine made from pears to that of apples, but the fermented juice of apples or pears was not of major importance either in Rome or Roman-occupied Europe.

One of the earliest references to cider in Europe was by Charlemagne at the beginning of the ninth century but, although it may have been made in a few monasteries in England at that time, the monks usually drank ale or wine.

INFLUENCE OF THE MONASTERIES

After the Norman Conquest there are definite records of cider production in the monasteries of England. The *pomerium* in the plan of the grounds adjoining the monastery at Christ Church, Canterbury, in 1165, probably included apples for cider, as did the *pomeria* attached to other monasteries. The Normans brought to Britain many varieties of fruits of which Lambard wrote in 1570: 'Those plantes which our ancestors had brought hither out of Normandie, had lost their native verdour, whether you did eat their substance or drink their juice, which we call Cyder.'

The record of 1204 relating to the use of the Old English Pearmain for making cider by the manor of Runham in Norfolk, to be supplied to the King, is one of many accounts of cider production by manors and monasteries during the thirteenth to fifteenth centuries. In the main apple-growing counties, including Kent, Somerset and Hampshire, most manors had their own cider presses and made their own cider. In 1282, the tenants at the manor of Crawley in Hampshire had to collect the apples in the Waltham garden and take them to the cider-mill for pressing, for which they received each day, as part of their wages, ten apples and a meal.

As well as making cider for their own use, the monasteries regularly sold it to the public, as they did other farm products. The sale of cider from Battle Abbey in Sussex was recorded in 1275, as was the failure of the apple crop at Winchester in 1352, so that the almoner, in his accounts, noted that no cider had been made. This also happened at Battle Abbey in 1359, but in 1369 at Battle, 3 tuns of cider were sold for 55s, 12s being deducted for expenses and 20s for the purchase of barrels and the collection of the apples.

The planting of apples for cider received its first impetus with the arrival of the Norman monks and workers from France versed in the art of making cider, and gradually their planting spread to many parts of the country. In 1282 production of cider was noted in the accounts of the bailiff at Cowick in Yorkshire and, in Chaucer's time, cider was a common drink since, in 'The Monk's Tale' in *The Canterbury Tales* (1387) he wrote, 'This Sampson never Sider drank ne wine.'

In Medieval times the making of cider was an important industry in Kent, and the cider mills there were noted in the time of Henry II for their strong, spiced cider. This type of cider was also popular with the monks at Canterbury. As commercial production of cider increased, it became in great demand for supplying ships going on voyages abroad. From the west country, cider was sold to ships calling at Bristol and ports in Devon, while in Kent in the mid-fifteenth century there were no less than 13 suppliers of cider in New Romney.

A cider or cheese press, from a fourteenth-century MS.

While the wealthy drank wine, much of it imported, the drink of most people at this time continued to be ale, with increasing amounts of cider and perry drunk. Workers in the orchards of the monasteries in the thirteenth century received a daily allowance of cider as part of their wages, a practice which was continued on many farms in the west country until the present day.

The prosperity enjoyed by the manors and monasteries in the early centuries following the Norman Conquest was accompanied by the planting of considerable acreages of apple orchards, much for cider but also for market. However, this period of prosperity was followed by many years of decline and neglect during the depression of the fourteenth and fifteenth centuries, which seriously affected fruit production. The varieties of apples brought over from Normandy had, as Lambard said, deteriorated, and it was not until the new varieties were brought over from the Continent by Richard Harris in 1533 that fruit growing revived.

The great interest in the growing of fruit which was stimulated by these new varieties introduced by Henry VIII's fruiterer, and the model orchard which he planted at Teynham in Kent, extended to the planting of cider apple orchards, especially in the west country, though in Kent increasing quantities of apples were grown for market.

EARLY WRITERS ON CIDER MAKING

The importance of cider apple growing and cider were mentioned by most authors of books on fruit growing during the sixteenth and seventeenth centuries. In the sixteenth century, Mascall advised using selected varieties of merit for making cider and perry and the *Holinshed Chronicles*, while regretting the high consumption of imported wines, said that although beer was still the main drink, in some counties including Sussex, Kent,

A monastery cellarer caught in the act, from a fourteenth-century MS.

Worcestershire and others where fruit abounded, cider and perry were made.

Many writers praised the health-giving virtues of cider. Francis Bacon, in his *History of Life and Death*, noted how a little before his time (1561 – 1626), eight tenants of the Earl of Essex, who were constant cider drinkers and whose collective ages were more than 800 years, had danced a Morris dance! Several authors wrote that the saving of cereals used for making beer by the greater use of cider would help the economy, and the export of beer, so saved, to the Low Countries would be a further benefit.

Pounding apples to make verjuice, from a fourteenth-century MS.

In 1676, Austen wrote that the campaign for greater planting of fruit trees had been successful and that more trees had been planted within the past 30 – 40 years than in several hundred years previously, especially of cider apples.

DISTRIBUTION OF CIDER APPLE GROWING

Following the Norman Conquest, cider was made in the monasteries in many parts of the country. In 1600, Taverner said that Gloucestershire, Herefordshire, Worcestershire and a great part of Kent and Sussex had such a plentiful supply of fruit that it served the poor both for food and drink for the greater part of the year. The emphasis during the sixteenth and seventeenth centuries was on the importance of Herefordshire, considered the leading county both for the scale of production and the quality of its cider. However, the making of cider was already well established in Devon and some parts of Cornwall. Celia Fiennes, who was a connoisseur of cider, however made no reference to cider making when she visited these counties in 1698, but she did say that in Cornwall she was at last able to get what she had long sought, a west country tart or apple pie with custard on top!

It was not until Hugh Stafford started writing about cider orchards and cider making in the early eighteenth century, that there was much information about the Devon industry. Stafford wrote enthusiastically about his county in a 'Letter to a friend', dated 1727. This 'friend' was in fact Batty Langley, a nurseryman of Twickenham, who included the letter in his own *Pomona*, published in 1729. Stafford wrote of the importance of the 'South-hams', the area bounded by the rivers Teign and Dart. At the time of the survey of the county made for the Board of Agriculture at the end of the century, it was said that every valley throughout the South Hams was more or less filled with orchards, much celebrated for the excellence of their cider.

The trees in Devon were mostly relatively small and more closely planted, at 16 ft apart, than the larger trees grown in Herefordshire. The Devon trees were grafted on short, 3−4 ft stems, and it was said they were pruned to keep them fairly small so as to avoid the effect of the wind. While horses were allowed at this time to run in the cider orchards during the winter months and calves were sometimes allowed in, cattle were never grazed in the orchards in spring and summer, as was the practice in Herefordshire, owing to the likelihood of damage to the low branches.

The Devon cider apple orchards were generally quite small in area, much smaller than those of Herefordshire, but as each farm had its own orchard the total acreage was considerable. During the eighteenth and nineteenth centuries, cider was shipped from the Kingsbridge area and Salcombe to the London buyers. The use of the estuaries, allowing the convenient passage of small vessels, precluded the need for canals.

VARIETIES OF APPLES USED FOR CIDER

Although it is likely that the first cider was made from crab apples, the value of certain selected sorts for cider was appreciated very early during its history in Britain. The Old English Pearmain, first recorded as being used for cider in 1204, was still highly rated for cider by Austen in 1657 and probably exists today in the National Fruit Trials.

From the very earliest times, seedlings of crab apples or seedlings of cultivated varieties were used as rootstocks. Crab apple seedlings were generally preferred for producing large, long-lived standard trees, but trees on seedlings from cultivated varieties were thought to come into crop more quickly. It was common practice, especially in the west country, to raise the seedlings and to plant them out in the fields or hedgerows, where they were allowed to bear their first fruits before a decision was made as to whether they should be grafted or not. If the fruit showed signs of promise, the stocks were left ungrafted. In this way, numerous new varieties were introduced, though the majority soon disappeared. This practice was advised by William Lawson in 1618 and persisted for over 200 years.

Parkinson, in 1629, said that the apple varieties not fit to eat raw or to roast were best for making cider, though in his time two varieties widely used for cider, Genet Moyle and Codlin, were also popular in the kitchen. Other writers in the seventeenth century were much concerned about the poor quality of apples generally used for making cider. This was emphasized by Samuel Hartlib, a life-long advocate of cider, in his book *Discourse of Husbandrie used in Brabant and Flanders*, published in 1645. After praising the quality of the cider and perry made in Normandy and northern Spain from specially selected varieties, he said that if only in England cider and perry were made of good-quality fruits we might make drinks in no way inferior to the French wines which were usually spoiled before they came over to Britain.

In 1657 Austen also said that there was general neglect in choosing the apples for cider and many thought that so long as the apples were ripe, it did not matter what kinds were used and all were ground together, good and bad, sweet and sour, so that much of the cider was poor, weak, heartless liquor. However, some growers sorted their apples when making cider, separating the best varieties to make into cider on their own, knowing that the product would be of strength and goodness according to the flavour and quality of the apples used.

Austen praised the 'Pearmaine' as making a very excellent cider of a pleasant vinous taste, while he considered some of the pippins also very good but the 'Gennet-moyle' even better and noted that some said that Redstreak was best of all. He said that in some places there was very little good fruit because the trees were old and the varieties grown in the past had been generally poor but of recent years cider made from better varieties was not inferior to French wines.

REDSTREAK

Austen's reference to Redstreak, which he had apparently heard recommended but had not grown himself, was the first recorded mention of this variety which was regarded as the most important cider apple in the seventeenth century, not only in Herefordshire, where it was first planted, but, according to Worlidge writing in 1687, it had spread to all parts of England.

The introduction of Redstreak is attributed to Lord Scudamore, and in his own county of Herefordshire it was also known as the Scudamore Crab. Lord Scudamore served for some time, during the reign of Charles I, as ambassador to the court of Louis XIII and his travels in France doubtless enabled him to observe French orchards. At Holme Lacey, where he lived after 1628, he developed great interest in the culture of fruit trees, especially in cider apple orcharding, and selected and introduced new varieties of considerable merit. The most famous of these was Redstreak which was acclaimed by all writers in the seventeenth and eighteenth centuries, as being the most outstanding cider variety of that time. In the poem on cider written by the Herefordshire poet Phillips in 1700, he mentioned most of the important apple varieties then used for cider, but especially praised Lord Scudamore for his introduction.

Redstreak seems to have been a 'wilding', but so impressed Lord Scudamore that he made wide use of it in his own orchards. It quickly became accepted in Herefordshire, Gloucestershire and the adjoining counties, while its fame spread as far as Devon where they were also selecting their own varieties. Redstreak was described as having rough and smooth blended in such proportion as to make it palatable to all. It was also considered by Worlidge especially suitable for planting in orchards remote from the farmhouse as the fruit was harsh and unpleasant, not tempting to the palates of 'lewed persons'.

OTHER CIDER APPLE VARIETIES

The increasing interest in good-quality cider resulted in the selection and introduction of many new varieties during the seventeenth and eighteenth centuries. In Gloucestershire, the Bromsbury Crab and Must cider apples, and the dual-purpose Harvey, were popular. Golden Pippin, a high-quality dessert apple for several hundred years, was very extensively planted in Herefordshire before the end of the seventeenth century, and many large orchards of it still remained in the middle of the next century.

Foxwhelp also appeared at this time in Herefordshire and has continued in use until the present day. John Evelyn included it in his *Pomona* in 1664 in the list of varieties grown in Gloucestershire. Hugh Stafford in 1755 said that Foxwhelp had lately acquired a greater reputation and had been told that a hogshead of its cider had been sold in London for £8 or £8 8s, and that often a hogshead of French wine had been given in exchange for one of this cider. Thomas Andrew Knight wrote in 1809 that Foxwhelp entered into many of the finest ciders in Hereford as it imparted strength and flavour.

According to Stafford, the Styre or Stiar apple was also noted for producing a bold, masculine and strong cider, and at one time was almost the only apple esteemed for making rough cider. It was praised by Phillips in his poem on cider. In Devon at the beginning of the eighteenth century, Royal Wilding came into much prominence. This was a chance seedling found in a garden at St Thomas, a parish on the Exeter—Okehampton road, towards the end of the seventeenth century. It was the interest in its merits by the Rev. Robert Woolcombe, rector of the adjoining parish of Whitestone, that attracted attention to it. As Hugh Stafford said, 'Mr Woolcombe was very pleased with it and talked about it in all his conversation. At first this created much amusement but when, in time, he produced a hogshead of cider, the raillery changed to serious attention, and every one fell from laughter to admiration.' Royal Wilding soon established in its own county the same kind of reputation enjoyed by Redstreak in Herefordshire. Other varieties grown in Devon at this time were Meadgate, White-sour, the Irish Cockagee and Elliot from Hereford.

In Somerset during the seventeenth century, most of the cider orchards consisted of seedling, ungrafted trees and there was not the same attention given to selected varieties as in other counties. John Evelyn wrote in 1664 that in Somerset they had a generous cider made with the apples from ungrafted trees and were satisfied that no other cider exceeded it for strength and vigour.

In 1696, Celia Fiennes criticized Somerset growers for not planting the best sorts of apples and for pressing all kinds together. However, the reputation of Somerset was later somewhat redeemed since it was in this county that the famous Kingston Black cider apple appeared. The date of its introduction is uncertain but it was probably during the latter part of the eighteenth century. By tradition, it is believed to have been raised at Kingston, near Taunton, and although there is no record of its origin, its synonym, Black Taunton, supports this. About 1820, Kingston Black was brought to Herefordshire by Thomas Reynolds, a nurseryman at Ross-on-Wye. He supplied trees of it to Palmer, a noted cider apple grower of his time and, within a short while, its good reputation resulted in it being planted throughout the county and it soon spread to most of the other cider-producing areas. Although still much valued for its high vintage qualities, Kingston Black is not now grown nearly so extensively as in the past.

CIDER ORCHARDING IN THE EIGHTEENTH CENTURY

The encouragement given to the planting of new orchards in the seventeenth century after the Restoration of the Monarchy resulted in a considerable increase in cider apple production, especially in the west country. These orchards, particularly in Herefordshire, were usually planted with care, using the better varieties as they became available, and were well maintained. As imports of wine were sometimes limited, there was good demand for cider. Provided transport was available to take it to the towns, cider making was generally profitable. This was in fact the heyday for cider and the hundred years from about the middle of the seventeenth century was probably the period when the industry was at its most flourishing.

However, the position changed dramatically during the second half of the eighteenth century when the relative profitability of growing apples and making cider, compared with producing corn and cattle, changed in favour of the latter. Orchards became neglected, diseases including apple canker were rampant and the quality of the cider declined so that, in turn, its sale was severely affected.

At the end of the eighteenth century, the important books by William Marshall on the rural economy of the west of England were published, and these were followed, in the early years of the nineteenth century, by the county reports of the nationwide survey of agriculture initiated by the newly formed Board of Agriculture. Nearly all these reports showed a marked decline in the condition of orchards in the west country. In his report on Herefordshire, included in the review by William Marshall in 1818, Duncomb said that the decay of the old and valuable fruits was generally acknowledged and lamented and that the renovation of the trees or the introduction of other, equally good varieties was strongly urged.

In the report for Gloucestershire it was observed that there had not been a 'hit', or generally good crop, more than once in four years, that the trees did not flourish, that canker was rife and that the experiment of having grafts and stocks brought from Normandy had totally failed. The idea had been suggested that the land was tired of fruit. The reporter observed that in his youth the leading farmers rivalled each other in their ciders, but now cider and perry were seldom introduced at dinner and then only for a draught as was small beer. The host had to serve foreign wines or incur the reputation of not making his friends welcome.

The report for Worcestershire was rather more optimistic as this county did not depend so much on its cider apple orchards as did Herefordshire. The orchards included plums and cherries as well as apples, which meant that there were fewer replant problems resulting from the repeated planting of apples. This county also had better outlets to the Midland and northern markets through the use of its canals. About half the fresh fruit sold in Worcester market, together with some fruit from Hereford, went by water to the large manufacturing towns of the north and Midlands.

The cider orchards of Somerset at this time also seem to have been in a better condition than those of Herefordshire. Many trees were still grown in the hedgerows, surrounding arable or pasture fields. The reporter was, however, worried about excessive drinking of cider which resulted in idleness, drunkenness and debauchery, not only among the lowest class but also among the yeomanry who, at times, spent successive days and nights at each others houses drinking and guzzling! Concern about excessive drinking of cider was constantly expressed during the seventeenth and eighteenth centuries. Marshall was critical of the way farm labourers were given to drunkenness as a result of their obtaining a free daily allowance of cider.

The state of cider orcharding in Devon, as reported by Marshall in 1796, was much the same as at the beginning of the century, and there was not the same decline as experienced in Herefordshire. There seems to have been less of a problem over gapping up or replanting orchards on the same site as occurred in Herefordshire. Canker, the scourge of young trees in Hereford, was also an insignificant problem in Devon. The number of cider apple varieties in Devon was numerous but not so considerable as in Herefordshire, where the use of seedling trees was commonplace in an effort to overcome the problems of canker and deterioration of the older, established varieties such as Redstreak, though the latter still grew successfully in Devon.

CIDER APPLE ORCHARDS IN THE NINETEENTH CENTURY

The depressed state of the cider industry, as shown by the Board of Agriculture and other surveys, was made even worse by adverse weather conditions which were referred to by William Salisbury in 1816 and again by William Speechly in 1820. Speechly wrote that, since the beginning of the century, severe weather in the spring had destroyed all the blossoms until 1818 when there was a very heavy crop.

Further difficulties were experienced at the end of the war with France in 1816. This resulted in a renewal of large-scale imports of wines and apples from France which had been cut off during the long conflict with Napoleon.

As Herefordshire had, since the sixteenth century, been the leading county for cider apple orcharding, the decline in the industry was of especial concern to their growers. The theory put forward by Thomas Andrew Knight as to the natural limitation in the life of varieties led to the Herefordshire Agricultural Society proposing, in 1798, to give annual prizes for the best new apple seedlings. Knight himself won their award on several occasions. He also edited the *Pomona Herefordiensis*, published by the Agricultural Society, which included engravings of the old cider and perry fruits of the county together with new promising varieties.

In spite of the efforts of this society, the cider apple industry showed little improvement, and most orchards continued to decline. In 1872, the Woolhope Naturalists' Field Club drew attention to the chronic state of neglect into which the orchards of Herefordshire had been allowed to fall, with many dead and decaying trees. It was decided to carry out a survey of the orchards in the county, and the Club appointed Dr Robert Hogg. A major result of the survey was the publication, between the years 1876—85 of the illustrated *Herefordshire Pomona*.

One of the first actions of the Club was to distribute grafts of 92 different varieties of apples supplied to them from the Royal Horticultural Society's garden at Chiswick. They also carried out a trial to see if the old, valued varieties of cider apples, Foxwhelp and Skyme's Kernel and Taynton Squash pear, could be brought back into cultivation. This they did successfully, once again disproving Knight's contention about the limited life of varieties. The Club distributed hundreds of trees of these three fruits to growers in the county.

In order to see whether cider apples with the prefix 'Norman' had really come from Normandy, some members of the Club visited Rouen in 1884. They were able to show that virtually all the 'Norman' varieties grown in Britain were, in fact, unknown in France. Possibly some had originally come from France and had since been lost in that country or 'Norman' had been used as a prefix for local seedlings.

During their visit to France, the Club members selected certain Normandy apples for introduction to Herefordshire. These included Medaille d'Or and Michelin, still grown today. One of the members of the Club who took an active part in the preparation of the *Pomona* was the Rev. C. H. Bulmer, who wrote a valuable paper on 'The orchard and its products, cider and perry'.

THE CIDER APPLE INDUSTRY

The first returns of orchard acreages were collected by the Board of Agriculture in 1877, but at first only referred to any acreage of arable or grass which was used for fruit trees of any kind. However, by a comparison with later figures for separate fruits, it is possible to estimate that in 1877 there were 23,000 acres of apples in Devon, 22,000 in Herefordshire, 21,000 in Somerset, 9,000 in Worcestershire, 8,000 in Gloucestershire and 6,000 in Kent. Of these acreages, the greater part in Devon, Herefordshire and Somerset were of cider apples and, while Gloucestershire and Worcestershire sent apples to market, they too grew many cider apples. Kent at this time came quite low in its acreage of apples, grown virtually entirely for market.

With some recovery in the cider industry, the orchard areas in the main cider-producing counties of the west continued to increase up to the beginning of the present century and then remained relatively stationary until 1920. After this date, the acreage began to decline, mainly the result of the grubbing up of old cider apple orchards. There was an even more marked decline following the Second World War so that, although Herefordshire maintained its position as the leading county for cider apple production, by 1979, together with that of Worcestershire, its acreage of cider apple orchards was just over 6,000. Although the acreage has fallen even more dramatically in the other counties of the west, the collective production of cider apples has been virtually maintained as the result of improved modern methods of cider orcharding.

Away from the west and south-west, apples from Kent and other areas, surplus to the requirements for market and other forms of processing, are often sold to the west-country cider makers for blending with cider apple varieties. In addition, cider factories in Kent, Sussex and Norfolk make cider from regular market varieties.

NATIONAL FRUIT AND CIDER INSTITUTE

In the nineteenth century, the great bulk of cider was made on the farms producing the apples, just as it had been for many hundreds of years. The methods used were often crude and the resulting product very variable. Much of the art of cider making which had been developed during the seventeenth and eighteenth centuries seems to have been lost. Revival of interest in cider apple and perry pear orcharding was encouraged by G. W. Radcliffe Cooke of Hellens, Herefordshire who, in 1898, wrote *A Book about Cider and Perry*. At that time, he calculated that the acreage devoted to cider apple and perry pear orchards in the principal counties of Devon, Herefordshire, Somerset, Gloucestershire, Worcestershire and the minor counties of Cornwall, Dorset, Monmouth, Shropshire and Wiltshire amounted to 112,000.

It was, however, the obvious lack of knowledge of the underlying principles of cider making which concerned Neville Grenville of Butleigh Court, near Glastonbury in Somerset, where, in cooperation with the Bath and West and Southern Counties Society, aided by small grants from the Board of Agriculture, he began experiments on this subject in 1893 which continued until 1903. This led, in that year, to the setting up of the National Fruit and Cider Institute. This in turn, following amalgamation with the University of Bristol in 1912, became Long Ashton Research Station.

In 1903, when the Institute began its work, there were about 70,000—80,000 acres in the farm orchards of the west of England consisting mostly of so-called cider apples and perry pears, many local seedlings of relatively little value. There were, however, some varieties of outstanding value in certain areas, as Foxwhelp and various members of the Norman family in the orchards of Herefordshire and adjacent areas of adjoining counties. Sweet Alford and Woodbine were common in Devon and Morgan's Sweet was found in Somerset in addition to the famous Kingston Black. Apart from these named sorts, there were uncountable numbers of different seedling varieties whose distribution was often limited to the farm on which they were raised.

Professor T. P. Barker, the first Director of Long Ashton Research Station, was anxious to encourage the cultivation of the better-quality cider apple varieties and to hasten and improve their cropping. The Research Station therefore arranged, during 1935—6, for the planting of nine trials of selected varieties in the various counties with trees raised at Long Ashton and trained in bush form. In this way valuable information on the performance and uses of the varieties was obtained. An outstanding variety which came into prominence during this period, and is now widely grown in all the cider-making districts, is Yarlington Mill, a seedling raised in Somerset at the end of the nineteenth century.

The initial work of the Research Station was centred on cider making and the suitability of different varieties. Investigations were, however, soon begun into orchard management, nutrition and pest and disease control. From that time onwards, Long Ashton proved of inestimable value to both growers and to the rapidly expanding cider factories. Although there had been some cider production on a relatively small factory scale in the past, the bulk of the cider had been made on farms from locally grown apples. During this century there has been a marked change to factory production for most of the cider made in Britain. While for many years the factories have obtained some of their supplies by buying fruit from France and now buy concentrated apple juice from abroad, they have also taken a marked interest in improving material bought in Britain. This has included supplying trees of approved varieties and giving advice to growers on the planning of cider apple orchards. More recently, some factories have extended production of cider apples on their own farms. In all this work there has been very close cooperation between the cider industry, the cider apple growers and the Research Station. The result has been a marked improvement in the quality and standardization of most ciders, accompanied by a decided increase in public demand.

Modern Trends in Cider Apple Orcharding

Traditional methods of cider apple production were normally based on relatively large trees growing in orchards grazed by livestock; these were slow to come into full crop and today are proving uneconomic. As with dessert and cooking apples, the modern trend has been to plant the trees, worked on growth-controlling rootstocks, more intensively, to train them with a central leader and to prune them lightly so that they come into crop relatively early. The trees remain smaller and are more easily managed than the old standard ones.

In place of the seedling apple rootstocks, generally raised from seeds in the apple pomace, the trees are worked on virus-tested, vegetatively propagated stocks, the scion varieties also being taken from the healthiest material available. Here, as with other fruits, the research stations have cooperated with nurserymen and others in providing virus-tested plants. By using this material and growing the trees more intensively, much heavier crops are obtained.

In most modern orchards, the trees are spaced relatively more closely in than between the rows and the grass is cut rather than grazed, while herbicides are also used to control grass and weeds. Whereas in the past, little attempt was made to control pests and diseases by spraying, modern cider apple orchard management demands an economic level of control of any trouble which may influence cropping.

The cider apple varieties being planted today are nearly all ones which would have been well known to the grower in the past, and include Brown Snout, Chisel Jersey, Dabinette, Harry Master's Jersey, Michelin, Nehou, Taylor's Bitter Sweet, Tremlett's Bitter, Vilberie and Yarlington Mill. Virus-tested strains of several varieties such as Harry Master's Jersey, Chisel Jersey and Dabinette are of increasing importance. At Long Ashton, where valuable work on the pollination of both eating and cider apples has been done, it has been found that some varieties, including Dabinette and Chisel Jersey, are cross-incompatible and others, such as Harry Master's Jersey are self-incompatible. Other varieties, including Nehou, Reine des Hatives, Vilberie and Tremlett's Bitter, tend to be strongly biennial in their cropping and attention has been given to encouraging more regular cropping in these valuable varieties. Methods include chemical treatment to reduce flower initiation in the 'off' year.

The large fluctuations in yield from year to year continue to be a major problem both to the cider apple growers and the cider makers, just as it was in the past when a 'hit' was followed by light yields and this, and the ever-continuing search for the best varieties, will remain dominant aspects of future cider apple production. Where the apple crop is the only source of income from the orchard, as it is in the modern bush plantation, and is not supplemented by the grazing of livestock as it was in the past, the use of the best-quality vintage varieties which give regular crops is essential for economic success.

Although the modern cider apple orchard, with its mechanized crop-harvesting and handling equipment, and the cider factories are so different from anything known to John Evelyn and his contemporary protagonists of the virtues of cider, they would surely approve of the present popularity of their favourite drink.

PEARS

The pears cultivated in Europe are thought to have arisen from the species *Pyrus communis* which is a native of Europe and Northern Asia and is found growing wild in Britain, but it is doubtful if this species was indigenous to Britain. It is found growing wild in the woods and forests of the Caucasus and Turkestan and over a wide area extending beyond this region. Workers there have considered there is evidence of hybridization between *P. communis* and other *Pyrus* species, *P. korschinskyi* and *P. heterophylla*, and think that it is not improbable that several species have contributed to the development of cultivated pears. The pears growing wild in the forests, like the apples, show considerable variation, and the better forms have been selected by the local population for the preparation of food dishes and the making of drinks.

In Japan, China and other countries of the Far East, the cultivated varieties of pears have been derived from *Pyrus serotina*, but this species has played no part in the origin of the types grown in Europe. However, in the United States, a form of *P. serotina*, the Chinese Sand pear, was one of the parents of Kieffer, a variety which was much used for canning and, in spite of its poor quality, for dessert. Kieffer arose as a chance seedling in the nursery of Peter Kieffer, who lived near Philadelphia, where he grew the Sand pear as an ornamental tree and also had nearby trees of the Williams' Bon Chrétien or Bartlett pear. The hybrid pear first fruited in 1863 and was the first of such hybrids to be grown commercially, but since that time many such crosses with *P. serotina* have been made.

PEARS IN ANTIQUITY

There is little evidence of the use of the wild pear as food by the prehistoric peoples of Europe. The fruits of *Pyrus communis* are small, hard, gritty, sour and astringent and are not improved by cooking, and so would be unattractive to seekers of food. Very few examples of the remains of the wild pear have been found during excavations of prehistoric lake dwellings in Switzerland and none has been found in Britain.

There is no reference to the pear in the Bible but there are frequent references to it in the writings of the ancient Greeks and Romans. As with several other fruits, pears were mentioned in Homer's *Oddyssey* as being grown in the garden of the Palace of Alcinous. Theophrastus, the Greek botanist, distinguished between wild and cultivated pears and said that the latter had been given different names. He wrote of the propagation and cultivation of pears and it is obvious that their use was well established in his time. It is likely, as with apples and stone fruits, that the cultivated forms of pears spread from southern Russia into the Fertile Crescent and from there to Greece and later Rome.

The first Roman writer to speak of pears was Cato the Elder, a leading statesman, who wrote about farming, fruit growing and gardening in a way which would be quite acceptable today. Describing the management and layout of a suburban farm he said: 'Plant all kinds of fruit . . . of pears the Volema, the Anician frost pears (these are excellent when preserved in boiled wine), the Tarentine, the Must pear, the Gourd pear and as many other varieties as possible.' It would seem that at this time farmers and fruit growers had a good selection of pear varieties available for planting. Cato also described sowing apple and pear seeds in the nursery.

Another Roman, Varro, dealt with the propagation of pears: 'No matter how good the pear shoot which you graft on a wild pear, the fruit will not be as well flavoured as if you graft on a cultivated pear.' It is well established that pears on seedling pear stocks are different in appearance, texture and flavour from those grafted or budded on quince or when worked onto other pears.

Pliny the Elder also discussed pear varieties:

Of all the varieties of pears, the Crustumian is the nicest. Next to this are Falernian pears, used for wine, as they contain such a quantity of juice — this is called being 'milky' — and among these are some others of a very dark colour, given us by Syria.

The names of the remaining varieties are designated differently in various different localities; but pears that have advertised their producers by the accepted designations of Rome, are the Decimian, and the offshoot from it is called the Sham Decimian, the very long-stalked one called Dolabellian, the kind of Pomponian called breast-shaped, the Licerian, the Sevian and the Turranian, a variety sprung from the Sevian but differing in length of stalk. The Favonian, a red pear a little larger than the 'proud' pear (one of the earliest but of poor quality), the Laterian and the Anician which comes when autumn is over and has an agreeably acid flavour.

One pear is called the Tiberian, which was a special favourite of the Emperor Tiberius; it is more coloured by the sun and grows to a larger size, but otherwise would be the same as Licerian. Pears having the name of their place of origin are the Amerian, the latest of all kinds, the Picentine, the Numantine, the Alexandrian, the Numidian, the Greek, a variety of which is the Tarentine, and the Signine, which some people call the tile pear from its colour; like the Onyx pear and the Purple pear; while named for their scent are the Myrrh pear, the Bay-leaf pear and the Nard pear; named from its season the Barley pear; from its long neck, the Bottle pear; and the Coriolan and Bruttian pears are so called because of their connection with certain races, and the Gourd pear and the sourish pear from their juice.

Pears, the reason for the names of which is uncertain, are the Barbarian, the variety of Venus called Coloured Venus, the royal pear called the Squat pear because of its very short stalk, the Patrician pear, and the Vocimum, a green kind of oblong shape.

Virgil has also mentioned a warden pear which he gets from Cato who also specifies a 'seed time' pear and a Must pear.

Pliny also wrote that the Greek pear, the Bottle pear and the Bay-leaf, could be left on the trees until the first frost when they would be ripe. His reference to Virgil was to the *Georgics*, published 30 BC, in which he said: 'Nor are all the pear tree scions the same, Crustumian, Syrian and the Warden large.'

The account given by Pliny is of great interest for several reasons. It shows that a wide range of pear varieties, differing in colour, flavour, texture, season and keeping qualities, was already available to the Roman grower, that use was already made of mutations of existing established varieties, as the Turranian which had 'sprung from the Sevian', but differed in length of stalk; and that use was made of one very juicy pear, the Falernian, for wine or possibly a form of perry.

Pliny also included two pears, the Tarentine and the Gourd, which Cato had mentioned 200 years earlier and two which had obviously been imported, the Greek and the Syrian. He added some remarks about the uses of pears:

All kinds of pears as an aliment are indigestible, even to persons in robust health; but to invalids they are forbidden as rigidly as wine. Boiled, however, they are remarkably agreeable and wholesome, those of the Crustumian in particular. All kinds of pears, too, boiled with honey, are wholesome to the stomach. Poultices are made with pears and a decoction of them is used to disperse calluses.

The idea that pears could be harmful to the consumer was repeated in several proverbs current in the sixteenth and seventeenth centuries. Thomas Cogan in his *Haven of Health* of 1588 wrote, 'That saying which is commonly used, that pears without wine are poyson', while Randle Cotgrave in his *Dictionary* of 1611 said, 'After a peare wine or a priest' and another proverb said, 'A pear must have wine after it, and a fig, water.' The origin of this attitude to pears is somewhat obscure, but it is possible that it arose following the use of hard wild pears or ones which were eaten straight off the tree without allowing time for ripening; these would certainly be indigestible.

Nevertheless, pears were certainly appreciated by the Roman legionaries, whose diet in peacetime in Europe included apples, pears, plums, cherries, peaches, grapes and elderberries as well as nuts of various kinds. Murals from the walls of ruined villas in Pompeii include paintings of pears which seem to be as large and as attractive as modern-day varieties.

Columella, who was a contemporary of Pliny, in a poem advising on the choice of site for a garden, recommended ground which is naturally covered with wild vines and is thick with groves of wild pears, plum and apple trees. There are other indications that at this time wild fruits of all kinds were to be found in the countryside of central Italy. Columella also gave a list of pear varieties which he regarded as the most excellent kinds. He, like Pliny, headed his list with Crustumian which he said had come from Crustmium in Etruria, part of the ancient Etruscan city states.

PEAR CULTIVATION IN BRITAIN

No excavations of ancient British or Roman sites have yielded definite evidence of the cultivation of the pear before or during the period of Roman occupation but, in view of the great popularity of the pear in Rome at this time, it would be surprising if no attempts had been made to introduce the fruit to Britain. The fact that the Saxon name for the pear, 'pirige', is thought to have been in use before the end of the Roman occupation supports this view. Again, as with other fruits, since Tacitus wrote that the soil of Britain would produce good crops with the exception of olives, vines and others requiring a warmer climate, the implication is that pears and other temperate fruits were grown in Britain.

It is not until after the Norman Conquest that there is definite recorded evidence of pears being cultivated in England, although pears were certainly being grown in Europe towards the end of the Dark Ages, as this fruit was included in the list of plants to be cultivated by the orders of the *Capitulare* issued by Charlemagne c.800. The *Capitulare* said, 'Plant pear trees whose products, because of pleasant flavour, could be eaten now, those which will furnish fruits for cooking and those which mature late to serve for winter use.' This indicates that a number of different varieties were being grown in

France at the beginning of the ninth century, and there seems to have been no fear of eating them raw!

There is evidence that pears were planted, along with the other fruits mentioned in the *Capitulare*, a few years after its publication, in the gardens of the Abbey of St Gall in Switzerland. Since the abbeys and monasteries of the Continent were in communication with those in Britain, it is likely that pears were brought over to Britain and grown at this time even if others brought over by the Romans had disappeared during the Dark Ages. Pear trees have a long life, much longer than that of apples, some of the perry pear trees in Gloucestershire being between 200 and 300 years old. In *Domesday Book* of 1086 old pear trees were several times noted as boundary marks, so that these trees must have been in existence for many years before the Norman Conquest.

PEARS AFTER THE NORMAN CONQUEST

To what extent pears were brought over from Normandy following the Conquest is not known, but the court accounts during the early years of the reign of Henry III (1207−72) show that pear fruits were being imported from France, and for many years French varieties dominated British orchards. There are accounts for the year 1223 of fruits bought in Paris for supplying Henry III during his travels through France to England. These included one hundred 'S.Rule' pears costing 10s, and 600 apples which cost 12s − pears were obviously more costly than apples. La Rochelle in France was celebrated for its pears, and from this region the Sheriffs of London imported pears to present to Henry III; it appears that the king was particularly fond of this fruit.

A Wardrobe account for Henry III for 1252 records that a 'Janettar' pear was bought, together with 'Sorelles and Cailloels', both popular pear varieties, from John the Fruiterer of London. In 1236, Henry III married Eleanor of Provence, who was a keen gardener, and from this time they developed extensive gardens and orchards. The royal accounts record the purchase of pear trees: in 1262, a writ of Henry III directed his gardener to plant six 'Cailhou' pear trees at Westminster and the same variety in the gardens of the Tower. This was the same as the 'Cailloels' recorded earlier, so they must have been well liked by the royal family! William, the Gardener, who was responsible for planting them, was paid 3d a day.

Edward I, who succeeded his father Henry III as king in 1272, married Eleanor of Castille who was also a keen gardener. She herself created a new garden and planted orchards at Kings Langley in Hertfordshire, bringing gardeners over from Aragon especially to do this work.

The accounts of the king for 1276−92 show that young pear trees were produced for the royal gardens at Westminster, the varieties being 'Kaylewell' or 'Calswel', 'Rewel' or 'de Regula' and 'Pesse-pucelle'. 'Kaylewell' was a synonym for 'Caillou', the Burgundy pear which, though a hard, rather inferior fruit only fit for baking, seems to have been the most generally planted in England and was certainly popular with the royal family. From the time of the Romans right up to the Middle Ages pears for baking were much more important than they are today. The 'Rewel' or 'St Rule' was probably named after St Regolo or Rule, who was Bishop of Arles. This variety had been noted by Neckham, Abbot of Cirencester (1157−1217). The 'Pesse-pucelle' may have been the variety known in ancient France as Pucelle de Saintonge. All these pears were of French origin.

Information about other pear varieties can be found in the fruiterers' bills of Edward I for 1292. Among the varieties named were 'Martins, Dreyes, Sorells, Gold-Knopes, Regul and Chyrfall'. The following is an example of one of the entries from these accounts: 'Sent to the Lord the King at Bernwell, on Monday next after Palm Sunday, 800 and a half Regul pears, price of the hundred, 10d, also 900 apples, price of the hundred 3d. Also Chasteyns [chestnuts] of the hundred 2d. In paniers and cords 6d. In the hire of one horse and expenses of the same, and of one groom going and returning 2s 1d, sum 13s 11d proved.' This account shows that the 'Regul' or 'Rewel' pear must have been a long-keeping variety to have been in good condition by Palm Sunday. Other accounts show that Regul and Pesse-Pucelle pears seem to have been the most esteemed as they cost 10d to 3s a hundred, Martins were 8d and Caillou 1s. The rest were 2d to 3d a hundred.

In the accounts of William de Donyncton, Sergeant to the Earl of Lincoln, for the garden belonging to the Earl, for 1295−6, the following items relate to the propagation of pears: '3s 2¼d for 2 insitis [grafts] de Rule, 2 de Martin, 5 de Caloel et 3 de Pesse pucele, bought for planting.' However, the Earl's garden does not seem to have had pears in crop as 27s was spent for '100 Caloels, 100 Pesse-puceles, 200 Rules, 300 Maryns and 300 Quoynz [quince] bought and sent to the Earl of Ambr. [Amesbury?] with carriage of the same . . . 17s ¼d.'

AN EARLY ENGLISH VARIETY

The thirteenth century was a period when there was a marked development in the laying out of gardens and a general advance in horticulture and fruit growing. There are many records of the sale and purchase of 'grafts' (scions) of apples and pears and their rootstocks for use in planting up new orchards. Confirmation of these advances was given by Harrison in 1580 who, when reviewing the past, wrote that fruits and other crops grown in gardens had been very plentiful at the time of Edward I and following his time but that they had been gradually neglected, especially after the end of the fourteenth century.

Contributing to the development of gardens and orchards in the thirteenth century were the plants, including pears, which were imported from the Continent. However, during the following century an important English pear, the Wardon, was introduced. This was said by Hogg to have been raised by the Cistercian monks of Wardon in Bedfordshire, a foundation of the twelfth century, some time before 1388. It was a baking pear of great repute and was used for making the celebrated 'Wardon pies', as in Barham's *Ingoldsby Legends*:

> *The Canon sighed, but rousing cried, I answer to thy call,*
> *And a Warden pie's a dainty dish to mortify withal.*

From the fame of these pears, the name Wardon or Warden came into common use for all kinds of large baking pears which required keeping. Warden pears were favourites for centuries for pies and pastries which every early cookery book described. In the early literature, the Warden was considered a distinct type of fruit and lists of fruit varieties included both pears and wardens.

In the account of Henry IV's wedding feast, 'Wardon' pears in syrup occurred twice and were served in the same course as venison, quails, sturgeon, fieldfare and other dishes. In the Middle Ages, when meats and game of many kinds were freely available to the wealthy, their gardens mainly supplied herbs of various kinds and any vegetables were usually cooked with the meats. The same applied to fruits. In a cookery book of 1450, recipes included such mixtures as meat or fish cooked with pears or apples, spices and sugar, to which leeks, ground small, whole onions or garlic sauce were added.

PEARS IN THE FIFTEENTH AND SIXTEENTH CENTURIES

Pears were included by 'Mayster Ion Gardener' in his poem 'The Feate of Gardeninge' (1440−50). He advised grafting the pear on hawthorn, a practice continued for many centuries:

> *Of pere y mynde zorne*
> *To graffe hym a-pon a haw-thorne.*

Pears were among the fruits introduced from France and the Low Countries by Harris, fruiterer to Henry VIII, in 1533 for planting at Teynham in Kent, whence they were distributed to other parts of Kent and the rest of the

country. Although many varieties of pears had been brought over from
France during the thirteenth and fourteenth centuries, there seems to have
been a marked deterioration in the orchards until the revival of the fruit
industry in the sixteenth century. The improvement in the varieties then
available was commented on by William Turner in his *Herbal* of 1568:

> *We have many kyndes of garden Peares with us in England / and*
> *some kyndes better then ever I saw in Germany for holsomnes / and*
> *som in Germany more pleasant and greater then ever I saw in*
> *England. I have red in no old boke so many kyndes of peares / as I*
> *rede of in Plini / here I will show certayn Latin names / and*
> *compare them with our English peares and Dutch peares / as well I*
> *can.* Pyra superba / *that is to say / proud peares / are little and*
> *soonest rype / and these are called in Cambridge / mid-summer*
> *peares.* Falerna pira *have theyr name (sayeth Pliny) of drinck /*
> *because they be ful of iuce. These are called in some places watery*
> *peares /* Dolobeltiana *are the peares that have the long footstalkes. I*
> *remember not how they be named in England.*

Turner's reference to pears in Germany at this time is supported by
Valerius Condus, a botanist and the earliest German writer on fruit who
made a special study of apples and pears being grown in Germany and
included the results of his work in his *Historia Plantarum* 1561, which
included full descriptions of 50 different pear varieties. From his account it
is clear that the varieties then in existence, possessed all the characteristics
found in modern pears, just as these basic characteristics could be seen in
the pears grown by the ancient Greeks and Romans.

Among the varieties described by Cordus were ones covering the whole
year from the small Musk, ripening in June, and the Augustbirn, ready in
August, both of which, like our present-day early varieties, had a very short
season, to the Bratbirn gross, an enormous cooking pear, averaging about
1 lb in weight. He also included the Schmalzbirn, the Butter pear, a pear with
melting flesh. This character differed from those of the majority of pears
cultivated in the past and which had firm, crisp flesh even when ripe, and
was to be an important character in the evolution and breeding of modern
pears.

Thomas Hill in 1579 said there were several good sorts of Wardens or
baking pears, and Thomas Tusser in 1580 listed white and red wardens
separately from other varieties of pears. John Gerard in 1597, showed that
the number of different varieties of pears, as of other fruits, had considerably
increased since the beginning of the century. As he said, to list all the pears
would require a whole volume as every county had its own varieties. A friend
of his had in one orchard, 60 kinds of the best-quality pears and could easily
plant as many again of ones of lesser value. He mentioned that some had

little or no taste but were very watery and seemed similar to the watery Falernian referred to by Pliny and later writers.

Gerard illustrated eight pears: the Jennetting, the Pear Royall, the Quince Pear, the Katherine, Saint James, the Burgomet, the Bishops and the Winter Pear. The Jennetting was doubtless the same as 'Janettar' supplied to Henry III in 1252. He also illustrated a number of wild or hedge pears including the Great Choke, the Small Choke, the Wild Hedge pear, the Lowsie wild and the Crow pear. He said that many of these wild pears were harsh and bitter and others of such a choking taste that they were not to be eaten by man or beast. These wild and Choke pears were often used for making perry.

The great expansion in fruit growing in Britain during the sixteenth century was reflected in the establishment of many nurseries for supplying the needs of growers and gardeners around London. These nurseries, however, often supplied wrongly named plants so that authors of books on horticulture at this time felt it necessary to include the names of nurseries which could be trusted. As Gerard said:

> All these and many sorts more, most rare and good, are growing in the ground of Master Richard Pointer, a most cunning and curious graffer and planter of all manner of rare fruites, dwelling in a small village neere London, called Twickenham; and also in the ground of an excellent graffer and painfull planter, Master Henry Banbury of Touthill Street into Westminster; and likewise in the ground of a diligent and most affectionate lover of plants, Master Warnar neere Horsey Downe by London; but beware the Bag and Bottle; seek elsewhere for good fruit faithfully delivered.

SEVENTEENTH-CENTURY PEAR GROWING

By the beginning of the seventeenth century numerous new varieties were being introduced, both the result of seedlings raised in Britain and a constant influx from Europe, including ones brought over by John Tradescant for which he paid 2s to 4s each. Parkinson said that, as with apples, there were so many varieties that they could not be numbered:

> The most excellent sorts of Peares serve to make an after course for their masters table whereof the goodness of his Orchard is tryed. They are dryed also and so make an excellent repaste. They are eaten familiarly of all sorts of people — of some for delight and of others for nourishment, being baked, stewed or scalded. The Red Warden and Spanish Warden are reckoned among the most excellent of Pears, either to bake or to roast, for the sicke and the sound.

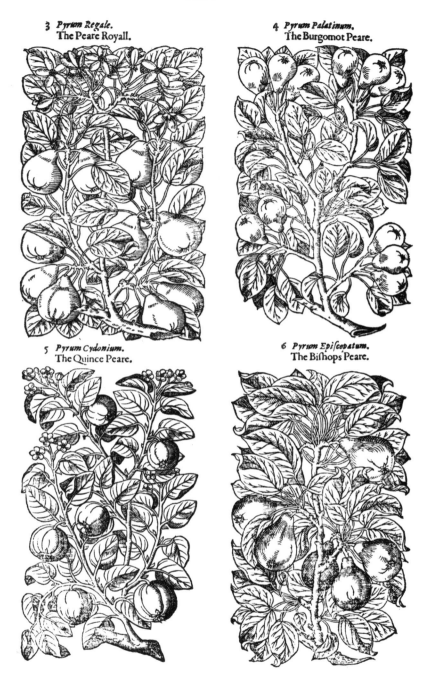

3 *Pyrum Regale.*
The Peare Royall.

4 *Pyrum Palatinum.*
The Burgomot Peare.

5 *Pyrum Cydonium.*
The Quince Peare.

6 *Pyrum Episcopatum.*
The Bishops Peare.

Pear varieties grown in nearly all gardens by the sixteenth century.

The Spanish pear had been introduced by Tradescant in 1611. Apart from this, Parkinson described 65 other varieties. Among these were the Pucell and Sorrell bought for Edward I in 1292 and Rewell or Rewl which had been known even earlier in the twelfth century. Apart from these old varieties, most of Parkinson's list seemed to consist of more recent introductions. From the names of some of them, 'the Norwich, the Worcester, the Warwicke, the Arundel and the Petworth', it is clear that pear culture must have been practised in many parts of the country.

The keenness of garden owners to obtain varieties of note from the Continent is illustrated by Parkinson's description of the 'Ten pound' pear. This he said was the best Bon Chrétien grown at Syon, so called because the grafts cost the owner so much in expences in importing them. Few in Parkinson's list of pears are still grown today, though his 'Gergonell' is Jargonelle, and Catherine, Winter Bon Chrétien, Windsor and Bergamot were being grown within the past hundred years. Jargonelle is still grown in England and America.

The *Garden Book* of Sir Thomas Hanmer, which was mostly written in 1659 but not published at the time, included information about the varieties of fruits he grew at Bettisfield in Wales. Of pears to be grown on walls he gave Winter Bon Chrétien and the Winter Bergamots. The other varieties which he said bore well enough as standards in the orchard were, 'the Early Katherine, the mid-season Surmer Bergamot, the Summer Bon Chrétien, the Norwich, the Winsore, the Slip pear, the Binfield or Dove, Messire John, Roy d'Este, the Lewys, Long Greene, Bishops, Double Flower'd, the Wynter Thorne and Spanish Warden'.

Hanmer gave a list of fruit trees and their prices to be obtained from George Ricketts of Hogsden, London. The most expensive trees were peaches, some priced at 3s each, but the majority were 2s. Cherries and apples were 8d a tree and pears 12d. In this list he added another pear, the King's pear, so-called by Rose, gardener to Charles II, because, he said, the king liked it.

In 1691, Worlidge listed 129 varieties of pears for the table which would provide fruits to eat throughout the year. The names of most of these suggest an English origin but there were a number which were obviously imported, as Russet of Remes, Beurré du Roy, Montpelier, Pear of Lyons and Brunswick. Beurré du Roy he described as the best summer pear, melting in the mouth and therefore called the 'butter-pear'. It bore best against a wall. De la Quintinye, who gave more information about varieties of pears than any other writer of his time, regarded this pear, later known as Beurré Brown, as his second choice after Bon Chrétien. It had first been described by Olivier de Serres in 1608 and seems to have been one of the first of the melting fleshed pears to be planted on any scale both on the Continent and in England. It probably played a most important part in the later development of new varieties having this desirable character.

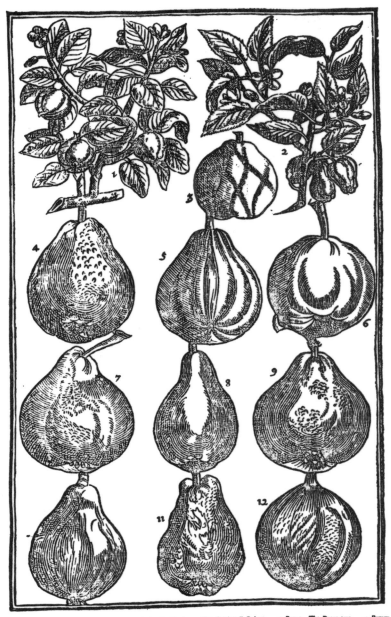

1 *Malus Cotonea*. The Quince tree. 2 *Cydonium Lusitanicum*. The Portingall Quince. 3 *Pyrus*. The Peare tree. 4 *Pyrum Pompeianum, siue Cucumerinum hyemale*. The Winter Bon Chretien. 5 *Pyrum pictum vel striatum*. The painted or striped Peare of Ierusalem. 6 *Pyrum Palatinale*. The Burgomot Peare. 7 *Pyrum Cucumerinum siue Pompeianum æstivum*. The Summer Bon Chretien. 8 *Pyrum Volemum*. The best Warden. 9 *Pyrum Librale*. The pound Peare. 10 *Pyrum Windsforianum*. The Windsor Peare. 11 *Pyrum Cucumerinum*. The Gratiola Peare. 12 *Pyrum Caryophyllatum*. The Gilloflower Peare.

Pear and quince varieties. The quince reached the height of its popularity in the seventeenth and eighteenth centuries.

De la Quintinye included a whole chapter on the Winter Bon Chrétien which he considered the best of all pears. He said it had been known to the Romans as Crustumium or Volemum and featured in their entertainments. It is difficult to be certain as to its origin but Robert Hogg also thought it probable that it was synonymous with Crustumium. It was imported into France from Italy in 1495 by Charles VIII on his conquest of the Kingdom of Naples. Though not now regarded as of first quality for dessert, it is still, as it always was, considered one of the best for cooking. This was probably the 'Ten pound' pear described by Parkinson as the best Bon Chrétien of Syon.

PROPAGATION OF PEARS

In the fifteenth century, Jon Gardener advised grafting pears on the hawthorn. In 1523 Fitzherbert said: 'A peare or a warden wolde be graffed in a pyrre stocke; and if thou canst get none, then graffe it in a crabbe tree stocke, and it wyll do well; and some men graffe theym in a whyte thorne, and than it wyll be the more harder and stonye.' In 1575, Mascall's book, mostly translated from one by a French monk suggested, 'For to have the Peare of Anguisse, or Permain, or Satigle a moneth or two before others, the which shall endure, ye shall graffe them upon a Quince tree.' However, no other English writer at this time recommended the use of quince, and the first reference to its use in the following century was in the unpublished book of Thomas Hanmer in 1659 who suggested using it for vigorous growing pear varieties trained on walls. John Evelyn, who was a friend of Hanmer, was also aware of the value of the quince since this was referred to in *The French Gardiner*, translated by Evelyn in 1658. This said that all sorts of pears succeeded incomparably on quince, producing earlier fruit, of better quality and better size, than when grafted on seedling pear stock, with the exception of the Portail variety which often failed on quince and so was better on pear. It is well known that a few varieties of pears are incompatible with quince and so require double working on an intermediate of another, compatible pear. Evelyn went on to describe how, in order to raise quince rootstocks, any quince on which the buds have failed should be earthed up like a mole hill to encourage rooting of the new shoots. This is similar to the present-day method of 'stooling' rootstocks.

As had happened after the Norman Conquest, when new varieties of pears and other fruits were introduced from France, once more it was French influence which led British growers to adopt the new rootstock. The opposition to its use had been fairly strong. In 1657, Austen, the noted Oxford nurseryman, said that the only stock for pears was the pear seedling and he disliked the whitethorn or any other kind of rootstock. However in 1676, John Rea, a friend of Thomas Hanmer, advised the use of quince saying that these stocks, like the Paradise apple, have the effect of dwarfing the trees and are therefore useful for trees trained on walls where on pear stocks they grow too strongly.

By 1681, Langford was quite definite in his advice, saying that the quince was generally used for dwarf trees growing in borders and those trained on walls. However, in spite of the advice of Rea and Langford, some nurserymen could not be trusted to supply trees on the correct rootstocks, as Switzer observed in 1724. He said that because the considerable demand for trees on quince or pear exceeded supply, some unscrupulous nurserymen worked trees on whitethorn which gave stony, gritty fruits, good for nothing, or on wild ash which never bore well. The worst of it was that the buyers often never realized the reason for the poor cropping of the trees and poor quality of the pears until many years later when the nurseryman was dead or the account forgotten.

PEAR PRODUCTION IN FRANCE AND BELGIUM

The production of pears was of particular importance during the Middle Ages in France and Belgium. One of the earliest writers on pears was Charles Estienne who published his *Seminarium* in 1540. De Serres, who wrote in 1608, was also a keen advocate of pear growing but his enthusiasm for this fruit was exceeded by Le Lectier, attorney to the king at Orleans, who collected and grew fruits of all kinds, but above all, pears. Le Lectier stimulated such interest in pears that their culture became a craze and everyone began planting them and collecting different varieties. Le Lectier started his collection in 1598, and in 1628 circulated a catalogue of his varieties with the request that anyone who had ones not in his collection would supply grafts to him and he would be glad to send others in exchange. From Le Lectier's time fruit growing in France occupied a place of major importance, especially with the king and court. De la Quintinye, working as head of the royal gardens at Versailles, wrote his famous book, published in England in 1693, which included full descriptions of 67 varieties of pears.

While the French played an important part in popularizing the pear, it was in Belgium that serious attention was given to the breeding of new and improved varieties which resulted in many of the types we have today. The first of these breeders was Nicolas Hardenpont (1705–74), a priest at Mons, who began sowing pear seeds and selecting ones he thought showed improvement. After 30 years' work, he introduced his first new variety in 1758, to be followed by a dozen or more other varieties. One of these, raised in 1750 but not distributed until 1806, was Glou Morceau, still cultivated today, sometimes as a pollinator for Doyenné du Comice.

Hardenpont selected the parents for his new varieties with great care and increased the interest in the 'beurre' or buttery textured fruits. Just as the work of Le Lectier had stimulated interest in growing pears in France during the previous century, so the work of Hardenpont started off a craze for breeding pears in Belgium, rather like the tulip craze in Holland and the breeding of gooseberries by the gooseberry clubs in the north of England. Breeding pears became a hobby with priests, physicians, scientists, apothecaries and many others who gave their names to new varieties. Medals were awarded for the best seedlings and though the majority of these proved of little merit, the whole impetus given to breeding, which continued into the first half of the nineteenth century, resulted in a marked improvement in the fruit.

Among those who were influenced by Hardenpont was Dr Van Mons, a pharmacist and physician of Louvain, who developed his own theories about the breeding of plants and the importance of selection, which he put into effect by sowing the seeds of many wild or little-improved pears, raising something like 80,000 seedlings. By continuous selection, he bred numerous new varieties, some 400 in all, of which a number are still cultivated including Beurré d'Anjou.

PEARS IN BRITAIN IN THE EIGHTEENTH CENTURY

As many English writers showed, before Belgian pears became of importance, Britain already had a great many varieties, whether imported, the result of chance seedlings or the selection of seedling pears grown for rootstocks or for perry. An example of selection was given in 1812 by Thomas Andrew Knight. He said that he had found the Elton pear, which he introduced, in an orchard of seedling pears, probably planted 140 years earlier in the parish of Elton in Herefordshire.

In 1724, Switzer described 72 varieties. His list included Jargonelle, long established in England but of French origin; Uvedale's St Germain, a large cooking pear raised by Dr Uvedale, a schoolmaster at Eltham, Kent in 1690; and two other culinary varieties, Warden and Cadillac, the latter supposed to have been found near Cadillac in the Gironde and later, in England, called Catillac. Of the many dessert pears, Switzer said that Ambrosia had been brought from France amongst a collection of fruits which had been planted after the Reformation in the royal gardens in St James' Park. The Autumn or English Bergamont he thought had been in existence from or before the time of Julius Caesar and was possibly the Assyrian pear of Virgil, though there is little supporting evidence for this. The Easter Bergamot he said had been at Hampton Court at the time of Elizabeth I, and, like De la Quintinye, considered Winter Bon Chrétien one of the best of the very ancient varieties.

In 1770 a new pear was raised in England which was to become one of the

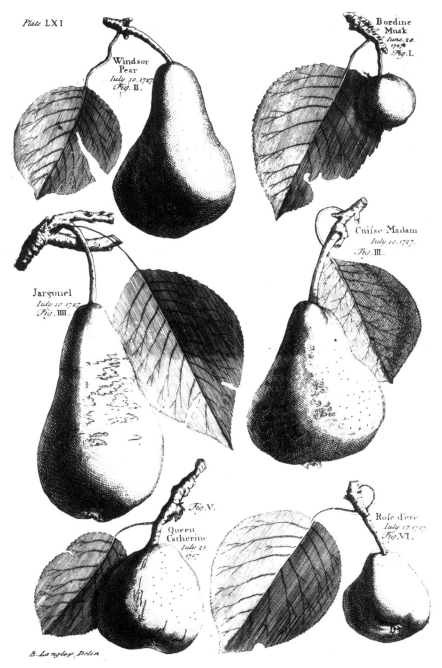

Plate LXI

Bordine
Musk
June. 20.
1727.
Fig. I.

Windsor
Pear
July 10. 1727.
Fig. II.

Cuifse Madam
July 10.1727.
Fig. III.

Jargonel
July 10. 1727.
Fig. IIII.

Fig. V.

Queen
Catherine
July 25
1727.

Rofe d'ete
July 17.1727.
Fig. VI.

B. Langley, *Delin*

Of the early eighteenth-century varieties of pear, some are still known today.
Jargonelle has been especially popular.

most important varieties still in cultivation today. This was Williams' Bon
Chrétien bred by Stair, a schoolmaster at Aldermaston in Berkshire. It took
its name from its distributor, Williams of Turnham Green, Middlesex. In
1797 this pear was taken to America by James Carter of Boston for Thomas
Brewer who planted it in his grounds at Roxbury, Massachusetts, under its
original name. In 1817, Enoch Bartlett of Dorchester, Mass., took over the
Brewer estate and, not knowing the name of the pear, sent it out under his
own name of Bartlett and it quickly became one of the leading varieties in the
USA, especially for canning in California.

The catalogues of pears available towards the end of the eighteenth
century included a very wide range, far greater than are grown today. During
1775–89 Richard Weston published his *Flora Anglicana* in four volumes
which included lists of all types of garden plants and fruits then cultivated in
England. He gave 120 varieties of pears, adding that any of the French ones
could be procured from London nurserymen who had correspondents in
France. In 1779, John Abercrombie, in his *British Fruit-gardener*, gave
information on the different fruits approved and then available from British
nurseries. He had 26 summer, 18 autumn, 21 winter and 4 cooking varieties
of pears. In 1783, the catalogue of Luker and Smith, nurserymen of Covent
Garden and Dalston, offered 49 of the best kinds. Very few of these still exist
except in the collections in the National Fruit Trials.

The Nineteenth Century

At the beginning of the nineteenth century, Thomas Andrew Knight was
involved in his important work of breeding a number of different fruits and
had, in fact, begun the breeding of pears in 1797. He used Bergamot as the
female parent crossed with pollen from St Germain and advised using such
regular cropping varieties as parents by others who might try to raise new
pears. This breeding was encouraged by the Horticultural Society which, in
1811, proposed giving medals and premiums for new fruits, including pears,
which should be of a type similar to those imported from France but which
were hardy and could be kept for marketing in winter and spring.

Although Knight introduced several pears, including the old seedling
Elton and others such as Downton, none of them was very successful. In
1826, the RHS had 622 pear varieties growing in the gardens at Chiswick
and these had increased to 627 by 1831. However, in spite of the
encouragement given by the Society and others, it was another French pear
which created much interest among fruit growers and became one of the
major varieties both in Britain and in other pear-growing countries of the
world. This was Doyenné du Comice, one of the best flavoured pears raised
from seed sown in the fruit garden of the Horticultural Society of Maine et

Loire at Angers which first fruited in 1849. It was immediately recognized as a variety of great merit and, the next year, was distributed in France and other countries, including America. It was brought to England in 1858 by Sir Thomas Ackland.

Following the example set by Van Mons, other varieties of importance were raised in Belgium. Durondeau was bred by M. Durondeau at Tongre, near Tournai in 1811, Easter Beurré by M. Vilain, a solicitor of Mons about 1804, and Beurré Hardy by M. Bonnet, a friend of Van Mons, at Boulogne about 1820. This last variety was acquired in 1830 by M. J. Jamin, a nurseryman near Paris, who named it after M. Hardy, Director of the Luxembourg Gardens, and distributed it about 1840.

The first English pears of note to result from controlled breeding came from the two famous nursery firms of Rivers of Sawbridgeworth and Laxton Brothers of Bedford. Fertility was raised about 1875 by Rivers from seed of Beurré Goubault, and, though of rather poor quality, was planted both commercially and in gardens. Improved Fertility is a tetraploid mutation discovered by Seabrooks in their nurseries at Boreham, Essex in 1934.

Conference, the most widely planted commercial pear in England in the twentieth century, was introduced by Rivers in 1894. Its parent was an open pollinated blossom of Leon le Clare de Laval, a culinary variety, one of the many pears raised by Van Mons in 1825. The first 25 trees of Conference were a gift in 1895 from Francis Rivers to Messrs Edmonds of Allington, Maidstone, who tried them on their Allington farm where they proved so successful that within a few years they planted up the first commercial orchard. Conference soon established itself as the leading commercial pear in England, mainly on account of its heavy cropping and good storage capabilities, especially in refrigerated and controlled atmosphere conditions.

Of the other pears raised in the past century, and still grown on a limited scale in Britain, are Dr Jules Guyot and Packham's Triumph. Dr Jules Guyot, raised by M. Ernest Baltet of Troyes in 1870, is rather similar to Williams' in appearance but is of inferior quality. Packham's Triumph is an Australian pear raised by Packham of Malong, New South Wales about 1896 and thought to be a seedling of Uvedale's St Germain crossed with Williams'.

At the Royal Horticultural Society's Apple and Pear Conference held in 1888, W. Paul gave a talk on varieties of fruits to be grown profitably for market and included the following pears: Aston Town, Eyewood, Hessel, Williams' Bon Chrétien, Beurré Capiamont, Beurré d'Amanlis, M. le Curé, Vicar of Winkfield, Doyenné d'Eté, Mdme Treyve, Marie Louise d'Uccile, Louise Bonne of Jersey and Marie Louise. Of these only Williams' Bon Chrétien is still grown commercially today.

Pear Breeding in the Twentieth Century

The breeding of pears was continued by Laxton Brothers of Bedford. Making use of some of the leading varieties, Marie Louise, Doyenné du Comice, Williams' Bon Chrétien, Beurré Superfin, Fertility, Doyenné d'Eté and Durondeau, many seedlings were raised and seven varieties were named. Those bearing the prefix Laxton's were Early Market, Foremost, Progress, Record, Superb and Victor and another was Beurré Bedford. Laxton's Victor was the first raised, in 1900, though it was not introduced until 1933. Two other varieties were raised in 1901, Laxton's Foremost and Laxton's Superb, but the latter, a cross between Beurré Superfin and Williams' Bon Chrétien and introduced in 1913, was their only variety which had much impact on the commercial market.

Laxton's Superb, an early variety ready in late August, proved useful as a pollinator for Doyenné du Comice but, during the 1960s, its extreme susceptibility to the bacterial disease, fireblight (caused by *Erwinia amylovora*) due to the tendency of Superb to produce secondary blossoms, resulted in it being generally given up as a commercial variety.

The breeding of pears at the research stations has not received the same attention as apples, but some new pears have been introduced by both John Innes and Long Ashton Research Station and breeding of this fruit is being undertaken at East Malling. Spinks at Long Ashton raised Bristol Cross, Williams' crossed with Conference, bred in 1921 and introduced in 1931, which was planted on a limited scale but proved incompatible with quince rootstocks and the fruit has a short shelf-life.

Merton Pride, a triploid variety, was raised at John Innes by M. B. Crane in 1941 from Glou Morceau crossed with Double Williams', a form of Williams' Bon Chrétien having a double set of chromosomes. This was introduced in 1959 but, though excellent in eating quality, it proved rather a light cropper and the buds are especially attractive to bullfinches. Another variety raised by Crane was Merton Star, Marguerite Marillat crossed with Conference, raised in 1933 and named in 1967. This has not attracted commercial attention.

Onward was raised at the National Fruit Trials at Wisley in 1947 from Laxton's Superb crossed with Doyenné du Comice, and was introduced in 1967. The fruit has a very short shelf-life but is of good quality. Beth, a September pear, was bred at East Malling by Tydeman in 1938 and named in 1974; it was suggested for garden use.

At the 1934 Apple and Pear Conference of the RHS, the leading commercial pear grower, Thomas Neame, spoke of the pear varieties which he considered of commercial importance. He recommended planting

Conference and Fertility with lesser numbers of Pitmaston Duchess and possibly Williams' Bon Chrétien, Dr Jules Guyot and Laxton's Superb. But by the 1980s the number of varieties grown commercially has become even more limited and Conference is now the leading variety with smaller acreages of Doyenné du Comice and some Williams' and Beurre Hardy. All other varieties are now grown to a very limited extent.

The only American pear imported in this century which has received any attention is Gorham. This was raised at the New York State Agricultural Experiment Station, Geneva in 1910 from Williams' Bon Chrétien crossed with Josephine de Malines and introduced in 1923. It is of good quality but has a short season, in early autumn, and has proved of little commercial appeal.

As with many other fruits, the gardens of enthusiasts are the only places where many of the old varieties of merit are still to be found. These include Doyenné d'Eté, Beurré d'Amanlis, Fondante d'Automne, Beurré Superfin, Louise Bonne of Jersey, Durondeau, Emile d'Heyst, Glou Morceau, Winter Nelis and Josephine de Malines.

The acreage of commercial pear orchards in Britain has been severely reduced during recent years and the English grower has had to meet increasing competition from other countries who send over large quantities of Passe Crassane and Williams' from Italy and France, and Doyenné du Comice from Europe, America and the southern hemisphere. The use of controlled atmosphere and refrigerated storage has enabled both Conference and Doyenné du Comice to be kept and marketed over an extended season and has removed any necessity to grow naturally long-keeping varieties as was done in the past.

FACTORS AFFECTING PEAR CULTURE

The satisfactory commercial production of pears in England is generally limited to those areas where climatic conditions are especially favourable, where there is relatively warm, sunny weather in summer. Pear growing in areas of high rainfall and cool summer temperatures is highly speculative. The trees are often more subject to disease and the fruits are of poor eating quality and may fail to ripen satisfactorily.

Two other factors which have affected successful cultivation of pears are attacks by the fireblight bacterial disease and the eating of buds by bullfinches. Fireblight made its first appearance in England in 1957, apparently having come from the United States where it was already well established. The variety Laxton's Superb proved very susceptible, which led to its elimination from most orchards, but the disease is now endemic and, under favourable climatic conditions, attacks both apples and pears as well as many kinds of shrubs and hawthorn hedges.

Bullfinch attacks on fruit buds have been reported by most writers on fruit growing. The severity of the attacks has varied considerably from one age to another and has been especially severe during the past 30—40 years. The destruction of pear buds during the dormant season often results in no crop on badly affected trees. The buds of Conference, Williams' Bon Chrétien and Merton Pride are particularly attractive to bullfinches, whereas those of Doyenné du Comice and Beurré Hardy are often left alone.

Modern Rootstocks

The use of quince rootstocks for some pears was recommended by Mascall in the sixteenth century and, although seedling pear stocks were still used for large standard trees right up to the present century, quince stocks have been used for well-trained trees and those grown in pyramid or bush form for several centuries. Various types of quince have been used for stocks, the majority coming from the Angers region of France. A French writer in the seventeenth century advised choosing certain types by the shape of their leaves. When Hatton at East Malling Research Station was investigating the comparative behaviour of different types of apple and plum rootstocks, he also compared a number of vegetatively propagated quince stocks. From these he selected three in particular which he labelled Quince A, B and C. A and B proved to be rather similar in the degree of vigour they imparted to the tree, but Quince C proved to be somewhat dwarfing. Quince A (Angers quince) became the stock mainly used and once Quince C was freed of virus infection, its value as a more dwarfing stock was increased. There are other quince stocks which are used on the Continent and a number of these have been examined and tested at East Malling. A few pear varieties are incompatible on quince, and so need to be double worked using a variety such as Beurré Hardy as an intermediate. This practice was well known to pear growers in the seventeenth century.

Little use is now made of seedling pears as rootstocks as these tend to produce trees showing too much vigour while the quality of the fruits is often adversely affected. Such stocks were often grown from the seed of perry fruits or sometimes from the seed of dessert varieties of pears, especially of Williams' Bon Chrétien. Seedling stocks are still used for some perry pear trees.

Perry Pears and Perry Making 16

The earliest reference to the use of pears for making a fermented drink was by Pliny who said that the Falernian variety, being very juicy, was used for making wine. Palladius, in the fourth century, wrote of pears being used, like apples, to make both a drink and a sauce, and said that the Romans preferred wine made from pears to that of apples. He also gave instructions how to make perry, then called Castomoniale.

In France in AD 513, according to Fortuneatus, Bishop of Poitiers, after her retirement to the convent she had founded, St Radegonde, wife of King Clotaire, drank nothing but mead and perry. In the eighth century, St Segolene, Abbess of Troclar, refused all drinks during Lent except water and perry; while Charlemagne in the ninth century advised the employment on an estate of persons who could make wine, beer, cider, perry and other drinks.

It therefore seems that during the centuries following the collapse of the Roman empire, the production of perry was well established in France but there is no similar evidence in Britain. After the Norman invasion, new varieties of pears were introduced, and pears were planted in the orchards and gardens of the royal families and the aristocracy, but these were mostly hard varieties used for cooking, with a few, such as the early Janettar, being eaten fresh. However, although in later centuries, perry was generally made from the fruits of the wild or 'choke' pears, there is little evidence that this was done during the Middle Ages when there was considerable planting of apples for making cider. Where perry was made, it was certainly on a much smaller scale than cider.

There is virtually no reference to any drinks made from pear juice before the introduction of printed literature in the sixteenth century. Harrison, in 1580, said that 'pirrie' was made from pears, along with cider, in Sussex,

Kent, Worcestershire and other counties. Orchards of pears for making perry were planted, though on a smaller scale, with apples for cider, during the sixteenth and following centuries, especially in Gloucestershire, Herefordshire and Worcestershire. In general, perry pear trees grew to a much larger size and lived longer than those of the cider apple and so were widely spaced at 60 ft or more apart. For some years, intercrops of cereals or other arable crops were taken but, eventually, the orchards were grassed down and grazed by livestock. In Worcestershire, the importance of the pear was recognized by the incorporation in the city arms of 'three pears sable', at the direction of Queen Elizabeth I when she visited the city in 1575.

PERRY IN LITERATURE

Gerard in 1597 wrote: 'Wine made of the iuce of Peares, called in English Perry, is soluble, purgeth those that are not accustomed to drink thereof; notwithstanding it is as wholesome a drinke being taken in small quantities as wine; it comforteth and warmeth the stomacke, and causeth a good digestion.' Parkinson, in 1629, referred to the 'Choke' pear which in his time was the principal pear used for perry. The name 'Choke' seems to have been applied to any wild, very astringent type of pear.

> Perry, which is the juice of Peares, pressed out, is a drinke much esteemed as well as Cyder, to be both drunke at home and carried to the Sea and found to be of good use in long voyages. The Perry made of Choke Pears, notwithstanding the harshness and evill taste, both of the fruit and juice, after a few months, becomes as milde and pleasante as wine.

In 1652, Samuel Hartlib, encouraging the greater planting of orchards in England, suggested that Normandy should be taken as an example:

> Normandy, which produceth but little wine, maketh abundance of Cider and Perry, which they estimate equally to Wine, if it be made of good fruit. The ordinary Perry is made of Choaky Pears, very juicy, which grow along by the High-way sides, which are not to be eaten raw.
>
> There are two wayes of making Cider and Perry; one by bruising and beating them, and then presently to put them in a vessel to ferment or work of themselves. The other way is to boil the juice with some good spices, by which the rawness is taken away and then to ferment it with some yeast if it work not of itself.

1 *Pyrum ſtrangulatorium maius.*
The great Choke Peare.

2 *Pyrum ſtrangulatorium minus.*
The ſmall Choke Peare.

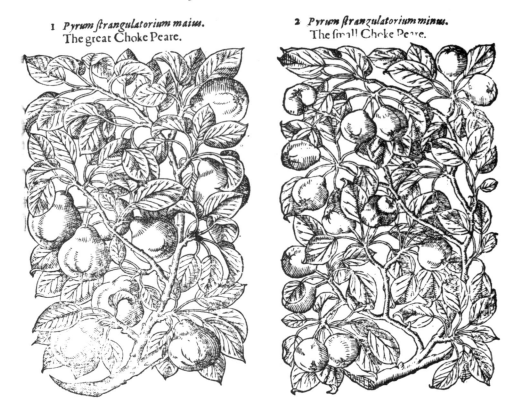

Wild Choke pears used for making perry.

Writing later, Hartlib said:

> *Perry is most pleasing to the female Palate, having a relish of weak*
> *Wine mixed with Sugar. The White Horse-pear yields a juice*
> *somewhat near to the Quality of Cyder; and the neighbourhood of*
> *Bosbury is famous for a peculiar Perry, which hath many of the*
> *Masculine Qualities of Cyder. This Bosbury pear is there called*
> *Bareland Pear.*

Austen, in 1657, suggested that Choke pears, because of their unpleasant taste, might safely be planted in fields and hedges without fear of their being stolen, and Hartlib advised planting perry pears and cider apples alternately in the rows as the pears would outlive the apples. By the end of the century, the number of pear varieties considered suitable for making perry had increased. Worlidge in 1691 said:

> *Pears that are esteemed for their Vinous Juice in Worcestershire and*

those adjacent Parts, are the Red and Green Squash-pears, the John-pear, the Green Harpary, the Drake-pear, the Mary-pear, the Lullam-pear, but above the rest are esteemed the Bosbury and the Bareland pears and the White and Red Horse pears.

As for the Turgovian-pear that yields that most superlative Perry the world produces, I only wish it were more generally dispersed.

PERRY PEAR CULTIVATION

As with cider apples, seedling pears were usually allowed to crop to see if they were of any value before a decision was made to graft them to other varieties. In this way, numerous new varieties were raised, many of which had only a local distribution. If any of these received local acclaim they might receive wider distribution.

Some of the pears in the seventeenth century, though astringent, might be used for eating fresh or for cooking and the surplus sent to the mills to be made into perry. Examples of pears used in this way were Thorn, Hastings and Brown Bess. The planting of dual-purpose pears was fairly common during the nineteenth century when Blakeney Red was a popular choice.

As in the case of cider, the planting of new pear orchards and the making of perry reached the peak of its importance during the seventeenth and early eighteenth centuries, followed by a decline from the end of the eighteenth and throughout the nineteenth centuries. However, owing to the longevity of the perry pear trees, many of those planted in the seventeenth and eighteenth centuries still exist today.

There was a concentration in the planting of perry pears in the areas of Gloucestershire adjoining the Herefordshire border. Here an example of an orchard planted towards the end of the eighteenth century was at Knap Farm which consisted largely of local varieties, Knapper, Tumper and Late Treacle. In another orchard, Thorn dominated. Other varieties planted at this time were Thurston's Red, New Meadow, Newbridge, Turner's Barn, Oldfield, Red Pear, Moorcroft and High pear.

DECLINE IN PERRY ORCHARDS

The decline in the health of the orchards and the poor quality of much of the cider and perry in his time was of great concern to Thomas Andrew Knight who considered that the poor quality of the cider and perry was often due to the use of inferior varieties. To try to correct this, he spent 15 years examining a large number of seedling pears and grew many on his own farm but he only found one, Holmer, capable of making a fine perry. This had been found growing in a hedge on the estate of Charles Cook of the Moor in the parish of Holmore. Knight encouraged its planting and it is still grown today though, owing to its small fruits and poor cropping, it is not being planted in new orchards.

In spite of the encouragement given by Knight, there was a further decline in the planting of perry pears during the nineteenth century and neglect of many of the old orchards. The Woolhope Naturalists' Field Club and the work of Robert Hogg did much to try to improve the cider and perry industry and reintroduced a number of the valuable old varieties, including the famous Taynton Squash perry pear.

When Radcliffe Cook, a Herefordshire grower, campaigned for the revival of cider production at the end of the nineteenth century, he also expressed concern about the state of the perry orchards. Cook himself selected the variety Hellen's Early, named after his own estate, which is still regarded as one of the best early varieties. Other varieties he selected for planting were Taynton Squash, Barland, Thorn, Moorcroft, Red Pear, Yellow Huffcap, Winnal's Longdon, Oldfield, Pine, Butt, Rock and Blakeney Red. All of these, with the exception of Barland, Yellow Huffcap and Pine are still recommended for planting to a greater or lesser extent, which illustrates the great foresight shown by Radcliffe Cook.

Professor B. T. B. Barker included the study of perry pears and perry in the work of the newly established National Fruit and Cider Institute in 1903 and encouraged the planting of trial orchards of selected varieties throughout the counties of the West Midlands and the south-west. Over the succeeding years these orchards provided valuable information about the varieties, the effect of different soils and orchard management, in addition to the information obtained at the Research Station on the production of perry.

However, there was still very little interest in the planting of new perry orchards until the pioneer work of Messrs Showerings of Shepton Mallet in Somerset in the late 1940s, producing a perry by controlled fermentation. This firm planted experimental orchards including trees worked on quince rootstocks and planted in hedgerows. The initiative of Showerings has resulted in some limited revival of interest in the planting of perry pears by other firms and growers and the work of R. R. Williams at Long Ashton, who has studied the many — possibly 100 — varieties of perry pears still in existence, has done much to further this interest in the selection of varieties to plant.

Several species of *Prunus* were involved in the development of plums and allied stone fruits. Of these the blackthorn or sloe, *Prunus spinosa*, is found growing wild in Britain, in many parts of Europe and in northern Asia. It grows in hedgerows and in woodlands and as a scrubby bush on poor soils. This species is a tetraploid, having three sets of chromosomes. The wild fruits are sometimes collected for making a fermented drink but their astringency generally makes them unacceptable as food.

Prunus cerasifera, syn. P. divaricata, the cherry plum or Myrobalan, is not a native of Britain or northern Europe but, along with other species of *Prunus*, including *P. spinosa*, is found growing in considerable numbers in the forests of southern Russia. It has two sets of chromosomes. The cherry plum, as cultivated in Britain, is usually a red-fruited type but there are also yellow forms. On the coast of the Caspian Sea, in Daghestan, black-fruited types predominate; in the central and southern parts of the Black Sea coast, red and purple forms occur, while in western and eastern Transcaucasia and the northern Black Sea coastal areas, the yellow colour, which is a recessive character, is common.

For many centuries, improved forms of wild *P. cerasifera* were selected by the local Caucasian inhabitants as food, cooked and dried and made into meal by mixing with wheat or barley flour. In the early years of this century, up to 700 tons of the dried fruits were exported annually from Transcaucasia. As a result of its early flowering, in February or early March, the cropping of the cherry plum is uncertain in Britain, but seedling and selected vegetatively propagated forms are often used as rootstocks.

Prunus institia occurs as a wild form, the bullace, in Britain and other countries of Europe. It has six sets of chromosomes and has round, black, red or paler coloured fruits. This is the Mirabelle of France, and it is thought that damsons have been derived from this species and took their name from Damascus where this fruit was grown before the Christian era and was originally known as the 'damas cene'.

From another species, *Prunus triflora*, the Salacine plum, Japanese plums have been developed. This species is a native of China and, though widely cultivated in Japan, does not occur there in a wild state. It flowers very early in the year and so is very subject to frost damage, though the trees themselves are relatively hardy. For this reason, Japanese plums are only cultivated in the milder regions of the world, including California, South Africa and parts of southern Europe; they usually fail to crop well in England.

ORIGIN OF THE DOMESTIC PLUM

Most of the plums cultivated in Britain and in many parts of Europe and the rest of the world are grouped as derivatives of *Prunus domestica*. The domestic plum is considered to have arisen as a cross between *P. cerasifera* and *P. spinosa*. This hybridization could well have occurred in the Caucasus region where many different forms of the cherry plum grow wild in the forests together with trees of *P. spinosa* which also shows many variations. In *P. spinosa*, the ground colour of the fruits is green and the anthocyanin blue, while in *P. cerasifera* the ground colour is yellow and the anthocyanin red. The combination of these various characters, as the result of hybridization between the two species, has resulted in a great range of types of plums showing considerable differences in skin colour, fruit size, shape and flavour.

It is known that the two species hybridize freely in the forests of Maikop, in the north Caucasus but may well have occurred in other regions. Dr Rybin of the USSR himself raised seedlings from crosses between these species.

GROUPS OF PLUMS

The plums of Europe, in spite of the hybridization between varieties which has taken place in the past, can in general be divided into a number of fairly distinct groups. Damsons, derived from *P. institia*, have small, purple-coloured fruits with an astringent, sour or acid flavour. Cherry plums, having round, mostly red fruits, remain a distinct group and other minor groups have been derived from the bullace and the Mirabelle.

The domestic plums form the major part of the European plums, but within this classification certain distinct types can be recognized. The Reine-Claude or Green Gage group is characterized by more or less round fruits of a green, yellow or slight red colour. The flesh is sweet, tender and juicy. This characteristic is frequently shown by their offspring. The Transparent gages are those having transparent or semi-transparent skins, allowing the stones to be seen within the fruit.

The prunes have always formed an important group, comprising plums which usually have a high sugar content and purple-coloured fruits which can be successfully dried. Other types of plums, such as the Yellow Egg, are sometimes distinguished. These varieties, mostly of the culinary and canning group, are characterized by the colour of the skin and shape of the fruit. These different groups of plums and other *Prunus* fruits have probably existed for several thousand years.

PLUMS IN ANTIQUITY

In Britain there are numerous records of the discovery on prehistoric sites of the stones of the sloe, *Prunus spinosa*. The earliest fossils are five from inter-glacial sites at Clacton and Cromer in East Anglia, and many stones have been found on sites dating from the Neolithic period. These have often been associated with remains of human settlements as at Glastonbury lake village. The fruits of the sloe are astringent and would therefore have been unpalatable as food unless cooked and sweetened in some way. There is a possibility that they were used in dyeing. Other sites where sloe stones have been found date from the Middle Bronze, Bronze and Iron Ages, as well as from Roman sites at Silchester, Manchester and Caerwnt in Monmouthshire.

There are also many records of the discovery of stones of the bullace, *Prunus institia*. These have been found at prehistoric Swiss lake sites, and appear to have been part of the diet since, unlike the sloe, the bullace is palatable when eaten raw. In Britain, charcoal remains of the bullace dating from the Iron Age were found in Norfolk, from the Roman period at Silchester and from the Anglo-Saxon period at Hungate in Yorkshire.

The domestic plum is not thought to be indigenous to Britain. Although hybridization between the cherry plum (*P. cerasifera*) and the sloe (*P. spinosa*) probably occurred in other places besides the Caucasus region, the cherry plum is not a native of Britain. However, stones of the domestic plum have been excavated from the Late Iron Age settlement at Maiden Castle in Dorset and from the Roman site at Silchester, so it certainly seems that plums were growing in Britain, either cultivated or in a wild state, before the Roman occupation. Damson stones dating from the Roman period were also found at Silchester.

The plum is now found growing wild in many parts of Britain and occasionally forms of it are found which are suitable for bringing into cultivation.

CULTIVATION OF THE PLUM IN ANCIENT ROME

The only brief reference to the plum by the Greek writer Theophrastus was to say that the fir-plum had few and shallow roots. There was no mention of it by the Greek poets, Homer or Hesiod, nor does it feature in the books of the Roman authors Cato and Varro who wrote in the pre-Christian age. It was not until the first century AD that Pliny and Columella spoke of plums.

Columella, in an introductory poem to one of his books, describing the orchard harvest wrote:

> *. . . and the panniers are piled high*
> *With apricots and plums and damsons too*
> *And fruits once sent by Persis barbarous.*

Pliny described 12 different varieties of plums:

> *Afterwards comes a vast crowd of plums. There is the parti-coloured plum, partly black and partly white in colour, which is called the Barley-plum because it ripens at barley harvest; and another of the same colour, which is later and is larger in size, called the Donkey-plum from its inferior value. The Wax-plum and the Purple plum are smaller in size but more esteemed; and there is also the Armenian plum, imported from foreign parts, and the only plum that recommends itself even by its scent . . . the peach and the Wax-plum and the wild plum, if stored in casks like grapes, will prolong their life till another crop begins to come into existence, but the remaining varieties, ripening quickly, speedily pass off. Among our foreign trees, we have already spoken of the Damson, named from Damascus in Syria; it has been grown in Italy for a long time, though it has a larger stone and less flesh here than in its country of origin, and here it never dries into wrinkles, because it lacks its native sunshine.*
>
> *The Persian plum or peach, it is true, is shown by its very name to be an exotic even in Asia Minor and in Greece, and to have been introduced from Persia. But the wild plum is known to grow everywhere, which makes it more surprising that this fruit is not mentioned by Cato, especially as he pointed out the way of storing some wild fruits.*

Pliny's account demonstrates that plums were commonly grown in Rome in his time; he was surprised that this fruit had not been mentioned by Cato, writing about 250 years earlier, especially as plums commonly grew wild in Italy and damsons, originating from Damascus, had been grown in Italy for a long time. Possibly the plum was regarded as an inferior fruit by the earlier writers and so did not merit mention.

THE PLUM IN BRITAIN

Stones of plums and sloes were found on Roman sites, such as Silchester, and plum stones were also found, along with remains of other fruits, in a pit near a second-century building in St Thomas Street, Southwark. It is known that plums formed part of the diet of Roman troops in various countries in Europe, and in Britain an amphora of plums, probably sent over from Spain, was found at Brough-on-Noe. Stones of various fruits of *Prunus*, resembling those of the bullace and damson, were excavated from New Wharf, a second-century Roman waterfront near Upper Thames Street in London. At Silchester, Reid identified a plum stone which was similar to that of the ancient black plum of Cornwall of the Orleans type, an old French variety.

From these discoveries and in view of the popularity of plums in Rome at the time of the Roman invasion, it seems likely that this fruit and other *Prunus* species were used as food and cultivated here during the occupation. Even during the Dark Ages, plums would have continued to grow in a wild state, and as the life in the monasteries developed would have been one of the fruits cultivated by the monks. Plums were included in Charlemagne's list of fruits to be grown in the early ninth century.

Recent excavation of the Viking settlement at York has indicated that the inhabitants had a varied diet, including fruits and nuts. Among the fruit remains found were stones of sloe, a cultivated plum and probably those of a damson. From an Anglo-Saxon herbal, written early in the tenth century and originally held at Glastonbury Abbey, it is apparent that plums were cultivated in the gardens and were grafted on the sloe as rootstock.

There are relatively few references to plums and allied stone fruits in the records of the thirteenth and fourteenth centuries and no reference to individual varieties as there is for apples and pears. In 1270 the Westminster Abbey Customary required the monk who was gardener to supply the monastery with plums as well as apples, cherries, pears, nuts and medlars. Plums were also grown in other monasteries as far north as Scotland. However, although they were cultivated in some of the monastery gardens, the majority of people still relied on wild plums, bullaces and sloes for their fruits; their sourness made them especially suitable for making into verjuice. The inclusion of plums in William Langland's, *Piers Plowman*, in 1362, and in Chaucer's translation of the *Roman de la Rose* in 1372 indicates their importance.

PLUMS IN THE SIXTEENTH CENTURY

Even if more varieties of plums were planted during the thirteenth and fourteenth centuries, when there was increased interest in the development of gardens and the planting of fruit trees, they must have disappeared during the depression of the fifteenth century, judging by the account of plums given by Peter Treueris in his *Grete Herball* in 1526:

> *Plomes be colde and moyst / there be two sortes of them / blacke and reed. The blackes be somewhat harde and amonge them the best be those y be called damaske plommes or damassons. They ought to be gaded when they be rype / If they wyll kepe them must cleve and dewe they with vyneygre / so they may be kep in a vessell of wood. But when they be cloven they must be dryed 15 days in the sonne / and then put in syrope. They have vertue to smothe and polyshe y bowelles.*

The emphasis still seems to have been on the preserving and drying of damsons and plums as it had been from the earliest days of their cultivation. When William Turner published his *Names of Herbes* in 1548 he wrote of rather more varieties:

> *Of the plum trees, bulles trees and slo trees.*
> *Ther ar a greate sorte of divers kyndes of plumbes / one with a diverse color / an other blacke, an other whytishe. Ther ar other that they call barley plumbes of the folouring of that corn. There are others of the same color later and greter. They are called ay asse plumes of the evil esycenes. There are also som that ar black and more commendable / and purple plumbes.*
> *These kyndes of garden plumbes (if a man may trust Pliny) were not known in Itali in Catoes tyme.*
> *Ther ar divers kyndes of wilde plumbes and plum trees. Wherof I knoe two severall kyndes at the leste. The one is called the bulles tre or the bullester tre / and the other is called the slo tre on the blak thorn tre. The bulles tre is of two sortes / the one is removed in the gardines / and groweth to the bygnes of a good plum tre. The other groweth in hedges / but it never groweth in to y bygnes of any grete tre / but abideth betwene the lygnes of a tre and a great bushe. I never saw in all my lyfe more plenty of thys sorte of bulles trees / then in Somersetshire.*

New varieties of plums were among the trees and scions of fruits brought over from the Continent which contributed to the revival of fruit growing in

Britain during the reign of Henry VIII. As Harrison commented in 1580, Britain had never been better supplied with good fruit, including the most delicate varieties of plums, than during the previous 40 years.

In spite of Harrison's comments, however, the damson still seems to have been regarded as the best of the stone fruits as it was by Mascall in 1575. He advised gathering other varieties when ripe and drying them in the sun or in a hot bread oven; in this way they could be kept for a year. Heresbachius in 1578 also said that the damson was the principal variety of plum but there were many others, some white, black, purple or red. The Wheat and Horse plums were used to fatten pigs. He recommended the Finger plums which were the length of a man's finger and had been brought over from Bohemia and Hungary, the source of many new plums. He also recommended the Julians and Noberdians varieties, both blue in colour. Like Mascall, he described the drying damsons in the sun, spread out on lattices or on the roof leads. The Wheat plum was later described by Hogg in 1875 as a very old dessert variety of fair quality. The Noberdian was probably the Norbert or Prune de Lepine, which Hogg said was a beautiful little purple plum about the size of a bullace, round in shape and ripe in October but would hang until it shrivelled, when it became like a raisin. The Julian or St Julien is also a late-ripening purple plum which was once much used for preserving, as were the majority of plums grown at this time. Tusser in 1580 included the Wheat plums separately from the green and grafted varieties.

These early writers suggested that some plums could be propagated from their own suckers, a method still continued to this day for certain varieties, as Pershore Yellow Egg. As time went on the St Julien became one of the most popular rootstocks for grafting or budding plums onto.

Gerard on Plums

Gerard, in 1597, was the first writer to have very much to say about plums, and it seems that the number of varieties had increased very considerably by his day. He said he had 60 of the best and rarest varieties in his garden and every year he received new ones not previously known. He included illustrations of a number of different types. The heading of 'Prunus Domestica' was given to the 'Damson Tree' and 'P. Damasceena' was called the 'Damson Plum Tree'. The latter was the damson as known today which had come from Damascus but the name 'Damson' was also given to other varieties of plums.

According to Gerard, there were many different kinds of black plums or prunes. The dried Damask prunes were more astringent than those of Spain which were sweeter, but those of Hungary which were long and sweet and those of Moravia were the best. Gerard said that the Almond plum was long, having a cleft down the middle, of a brown colour and pleasant taste. The 'Mirobolan' was round, full of juice and of good flavour. Wild plums were to be found in most hedges throughout England.

His account shows that new varieties of plums were being imported from many countries of Europe and that, as today, some of the best prunes came from the Balkan countries and southern Europe. Parkinson in 1629 described no fewer than 61 varieties of plums and emphasized the important part played by John Tradescant in bringing in new ones.

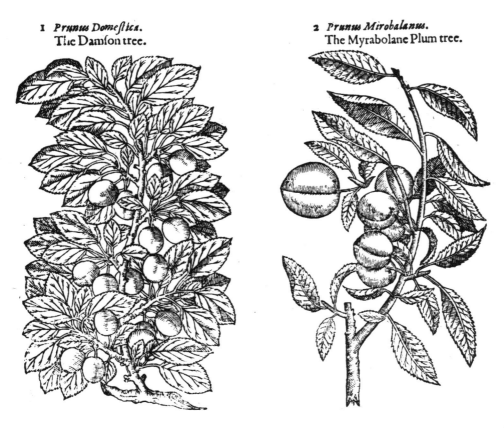

1 *Prunus Domestica.*
The Damson tree.

2 *Prunus Mirobalanus.*
The Myrabolane Plum tree.

The Damson was popular in ancient Rome. The Myrobalan, or cherry plum, originated in the forests of southern Russia.

Writing of dried damsons and plums, Parkinson said that the great Damask or Damson plums were dried in France in great quantities and brought to Britain in hogsheads (large barrels) and sold at grocers. The Bruncola plum was dried, the stones removed and imported in small boxes and sold at 'Confitmakers'' shops, to be served as a sweet course, being much appreciated for its pleasant tartness. The Great Damask was one of the plums, according to Parkinson, now called German Prunes which include the Quetsche, Zwetsche or, as they are called in Kent, Switzen, types. This kind of plum is thought to have originated in Asia and have been grown by the Romans and is still an important processing fruit.

From the description of varieties by Parkinson and other writers in the sixteenth and seventeenth centuries, all the characters shown by present-day plums can be seen to have existed then and a number of the varieties popular in their time are still in existence, several of them of commercial importance. Of those mentioned by Parkinson, Amber Primordian is considered to be Catalonia which still exists and is one of the earliest of all plums. It received a First Class Certificate of the RHS in 1901. It probably came from the Catalan region of Spain. Blue Perdrigon, which Parkinson called a dainty good plum, was introduced from Italy about 1582. It is still grown today and for centuries has been the basis of the manufacture of Brignole prunes in the Basse Alps. Morocco still existed earlier in this century and Winter Creke is Black Bullace.

Parkinson's Verdoch is the original name of our present-day Green Gage or Reine-Claude of France, which comes fairly true from seed and so the name has been used for a number of almost identical varieties. The original type is thought to have come from Armenia and was taken to Greece and then to Italy, where it was called Verdocchia, and to have reached France during the reign of Francois I (1494—1547), being named after his wife, Reine Claude.

The Green Gage probably first reached England direct from Italy since it was known to both Parkinson and to Leonard Meager in 1688 by its Italian name, though Worlidge in 1691 described Verdoch as good only to preserve which suggests the name had been used for another variety. The English name Green Gage came about by accident. Some time before 1724 this plum was sent with others by John Gage, a Roman Catholic priest near Paris, to his brother Sir Thomas Gage at Hengrave Hall, near Bury St Edmunds. Apparently the label on the Reine-Claude trees was lost and so the gardener simply called them 'Green Gage'.

By 1729, the London nurseryman, Batty Langley listed both Reine-Claude and Green Gage separately; in 1731 Miller described the Green Gage as one of the best plums in England, and the same name was used by Professor Bradley in 1739, since when it has been sold under this name.

A form of the Green Gage was among the stones of plums recovered from the wreck of the Mary Rose, the flagship of Henry VIII, which sank in 1545 and was raised in 1982. The wreck revealed a basket containing the remains of rather more than 100 plums. Examination of the stones resulted in the identification of five different species and varieties of plums. These were Green Gage and Catalonia, together with the Mirabelle (*Prunus institia*), the Myrobalan (*P. cerasifera*) and its yellow form, the yellow cherry plum. All

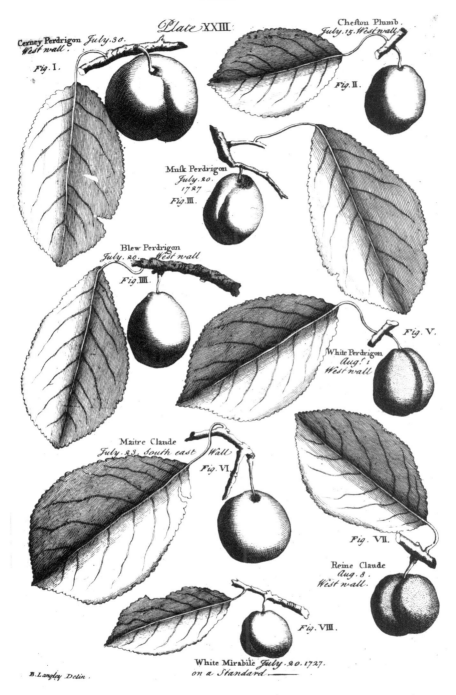

Plate XXIII

Cerney Perdrigon *July.30.*
West wall.

Fig. I.

Cheston Plumb.
July.15.West wall.

Fig. II.

Musk Perdrigon
July.20.
1727

Fig. III.

Blew Perdrigon
July. 20. West wall

Fig. IIII.

Fig. V.

White Perdrigon
Aug.ᵗ 1
West wall

Maitre Claude
July.23. South east Wall

Fig. VI.

Fig. VII.

Reine Claude
Aug. 8
West wall.

Fig. VIII.

White Mirabile *July. 20. 1727.*
on a Standard.

B.Langley *Delin.*

Plum varieties: the French Perdrigon was raised from its stone and often used for drying. Maître Claude, Reine Claude and Green Gage also came from France.

these plums were known and grown by gardeners and others in Europe before any of them were described by the English writers, Turner, Gerard and Parkinson in the sixteenth and seventeenth centuries. This discovery confirms that they were also grown here early in the sixteenth century.

ROOTSTOCKS FOR PLUMS

The Romans grafted or budded their selected varieties of plums onto rootstocks, and for many centuries suckers were used for propagating particular varieties or were used for budding or grafting with different kinds. Both Mascall and Heresbachius had advised using suckers, but Mascall had also suggested using seed taken from good-quality plum trees to raise seedling stocks. Later writers advised using seed from special varieties. Austen in 1657 said that the White Pear plum stocks were the best and damson stocks the worst as they were too dry and the grafts did not take satisfactorily on them. The *French Gardiner* in 1669 recommended using seedlings or suckers from the Damask plum which would give abundant crops but wild plum stocks were to be avoided as they were incompatible with many stone fruits.

Miller in 1731 favoured the White Pear plum but also suggested using seedlings of the 'Muscle, St Julian, Bonum Magnum or any other sort of Free shooting plum'. The 'Muscle' of Miller is the Mussel plum which is still used as a rootstock, its chief merit being its compatibility with all varieties of plums and other stone fruits.

The St Julian or Julien was cultivated in the sixteenth and seventeenth centuries as a plum for drying and is considered to be a form of *Prunus institia*. As a rootstock it has long been popular on the Continent, especially in France. Since it has frequently been grown from seed, variations have occurred which can affect the vigour and general behaviour of the trees worked on it.

PLUM VARIETIES IN THE EIGHTEENTH CENTURY

In 1657 Austen wrote that there were very many varieties of plums, more than of cherries. In 1669 John Evelyn included 75 and in 1691 Worlidge 70 varieties in their books. So, by the beginning of the eighteenth century, gardeners and market growers had a wide selection of plums to choose from. Switzer, in 1724, considered that the varieties available in his time were far superior to those of the past although, in fact, many he mentioned had been described by Parkinson a hundred years earlier. Switzer wrote: 'It is manifest to all Lovers of Planting, that we are very much improv'd in our Collection of

Plums within these twenty or thirty years, there being at least twenty Sorts that are tolerably good. A good Plum should have a sweet sugar'd Juice, a tender melting Pulp and a rich and Exquisite Taste something perfum'd.' These aims might well be a guide to modern plant breeders! Switzer's list included 'St Katherine, Reine Claud, Maitre Claud, Drap-d'or, Jeanne Hative, Mirabel, La-Royal, Blue Perdigon, Orleance, Red Fotheringham, Black Damaseen, Morocco and St Julian'.

In 1779, the varieties of plums in John Abercrombie's list of those approved and available in nurseries consisted almost entirely of ones which had been grown 50 years earlier, including Black Damask, Orleans, Queen Claude, Green Gage, Perdrigon, White Magnum Bonum, Fotheringham, St Catherine, Mirabelle, Muscle, St Julian, Damascene and the cherry plum. A very similar list appeared in the catalogue of Luker and Sons, nurserymen of Covent Garden, in 1783.

Fotheringham is a good-quality plum of English origin still in existence, and mentioned by Rea in 1665. St Catherine, synonymous with Red Magnum Bonum, also still exists. It is an old French plum know to Parkinson in 1629 as Imperial. Jeanne Hative was Catalonia.

One of the few plums of note bred in England during the eighteenth century was Coe's Golden Drop. This was raised by Jervaise Coe, a market gardener at Bury St Edmunds, Suffolk, who bred several new plums during the latter half of the century. He believed that Golden Drop, which grew from a stone of Green Gage, had been pollinated by White Magnum Bonum which grew nearby. It was introduced in 1800. It is an excellent quality late dessert plum which, in the past, was often picked and stored for winter use. Apart from its intrinsic value, it has been much used by other plant breeders endeavouring to raise late good-quality varieties. A damson which came into prominence in the eighteenth century was the Damascene or Shropshire Damson, which had fruits much larger than the common type.

THE NINETEENTH CENTURY

In 1806, William Forsyth, gardener to George IV, gave a description of the 27 varieties of plums then most commonly grown in England. All of these had been well known in the previous century or earlier. But when the Horticultural Society published its catalogue of fruits planted in the gardens at Chiswick, it included 281 varieties, though many of these proved to be synonyms or of little value.

The breeding of new varieties of plums was one of the objectives of the Horticultural Society, in encouraging the introduction of new fruits. There was a need for plums with hardy blossoms which would be less subject to frost damage. The Society thought that several native *Prunus* species which

F

were hardy and rarely injured might be used by crossing with pollen from the high quality but tender varieties, in the same way as had been done with apples by crossing with the Siberian crab as reported by Thomas Andrew Knight in the *Herefordshire Pomona*. These objectives in breeding plums still apply today when plant breeders at Long Ashton Research Station have endeavoured to raise varieties less liable to frost damage.

After a long period of stagnation in the introduction of new varieties of plums, extending over more than a hundred years during which time growers in Britain depended on old varieties mostly imported from Europe, many by John Tradescant at the beginning of the seventeenth century, the position was radically altered. Knight himself included the breeding of plums in his other work of raising new varieties by controlled fertilization, but was not particularly successful. He did introduce one variety, Downton Imperatrice in 1823, raised from Magnum Bonum crossed with the pollen of Blue Imperatrice, the latter a very old dessert plum, but the new variety was only of preserving quality. However, Knight's work and the influence of the Horticultural Society did much to foster a new approach to fruit breeding especially by the leading nurserymen in England, Thomas Rivers and Thomas Laxton.

The pioneer was Thomas Rivers who was responsible for the introduction of several new plums which are still of major importance today. The first of these was Early Rivers, originally called Rivers Early Prolific, raised in 1820 from the seed of the early Précoce de Tours, and introduced about 1834. This quickly became popular as an early culinary variety and has maintained this position for 150 years.

While on a visit to a French nurseryman, Thomas Rivers was struck by the quality of a plum, Reine-Claude Diaphane (Transparent Gage) but as this proved a poor cropper at Sawbridgeworth, he planted seed from it and raised Early Transparent Gage, introduced in 1873. This was awarded a First Class Certificate by the RHS in 1898.

Encouraged by the success of Early Rivers, Rivers crossed this with Prince Englebert, a heavy-cropping, dual-purpose variety raised in Belgium in 1843, and bred the famous Czar, named after the Czar of Russia who was visiting England. Czar was introduced in 1875 and soon established itself as a heavy-cropping, self-fertile, August cooking plum, a position it still maintains.

Many other varieties of plums and gages were raised by Thomas Rivers and introduced by him or his successors, including the high quality Golden and Late Transparent gages and the cooking plums, Monarch and President, both of which received First Class Certificates from the RHS. Rivers were also responsible for introducing, though not raising, several other plums. Of these Wyedale, raised at Swainton in Yorkshire and introduced by Rivers in 1869, is a heavy-cropping cooking plum of poor quality, its only virtue being its late ripening in October.

Oullins Gage was a chance seedling found in France at Coligny and introduced by M. Massot, a nurseryman at Oullins near Lyon, as Reine-Claude d'Oullins. It was brought to England by Thomas Rivers some time before 1856. Though not of gage flavour or quality, this yellow, August plum is still of commercial importance in England. A much better quality real gage type is Count Althann's, which was raised in Bohemia by the gardener to Count Althann between 1850 and 1860 and introduced to England by Rivers before 1867.

In 1840 one of the most important plum varieties grown in Britain was introduced. This was Victoria which was found as a seedling in a garden at Alderton in Sussex. It became known as Sharp's Emperor and was ultimately sold to a nurseryman Denyer, at Brixton, and was sold by him in 1844 at a high price to customers as Denyer's Victoria. As a self-fertile, heavy-cropping, dual-purpose variety, it was soon planted both in gardens and on commercial farms in Kent, the Evesham Valley and most other areas of plum production.

Diamond was also a chance seedling found in a hedge at Brenchley in Kent by a farm worker, Diamond, and introduced by Hooker, a Brenchley nurseryman, in 1830. It is a black, August, cooking plum, which was widely planted in Kent and even spread to the United States where it was grown commercially.

In the last century a number of plum varieties of importance raised in the United States were brought over to England. Imperial Gage, wrongly named Denniston's Superb in this country, was raised on Princes' nursery at Flushing, Long Island about 1790. This was selected from seedlings raised as the result of sowing 25 quarts of Green Gage stones. This is still grown as a self-fertile, August, gage-quality plum. Jefferson is another dessert plum raised about 1825 by Judge Buel in Albany, New York, and brought to England about 1840. Ontario, a yellow plum, was raised at Rochester, New York and described in 1874. It has been planted to a limited extent in England during the present century.

LOCAL ENGLISH VARIETIES

A number of plums and damsons have arisen in different plum-growing counties in England where they have become of importance in their own area and have often been distributed to other parts of the country. Cambridge Gage is of unknown origin but was probably a seedling of the Green Gage, showing somewhat greater vigour and better cropping. It probably arose in the Cambridge area where it is extensively grown for market.

Aylesbury Prune is a black plum which may have arisen as a chance seedling from *Prunus institia* and has been widely grown in the Valley of Aylesbury. Like many other local seedlings, it is propagated from suckers. Blaisdon Red was a seedling discovered by a Mr Dowding of Blaisdon in

Gloucestershire and first recorded in 1892. It is a red—blue plum mainly used for processing and has been grown especially in its native area of Huntley. Pershore, or Yellow Egg, was a seedling found by George Crooke in Tiddesley Wood, Pershore, in 1827, and is of importance especially in the Evesham area for processing. It is mainly propagated from suckers and is often used as a rootstock.

Purple Pershore was raised by Walter Martin of Pershore Fields, Drakes Broughton, near Pershore c1877, from a cross between Early Rivers and Diamond. It was at one time planted extensively around Evesham.

Kea is a chance seedling found and grown at Crome and Crowland, near Truro in Cornwall. There are black and red forms. The Dittesham Small Red is indistinguishable from Kea and Dimmock Red is a seedling often grown in the hedgerows at Dimmock and Newent in Gloucestershire.

Winesour is a small, black cooking plum of unknown origin which is believed to have been first grown near Rotherham. According to John Harvey, it grows in the neighbourhood of Sherburn in Elmet, the site of an ancient hill settlement dating back to the seventh century; he therefore wonders whether this variety is a survival from the time of the Roman occupation.

Warwickshire Drooper is also of unknown origin but has been much planted in parts of the county where it is known as Magnum or Magnum Bonum but has no connection with the old White Magnum Bonum. It has also been planted in Kent and is sometimes sold as a gage, on account of its yellow—green appearance but is not of gage quality.

Marjorie's Seedling is one of the few local seedlings found during this century which has proved a commercial success in many parts of the country. It was found by G. W. Langley at Hillfoot Farm, Beenham in Berkshire in 1912 and was introduced in 1928. It was distributed by Burleydam Nurseries in 1943.

DAMSONS

The damson is a fruit which has been more widely cultivated in Britain than in the other countries of Europe. As it is derived from *Prunus institia* which is native to Britain, it is not surprising that improved wild seedlings should have been brought into cultivation. The Farleigh Damson was a wild seedling found by James Crittenden of Farleigh, Kent, and introduced about 1820. It is somewhat larger than the wild forms.

Bradley's King has a comparatively large fruit and is thought to have been raised by Bradley of Halam, Nottinghamshire and first recorded in 1880. The Merryweather Damson was raised on the nurseries of Merryweathers of Southwell, Nottinghamshire, and introduced in 1907. Its origin is not known but the size of the fruit suggests it was a hybrid between a damson and a plum.

The Prune Damson is known by different names according to the area where it is grown, for example the Shropshire, the Cheshire and the Westmorland, all types selected from the wild on account of their improved size.

THE TWENTIETH CENTURY

In 1888, in a paper read at the RHS Apple and Pear Conference, W. Paul spoke of profitable plums to grow for market. His list was: Early Prolific, Early Orleans, Czar, Diamond, Belle de Septembre, Pond's Seedling, Prince Englebert, Victoria, Purple Pershore and the Farleigh damson. All of these varieties, with the exception of Early Orleans which was grown over 300 years earlier in England, had been introduced during the 50 years before the Conference, three of them by Rivers. After the long period of inactivity, the range of plum varieties grown in Britain had changed.

The present century has seen the introduction of new varieties raised by Laxton Brothers. One which was planted to some extent commercially was Early Laxton raised in 1902 and introduced in 1919. This was bred from a cross between the old early variety, Catalonia, known to Parkinson in 1629 as Amber Primordian, and Early Rivers. Early Laxton is a good-quality very early plum, but has proved susceptible to bacterial canker infection.

Other varieties introduced by Laxtons included Utility, Bountiful, Laxton's Gage, Delicious, Goldfinch, Blue Tit, Black Prince and Laxton's Cropper. Of these, Cropper, Victoria crossed with Aylesbury Prune, was introduced in 1931; Laxton's Gage, Green Gage crossed with Victoria, was introduced in 1922; and Bountiful, Victoria crossed with Red Magnum Bonum, in 1926. Other varieties had Victoria as one parent crossed with Imperial Gage (Denniston's Superb) and Green Gage. However, in spite of the wide range of good-quality varieties bred by this firm, few have maintained a position of commercial importance, though several are grown in gardens.

As with other fruits, during the early years of this century, the breeding of new varieties of plums passed from the hands of the leading nurserymen to the recently established research stations. At Long Ashton, Spinks made use of the good-quality gages and plums as one parent, as experience has shown that these are most likely to give rise to good-quality progeny. Of the four varieties he introduced, Avon Cross was raised in 1920 from Jefferson crossed with Victoria and released in 1931; and Severn Cross, raised in 1921 from Coe's Golden Drop crossed probably with Giant Prune, was introduced in the same year. Both Thames Cross and Frome Cross were bred from Coe's Golden Drop, the first crossed with Giant Prune and the second with Merryweather Damson, released in 1947 and 1948 respectively. All of these plums were of some merit but none of them has been accepted commercially.

More recent work by Wilson at Long Ashton resulted in several promising varieties of plums, extending the season of flowering and harvesting. This work is now being continued at East Malling Research Station.

At John Innes, M. B. Crane bred three varieties which have been released, Merton Blue, Merton Gage and Merton Gem. Like Spinks, Crane used good-quality gages and plums as one parent. All three were raised in 1923, Merton Blue from Late Orleans crossed with Bradley King Damson and named in 1956; Merton Gage, Pond's Seedling crossed with Transparent Gage, named in 1952; and Merton Gem, Coe's Violet crossed with Victoria, named in 1965.

MODERN ROOTSTOCKS FOR PLUMS

For many hundreds of years certain types of *Prunus* rootstocks have been preferred. These were often selected from wild seedlings of species such as *P. cerasifera*, the Myrobalan, and which come relatively true from seed as does the St Julien, a form of *P. institia*. Other rootstocks were of varieties of plums which readily formed suckers which could be used for propagating the variety itself or as a rootstock for budding or grafting, as for example Pershore and Blaisdon Red.

In 1826 the fruit collection of the Horticultural Society at Chiswick included Common Plum, Brompton, Brussels, Mignonne, Mussel, White Pear, Black Damas and St Julien rootstocks. The White Pear plum and St Julien had been used for many hundreds of years.

The sorting out and testing of plum rootstocks formed part of the work of Hatton at East Malling during the earlier years of this century. Here he selected a number of rootstocks which could be propagated vegetatively including Myrobalan. Of the latter, Myrobalan B proved suitable for the production of large trees, though rather slow to come into cropping. It is also incompatible with some plum varieties, Oullins Golden Gage, Count Althann's Gage and Marjorie's Seedling. Myrobalan B has now lost popularity in favour of the Malling selection of St Julien, St Julien A, which is compatible with all plums and peaches and makes an earlier cropping and smaller tree than Myrobalan.

Of the other rootstocks grown in 1826, forms of Common Plum, Brompton, Brussels, Mussel and Black Damas were still being used well over a hundred years later, including a Malling selection, Damas C, but most of these have given place to St Julien, which was in fact one of the earliest used rootstocks for plums. The breeding of new rootstocks at East Malling resulted in the

release of Pixy, selected from seedlings of the French St Julien d'Orleans.
Seed from this selection is considered to have some dwarfing properties and
Pixy does make a rather smaller tree than St Julien A, but there are still no
plum rootstocks in use which are the equivalent of the dwarfing apple
stocks.

PLUM GROWING TODAY

From the sixteenth and seventeenth centuries, the cultivation of plums has
been associated with certain parts of the country. Like other fruits, plums
have long been grown in Kent for supplying the fresh-fruit markets in
London with smaller quantities for processing. In the Vale of Evesham in
Worcestershire, the decline in farming following the repeal of the Corn Laws
in 1846 was followed by a marked increase in market gardening. The
cultivation of plums in Worcestershire was already important for sypplying
the markets of the Midlands and their cultivation fitted in well on the new
holdings. The use of the local Pershore plum, which was readily propagated
from suckers, was of particular value to the smallholders.

The growing of plums has also long been a feature of the smallholdings of
Cambridgeshire, and here there has been specialization in the growing of the
Cambridge Gage, a local variety propagated by suckers.

There was a considerable extension in plum growing during the second
half of the nineteenth century, with the great increase in the demand for fruit
for jam and other forms of processing. Plums were a relatively cheap fruit for
making jam and this became a staple part of the diet of those who could not
afford the more expensive strawberry and other jams. During the Great War
plum and apple jam was regularly supplied to the British troops.

Since the middle of this century, there has been a marked decline in the
acreage of plums grown commercially in Britain. With the rise in the
standard of living and the greater availability of many alternative products,
the demand for jam has fallen dramatically as it has for canned plums. On
the fresh-fruit market in Britain, plums grown here have met with competition
from the imported large Japanese varieties which are available throughout
the year from different countries of the world.

In spite of many attempts to develop the production of the better-quality
gages on a larger scale for market, their cropping has remained erratic and
their fruits are subject to splitting in showery weather and also to bruising
unless picked when very under-ripe. Also, despite the efforts of the plant
breeders, the main plum varieties grown commercially are the same as those
used a hundred years or more ago. Pershore was introduced in 1827,
Victoria in 1840, Czar in 1875, Oullins Golden Gage in 1856, Early Rivers
in 1834, Purple Pershore in 1877, and the Green Gage existed before the

fifteenth century. Commercial growers are therefore depending mainly on varieties which resulted from the enthusiasm of growers and breeders engendered in the early years of the past century.

For the garden, there are still many good-quality varieties available which far exceed in flavour the average commercial ones, varieties which were of great appeal to the more fastidious consumers of the past.

CHERRIES 18

The cherries cultivated for their fruits in Britain have been derived from two species of *Prunus*: the sweet cherries from the diploid, *P. avium*, and the acid varieties from the tetraploid, *P. cerasus*. The Duke cherries are tetraploids, considered to have arisen from crosses between the sweet and acid types. The hybrid constitution of these cherries is confirmed by the fact that they give rise to sterile seeds or to defective seedlings, lacking vigour.

Seedlings of *Prunus avium*, often referred to as 'geans' or 'mazzards', grow wild in woodlands of Britain and many other parts of Europe and may reach a height of 60 ft. Apart from being a parent, or one of the parents, of cultivated cherries, for many hundreds of years *P. avium* seedlings and suckers have been used as rootstocks on which cultivated varieties have been budded or grafted.

Prunus cerasus is a dwarf-growing acid cherry which makes a bush or small, rounded tree, lacking the vigour of *P. avium*. It is found wild in woods, thickets and hedgerows in Britain, central and southern Europe and temperate Asia, extending northwards to Scandinavia. *P. cerasus* is the parent of the acid, Morello cherries.

Another species of cherry, *P. mahaleb*, a native of Europe, has often been used as a rootstock for sweet cherries both in Europe and America, though it has not been popular in Britain. Three other species with edible fruits which are sometimes grown in gardens are *P. pseudocerasus*, the Chinese Early Cherry, *P. tomentosa*, a native of Central Asia, and *P. besseyi*, the Western Sand Cherry of North America.

CHERRIES IN ANTIQUITY

The history of cherries goes back as far if not farther than most of our other fruits. The Danes of the Mesolithic period used cherries as food, as did Swiss prehistoric lake dwellers who ate the fruits of *P. avium.*

Cherries seem to have been cultivated first in the orchards of Mesopotamia where Sargon II of Assyria in the eighth century BC liked their sweet fragrance. The Akkadian name for the cherry, 'karshu', has survived in the European languages: in Greek 'kerasos' and in German 'kirsche'.

The Greek historian, Herodotus, in the fifth century BC, mentions a cherry called 'ponticum' which was part of the staple diet of a Scythian race, north of the Black Sea, named Agippaei, who all had their own 'ponticum' trees which they protected from winter frosts by binding thick white felt around them. Herodotus says that the cherries were pulped to make a thick juice called 'aschy' which they drank, while the sediment was formed into cakes and used as food.

At this time, apples, pears, medlars and plums, as well as cherries, were grown in Greece and it was from Greece that, according to Pliny the Elder, cherries were brought to Italy:

> *Before the victory of Lucullus in the war against Mithridates, that is down to 74 BC, there were no cherry trees in Italy. Lucullus first imported them from Pontus and in 120 years they have crossed the ocean and got as far as Britain; but all the same, no attention has succeeded in getting them to grow in Egypt.*

As it is known that wild cherries existed in many parts of Europe before the dates given by Pliny, it may be presumed that he was referring to cultivated forms of the fruit and, in particular, to the variety or varieties growing in Pontus, a state on the Black Sea, part of Armenia. Lucullus had won a major victory against King Mithridates VI of Pontus, which resulted in the reorganization of the Near East, with Rome being left in possession of a coast running from Egypt to the Black Sea. It was of this region of Pontus that Herodotus, nearly 400 years earlier, had written of the 'ponticum' cherry which was so important to the local economy. One of the towns which the army of Pontus had destroyed was Cerasus, later called Keresoun, from which the cherry is believed to have derived the name of 'Cerasus'.

ROMAN VARIETIES OF CHERRIES

Pliny described the cherry varieties grown in Italy in his day:

> *Of cherries, the Apronian are the reddest, and the Lutatian the blackest, while the Caecilian kind are perfectly round. The Junian cherry has an agreeable flavour but practically only if eaten under*

the tree on which it grows, as it is so delicate that it does not stand carriage. The highest rank, however, belongs to the bigaroon (Duracina, the hard-berry) cherry, called by the Campanians, the Plinian cherry; but in Belgium and on the banks of the Rhine, the Lusitanian is held in highest regard. This cherry has a third kind of colour, a blend of black, bright red and green, which looks as if the fruit were always not quite ripe.

It is less than five years ago that what is called the laurel-cherry was introduced, which has a not disagreeable bitter flavour, and is produced by grafting a cherry on a bay tree. There are also Macedonian cherries, grown on a tree of small size and rarely exceeding four and a half feet in height, and ground cherries, with a still smaller bush.

The cherry is one of the earliest fruits to repay its yearly gratitude to the farmer. It likes a north aspect and cold conditions; moreover it can be dried in the sun and stored in casks like olives.

It is not possible, with any certainty, to identify the varieties mentioned by Pliny but, according to Gibson, the author of *The Fruit Gardener* in 1768, the Apronian was the Cluster cherry, the Lutatian probably the mazzard (*P. avium*), the Caecilian, the Kentish or Common Red, the Junian, the French guigne, and the bigaroon or Duracina, in English the firm-fleshed bigarreau heart-cherry. The ground cherries Pliny refers to were probably *Prunus fruticosa*, a native of Continental Europe which has been cultivated in England for nearly four centuries under the name of 'ground cherry'.

EVIDENCE OF CHERRIES AT ANCIENT SITES IN BRITAIN

Although the identification of the species of *Prunus* based on charcoal remains alone may be subject to some doubts, evidence of the presence of the wild, sweet cherry, *P. avium*, has been found during several excavations in Britain. The Late Iron Age site at Maiden Castle in Dorset and a Neolithic site, Nympsfield Long Barrow in Gloucestershire indicated remains of this species, while remains of what were considered stones of the sour cherry, *P. cerasus*, were also found at Nympsfield and at a Middle Bronze Age site at Haugh Head in Northumberland.

It is known that the diet of the Roman troops, stationed in countries under their control, included fruits and nuts. In peace time at Vindonissa the legionaries ate apples, pears, plums, cherries, grapes and elderberries as well as sweet chestnuts, walnuts, hazel nuts and beech nuts. At Saalburg the garrison ate plums, damsons, wild cherries, peaches, walnuts and hazel nuts, all of which could have been grown locally. In Britain, the auxillary troops manning the fort at Caerws in Wales ate cherries and blackberries, both of which were also probably wild fruits.

Cherry stones have been excavated from Roman sites at Silchester, Selsey and West Wittering and also from waterlogged Roman sites near the Thames in London. It proved difficult to identify the stones from these sites with any certainty but they most closely resembled those of modern cultivated forms of the sour cherry. Excavation of the site of a second-century building in St Thomas Street, Southwark, revealed the remains of fish and fruits, including cherries.

Since Pliny said that cherry trees had been imported to Britain as early as AD 46 and Tacitus, writing in AD 79 of Britain, said that 'The soil will produce good crops except olives, vines and other plants which usually grow in warmer climates', it is likely that cherries were planted, probably in Kent, for supplying the needs of the Roman troops and markets of the rapidly developing rebuilt London. During the Roman occupation of Britain, considerable quantities of cereals were grown here for feeding the troops and there would obviously be a good demand for any locally grown fruits.

The finding of the remains of cherries and other fruits near the second-century waterfront and wharf areas in London could suggest that some of them were brought up the Thames from Kent. In later ages, before transport by road was efficiently developed, produce from Kent was regularly sent by boat from Gravesend to the London markets. At the time of the Roman occupation of Britain fruits were transported packed in amphorae, as were some plums which it is thought had been imported to Britain from Spain.

EARLY CULTIVATION OF THE CHERRY

What may have happened to cherries or any other fruits grown on farms or in villa gardens during the unsettled times after the Romans left Britain in the early years of the fifth century is not known. Some consider that they disappeared completely and had to be reimported in later centuries, but some fruits must have persisted in a wild state.

Cherries were a popular fruit in the Middle Ages and the 'ciris beam' or cherry tree was grown in Saxon times. In the twelfth century it was one of the fruit trees praised by Necham, Abbot of Cirencester, in his poem, 'De laudibus divinae Sapientiae'.

The cherry was regularly grown in the gardens and orchards of the monasteries. At Norwich, besides the 'Pomerium', the appleyard or orchard, there was a 'cherruzerd' or 'orto cersor', the cherry garden. At Ely, besides the famous vineyard planted in the gardens of the bishop, the 1302 records of sales show that cherry trees were also grown in the vineyard area: 'Of 20d from cherries in the vineyard sold'. However, cherries were so popular that from time to time they had to be bought for supplying the convent.

Cherries were also grown in private gardens. The accounts, 1295–6, for the Holborn gardens of Henry de Lacy, Earl of Lincoln, include an item, 'Of 2s 3d for cherries of the garden sold, the tithe being deducted.' Cherries were often cultivated in the gardens on Tower Hill and adjoining areas running down to the Thames, and were commonly sold from the street stalls on the site opposite St Austin's near St Paul's churchyard which had been the subject of much dispute in 1355. Cherries were specifically mentioned in the records of this incident.

FOURTEENTH AND FIFTEENTH CENTURIES

Confirmation that cherries were popular and cultivated extensively at a time when many other fruits were still in short supply is given by references to this fruit in *Piers Plowman* by William Langland of Malvern in 1362. Writing of the poorer classes who were living chiefly on vegetables, he said that the housewives used many ripe cherries as well as peas, beans and baking apples. The season of cherry gathering, 'the cherry-time', coming at the height of the summer, was a time for merry-making. Gower in *Confessio Amantis* compares the briefness of human life with the cherry harvest:

> . . . *endureth but a throw*
> *Right as it were a cherry feast.*

Chaucer, rather in the same vein as Gower, wrote:

> *This world is but a cherry fair.*

In his *Roman de la Rose*, 1372, Chaucer included cherries with other fruits:

> *And many hoomely trees there were*
> *That peaches, coynes [quinces] and apples bere*
> *Medlers, ploumes, peres, chesteynis,*
> *Cheryse, of which many one fayne is.*

During the fourteenth century, cherries, like strawberries, were hawked through the streets of London by the market women who were referred to in 'London Lickpenny', the poem by John Lydgate (1330–1400):

> *Then unto London I dyd me hye*
> *Of all the land it beareth the pryse*
> *'Hot pescodes' one began to crye*
> *'Strabery rype' and 'cherryes in the ryse'* [on the branch or twig]

Such frequent references to cherries at this time indicate that they must have been widely grown and also picked from the wild. They are a fruit which does not travel well and with the limited transport of the Medieval period would have to have been picked within a few miles of the market.

THE SIXTEENTH CENTURY

Tusser included red and black cherries in his list of garden fruits and, during the sixteenth century, the fruit became of increasing importance in Kent where it flourished, along with apples, pears and plums, as in no other part of the country and impressed both William Lambard in 1576 and William Camden in 1586. A particularly successful cherry orchard was one planted at Sittingbourne for the Earl of Leicester, extending to 30 acres, and which Hartlib later said had produced a thousand pound's worth of cherries in one season. Though he doubted whether anyone would believe this, even in 1652 £10–15 an acre had been given for the crop on other farms.

The variety at Sittingbourne was one of the first to be planted with the Flemish cherry which, over a century later, impressed Celia Fiennes when she saw it growing in the Gravesend area. From there, she said, the cherries were taken up the Thames to supply the London markets.

The Flemish cherries were probably the variety known for many centuries, up to the present day, as Flemish or Flemish Red. This is a rather small red, acid cherry ready at the end of July. Kentish Red is very similar but has rather larger fruits, ripe earlier in the month. Both varieties are derivatives of the acid *Prunus cerasus* and are classified as 'Amarelles' to distinguish them from the 'Morello' types. The latter have coloured juice while that of the Amarelles is colourless. On the other hand, the variety may have been one of the other cherries imported from Flanders by Harris in 1533 and so given the general name of 'Flemish' fruit.

The first description of the cherry varieties being grown in England was in Gerard's *Herball*, which included illustrations of most of the types described. The picture of the Flanders cherry shows that it was a 'heart' type of fruit, distinct from the round English varieties and was probably a forerunner of a number of heart cherries which became popular in later centuries.

The Spanish cherry, later named the Spanish Amber, was the Bigarreau, an early form of what became some of the most important and valuable kinds of sweet cherries with their large size and firm flesh. This type was known to Pliny as the Duracina, the hard-berried or bigaroon.

The Gascoine, later named Gascoigne's Heart, synonymous with Bleeding Heart and Herefordshire Heart, was cultivated on a limited scale until this century. The Bird cherry or Black cherry, a form of *P. avium*, grew wild in

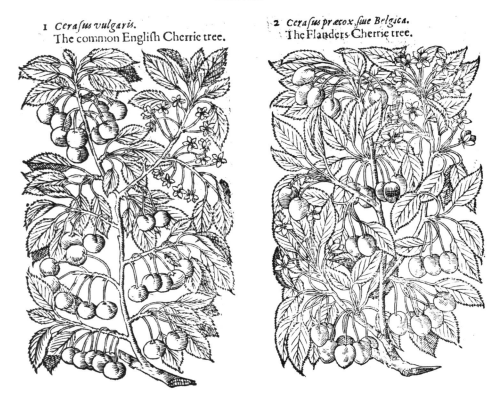

Sixteenth-century cherries: the Common English, often growing wild, and the Flanders, introduced for Henry VIII.

the woods of Kent according to Gerard, and was used as a rootstock for better-quality cherries, in particular Flanders. A later edition of Gerard included several more cherries which had been imported from Italy. Luke Ward's, held in high esteem for over 300 years, but a poor cropper, and Naples, both came from Italy.

SEVENTEENTH-CENTURY CHERRY CULTIVATION

Parkinson listed 30 varieties of cherries. One of these, John Tradescant, thought to have been imported in 1611 by Tradescant, was later known as Tradescant's Heart and was identical to Noble, grown until recent years for its high quality. Parkinson, like others after him, complained bitterly of the difficulty of obtaining varieties true to name, as for example John Tradescant, sometimes sold wrongly as Archduke which was of great antiquity and which Bunyard thought might even be the Lusitanian of Pliny. In the

3 *Cerasia Hispanica.*
The Spanish Cherrie tree.

4 *Cerasis Gasconica.*
The Gascoine Cherrie tree.

5 *Cerasus Serotina.*
Late ripe Cherrie tree.

6 *Cerasus vno pediculo plura.*
The Cluster Cherrie tree.

Cherry varieties: the Spanish was known in ancient Rome; the Gascoine was grown on a limited scale until this century.

seventeenth century many trees and other horticultural products were still imported from the Continent, as they had been in Queen Elizabeth's time when even garden tools were brought over from Holland.

One of the most reliable nurserymen in the mid-seventeenth century was Ralph Austen who wrote that the Flanders variety was the most planted cherry and sometimes it was as early as the May-cherry, but the latter was tender and needed some shelter, whereas the Flanders would do well in open fields or orchards. The Black-heart cherry was a very good, heavy-bearing variety which was useful for pressing for wine, either to drink by itself or to add to the unfermented juice of cider to give it the colour of claret. A small quantity of the juice would colour a gallon of cider or white wine. Another variety, Miller's Great Bearing, was also very good for colouring cider, perry, white wine or similar drinks.

John Rea, in 1665, recommended 16 varieties. He was the first to include Carnation, a good-quality but light-cropping variety which still exists in some Kent orchards today. He was also the first to mention the Duke, later called May Duke, an early representative of the 'Duke' cherries, hybrids between the sweet, *P. avium*, and the acid, *P. cerasus*. Several Dukes were known in the seventeenth century and probably had their origin in England since in France they were known at this time as 'Anglais'. This means that they represent the few varieties raised in Britain as most cherries grown in Britain in the sixteenth and seventeenth centuries had been imported from the Continent.

PROPAGATION OF CHERRIES

Gerard and Austen considered the black cherry, a type of *P. avium* or mazzard, as the best rootstock for large trees but the acid, red cherry, *P. cerasus*, was often thought to be best for the May-cherries. Until the twentieth century the mazzards or geans, seedlings from the woods in Kent, were the most popular rootstocks for sweet cherries, but these have been replaced by selected, vegetatively propagated *P. avium* stocks introduced by East Malling. One of these, known as F 12/1, was the principal one used for large trees of sweet cherries, though recently the demand has been for smaller trees and less vigorous rootstocks and so other species and hybrids have been used.

The demand for smaller or dwarf cherry trees also existed in the early eighteenth century when Bradley wrote, in 1726, that to produce such trees the scion variety should not be grafted direct onto the black cherry but on the latter already grafted with another cherry, chiefly the Morello, this acting as an intermediate and checking the vigour of the black cherry stock. Bradley's suggestion of using an intermediate had already been advised in the previous century to reduce the vigour of seedling apple rootstocks by inserting a bud of a Paradise dwarfing stock between the seedling and the scion. The use of intermediates in this way has become popular during recent years for apples and has also been tested for sweet cherries.

There was a special need to curb the vigour of cherries in Bradley's time because, although sweet cherries were grown as large standards in farm orchards, in gardens attached to the mansions of the more wealthy all kinds of fruit trees were trained on walls. Other trees were planted alongside the paths and walks dividing up the garden beds and often trained as espaliers. Switzer in 1724 said that garden walls, especially those facing north, were most useful for the Morello or, as he called it, 'the Morella or Milan' cherry — just as they are today. Although known to both Gerard and Parkinson, the Morello gained in popularity in Switzer's time. He held it in great esteem as the richest cherry both for eating raw with sugar or for conserving.

The enthusiasm for cherry growing in England was not shared by Gibson from Scotland, who in 1768 emphasized the problems of frost, damage by birds and the perishable nature of the ripening fruits. To control attacks by birds he said that nets could be spread over the trees but, though effective, the cost and trouble of doing this was great. During the present century, the use of nets to protect cherries has been used in some countries, including New Zealand, and more recently in England for covering the smaller trees grown on less vigorous rootstocks.

EIGHTEENTH-CENTURY VARIETIES

The lists of varieties recommended by writers in the eighteenth century show that these had settled down to ones found most reliable. Those suggested by Thomas Hitt in 1757 were typical. These were 'Small May, May Duke, Kentish, Flemish, Morello, Black and White Heart, Black Carroon, Lukeward, Amber, Carnation and Gascoin'. Other writers added the Cluster cherry.

The Caroon or Carone name was given to a black cherry which came fairly true from seed and so was applied to several varieties of the same type. These were widely grown in Hertfordshire and Norfolk and known, before 1725, as Kerroon. Another variety introduced in the eighteenth century was Black Tartarian, a good-quality, very large, black cherry. It came to this country from Russia where it had apparently been introduced by Prince Potemkin, the chevalier of Catherine the Great, from Pontus after the conquest of the Crimea in 1783. According to Forsyth in 1824, Tartarian had been brought over from Russia in the autumn of 1796 by John Fraser of Sloane Square, Chelsea, well known for his industry in collecting plants in North America and the West Indies. He said that these cherries were natives of the Crimea and he purchased them from a German who cultivated them in

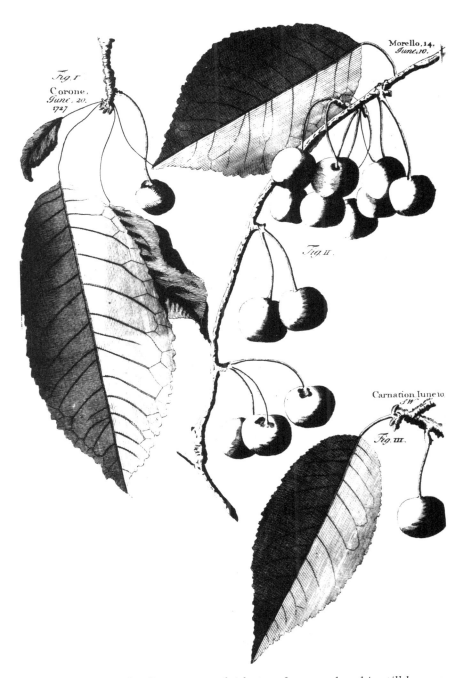

Cherry varieties: the Corone came fairly true from seed and is still known in English orchards; the Morello has long been popular for preserving and cherry brandy; the Carnation has also been popular since the seventeenth century.

his garden near St Petersburg. Later he saw them in the Imperial gardens where they were forced in pots.

Another nurseryman at Brentford, Ronalds, also introduced new cherries from the Circassian region, at the eastern end of the Black Sea, still important for cherries as it had been in the time of the ancient Greeks. Two varieties introduced by Ronalds were a form of Morello from Circassia, Late Duke and Ronalds' Heart.

THE NINETEENTH CENTURY

At the beginning of the nineteenth century, Thomas Andrew Knight was engaged in his valuable work on the breeding of new varieties of a number of different fruits by using controlled hybridization. He was particularly successful with cherries, and several of his new varieties were introduced in the early years of the nineteenth century and are still of importance today. The most important of his varieties were Knight's Early Black, raised about 1810 from Bigarreau crossed with May Duke, Elton Heart, raised in 1806, from the Graffion pollinated by White Heart, and Waterloo, one of the best quality though, erratic cropping, black cherries, raised from Ambree crossed with May Duke and introduced in 1815. Downton was bred from seed of Waterloo or Elton and first exhibited in 1815. Black Eagle was raised about 1806, not by Knight himself but by his daughter, Elizabeth, from Bigarreau crossed with May Duke, the same parentage as Knight's Early Black.

By 1827, when the Horticultural Society published its lists of the different fruits in its collection at Chiswick, these included 246 cherries. Many of these were synonyms and of that number, relatively few were being grown commercially or in gardens.

Apart from Knight's varieties, several others of importance were introduced during the past century. Bigarreau Napoleon is of unknown origin but was first recorded in Germany under the name of Bigarreau Lauermann and introduced into England in 1832. It was given the name Napoleon at a later date, though it is doubtful if the variety grown today as Napoleon is in fact the original. There has been some confusion with the variety Wellington and it has been suggested that the name Wellington was substituted for that of Napoleon due to the unpopularity of the French hero!

A variety which became important, both for the commercial grower and the gardener, was Frogmore Early, introduced about 1864. Though not a cherry of the highest quality, it proved valuable as a regular and heavy bearer, popular on the London markets. It was raised by Thomas Ingram who was head gardener to Queen Victoria at Frogmore. Ingram was an outstanding horticulturist and was one of the first to grow and recommend the apple Cox's Orange Pippin. Frogmore Early is still grown in Kent orchards.

The famous nurseryman, Thomas Rivers of Sawbridgeworth, raised Early Rivers from seed of Early Purple Guigne. This first fruited in 1869 and was introduced in 1872. This black cherry rapidly became the best-quality early variety in commercial use, though its early flowering, with liability to poor pollination, makes for erratic cropping. A variety often used as a pollinator for Rivers is Noir de Guben, raised by Herr Groth of Guben in Germany.

During the nineteenth century, the production of cherries in the United States was developed on a considerable scale and many new varieties were introduced there. Several of these were brought over to England and became of commercial importance. Governor Wood was raised by Prof. Kirtland of Cleveland in 1842 and named after Reuben Wood, Governor of Ohio. It proved to be a heavy and regular bearer in England and, like Frogmore, provided much of the bulk of the second early white cherries for the London and other markets. Another variety raised by Prof. Kirtland was Ohio Beauty, introduced in 1847. Windsor is a dark-coloured late variety raised on the farm of James Dougall of Windsor, Ontario and introduced in 1881.

CHANGES IN CHERRY ORCHARDS

As evidence over the past 600 years has shown, cherries have always been an important crop for market, whether by local sales from monasteries or private gardens or, on a larger scale, from the commercial orchards of Kent. Throughout history, Kent has been the leading county for cherry production and it was doubtless here that the cherries imported during the early years of the Roman occupation were planted, as were those brought from Flanders by Harris for Henry VIII.

There is evidence from the fourteenth century, at a time when the transport of produce over any distance was very difficult, that the distribution of cherry cultivation was more widespread than it is today but, at the same time, large quantities of cherries and other fruits were imported from the Continent, especially from Flanders. As the varieties have grown and their production improved, reliance on imports was reduced and, by 1794, the report made to the Board of Agriculture by Boys said that the cultivation of cherries in the neighbourhood of Maidstone in Kent was very profitable because of their easy transport by water from the Medway and up the Thames to the London markets, as it had been in the time of Celia Fiennes. Apart from cherries sent to London, others were sold direct to the 'higlers' who retailed them in the coastal towns. The young cherry orchards were mostly interplanted with hops and filberts until the trees required all the room and the orchards were grassed down. The varieties at the end of the eighteenth century were mainly Black Heart, White Heart, Flemish or Early Kentish, Caroon, Hertfordshire Black, together with wild black and red types.

A hundred years later, at the end of the nineteenth century, sweet cherries grown as tall standards to allow sheep or cattle to graze underneath, were grown to perfection in Kent and the other important cherry orchards in Buckinghamshire, Worcestershire and, to a lesser extent, in Cambridgeshire. In Kent, plantations of Kentish Red or Morello cherries, grown on pyramid-trained trees, supplied the London markets, while there was an important outlet of a local Morello for making into cherry brandy. In East Sussex a specialized production involved cutting the trusses of the Morello cherries from the branches with scissors and sending the cherries to London with their stalks attached, so as to minimize damage. The tradition in Kent of grazing the cherry orchards with sheep was continued into the twentieth century. Sheep from the Romney Marsh were moved up to the orchards of east Kent in the autumn and moved back again as the cherries developed.

More Recent Varieties

During the 1920s and 30s, breeding of cherries was begun at the John Innes Horticultural Institute, using as parents some of the best commercial sweet varieties. After a long trial in Kent, the new varieties were introduced in 1947. These included Merton Bigarreaù, raised in 1924 from Knight's Early Black crossed with Bigarreau Napoleon, and Merton Glory, Ursula Rivers crossed with Noble. Unfortunately, Merton Bigarreau, although a black variety of excellent quality, proved susceptible to bacterial canker, but Merton Glory, a very large, early, heavy-cropping white variety, has proved very popular. The spreading habit of Merton Glory is conducive to early fruiting, whereas another variety, Merton Heart, has a very upright habit which delays cropping and so this variety has been little planted.

The breeding of these cherries was the beginning of work which spanned the next 50 years. A number of new varieties having Merton Glory as one parent, to induce early cropping, together with resistance to bacterial canker, have been introduced. Three having high resistance to this disease are Mermat, Merpet and Merchant. The moist British climate makes the disease especially rife in English cherry orchards, much more so than in those growing in the drier areas of France and Italy.

When planning new cherry orchards and planting cherries in gardens, special attention has always been paid to ensuring adequate pollination, complicated by the fact that most sweet cherries are self-incompatible and fail to set a crop with their own pollen. Moreover, sweet cherries fall into groups of varieties within which the different varieties are cross-incompatible, and so must be pollinated by those from another group which both flower at the same time and are compatible with each other. A few varieties are cross-compatible with all other varieties. In recent breeding, attention has been given to raising self-compatible cherries, not requiring cross-fertilization. The first successful variety of this type was Stella, raised at Summerland, British Columbia, from a cross between the American variety Lambert and a John Innes self-fertile selection.

Another variety from Summerland, which has been planted both in America and in England, is Van. This was raised as an open-pollinated seedling of Empress Eugenie. The latter appeared as a chance seedling near Paris in 1845 and was considered a Duke type, that is, a cross between *P. avium* and *P. cerasus*. That a variety with such parentage can give rise to a new seedling with such large, firm, attractive fruits is especially interesting.

CHERRY CULTIVATION TODAY

After the 1950s, the high costs of growing and picking cherries from tall standard trees, plus the ravages of bacterial canker, virus diseases and attacks by birds, led to a dramatic fall in the acreage of cherries grown in Britain so that it is now only a fraction of what it was in the earlier years of the century. In an attempt to obtain earlier cropping and to reduce the costs of picking and general management, workers at East Malling have sought to breed new rootstocks which will give a smaller tree than the F 12/1 commonly used in England or the *P. mahaleb* used in several other countries. The stocks which have shown most promise have been hybrids between *P. avium* and *P. pseudocerasus*. One of these, named Colt, gives a somewhat less vigorous tree than *P. avium* and comes into crop more quickly, but this rootstock is still not really dwarfing. Other hybrid rootstocks as well as 'genetic dwarfs', naturally occurring dwarfing forms of *P. avium*, have been tested and others will be introduced in the future.

The smaller trees, earlier cropping and easier to pick and of better-quality disease resistant varieties, possibly self-fertile, should make the cultivation of cherries more profitable and also possible in smaller gardens, while netting can be used to combat bird attacks. Sadly, the cherry orchards of England today no longer occupy the place they did even 50 years ago, and imports of cherries from Europe invade the markets of Britain as they did in the fifteenth and sixteenth centuries before the Flanders fruit was replaced by that from the orchards of Kent encouraged by the lead taken by Henry VIII.

PEACHES AND NECTARINES 19

Cultivated peaches and nectarines have all originated from one species, *Prunus persica*. Although the name suggests that this had its origin in Persia, as was mistakenly thought by the Greeks and Romans, it was in fact a native of China. Here the peach is found growing wild in various parts of north China and Middle Manchuria and is also found in northern Korea. It is recorded that peaches were being cultivated in China some 2000 years or more before the Christian era.

Many different characteristics are shown by the wild peaches in China, including cling and free stone types, red or white skin, yellow or white flesh and fruits which are round, beaked or flat. The flat peaches from Shantung are much esteemed in China and forms have been distributed to other countries, including Britain. Evidence from the native peaches in China has demonstrated that all the characteristics seen in modern cultivated varieties can be found there. Smooth-skinned peaches, nectarines, are not common in eastern China but in Chinese and Russian Turkestan they are some of the most common forms.

In China the peach is the symbol of long life and immortality and peach blossom is the emblem of a bride. The peach is considered a potent force against demons, and branches or blossoms of the tree placed in front of the doorway of a house are thought to keep demons out. At the time of the Chinese New Year, many thousands of dwarf peach trees, in full blossom and growing in pots, are sold in Hong Kong. The nurseries supplying these trees are expert in growing the trees so that they are blooming at the time of the New Year although the date varies from one year to another.

DISTRIBUTION OF PEACHES

From China the peach was probably taken to Bokhar and Kashmir, along the ancient silk route, over the mountains of central Asia and so to Persia. The peach is readily raised from seed and so the distribution of the fruits and stones by travellers could have soon led to the establishment of the trees in new areas. Throughout Asia peach trees are still frequently raised from seed, without budding, just as they were for several centuries in North America after the introduction of the fruit to Mexico by the Spaniards.

In the Middle East peaches flourished in the Persian area of the Fertile Crescent and spread from there to other countries. They soon became naturalized in their new environment and were regarded as a native species. When peaches were first cultivated in Persia and adjoining areas is not known but, although there is no reference to the peach in the Bible, in Egypt it featured in offerings to the God of Tranquillity in about 1400 BC. The peach was also cultivated by the Assyrians and Babylonians.

Unlike many other fruits, *Prunus persica* is not one which occurs extensively in the forests of the Caucasus and Turkestan, but naturally occurring hybrids between the peach and the almond, *Prunus amygdalus*, have often been found in Armenia. Peaches grow widely in Mongolia, the north of India, in Russian Turkestan, northern Persia, Transcaucasia and other parts of Asia Minor.

The nectarine is a smooth-skinned form of the peach which normally has a downy skin. Smooth skin is a recessive character, as is yellow flesh colour and toughness of the flesh. When peaches are crossed with nectarines, the progeny are downy-skinned peaches and the smooth forms only reappear after further selfing of the first generation seedlings.

Following an experiment in which he fertilized an almond flower with peach pollen, Thomas Andrew Knight considered that the peach was a modified form of the almond, *Prunus amygdalus*, and he thought that continuous selection of almond seedlings would eventually result in peach type of fruits. Charles Darwin supported him in this view and Lindley, in 1856, wrote that the almond and peach bore the same relationship as the crab and the cultivated apple, while Thomas Rivers thought that peaches would degenerate into thick-fleshed almonds. These views have been refuted by modern plant breeders and, in any case, the almond was not known in China until shortly before the Christian era, some 2000 years after peaches had been first cultivated.

PEACHES IN ANTIQUITY

Since Theophrastus was the first writer to mention peaches, which he referred to as a Persian fruit, it is probable that the fruit was first brought to Greece by Alexander the Great from Persia. The Greek, Dioscorides, about 64 BC, referred to the medicinal uses of the peach.

Virgil in his *Georgics*, was the first Roman writer to refer to this fruit:

> *Myself will search our planted grounds at home*
> *For downy peaches and the glossy plum.*

Columella and Pliny, in the first century BC, also wrote of peaches. Columella said:

> *Peaches in Persia grow*
> *Bearing that country's name, with tiny fruit*
> *Are quick to ripen; huge ones by Gaul supplied*
> *Mature in season due; those Asia yields*
> *Are slow to grow and wait till winter's cold.*

The earliest ripening peaches, as Columella said, often had very small fruits. For many hundreds of years a very small-fruited variety, Nutmeg, was grown in England simply on account of its earliness. This was probably a descendant of the type known to the Romans. Columella's reference to peaches from Gaul suggests that this fruit may have reached France as soon as it spread to Italy.

At this time there was some confusion about the nature of the peach. Pliny, repeating the current view that peaches had originated in Persia, wrote:

> *The Persian peach is shown by its name to be an exotic even in Asia Minor and Greece and to have been introduced from Persia. The peach tree was only introduced lately and that with difficulty, inasmuch as at Rhodes, which was its first place of sojourn after leaving Egypt, it does not bear at all. It is not true that the peach grown in Persia is poisonous and causes torturing pain, and that, when it had been transplanted into Egypt by the kings to use as a punishment, the nature of the soil caused it to lose its dangerous properties; for the more careful writers relate this of the Persea. The Persea is the modern Mumusops Schimperi which is an entirely different tree, ressembling the Red Myxa and which has refused to grow anywhere but in the east. The Sebesten, the Myxa, also*

according to the more learned authorities, was not introduced from
Persia for punitive purposes but was planted at Memphis by Perseus.

This seems to be the explanation why the peach was considered to be
poisonous by some ancient Greeks and Romans, the result of confusion
between the names, Persea, Perseus and Persica.

Pliny also wrote of a number of varieties of peaches:

> *The palm among peaches belongs to the duracinus [the nectarine];*
> *the Gallic and the Asiatic varieties are named after their nationalities.*
> *The Asiatic peach ripens in summer; these were discovered within*
> *the last thirty years, and were at first sold for a denarius apiece. The*
> *Adriatic peach comes from Samnium, but the common peach grows*
> *everywhere.*
>
> *It is a harmless fruit in demand for invalids and peaches have*
> *before now fetched thirty sesterces each, a price exceeded by no*
> *other fruit, which may surprise us because there is none which*
> *keeps worse; the longest time that it will last after being plucked, is*
> *two days, and it compels you to put it on the market.*
>
> *Peaches are more wholesome than plums; and the same is the*
> *case with the juice of the fruit, extracted and taken in either wine or*
> *vinegar. Indeed what known fruit is there that is more wholesome*
> *for an ailment than this. There is none, in fact, that has a less*
> *powerful smell or a greater abundance of juice, though it has a*
> *tendency to create thirst. The leaves of it, beaten up and applied*
> *topically, arrest haemorrhage; the kernels, mixed with oil and*
> *vinegar, are used as a liniment for headache.*

The fact that the peach was distributed from its country of origin, China,
and reached Europe relatively late, has meant that no remains of peach
stones have been found in excavations of prehistoric sites in Britain or other
parts of Europe. The first discoveries of peach stones were associated with
the Roman occupation. In peace-time Vindonissa, the Roman legionaries ate
peaches in addition to other fruits, as did the garrison at Saalburg.

In England, peach stones were found during excavations of the waterlogged
site at New Fresh Wharf, just south of Upper Thames Street, west of the old
Billingsgate fish market, exposing a second-century waterfront. The peach
had not been found on Roman sites in Britain before this discovery and,
although it is possible that the peaches had been grown here, it is more likely
that they had been imported with other fruits.

EARLY RECORDS OF PEACH CULTIVATION

Apart from the finding of the peach stones at New Fresh Wharf, no other sites in Britain have yielded evidence that the peach was grown during the Roman occupation. In France there was a reference to the peach by Bishop Fortunat of Portiers in AD 530 and by the Abbot of the monastery of Saint-Denis, near Paris, in 784. The peach was also included in Charlemagne's *Capitulare de Villis* of 800.

One of the first references to peaches in England appears in the *Chronicle of Wendover* which records that King John, in the midst of his despair and disappointment, hastened his end by a surfeit of peaches and ale which resulted in a severe attack of dysentry. He died at Newark in Lincolnshire in October 1216. The account says that the peaches were green — not surprising for fruits grown outside without any protection as they would have been at this time, although the climate then was somewhat milder than today.

In 1275 the gardener to Edward I supplied various fruit trees for planting in the gardens of the Tower of London, including two peach trees which together cost 1s, compared with cherry trees which cost only 1s 6d for 100.

The Benedictine monk, John Lydgate (1330—1400), famous for his poem 'London Lickpenny' of the cries of London, said that peaches were among 'the fruits that common be'. Support for this suggestion in the fourteenth century is given in Chaucer's *Roman de la Rose*, in 1372, when he wrote:

> *And many homley trees there were*
> *That peaches, coynes [quinces] and apples bere.*

At this time surplus fruits and vegetables were sold from the large London gardens of the wealthy, and it is likely that peaches were grown on the walls surrounding these gardens and may have been grown in gardens in other parts of the country. In any case, these references prove that peaches were grown in Britain at an earlier date than the sixteenth century as frequently quoted.

The first mention of peaches in the early printed herbals was by Peter Treueris in 1526 in his *Grete Herball*:

> *Peches is a fruyte colde and moyste in y thyre degre, The Leues of the tre is lyke to leues of an almonde tre / but they be somewhat longer. This fruyte is pryncypally good yf they be eate fastynge. Oyle made of kyrnelles of peches is good agaynst payne of the eares.*

Turner in his 1568 *Herball* said:

> *The peches is no great tre in England that I could se / it hath long leues. The peche tre floureth with the / almond tre / but y floure is reder then the almond flour is. The apples [fruits] are soft and fleshy when they are rype somthyng ho without.*

IMPORTATION OF NEW VARIETIES

Although it is probable that the first peaches to be cultivated in Britain were brought to this country at least as early as the thirteenth century, improved varieties of peaches, as of other fruits, were imported during the reign of Henry VIII in the sixteenth century. Reference to this is made in Harrison's account of Britain included in the *Holinshed Chronicles* in 1586, when he wrote that although many fruits and vegetables had been plentiful during the reign of Edward I (1272–1307) — as had been shown by Lydgate and Chaucer — these had been neglected and had virtually disappeared during the succeeding centuries but had been brought back to Britain from France and the Lowlands during the first half of the sixteenth century. Harrison pointed out that many fruits, including the strange apricots, almonds, peaches and figs, had been introduced into the gardens of noblemen during the past forty years. Harrison, who was Dean of Windsor, was born in 1534 and died in 1593. He had himself lived through this period of change and reported his own observations.

The first reference to different varieties of peaches was in Tusser's list of 1580 when he spoke of red and white types. Gerard, in 1597, described four types, the white, the red, the 'd'aunt' (or avant) and the yellow peach. The white peach had white flesh, the red peach a red skin and red flesh, the 'd'aunt' had larger fruits than the others and a russet skin, coloured red on the sunny side and had a pleasant-flavoured, golden yellow flesh. The yellow peach had yellow skin and yellow flesh and a better flavour than any of the others. Its stone was serrated and rough. Gerard added that there were many other good-flavoured types not recorded by writers in the past.

A later edition of Gerard's *Herball*, revised by Thomas Johnson in 1633, gave more details of different varieties:

> *There are divers sorts of Peaches besides the foure set forth by our Author. The names of the choice ones to be had from my friend Mr. Miller in Oldstreet, are these; two sorts of Nutmeg peaches; the Queens Peach; the Newington Peach; the Grand Carnation Peach; the Carnation Peach; the Blacke Peach; the Melocotone; the White; the Romane; the Alberza; the Island Peach; the Peach of Troy. These are all good ones. He hath also of that kinde of Peach which we call Nucipersica or Nectorins, these following kinds; the Roman Red, the best of fruits; the bastard Red; the little Dainty Greene; the Yellow; the White; the Russet, which is not so good as the rest. Those that would see fuller discourse of these may have resource to the late works of Mr. John Parkinson, where they may finde more varieties.*

Parkinson, in 1629, had described 21 varieties of peaches which included both those listed by Gerard and later by Johnson and four others, the Durasme or Spanish, the Almond, the Man and the Cherry peaches. He added that there were many others 'whereunto wee can give no especial name; and therefore I passe them over in silence'. This was the period when many new varieties of all kinds of fruits were being brought over from the Continent, both by nurserymen and by individuals, in particular by John Tradescant who searched the gardens and nurseries of other countries for their best plants. In addition, peaches are readily raised from seed and are more likely to produce worthwhile progeny in this way than the majority of other fruits and so numerous new varieties came into existence.

The famous nurseryman, Austen, in 1657 favoured the Nutmeg and Newington peaches, the small size of the former being compensated for by its heavy crop and good flavour. He also recommended the Red Roman nectarine. Sir Thomas Hanmer, in his unpublished book in 1659 listed the Red and White Nutmeg, good but small, the Newington, Admirable, Primordian, Bellowes, Savoy, Pau, Persian, Ramboulion, Modena, Orleans, Superintendent, Smyna, La Varre, Sion, Lawrente and Magdalen. Of the nectarines he advised Red Roman, Murrey, Greene Nectoran and Elruge or Gurles. He said that peach and nectarine trees could be bought from George Rickett's nursery at Hogsden (Hoxton) in London; the peaches were 2s each and the nectarines 3s. Leonard Meager in 1688 suggested trees should be bought from Captain Gurle of the Great Nursery between 'Spittle fields and White Chappel', who had a collection of 39 peach and 12 nectarine varieties. The name of the Elruge nectarine which had been raised by Gurle was an anagram of his own name.

John Rea in 1676 listed 35 varieties of peaches of which he said the best were White Nutmeg, Orleance, Modena, Savoy, Morell, Violet Musk, Bordeaux, Billice, Isabelle and Royal Peach. He also gave 11 varieties of nectarines, the best being Red Roman, Murry and Tawny Red.

These seventeenth-century accounts show that by then the many different varieties of peaches and nectarines were, by experience, being sorted out and a limited number recommended. The Nutmeg, still considered the best early variety, was synonymous with the 'avant' of Gerard, a French variety. The names of most of the others indicate a French origin though the Melocotone had obviously come from Spain.

All writers at this time advised planting peaches and nectarines against south- or east-facing walls. Rea said both must be planted on the 'hottest' walls, and Worlidge in 1697 said that these fruits should either be grown on walls or in glasshouses.

1 *Malus Armeniaca ſiue Præcocia.* The Apricocke.   2 *Malus Perſica Melocotonea.* The Melocotone Peach.   3 *Perſica Moſchatellina.* The Nutmeg Peach.   4 *Perſica nigra.* The blacke Peach.   5 *Perſica Carnea longa.* The long Carnation Peach. 6 *Perſica Reginea.* The Queenes Peach.   7 *Amygdalus.* The Almond.   8 *Perſica du Troas.* The Peach du Troas.   9 *Nuciperſica rubra optima.* The beſt Romane red Nectorin.   10 *Nuciperſica rubra altera.* The baſtard red Nectorin with a pincking bloſſome.

An increasing number of peach varieties were introduced in the seventeenth and eighteenth centuries.

THE EIGHTEENTH CENTURY

The remark of Switzer in 1724, that it was a matter of some observation that peaches and nectarines were then so much in esteem, shows how interest in these fruits was still increasing. He recommended planting White Nutmeg, as the first to ripen, Red Nutmeg, Passe Violet, Ann, Royal George, Yellow Alberg, Mignon, Bourdin, White Magdalen, Mintaubon, Violet Hative nectarine, Chevereuse, Nobless, Newington, Elrouge nectarine, Rumbullion, Admirable and Bellegarde. Of these, Royal George, Admirable, Mignonne, Noblesse peaches and Violette Hative and Roman nectarines are still grown today. The Bellegarde peach, the Galande of France, and the Elruge nectarine, are still recommended for their fine flavour.

Flavour was of great importance to the grower in the seventeenth and eighteenth centuries. Switzer listed the points of a good peach, saying that the flesh should be firm but not hard so that it would not dissolve in the mouth, very fine grained and not tough or watery. The juice should be high in sugar and of a rich and vinous taste. The stone should not be too large nor the coat too downy or hairy. He did not consider the disputes as to the relative advantages of the cling (the Pavies) and the free-stone peaches justified, since the little extra trouble in getting the flesh off the stone of a variety like Newington, was more than repaid by the excellent quality of the latter compared with many of the free-stone French peaches. These standards enumerated by Switzer over 250 years ago could well be used by plant breeders today. An indication of the extensive planting of peaches in gardens is given in Switzer's advice that in small gardens no more than 20 peach and nectarine trees should be grown on the walls.

In 1777, Richard Weston included 35 varieties of peaches and 11 nectarines in his list of fruits then grown and available in Britain, while Luker and Smith's nursery catalogue of 1783, included 29 peaches. Hooker, in 1818, in his *Pomona Londoniensis*, recording the most esteemed varieties of fruits in British gardens, gave Galande (syn. Bellegarde), Royal George, Bourdene, Early Purple and Noblesse peaches. The Horticultural Society's list of fruits in their collection at Chiswick in 1826, had 224 peaches and 72 nectarines. By 1831, the sorting out of synonyms had reduced the number of peaches to 183 varieties. Of these, 60 varieties were then grown in England including Royal George, Hemskirk, Bellegarde and Barrington.

PEACH BREEDING IN THE NINETEENTH CENTURY

During the nineteenth century, the breeding of peaches received the attention

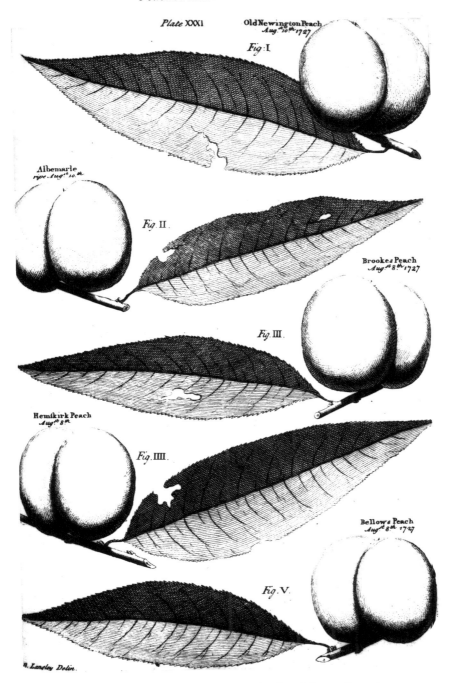

Some of the peach varieties grown in the eighteenth century.

of Thomas Andrew Knight and also those great nurserymen, Thomas Rivers and Laxton. Several of Knight's varieties were named. Spring Grove and Acton Scot, bred from Noblesse and Red Nutmeg, were introduced in 1814. The Downton nectarine, Elruge crossed with Violette Hative, was introduced in 1820. None of these proved very successful but Knight was hopeful that peaches might be bred which would be sufficiently hardy to be grown as standards out of doors.

Thomas Rivers, who was so successful in breeding many other new fruits, raised a large number of new peaches and nectarines, several of which soon established themselves as some of the most important varieties for use both outside on walls and under glass; they have maintained their position to the present day. Their number has been augmented by other varieties introduced by Rivers' successors.

One of the first nectarines bred by Rivers was Early Silver bred from the White nectarine in 1859, and this in turn gave rise to the better known Early Rivers in 1893. Lord Napier was bred from Early Albert peach which was raised in 1860, Pine Apple from Pitmaston Orange nectarine before 1870 and this in turn gave rise to Humboldt in the 1870s.

Of Rivers' peaches, Sea Eagle, bred from Early Silver nectarine, was introduced in 1881, but the outstanding peaches were introduced by Messrs Rivers in the early years of this century; Duke of York, bred from Early Rivers nectarine and Alexander peach in 1902 and Peregrine, a seedling from Spenser nectarine in 1906. Peregrine has long maintained its position as one of the best-quality peaches for use both under glass and on walls outside.

Messrs Veitch, nurserymen of Exeter, introduced a peach named Dymond after the gardener who raised it and Messrs Laxtons introduced Advance, bred from Early Rivers nectarine crossed with Hales Early in about 1910.

COMMERCIAL PEACH PRODUCTION

For many years peaches were grown by the rich, trained on the walls of their gardens and in their greenhouses, for their own use and any surplus fruit was often sold in the local market. In the seventeenth and eighteenth centuries peaches and other fruits were produced in the nurseries around London especially for sale in Covent Garden and other markets. In 1721, Bradley noted that the first Nutmeg peaches had arrived in Covent Garden on 20 July, and peaches continued to be sent to market until the beginning of November and were still 'in great perfection'.

To give added protection to peaches grown on walls outside, projecting glass copings were fastened to permanent brackets fixed to the tops of the walls. Canvas roller blinds fixed to the brackets could be let down at night to protect the blossoms from frost. After risk of frost had passed, the glass copings and blinds were removed.

In the nineteenth century the commercial production of peaches and nectarines in glasshouses reached major proportions, especially in the Worthing area of Sussex. These forced fruits received great care and attention and were carefully laid separately in lined baskets for sending to market. By the end of the century, the peach varieties recommended for this type of production were Amsden June, Duchess of York, Alexander, Condor, Mignonne, Princess of Wales, Prince of Wales, Exquisite, Barrington, Sea Eagle and Gladstone. The nectarines advised were Cardinal, Early Rivers, Rivers' Early Orange, Lord Napier, Pine Apple, Spenser and Victoria. Of the old varieties, Bellegarde peach known since 1732 and Royal George, believed to date from the days of George I, were still grown as they are today.

AMERICAN VARIETIES

Peaches have been grown in North America ever since they were introduced by the Spaniards in the sixteenth century. Their seedlings spread rapidly during the following centuries to become established in a wild state in the favourable climatic conditions existing in the south. Their fruits were used by the native Indians and the early settlers who also brought with them additional varieties. Until the end of the eighteenth century, the normal method of propagation was by seed so that many thousands of new seedling varieties were raised. In time the best of these were selected and further propagated by budding onto rootstocks. These varieties were supplemented by further importations of the best sorts from Europe and, during the nineteenth century, attention was paid to breeding new varieties by a number of nurserymen.

Several of the American peaches bred in the past century were brought to England where they proved very successful. Of these, one of the best was Hale's Early, raised from a seed planted in 1850 by a German settler at Randolph in Ohio. It was propagated and introduced a few years later by a nurseryman, Hale. Amsden June was another good variety raised in 1868 at Carthage, Missouri by L. C. Amsden, and for many years was the earliest peach. A rather more recent introduction from America has been Rochester raised in 1900 on the farm of Mr Waller near Rochester, New York. Although not always of first quality, this peach has been found to be very productive when grown on a bush tree outside in the more favourable areas of the country.

During this century, many new and valuable varieties of peaches and nectarines have been raised in the United States, mainly by the plant breeders in California, and these have dominated the other peach-growing areas of the world. These are the main varieties produced in the extensive new peach orchards of Italy. Vast quantities of Italian peaches are imported into Britain so that there is now little incentive to try to produce peaches commercially in English glasshouses since the costs are prohibitive. However, the peach or nectarine grown on the garden wall or in a greenhouse is still regarded by the owner as beyond compare. These fruits have had a very long period of history; they were appreciated by the Chinese 4000 years ago and are likely to be of major importance for the forseeable future.

Bush Peaches in the Open

Usually in Britain, peaches and nectarines have been grown with the protection of a glasshouse or on a south- or east-facing wall in the open. However, Thomas Andrew Knight thought that they might, in favourable situations, be grown as low espaliers and occasionally in the past they were grown as bush trees in the open. During this century, Justin Brooke began growing peaches for market on bush trees planted in open fields in Suffolk and encouraged others to follow his example. However, most of these attempts failed and within a few years, as a result of poor cropping and attacks by disease, most of the new orchards were pulled up.

One of the main causes of the failure was the choice of the peach variety, Peregrine, a most excellent peach for protected cultivation but a very uncertain cropping variety when grown out in the open. The use of the American Rochester ensures much better results and this variety has often been successful grown as a bush tree in favourable areas.

Rootstocks for Peaches and Nectarines

Since peach and nectarine seeds will often give rise to worthwhile seedlings, the chances of obtaining progeny of some value are better with these than with other temperate fruits. In addition, the seedlings of peaches and nectarines come into crop more quickly than other fruits. For these reasons they were often left unbudded, those showing fruits of some value being retained. Many of the new varieties were obtained in the early days of fruit growing in this way.

As improved varieties were found, these were propagated by budding onto rootstocks. Heresbach in 1578 advised the use of peach, almond or plum stocks. By 1657, Austen said that the rootstocks, normally obtained as suckers, from the White-peare plum should be used or alternatively peach seedlings. The use of the White-pear plum was also recommended by Worlidge in 1697. In 1731, Miller said that the Muscle and White-pear plum stocks were best but that some peach varieties would not 'take' (or prove compatible) on plum and so almond or apricot seedlings should be used. However, Switzer in 1724, said such incompatibility could be avoided by using an intermediate of apricot:

> *Many peaches take well on Shining Muscle or Black Damask but some will not take on any plum stock, for example Royal George.*
>
> *To remedy this misfortune as much as possible, I have advised a Method I have seen in Holland, and which I am told by one that has by my direction, done it in England and with good success. Let the ingenious Planter first of all bud his Plum stocks with some of the largest Apricocks and, in the ensuing year, rebud the Apricock likewise with such sort of Peaches as he cannot otherwise raise. But then the tree is as long again in raising and must of a consequence bear a double price. I recommende to all lovers of Propagating Fruit, the St Julian Stock, which is chiefly obtained from France.*

Thomas Rivers in 1865, advised Black Damask plum for peaches but said some varieties needed double budding, a practice he said was still neglected by some European nurseries. Today, the plum rootstocks Common Muscle, St Julien A and Pershore are all considered compatible with peaches and nectarines but Myrobolan B, Common Plum and Marianna are incompatible. Of all these, St Julien A is the most commonly used rootstock for peaches in England, the St Julien being generally favoured for all stone fruits as it was by Rivers and others in the past century. Peach seedling rootstocks are often found to give the peach tree a shorter life than plum stocks.

APRICOTS

The apricot, *Prunus armeniaca*, is found growing wild over a wide area of central Asia but, in spite of its name which denotes an Armenian origin, it is generally considered that it originated in China where, according to an account attributed to Emperor Yu, in 2205 – 2198 BC, the apricot was cultivated there in his time. It is still found growing wild in the mountains near Peking.

Like the peach, the apricot was probably spread by travellers along the ancient silk route from China to the West, through Asia Minor and Persia and was grown by the Assyrians and Babylonians. The wild peach and half-wild apricots grow in a wide belt from north China, through south Mongolia across the foothills and the high plateaux to the Caucasus. In Turkestan and Asia the wild apricot is found in Western and Eastern Tian-Shan and in the Namangan and Andijan mountains as well as in the mountains of the Trans-Ilian Plateau. The forests of wild apricot trees found in the mountains of Semirechye, not far from Alma-Ata, as well as in the Namangan mountains, comprise many forms, some being perfectly edible, differing from the cultivated varieties only in having smaller fruits and stones, chiefly containing bitter kernels. In comparison with cultivated forms, the stones of the wild fruits usually form a considerable part of their weight. All types of stones, including flat and pointed ones, with smooth or rough surfaces, are found.

The common apricot seems to be an intermediate between the peach and the plum. The plum and apricot have been hybridized to form the plumcot, while a supposed hybrid between the peach and apricot is called the peach – apricot. The flowers of the apricot are more like those of the plum than those of the peach, being white or whitish. They appear earlier than those of the peach or plum and the fruits ripen earlier.

Alexander the Great is said to have brought the apricot from Asia to

Greece, though Theophrastus, the Greek botanist who was his contemporary, did not mention it growing in Greece in his time, but it was referred to by another Greek, Dioscorides about 300 years later. From Greece, the apricot was brought to Italy where the first Roman writer to speak of it was Pliny, who referred to it as 'the Armenian plum, imported from foreign parts, the only plum that recommends itself even by its scent'.

At this time, the apricot was regarded as a type of plum and was called *praecocia* on account of its early ripening. There is no reference to the apricot in the Bible or in ancient Jewish records but later there was a major development in its cultivation around Damascus. The word 'mish mish' became established in Hebrew and Arabic for the apricot and the name Musch-Musch was given to the apricot of Alexandria. It was grown on a considerable scale in Upper Egypt where the fruits were dried for sale throughout Europe.

EARLY RECORDS OF APRICOT CULTIVATION

There are no records of apricots having formed part of the diet of Roman soldiers on active service and no remains of apricot stones have been found in excavations of prehistoric or Roman sites in Britain. This is indicative of the comparative late introduction of the apricot to Europe.

Similarly, the apricot was not included in Charlemagne's *Capitulare* of AD 800 or in any account of plants grown in Britain until the sixteenth century. The evidence is that apricots were included with other plants brought back to England in 1524 by Wolf, a priest who was gardener to Henry VIII, to furnish the gardens of the newly built Nonsuch Palace. In these gardens every type of decorative plant and fruit tree then available in Europe was grown. The *Holinshed Chronicles* of 1580 confirmed the fact that the apricot had only been introduced with other strange fruits and planted in the gardens of noblemen within the previous 40 years.

Turner, in his 1548 list of herbs grown in England, was the first English writer to speak of apricots:

> *Some englishe me cal the fruite an Abricock. Me thynkesing that we have very fewe of these trees as yet, it were better to cal it, an hasty Peche tree because it is lyke a peche and it is a great whyle rype before the peche trees wherfore the fruite of thes tree is called malum precox. There is in Colo great plentie of hasty peche trees.*

Turner had more to say about apricots in his *Herball* of 1551:

> *Abrecockes is rype before and are holsummer for the stomack then*

*the peches are. There is this difference betweene the abrecock / or
hasty peche tre and y other / and their fruites. The hasty pech tre
hath much broder leves then the pech tre / and hys fruite is a greate
tyme sonner rype then the peche is. I have sene meny trees of thys
kynde in Almany [Germany] and som in England / and now the
fruite is called of som Englishe men an abrock / but I thynk that an
hasty peche is a better and fitter name.*

These two accounts by Turner show that there were still very few apricots
being grown in England in 1551 but probably rather more 20 years later;
however, they were commonly grown in Germany especially near Cologne.
Turner's wish that the fruit should be called a hasty peach does not seem to
have been taken up by others. The name of apricot seems to have been
derived from the Latin *precoque* or *praecocia*. Mascall in 1575 called it
'abricote', Heresbachius and Gerard 'aprecocke', Parkinson in 1629
'apricocke' and Austen, Worlidge and Switzer, 'apricock', but from Bradley's
time in 1739 it was called 'apricot'.

In 1575 Mascall wrote that the great apricot should be budded on the
lesser type, indicating that a larger-fruited variety was available to be
budded on smaller, seedling rootstocks. Heresbachius said the plum was the
best stock, and Tusser included the apricot in his list of fruits to be grown in
the garden.

By the end of the century, Gerard reported that he, like many gentlemen
throughout England, grew apricots in his garden. This shows how much the
planting of the fruit had spread since it had only been introduced earlier in
the century. He described two types of apricot, the greater which he called
Armeniaca Malus maior, and the lesser, *A. Malus minor.* Parkinson also
mentioned these two types and added the White, Masculine and long
Masculine varieties. These latter had probably been introduced by John
Tradescant about 1620.

During the second half of the seventeenth century, interest in the cultivation
of apricots, as of peaches and nectarines, increased considerably, full use
being made of the walls around the gardens attached to the mansions of the
wealthy, upper classes. As Sir Thomas Hanmer wrote in 1659 apricots
required high walls, facing south or east and sheltered from the wind and
excessive rain. The varieties he recommended were the Great apricot, the
Masculine Early, the Orange and the Fruite de Noave. The Masculine only
had a small fruit but was one of the earliest, being ready in July.

In 1688, Leonard Meager of Brompton Park Nursery increased the number
of varieties offered for sale to seven, The Algar or Civet, Masculine, Orange,
Roman, Ordinary and the Great Turkey. The Algar or the Algiers was a
variety brought back from Algiers by John Tradescant, who had sailed to
North Africa as a voluntary passenger with the naval vessel which was
rounding up pirates in 1620. The Roman, synonymous with the Common or

2 *Armeniaca Malus minor.*
The leſſer Aprecocke tree.

*The lesser apricot grown in England
in the sixteenth century.*

Brussels, was a very old variety which may have gone back to Roman times. This seems to have been the first reference to the Turkey which doubtless had been introduced from that country.

Worlidge, in 1697, wrote of changes in the cultivation of apricots, saying that the fruit was well known almost everywhere. Although the tree could be grown as a standard, its fruits seldom matured unless it was planted against a wall; however, as with apples and pears, a recent development had been to grow apricots as dwarf trees, limited to 3 ft in height. Such small trees were less affected by the wind and had the benefit of heat reflected from the earth and so produced well-matured fruits early in the season.

THE EIGHTEENTH CENTURY

The popularity of apricots continued in the eighteenth century and Switzer, in 1724, like Worlidge, said they were so well known there was little need to

1 *Armeniaca Malus maior.*
The greater Aprecocke tree.

The greater apricot.

describe them. The Masculine, though early, was so small it was not so well liked as the large Dutch, the Orange, Turkey and Roman or Common varieties.

The Brussels, which was later described as synonymous with the very old Common apricot, was generally accepted as the most likely to succeed when grown in the open as a standard or dwarf tree. Apricots were often grown from seed and the progeny might be used for rootstocks or grown on for cropping so that numerous new varieties, often differing little from their parents, appeared.

In 1777, Richard Weston, in his nursery catalogue, gave Early Masculine, Orange, Algiers, Roman, Turkey, Breda, Lord Dunmore's Bride, Temple and Brussels as the varieties then grown in England. Temple was a synonym for Moorpark and this was the first reference in print to the variety which has dominated all others for over 200 years. In the *Pomona Britannica* of a nurseryman William Driver in 1788, in which he illustrated the leading varieties of fruits, he only included this apricot. He said this variety was

synonymous with the peach apricot, Dunmore and Lord Anson's. There has
been considerable confusion about the origin of Moor Park but the evidence
is that it was introduced in 1760 by the famous admiral, Lord Anson, and
first fruited at Moor Park, near Watford in Hertfordshire.

It is very similar to the peach—apricot and Driver considered them
synonymous, but Hogg later said that though for practical purposes the two
varieties could be regarded as identical, Moor Park could be budded on
Common Plum but the peach—apricot required the Brussels, Brompton or
Black Damas rootstock. For this reason, he thought Moor Park was a
seedling of the peach—apricot. This had probably been brought over from
France at the beginning of the eighteenth century as Switzer, in 1724, wrote
of a very large kind of apricot being cultivated at Woolhampton in Berkshire
which was as big as a large peach and was called the French apricot. The
peach—apricot is said to have originated as a seedling from Alberge.

Evidence of the high regard in which Moor Park was held in the past, as it
is today, is seen in Jane Austen's *Mansfield Park*, when Mrs Norris and Dr
Grant are discussing an apricot growing on a stable wall. Mrs Norris says:—

> *Sir, it is a Moor Park, we bought it as a Moor Park and it cost us —*
> *that is it was a present from Sir Thomas, but I saw the bill, it cost*
> *seven shillings and was charged as a Moor Park.*
>
> *You were imposed on, ma'am, these potatoes have as much the*
> *flavour of Moor Park apricot as the fruit of that tree.*

THE NINETEENTH CENTURY

W. Hooker in *Pomona Londoniensis* in 1818 only named Moor Park among
apricots, and Thompson, reporting on the apricots in the Horticultural
Society's collection in 1831, said that the Roman or Common variety had
been the most generally grown until the introduction of Moor Park.
Hemskerk, whose origin was unknown, was probably a seedling of the
latter and very similar to it. Thompson said that the nomenclature of
apricots was in a greater state of confusion than most other fruits. Out of the
70—80 so-called varieties planted in the trial, he found only 17 to be
distinct. Of other varieties grown in the past century, Kaisha, introduced in
1842, was sent to Hogg from Syria by the Consul at Allepo, and Shipley's
was later called Blenheim as it had been raised by Miss Shipley, daughter of
a gardener to the Duke of Marlborough at Blenheim, some time before 1830.

While most apricots in the past were grown on the walls around large
gardens or in glasshouses, during the nineteenth century their cultivation
was extended to the walls of cottages and houses in some of the villages of
Oxfordshire and the area of Northamptonshire adjoining its northern borders.

Their cultivation seems to have been encouraged by the owners of the large estates in the area, trees being supplied to their employees. *The Berkshire Gazette* of June 1839 said that the soil and climate of Kidlington-on-the-Green in Oxford appeared very favourable to apricots. The walls of every house and cottage were clothed throughout with apricot trees. It was estimated that 6,000 were grown in that year.

Thompson, in 1831, had said that in some parts of Oxfordshire a large apricot was grown under the name of Breda but was probably Roman. The trees were often planted near the warm chimney breast. Today, apricots are still grown in the village of Aynho in Northamptonshire. This village adjoins Croughton, the name of an apricot which has been tried in other areas without much success.

During the late 1940s and 1950, Justin Brooke experimented with growing apricots and peaches as bush trees in the open in Suffolk, and growers in other parts in the south of England also tried this system. Unfortunately most of these attempts failed, both the result of die-back due to infection by the fungus *Sclerotinia laxa* and damage to the flowers by early frosts.

APRICOT CULTURE TODAY

Today, probably fewer apricots are being grown in Britain than at any time since the eighteenth century. Few new houses now have suitable walls for their culture, and their cultivation in the gardens of older houses or in commercial glasshouses has been virtually given up due to the high cost of the labour involved and the relative cheapness of imported fruits. Where apricots are grown, the varieties recommended include New Large Early, raised by Rivers about 1873, Hemskerk and Moor Park. New Large Early is valuable for its earliness and fertility. It took the place of Masculine, whose only virtue was its earliness. Other varieties still grown are Breda, Early Moor Park and Shipley's or Blenheim. A few American varieties of apricots have been tested for cultivation as bush trees in the open with variable success. The lack of importance of the apricot in Britain has meant that no attention has been given to the breeding of new varieties, or other aspects of its cultivation, at any of the fruit research stations. Brompton and St Julien A plum rootstocks are recommended.

The fig, *Ficus carica*, is a native of western Asia and the eastern Mediterranean region and grows wild in an area extending from Syria to eastern Persia and to Afghanistan. It is found in the Caucasus and the lowest forest zone of Transcaucasia, where it is considered to have originated in the forests in the deep valleys and gorges of the Tajik mountains. Today figs also grow wild throughout the Mediterranean area and further to the Canary Islands, frequently growing on stony, rocky soils and are often found growing out of clefts between rocks where a little soil has built up.

Before domestication, the fig grew along the water courses and the banks of the Jordan and around the Dead Sea. Remains of figs, dating back to the Neolithic Age were found in excavations at Gezer. From the earliest records of civilization, it was of major importance as an item of food throughout Mesopotamia, Palestine and Egypt. In several countries, along with the date, the fig formed the basic diet, and was used either fresh or dried. When people travelled on long journeys or were besieged during battle they could subsist on dried figs.

In Greece and Crete, figs were known from very early times; remains from the Neolithic period were found at Olynthus and large quantities from the Late Bronze Age at Kakovantos (Pylos). In Crete, figs were found in the palace storehouse at Minoan Hafia Triada and appear in paintings at Knossus.

The earliest documented records of the use of figs as food are from Egypt from the days of Snefrou of the Fourth Dynasty (about 2700 BC); these mention the fig as a tree on whose fruit people live. On an inscribed stone stele of about 2400 BC, it is said that an army commander, Uni, was sent by Pepi I to Canaan to crush a vassal revolt and his troops returned in peace after cutting down their figs and vines. The Leningrad Papyrus of 1800 BC includes the story of a sailor saved from a shipwreck in the Red Sea, off the Sinai coast, by being thrown up on an island where he found wild figs, grapes and other fruits.

In the second and third centuries BC, the Papyrus of Zenon lists dried figs, oil, nuts and honey among other commodities bought from Syria. The Egyptians had two kinds of figs, the Sycamore, *Ficus sycamorus*, and the common fig, *F. carica*, the Sycamore being the more popular. As well as featuring in many pictures on tombs and other buildings, specimens of the fruits themselves have been found in many tombs as funeral offerings, sometimes threaded on strings and sometimes as entire baskets of fruits.

The timber of the Sycamore fig, also called the Egyptian or Pharaoh's fig, was used for making coffins for mummies as it proved resistant to rotting. This variety formed a very large tree valued for the shade it cast, much appreciated by travellers in the desert. Egyptian records show that idol worshippers offered wine and figs in sacrifices.

In the time of the Phoenicians, the fig was spread to China and India. In Mesopotamia it was also a staple item of diet. Sargon, the first king of the Akkadian dynasty about 2350 BC, said he had brought figs back from Anatolia, but these were probably new varieties as earlier records of Urukagina of Lagash had also mentioned figs.

There are frequent references to the fig in the Bible. The account of the fall of Adam and Eve in Genesis says that they sewed the leaves of the fig together and made themselves aprons to hide their nakedness. Some Jewish commentators consider the Tree of Knowledge in the Garden of Eden to be the fig. As well as being used for food, figs were used medicinally. The Bible mentions that the king Hezekiah was cured of a boil after his servant followed the advice of Isaiah and placed a cake of figs on it.

Muslims were also fond of the fig and spread it to every land of their wide conquests for Mohammed had said, 'If I desire a fruit of the Garden of Eden, I would choose the fig'.

FIGS IN GREECE AND ITALY

The fig had been known and used in Greece for many centuries before Homer included it in his account of the garden of the Palace of Alcinous in *The Odyssey*. Theophrastus wrote of propagating plants from cuttings and said: 'As for the fig, no cultivated kind is raised from its seed, but either the ordinary wild fig or some wild kind is the result, and this often differs in colour from the parent; a black fig gives a white and conversely.'

The fertilization of many of the fig varieties grown in Greece and Italy was aided by the small fig wasp, *Blastophaga psenes*. Aristotle described how the wasps came out of the male Capri figs, and then penetrated and fertilized the unripe female fruits. Theophrastus discussed this process of 'caprification' and Pliny devoted a whole chapter to the subject:

> *A plan was discovered of bringing branches of the wild fig, the Capri, from somewhere else and throwing them, tied in bundles, on to the fig orchard. A treatment which orchard figs do not require when planted on a thin soil with a northerly aspect, since they dry of their own accord owing to the situation of the place, and this cause, by making them split open, produces the same result as the action of the wasps.*

In Rome, figs were very popular with all classes. Cato gave advice on varieties to be grown for sale on a market garden: 'Plant Mariscan figs in chalky, open soil; the African, Herculanean, Saguntine, the winter variety and the black Tellanain, with long pedicels, in soil which is richer or manured.' Varro made an interesting point on the transportation of figs from one country to another:

> *It is better to plant in the nursery shoots from the fig trees than from the seeds of the fruit; unless this is impracticable, as when you wish to ship overseas or import from thence. In this case we pass a string through the figs when they are ripe for eating, and after they have dried they are tied in bundles and may be sent where we will; and these are planted in a nursery and reproduce. It was in this manner that the Chian, Chalcidian, Lydian, African and other varieties of overseas figs were imported into Italy.*

Varro seemed to be unaware of the fact that seedlings very rarely show similar characters to their parents, a point which Theophrastus had made 300 years earlier.

Both Columella and Pliny wrote of the different varieties of figs. According to Columella:

> *But 'tis beneath baleful Arcturus' star*
> *That Livian figs, which with the Chalcidian vie,*
> *And Caunion, rivals of the Chian, come*
> *To birth, and purple Chelidonian*
> *And fat Mariscan, Callistruthian*
> *Gay with rosy seeds, and that pale kind*
> *Which ever keeps the name of tawny wax*
> *And the cleft Libyan and the Lydian fig*
> *With spotted skin.*

He further advised planting chiefly the Livian, African, Chalcidian, Fulcan, Lydian, Callistruthian, Astropian, Rhodian, Libyan and Tiburnian and also those which crop twice or three times a year. Pliny wrote at length about figs, and he illustrates the high regard in which the Romans held this fruit:

> *The figs that are highly approved are given the distinction of being dried and kept in boxes, the best and largest growing on the island of Iviza and the next best in the district of Chieti; but in some places where there is a very large supply of them, they are packed for storage in large jars in Asia, but in casks in the city of Rusina in Africa, and when dry they serve the purpose of bread and other viands at the same time, inasmuch as Cato, as if laying down a law as to the proper rations for agricultural labourers, prescribes that they are to be reduced in quantity during the time when the figs are ripe.*
>
> *A plan has lately been devised to use a fresh fig instead of salt when eating cheese. To this class, as we have said, belong the Syrian and the Carian figs and the Caunean figs that, when Marcus Crassus was embarking to sail against the Parthians, gave him an omen by the voice of a man crying them for sale. All these varieties of fruit were imported from Syria to his country place at Alba by Lucius Vitellius, afterwards censor, when he was Lieutenant-governor of that province, in the latter part of the principate of the emperor Tiberius.*

Pliny wrote of the importance of the fig tree, apart from the use of its fruit, to the inhabitants of Rome and of the part it had played in the history of their city:

> *A fig-tree growing in the actual forum and meeting place of Rome is worshipped as sacred because things struck by lightning are buried there and still more as a memorial of the fig-tree under which the nurse of Romulus and Remus first sheltered those founders of the empire on the Lupercal Hill. The tree that has been given the name of Ruminalis, because it was beneath it that the wolf was discovered giving her rumis to the infants. And it is also a portent of some future event when it withers away and then by the good offices of the priests is replanted. There was also a fig-tree in front of the temple of Saturn, which in 404 BC, after a sacrifice had been offered by the Vestal Virgins, was removed, because it was upsetting a statue of Silvanus.*

Cato described six varieties of figs and Pliny 29. As Pliny said, since Cato's time so many new varieties had been introduced that this alone showed how their way of life had been transformed.

RECORDS OF FIGS IN BRITAIN

The fig formed an important part of the diet of the Romans, and their cultivation in Italy was supplemented by imports from Syria, Africa and other countries. Dried figs were taken by travellers on their journeys and were included in the rations of the Roman military forces when on active service. Excavation of the Roman fortress at Neuss near Cologne revealed the remains of figs, and these were also found on the site of the military hospital, suggesting that they had been prescribed by the medical authorities.

The seeds of figs have been excavated from several Roman sites in England, at Silchester, St Albans and, in London, at Bermondsey, Finsbury Circus and the wharf sites near the Thames. At the latter, fig seeds have been the most commonly found, both numerically and in the number of sites, at New Fresh Wharf and the nearby second-century site in St Thomas Street. The archaeologists responsible for the excavation of the wharf sites consider that the seeds were most probably imported dried fruits and not figs grown in this country. The seeds in fruits formed parthenogenetically, without fertilization, are somewhat vestigial while those recovered from the London sites were fully formed. At this time, the pollinating insect, the fig wasp, was unknown in Britain.

Although there is no evidence that the fig was planted in Britain during the Roman occupation, George Bunyard said that the variety Reculver was thought to have been named after Reculver in Kent, an important Roman port, and to have been introduced by the Romans. Hogg said that Reculver was Black Provence, synonymous with Black Marseilles, and so might well have been brought from Italy to the south of France and thence to England or direct from Italy.

Even if the fig had been planted in Britain by the Romans, it probably disappeared during the Dark Ages and, although in Europe the fig was included in Charlemagne's list of fruits in AD 800, the first evidence of its cultivation in England is in the sixteenth century. However, although home-grown figs were not available, they were appreciated at the court. In 1290 the wife of Edward I bought a 'frail' (a rush basket) of figs, together with other fruits which were part of the cargo of a ship from Spain.

Tradition has it that the first fig tree grown in England was introduced by Cardinal Pole and planted in the garden of the Archbishop's Palace at Lambeth by 1525. The Cardinal had long resided in Italy where he had probably developed a liking for the fruit. According to Miller, the trees were still growing in the Palace gardens two centuries later and were of the White Marseilles variety and bore delicious fruits. Loudon in 1834, repeating the account of their origin, said the trees still grew in the Lambeth garden and reached a height of 50 ft in spite of having been cut to the ground by severe winter weather on several occasions in the past, the last time being in the winter of 1813 – 14. He confirmed that the variety was White Marseilles, one of the few still recommended for planting today and described by Hogg as the most delicious fig in cultivation.

Doubt that the Lambeth figs were the first to be planted in Britain is cast by the fact that several authors in the sixteenth century wrote of figs as though they were a common fruit. Turner, in his herbal in 1568 wrote: 'A figge tree is no great highe tree / for the moste parte / but in some places some are founde as bigge and as high / as a pere tree. The figge tree is so well knowen / that it nedith no farther description.' This suggests that the trees had been established for some years and that the fig was commonly known to the readers of the herbal. Although Turner had travelled extensively on the Continent and sometimes described fruits he had seen growing there, he mentioned where he had found them.

In 1575 Mascall wrote of the propagation of the fig and then said:

> The black figges are the best, being dryed in the Sunne, and then layd in a vessell in beddes one by another. If a figge wyll not beare, ye shall dygge him all about, and under the rootes in Februarie, and take out all the earth and put unto him the doing of a privie, for that he lyketh best.

Thomas Hill in 1579 included two varieties of figs, the Greater Blue and the Dwarf Blue, and said there were several other varieties but the Greater Blue was best for the English climate. The trees, however, should be planted on a wall for protection. Tusser in 1580, in his list of fruits to be grown in the garden, did not include the fig but this is not perhaps surprising as he wrote as a farmer who had lived for most of his life in the eastern counties.

Gerard in 1597 wrote:

> The Fig trees do growe plentifully in Spaine and Italie, and many other countries, as in England; where they beare fruite but it never commeth to kindly maturities, except the tree be planted under an hot wall, whereto neither north nor north east windes can come.
>
> The dwarffe Fig groweth in my garden, and bringeth foorth ripe and very great fruit in the moneth of August, of which Figs sundrie persons have eaten at pleasure.

The dwarf fig tree, the French Figuier Nain, was described by John Merlet in Bradley's book in 1726, who said the tree had very short shoots with the buds very close together, but the fruit was of a fairly large size. This seems to have been a 'spur' mutation of a fig, similar to the spur forms of apples being planted today. By the time Parkinson wrote in 1629, the fig appears to have been quite widely planted:

> *The figge trees that are noursed up in our country are of three sorts,*
> *whereof two are high, the one bearing against a wall, goodley*
> *sweeter and delicate Figs called Figs of Albania, and is blewish*
> *when ripe; the other tall kinde is nothing so good and may be the*
> *white ordinary kind from Spaine. The third is a dwarf kind of Figge*
> *tree, not growing higher than a mans body or shoulders, bearing*
> *excellent good figges and blew, but not so large as the first kind.*
>
>   *Figges are served to the table with Raysins of the Sunne and*
> *blanched Almonds for a Lenten dish. The Figs that growe with us*
> *when they be ripe and fresh gathered, are eaten of divers with a little*
> *salt and pepper as a dainty banquet to entertain a friend, which*
> *seldom passeth without a cup of wine to wash down.*

During the seventeenth century relatively few varieties of figs were cultivated in Britain. Austen in 1657 said he only knew of one kind that ripened in England, the Great Blew which he said was as large as a Catherine pear and, when ripe, could be eaten fresh with pepper, salt and bread or could be dried to last the whole year. He said that figs grew in many gardens in Oxford and, provided they were trained on a south-facing wall, the fruits ripened perfectly. One celebrated fig tree brought from the East was planted in the garden of the Regius Professor of Hebrew by Dr Pocock in 1648.

The French Gardiner, translated by John Evelyn, in 1669 showed that more varieties were available in France at that time than in Britain. This listed nine varieties grown around Paris: White figs, Bourjassores, Bourno-Saintes, Flower-fig, Gourravaund of Languedoc, Marseilles, White Dwarfe, Violet Dwarfe and Violet fig. Of these, Marseilles, Violet Dwarfe or Dwarf Blue, and Violet or Greater Blue were probably already being grown in England but there was still not much enthusiasm for growing figs except in the gardens of the rich. In 1697, Worlidge, a very knowledgeable farmer and grower, said that as figs were of so little use in their rural habitation he would leave them out and consequently dismissed them from his book.

The Eighteenth Century

It was the initiative of Philip Miller, in charge of the Apothecaries' Garden at Chelsea, that resulted in the introduction of many new varieties of figs during the early years of the eighteenth century. As he said himself, up till that time most people in England were not lovers of the fig and there were not more than four or five kinds in the country. He therefore had a large collection of varieties sent to him by Chevalier Rathgeb from Venice which he grew and from which he selected those with the best flavour. These were the Brown or Chestnut-coloured Ischia, which was the variety with the largest fruits, Black Genoa, the small White Early, Large White Genoa, Black Ischia, Malta, Murrey or Brown Naples, Green Ischia, Madonna, also commonly called Brunswick or Hanover, Long Brown Naples, Yellow Ischia, Small Brown Ischia and the Gentile fig. The Madonna or Brunswick, the Murrey or Brown Naples, later called Brown Turkey, and the White Genoa, synonymous with White Marseilles, are the three varieties most generally recommended today.

Other writers began to speak of the new varieties brought over from Europe. Merlet in 1726 said that although they had not so many as were popular in Spain and Italy, Britain had 17 of which the White figs were valued for their delicate flavour and early ripening. Bradley said that although it was generally thought figs would only ripen their fruits when planted against walls, he had seen figs grown as standards in several gardens around London and they cropped better than when confined on walls by pruning. Switzer, writing at this time, described how to use mattresses of straw to protect fig trees planted on walls during the winter and how the Dutch planted the trees in pits made with sand walls, formed into squares or circles, and equipped with posts so that the whole pit could be covered over during the cold months. He also wrote of the use of glasshouses for forcing figs in which there were heated flues behind the brick walls. Switzer had apparently advised the Duke of Rutland at Belvoir Castle to site the hot-air flues lower down, near the roots of the trees rather than higher up, as this gave a more balanced growth when forcing.

Towards the end of the century, in 1777, Richard Weston gave a list of 15 varieties of figs which could be obtained from nurserymen. These were Early Long Blue, White Marseilles, Brown, Small, Black, Green and Yellow Ischia, Black Genoa, Large White, Malta, Brown Naples, Braunwic or Madonna, Large Blue, Large Brown and Black Provence. Large Blue was a synonym for Brown Turkey and Black Provence for Reculver, thought by Bunyard to be a Roman variety. The propagation of the fig at this time, as in the past, was by suckers, layers or cuttings.

THE NINETEENTH CENTURY

There were 75 varieties of figs in the collection of the Horticultural Society at Chiswick in 1826 but this included many synonyms and few of the varieties were being grown elsewhere in Britain. Phillips in 1827 and Loudon in 1834 wrote of the cultivation of figs as standard trees in the open at Tarring in Sussex. One orchard of about three-quarters of an acre had 100 trees which were the size of large apple trees. Their owner said he had gathered a hundred dozen figs per day during August to October, at a time when the neighbouring watering places were frequented by fashionable company which ensured a ready sale for the figs at a good price. As Phillips said, figs were only appreciated by the refined palates of the upper classes and, in Sussex, they were not only neglected by the middle and lower classes but even spoken of with derision.

Two of the trees at Tarring had been produced about 1745 by John Long who had raised them from old trees in a neighbouring garden near the ruins of the palace of Thomas à Becket, whom tradition said brought the trees from Italy and planted them himself. Other standard fig trees in the grounds of Arundel Castle grew to a height of 30 ft and cropped abundantly.

Phillips said he was convinced that figs could be grown more extensively in the coastal region of Sussex and sent to the London markets where, in September 1820, they fetched 6—8s a dozen.

A further account of the Sussex fig orchards was given in the *Garden* in 1890. This said that the most suitable variety had been found to be Brown Turkey and that the tree planted by Thomas à Becket had barely survived being struck by lightning in 1885. The ripening fruits had to be placed in bags to protect them from birds and they were so much appreciated that they sold for as much each as formerly for a dozen. By this time figs were also being grown in many parts of Kent as bushes or standard trees in the open and, in most large gardens, a fig-house was the rule. The hardiest varieties were considered to be Brown Turkey and White Marseilles.

During the nineteenth century, the production of figs was a major industry in the Argenteuil region of France where they were grown on low dwarf trees for market. The ripening of the latest figs was hastened by a drop of olive oil placed in the eye of the fruit by a woman who had a phial of oil at her waist and a piece of hollow straw in her hand. The same method was used in other parts of France and around Naples where the fruits were pricked with an ivory or bone pin. This technique, though it might well have proved useful, was not employed in England.

FIG GROWING TODAY

During this century there has been a marked decline in the cultivation of figs in Britain, and today they are generally only grown in the larger private gardens in glasshouses or on walls, comparatively few being grown as bush or standard trees in the open and then only in the most favourable situations. The three main varieties grown today are Brunswick, Brown Turkey and White Marseilles, the two former introduced by Miller in the early eighteenth century and White Marseilles at least a hundred years earlier. The lack of interest in the cultivation of figs in Britain, and the limits imposed by the climate, have meant that no attention has been given here to breeding new varieties. In addition, throughout the history of fig growing in Britain there has been no great enthusiasm by the public for the fresh fig, although dried figs have met with a much more ready sale.

The medlar, *Mespilus germanica*, is found growing wild in several countries of Asia Minor but is thought to have originated in Transcaucasia and from there spread to Persia. Wild medlars grow in the hedges and thickets of southern Europe and have been found in Kent and Sussex where they were probably escapes from cultivation. This fruit seems to have been taken to the United States by the French Jesuits and, in Florida, is commonly used as a hedge plant and often grows semi-wild.

Mespilus is closely related to *Crataegus* and *Pyrus*. It is separated from *Crataegus* by its very large flowers which are borne singly and have leaf-like sepals. At least two botanical forms can be differentiated, one a large-fruited form and the other a seedless type. These characters can be seen in the named varieties which now exist.

MEDLARS IN ANTIQUITY

The medlar was cultivated by the Assyrians and introduced to Greece at an early time. It was mentioned by Theophrastus who said the bird cherry had leaves like those of the medlar. From Greece it spread to Rome but, according to Pliny, was not grown there in the time of Cato who was born about 140 years after Theophrastus. Pliny wrote:

> *Fruits that must be included in the class of apples and pears, are the medlar and the service berry. There are three sorts of medlar, the Anthedon, the Setania and a third, rather inferior kind yet rather like the Anthedon, which is called the Gallic medlar. The fruit of the Setania is larger and of a paler colour, with a softer pip; the others*

have smaller fruit but with a superior scent and keep longer. The
tree itself is one of the most widely spreading, its leaves turn red
before they fall off; it has a great many roots, which go down deep
into the ground and consequently it is impossible to grub them up.

These two major types, the Setania, with larger fruit, and the others whose fruits are smaller but more highly flavoured, correspond closely to varieties known to have been widely planted for several centuries, the large Dutch and the smaller Neopolitan. The name Anthedon doubtless comes from a city of that name in Greece, the Gallic, according to Pliny, came from France and the Setania from the marshes of Setin.

MEDLARS IN BRITAIN

There are few records of the remains of medlars, and the only evidence of this fruit from the time of the Roman occupation of Britain is a single seed found at Silchester which might mean it had been grown in England at that time. It is somewhat unlikely, though possible, that the fruits had been imported.

The medlar, especially the large-fruited variety, the Dutch, which has been known since the seventeenth century and was quite likely a derivative of the Setania mentioned by Pliny, forms a large, handsome tree having very big, white flowers. For this reason it was often grown as an ornament. In 1326, when the palace orchard at Wells Cathedral was being partitioned, the medlar was reserved for the bishop. The beauty of the tree in full bloom was described in a poem 'The Flower and the Leaf', dating from about 1450:

And as I stood and cast aside mine eie
I was ware of the fairest medlar tree,
That ever yet in all my life I sie.
As full of blossoms as it might be
Therein a goldfinch leaping pretile
Fro bough to bough; and as him list, he cet
Here and there of buds and floures sweet.

Medlar fruits are normally left on the trees until late in the autumn and, after harvest, are left until they become brown inside and half rotten. In England, by tradition, they were eaten at the end of a meal accompanied by port wine. Their flavour is however disliked by many people, as it was by George Bunyard who said that the different varieties were all of equal unpleasantness.

In 1387 in 'The Reeve's Tale' in *The Canterbury Tales*, Chaucer refers to the custom of allowing the medlar fruits to become rotten before eating them:

> *But if I fare as doth an open-ers [a medlar]*
> *That ilke fruit is ever lenger the wers*
> *Til it be taten in mullock or in stre [rubbish and straw].*

In Shakespeare's *As You Like It*, Rosalind, replying to Touchstone, who said the tree yields bad fruit, remarked: 'I'll graff it with you, and then I shall graff it with a medlar; then it will be the earliest fruit i' the country; for you'll be rotten ere you be half ripe, and that's the right vertue of the medlar.'

There was much greater use of the medlar fruit in the Middle Ages than now, especially in Europe. In France it was the basis of the famous preserve made in Orléans, known as 'cotignac', which was always offered to the Sovereign when he entered the city and which was the first present made to Joan of Arc when she led her troops into Orléans. Medlars are still fairly common in the markets of France and Germany but are now only very occasionally seen in Britain.

CULTIVATION IN ENGLAND

The medlar was included in Charlemagne's list of fruits in AD 800 but the earliest reference to it in England was in the Westminster Abbey Customary of 1270, in which the gardener monk was instructed to provide the monastery with medlars along with other fruits. Among the Privy Purse expenses of Henry VIII there is mention of gifts of various fruits made to the king which included medlars. Treueris' *The Grete Herball* in 1526 said of medlars: 'Theyr propyete is to conforte the stomake and be more usefull for medycyn then for meate. For they nouryshe but lytell and be better afore meate then after / and be not grevous to the substance of the stomake and senewy sydes thereof.'

In Heresbachius' book, published in German and translated into English in 1577, the author said he had seen medlar trees growing in woods of oak trees and added that the wood of the trees was used for making the spokes of wheels while the twigs served for making whips for carters:

> *We have at this daie two kinds, the one havyng here and there prickles, growyng in every Wood and Thickette, very soure afore it is mellowed, and made soft with Froste, and cold of Winter; the other, havyng no prickles, and all with a greate fruite, which seemeth to be brought hereunto by diligent Plantyng and Graffyng.*

In 1579, Thomas Hill spoke of two varieties, the Greater and the Neopolitan while Gerard, in 1597, wrote:

> *There be divers sorts of Medlars, some greater, others lesser; some*
> *sweete and others of a more harsh taste; some with much core, and*
> *many great stone kernels, others fewer; and likewise one of Naples,*
> *called Aronia.*
>   *The Neopolitan Medlar tree, groweth to the height and greatness*
> *of an Apple tree, having many tough and hard boughes or branches,*
> *set with sharp thorns like the white Thorn.*

Although Gerard spoke of many varieties, which suggests that some of these must have been new seedlings raised in Britain, a medlar planted during the reign of James I at Hatfield House, Hertfordshire, and which still exists today, may well have been introduced by John Tradescant when he was responsible for the gardens. Obviously many of Gerard's varieties must have proved of little use as in 1629 Parkinson still only listed three varieties, the Greater and Lesser English and the Neopolitan. Even 80 years later in 1697, according to Worlidge, the medlar had not gained in popularity:

> *The Medlar is a Fruit of very little use, the reason I suppose they are*
> *no more multiplyed, yet have been of long standing; they are*
> *Pleasante to the Palate. This tree may well serve to fill a spare*
> *corner in your orchard. If we could obtain the Medlar without*
> *stones mentioned in the* French Gardiner, *they would be better*
> *worth the planting. The Great Dutch Medlar is best.*

The wish of Worlidge that the stoneless form of medlar could be available was fulfilled by the time Switzer wrote in 1724:

> *There are three sorts of Medlars that are raised in Gardens; the*
> *biggest Sort call'd the Great Dutch Medlar, without any Thorns*
> *upon the Branches is best and a good bearer. The Common Medlar*
> *has Thorns but the Fruit is good, and there is another Sort, though*
> *smaller, that has no Stones.*
>   *There is another Kind of Medlar call'd L'Azzercle or Neopolitan*
> *Medlar producing (in Italy from whence it comes), a very pleasant*
> *Fruit, and has of late Years been propagated in our English*
> *Gardens.*

This notion that the Neopolitan medlar had only recently been propagated in English gardens is not correct as Thomas Hill in 1579, Gerard in 1597 and Parkinson in 1629 had all included this variety in their books.

During the next hundred years, unlike the progress made during this period with other fruits, there was no further development in the production

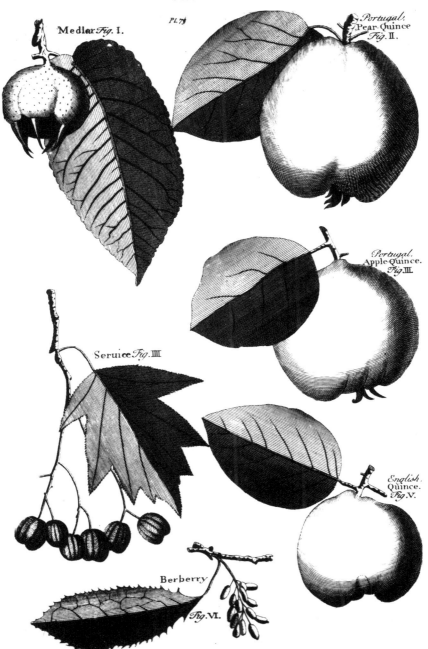

Pl. 79

Medlar *Fig.* I.

Portugal.
Pear-Quince
Fig. II.

Portugal.
Apple-Quince.
Fig. III.

Seruice *Fig.* IIII.

English.
Quince.
Fig. V.

Berberry

Fig. VI.

Medlars and quinces: the medlar was popular in ancient Greece and Rome,
and was much more widely grown in Britain in the Middle Ages and the
following centuries than today. Rowan berries were collected for food and
the quince was still widely cultivated in the eighteenth century.

of improved forms of medlar, nor did the fruit gain favour with consumers. Then, as today, the medlar in Britain seems only to have been grown by a limited number of connoisseurs. In 1777, Richard Weston listed the Dutch and Nottingham varieties, and the same types were offered by the London nurserymen, Luker and Smith, in 1783. This is one of the earliest references to the variety Nottingham which Bunyard considered a very old variety, the Common medlar, one of the first of the improved wild forms. Since the name of the Neopolitan, which had been grown for many centuries, disappeared from the literature about this time, it seems likely that the Nottingham was in fact this variety under a new name. This view is supported by the fact that their general description was similar and both had smaller, but better-flavoured, fruits than the Dutch.

Forsyth in 1806 said that Nottingham was much esteemed by some on account of its sharp and poignant taste and this variety was one of the three listed by Robert Hogg in 1875, the other two being the Dutch and the Stoneless on Sans Noyau, which had very small, poorly flavoured fruits, its only virtue being its lack of seeds.

The only new variety introduced into this country during the nineteenth century was the Royal, brought over from France by Thomas Rivers in 1860, its fruits being midway in size between those of the Dutch and the Nottingham.

Today, very few medlars are planted; the days of the drinking of port with the fruit have passed and few people have ever tasted it. In any case, the profusion of more exotic fruits means that the flavour of the medlar would now hardly appeal to the modern taste. The varieties still available are those which have existed for many centuries: the Dutch, the Nottingham and the Stoneless. There are two forms of the Dutch, the Narrow-leaved and the Giant or Monstrous. Some of these varieties probably date back to Greek and Roman times and are the oldest of any of our fruits.

PROPAGATION

Throughout recorded history, the usual advice has been to propagate medlars by grafting or budding rather than by seeds, cuttings or layering. In the past, the most commonly recommended rootstock was whitethorn but Austen, in 1657, said that pear seedlings were better and produced larger trees than whitethorn. Switzer, in 1724, said that although whitethorn or service tree stocks were generally used, of late they had found grafting or budding on pear excelled all others. Hawthorn, seedling medlar and quince rootstocks have all been used and today the quince is most commonly employed.

Mulberries belong to the genus *Morus* of which two species, *M. alba* and *M. nigra*, are the ones most usually cultivated. *Morus alba*, the white mulberry, is thought to have originated in the central and eastern mountainous regions of China and to have been cultivated there for at least 5000 years for rearing silk-worms which are fed on its leaves. Apart from its use for this purpose, the white mulberry is also grown to a limited extent in many parts of the tropics for its edible fruits which may be eaten raw or cooked. The bark has been used since early times in China for making paper. There are several varieties of the white mulberry, but *M. alba multicaulis*, which has leaves which grow up to 1 ft in length, is the most popular.

Morus nigra, the common or black mulberry, which is thought to have originated in the southern Caucasus or in the mountains of Nepal, is the one more usually grown for its fruits but is not so satisfactory for feeding silk-worms. The fruits are eaten raw or made into various conserves and drinks.

In the past, mulberries were grown in Mesopotamia, where seeds of the fruits have been excavated, and they have also been found in early Egyptian tombs. The trees are mentioned in the Old Testament of the Bible when David is told by the Lord to smite the Philistines 'over against the mulberry trees', and in the Psalms, 'He destroyed their vines with hailstones, and their mulberry-trees with frost.'

For many centuries China and Persia supplied the world with silk and, as a result of their monopoly, were able to sell silk in Europe, even as late as AD 526, at a price equal to its weight in gold. Later, other countries of the Far East and India became important for their silk production.

A third species, *Morus rubra*, the red mulberry, is a native of Virginia and was brought to England in the early seventeenth century. It is principally grown for its decorative value.

MULBERRIES IN ANCIENT GREECE AND ROME

Mulberry trees were spread from Persia to Greece and Rome before the Christian era but the art of silk production was jealously guarded for many centuries by both the Chinese and the Sassanid Persians living between China and Byzantium. Silk was first brought to Greece about 200 BC from Persia and to Rome from India about 160 BC.

There is no mention of mulberries by the Greek botanist, Theophrastus, but the Greek historian Diodorus, describing life in Egypt, said there were many kinds of trees and of the fig-mulberry trees, one kind bore black mulberries and the other a fruit resembling the fig. Ovid celebrated the mulberry in his poem of Pyramus and Thisbe:

> *The whiteness of the mulberry soon fled*
> *And ripening, sadden'd in a dusky red.*

Pliny included this description of the mulberry:

> *The flesh of the mulberry contains a vinous juice, and the fruit has three successive colours, first white, then red and when ripe, black. The mulberry is one of the latest trees to blossom, but among the first to ripen. The juice of ripe mulberries stains the hands, but the stain can be washed out with the juice of unripe ones. In the case of this tree the devices of the growers have made the least improvement of any, and the mulberry of Ostia and that of Tivoli do not differ from that of Rome by named varieties or by grafting or in any other way except in the size of the fruit.*

Pliny appears to have been writing of the black mulberry, *M. nigra* and this is confirmed by his remark that it was a fruit which showed no variations except in size and that it had not been improved through selection by growers. This has always been true of the black mulberry as compared with the white mulberry of which a number of named varieties exist. Pliny was the first to write of the production of silk:

> *The silkworm in Assyria is called Bombyx when a fly; it afterwards grows to a Bomylius, and then to a Necdalus of which in six months after, come the silk worm, Bombyces. These worms spin the silk of which our expensive ladies form their costly garments and superfluous apparel, which we call Bombycinca. The first that devised the means to unwind these webs of the silkworm, and to weave the same again, was a woman in Coos, named Pamphila,*

daughter of Latous; and we must not defraud her of due honour and praise for the invention of those fine, transparent silk fabrics which instead of apparel to cover and hide, show the person through them . . .

. . . they [the silk-worms] enwrap and enfold themselves in a round ball of thread; they are then taken up and put into earthen pots, and covered with bran to keep them warm. These balls are put into moisture before they are unwound by a spindle made of some light reed, and from this is made that fine silk cloth which even men are not now ashamed to put on and use in the summer, that they may go thinly clad. How could they carry armour on their backs, their common clothing being so heavy?

However, the Emperor Tiberius passed a law forbidding men to debase themselves by wearing silk. Apart from its uses as food and for silk production, the mulberry was much used by the Romans as medicine, especially for diseases of the mouth, the uvula, the windpipe and the stomach.

THE MULBERRY IN BRITAIN

From Rome the mulberry spread to other countries of Europe, including France and Spain, and the evidence from excavations in Britain is that the fruit reached this country during the time of the Roman occupation. Seeds of the black mulberry, *Morus nigra*, were found at Silchester, and seeds were also found in excavations of the first- second- and third-century remains at New Fresh Wharf and at nearby St Thomas Street — some one hundred incidents in all. Since the fruits of the mulberry are very soft and cannot be conveyed over any distance, and as there are no records of their having been preserved by the Romans, the likelihood is that mulberries had been introduced by them to Britain.

If the mulberry had been introduced by the Romans, it may or may not have persisted until the Middle Ages when it enjoyed a period of considerable popularity. The mulberry is very long lived and individual trees are known to have lasted for over 600 years; for example, the original mulberry planted when the Drapers Hall was built in 1364 lived until 1969. It would therefore be quite possible for mulberries planted during the latter years of the Roman occupation to have lasted until Anglo-Saxon times when the tree was called, 'mon-beam'; alternatively, as it comes true from seed, it could have persisted as seedlings.

Whether this fruit had existed since Roman times or been introduced later, it occupied a place of importance in Medieval gardens as the fruit was well liked. Its juice was used for adding colour and flavour to other wines or for making wine on its own. It was also used for making 'murrey', a kind of purée or pottage to be added to various spiced meats or used as a pudding. Other uses of mulberries were as a dye, the juice being added to that of other coloured wild fruits, including the elderberry and blackberry, both to give colour to Medieval dishes and also for painting and the preparation of manuscripts.

In 1241, the clerk to Henry III paid 6s 8d for mulberry and raspberry drinks for the King. Even earlier, in the twelfth century, Gerald of Wales, after visiting Canterbury Cathedral Priory, wrote of their use of mulberries for making wine. There was a mulberry tree growing in a York garden before 1361 and they were commonly planted in the gardens of the London livery companies.

In spite of this evidence for the earlier cultivation of the mulberry in Britain, for a long time tradition had it that the first tree was planted at Syon House in London in 1548. However, by this time it was already a comparatively common tree in England as Turner, in his 1548 lists of 'new founde Herbes whereof is no mention in any other ancient wryters', said: '*Morus* is in Englishe a mulberry tree . . . it groweth in diverse gardines in Englande.' In the 1551 edition of his *Herball*, Turner again wrote of the mulberry: 'It hath flory floures / and a fruite in proportion / somethyng long, in colour / when it cometh first furth whyte / in continuance of tyme it wareth rede / and after warde when it is full rype / it is black. The fruite of ye Mulberry tre louseth ye belly, and is good for ye stomach / but it is easeli corrupt or rotten.' From these references it seems that the black mulberry must already have been fairly common in England, a fact supported by the account given by Heresbachius in 1578:

> *The Mulberie is accounted of all other trees the wisest, because he never blossometh till all cold weather been quite paste: so that whensoever you see the Mulberies begin to spryng, you maie be sure the winter is at an ende: he is ripe with the first, and buddeth out so hastily, as in one night with a noise he thrusteth out his leaves: Of the Mulberie is made a very noble medicine for the stomake, and for the Goutes thei will longest endure kept in glasses. The leaves doe serve to feede silke wormes withall, wherof some make a very great gaine, and set them rather for that purpose, then for the fruite.*

This was the first reference in English literature to the use of the mulberry for feeding silk-worms but, from this time on for at least a century, this subject was constantly discussed by writers and others. In 1597 Gerard referred to both the black and white mulberries and illustrated both:

> *The Common mulberies . . . the fruite is long like unto a black Berrie, when it is ripe blacke, yet is the juice whereof it is full, red.*

The white Mulberie tree groweth almost as big as the former — the fruit is like the former but that it is white.

The Mulberie trees growe plentifully in Italie and other hot regions, where they do maintaine great woods and groves of them, that their Silk wormes may feede thereon. The Mulberie tree is fitly set by the slips; it may also be grafted on many trees . . . white Mulberies do growe in sundrie gardens in Englande.

Although both China and Byzantium had tried to prevent the spread of the knowledge of silk production, by the eleventh century silk was already being made in Sicily and Andalusia in Spain and, in the sixteenth century, spread to Tuscany, Venetia, Lombardy, lower Piedmont and along the Rhône valley. At the end of the sixteenth century, in an attempt to encourage the cultivation of mulberries and the production of silk in France, Henry IV had mulberry trees planted in the parks and along the highways. In England, in order to help the Huguenot refugees establish a silk industry, Elizabeth I encouraged the planting of mulberry trees at Rye in Sussex. The idea of making England self-sufficient in silk also appealed to James I. In 1606 a patent was granted to M. Vetron from Picardy and Mathew Stellende to import, each year, at least one million mulberry trees of one year's growth, to encourage their planting and to sell them at not more than a penny each. The first mulberry garden was established at Charlton Park, near Blackheath in Kent.

In November 1609, James I sent a circular letter to the Lord Lieutenants of the counties of England ordering them to make public the announcement that, in March following, a thousand mulberry trees would be delivered to each county town, and all who were able were persuaded and required to buy them at the rate of ¾d a plant or 6s a hundred. He also had a treatise on the cultivation of mulberries published.

The king himself set an example by having four acres of mulberry trees planted on the site of what is now Buckingham Palace and gardens. In the Exchequer Rolls for 1608, there was an item for £1000 for trees and plants for silk-worms and £935 was spent in levelling the ground, planting the mulberry trees and walling in the area. Later, in 1618, there was another item in the Rolls for £50 to the keeper of the gardens at Theobalds for making a place for the king's silk-worms and providing mulberry leaves.

For a brief period there seemed a hope that Britain might be able to produce at least some of her requirements of silk. The king and the whole royal family so persevered in feeding their silk-worms and preparing thread that the Queen had enough silk, which she wound herself, to make some yards of taffeta, which were used to make a complete set of clothes in which she appeared at court on the occasion of the king's birthday. Unfortunately, the mulberry plants imported were of the black species, *Morus nigra*, which is not satisfactory for feeding silk-worms which live on the leaves of *M. alba*, the white type from China. This, and the fact that the merchants who had

H

been importing silk made strong representations about their likely loss of trade, resulted in the complete collapse of the project and soon virtually no silk was being produced except in the place where it began, at Charlton Park. These trees were eventually cut down and sold by auction in 1821 when their timber was found to be still in a fine state of preservation.

The royal mulberry plantation became the celebrated Mulberry Garden referred to by Samuel Pepys and John Evelyn. The latter, in his diary for 10 May 1654, wrote: 'My Lady Gerrard treated us at Mulberry Gardens, now the only place of refreshment about for persons of the best quality to be exceedingly cheated at; Cromwell and his partisans having shut up and seized on Spring Gardens.' Samuel Pepys did not visit the gardens until 20 May 1668, by which time they seemed to have deteriorated as he wrote: 'To the Mulberry-garden, where I never was before; and find it a very silly place, worse than Spring-garden, and but little company, only a wilderness here that is somewhat pretty.'

OTHER USES OF MULBERRIES

Although with the coming of the Commonwealth, the cultivation of mulberry trees for silk production disappeared, there was still some interest in the fruit. Austen said it could be used to make wine or a spoonful of the juice would colour a quart of white wine or cider, this being a time when there was much adulteration of wine and the passing off of cider and perry as wine. A method of propagating mulberries was described in the *French Gardiner*, in 1669. This involved taking an old well-rope, rubbing it with ripe mulberry fruits and then burying the rope in the ground.

Several writers still hoped that the planting of mulberries for silk production might be revived. Worlidge thought that if the King or some other landowner did this, it would be an example to others. Bradley in 1739, after remarking that the mulberry fruit was so tender that it would not bear the most gentle carriage without bruising, also hoped that this country would follow Italy, where mulberry trees for feeding silk-worms were planted along the roads and in every vacant corner of their ground. Gerard had commented on the extensive planting of mulberries in Italy in 1597 so that this was a well-established industry there. In 1827, Phillips suggested the planting of mulberry trees on many parts of the South Downs, particularly in the vicinity of Brighton where, he said, less was done in the way of improving the neighbourhood by planting than in any other part of the kingdom.

Forsyth, in 1824, said that he thought mulberries had been introduced into cultivation in England earlier than was generally accepted, that is in the sixteenth century, as very old mulberry trees were often found growing in the gardens of ancient monasteries, abbeys and priories and had probably been planted there before the Dissolution.

The collection of mulberries in the garden of the Horticultural Society at Chiswick included five kinds in 1826, but the catalogue of 1831 stated that the Common or Black mulberry was the only one worth growing. Robert Hogg, in 1875, confirmed that this was the only one then grown in England but it was only in the southern counties that it ripened satisfactorily out in the open and in the Midlands needed the protection of a wall. It also cropped very satisfactorily trained as small bushes or as pyramids grown under glass.

During the present century very few black mulberries have been planted for their fruit alone though they are sometimes grown for their ornamental value. The same applies to the red mulberry, *Morus rubra*, a native of Virginia which Tradescant imported early in the seventeenth century. While the production of silk in Britain virtually disappeared during the nineteenth century, there was a minor revival during this century by Lady Hart-Dyke at Lullingstone Castle in Kent. However, the chance of any major attempt at the revival of the silk industry in England, such as was attempted by James I, seems most remote, though many of the trees planted in his time remain as a tribute to his initiative.

The common quince belongs to the genus *Cydonia oblonga*. Its origin is not known with any certainty but it occurs wild in Turkestan and Transcaucasia where many variations are found growing in the mountainous regions. It is also found wild in Persia, near the Caspian Sea, in Anatolia and grows on the banks of the Danube. Although now only cultivated to a limited extent in Britain, it was grown much more from the sixteenth to eighteenth centuries when it was commonly used for making quince marmalade which was also popular in other countries of Europe. Today, in Spain, the quince is much used for making a jelly, *membrillo*. It is also still an important fruit in southern Russia and countries of the Middle East. In France, it is cultivated extensively in the Angers area, especially for providing rootstocks for pears.

THE QUINCE IN ANTIQUITY

The quince seems to have been first cultivated in Mesopotamia and grew abundantly in Crete whence, according to Pliny, it was introduced into Greece. It derived its name, *Cydonia*, from the city of Cydonea, now Canea, a city on the island.

It was highly regarded by the ancient Greeks and Romans and was considered an emblem of happiness, love and fruitfulness. The quince was dedicated to Venus and the temples of Cyprus and Paphos were decorated with it. According to Plutarch, Solon enacted a law that this fruit should be the invariable feast of every newly wedded pair before they retired to the marriage bed.

The Greek botanist, Theophrastus, writing that plants propagated by cuttings or suckers are similar to their parents but when propagated from seeds could be of a wild type, said this applied to the quince. This establishes the existence of the quince in Greece in his time.

The Roman writers described quinces as 'apples', and Cato advised planting or grafting various kinds of fruits for preserving, including Sparrow-apples, Scantian and Quirinian quinces as well as the Must apple, another form of quince. Pliny had more to say about quinces:

> *There are several kinds of quinces; the Golden apple is cleft with incisions and has a colour verging on gold, a brighter tinge of which gives a name to our native quince and has an excellent scent. The Naples quince is also highly esteemed. The smaller variety of the same kind, the Sparrow-apple, gives out a rather pungent smell, and ripens late, whereas the Must quince ripens very early.*
>
> *Grafting the ordinary quince on the Sparrow-apple, produced a special kind of Mulvian quince, which is the only one of the quinces that is eaten raw; these at the present day are kept shut up in the gentlemen's reception rooms, and are placed on the statues that share our nights with us. There is also a small wild quince, the scent of which is the most powerful next to that of the Sparrow-apple and which grows in the hedges.*

The scent of the quince was also appreciated by the natives of Mesopotamia, where, in the region of Baghdad, it was the custom to place a highly perfumed quince fruit in their tents.

The Romans were especially adept at preserving all kinds of fruits and vegetables for use throughout the year. Columella recommended the Sparrow-apple, the Golden quince and the Must and gave detailed instructions for their storage:

> *Many people keep quinces in pits or barrels in the same manner as they preserve pomegranates. Some tie them up in fig-leaves and then knead potter's clay with lees of oil and smear the quinces with it and, when they are dry, store them in a cool, dry loft. Others put these same fruits into new pans and cover them up with dry plaster in such a way that they do not touch one another.*
>
> *Nevertheless we have not experienced any more sure and satisfactory method than, when the weather is calm and the moon waning, to pick quinces which are very ripe, sound and without blemish and, after wiping off the down which is upon them, to arrange them lightly and loosely, so that they may not be bruised, in a new flagon with a very wide mouth; then, when they have been stowed in up to the neck in the vessel, they should be confined with willow twigs laid across them in such a way that they compass the fruit slightly and do not allow them to be lifted up when they have liquid poured upon them.*

*Then the vessel should be filled up to the top with the very best
and most liquid honey, so that the fruit is submerged. This method
not only preserves the fruit itself, but also provides a liquor which
has the flavour of honey-water and can, without danger, be given at
their meals to sufferers from fever. It is called melomeli. But care
must be taken that the fruit which you wish to preserve in honey is
not stored before it is ripe; for if it is picked when it is unripe, it
becomes so hard as not to be fit to use.*

This method of using honey to preserve quinces was also used for other
crops.

QUINCES IN BRITAIN

Although the quince was a fruit of importance in ancient Greece and Rome,
no evidence of its remains has been found on prehistoric or Roman sites in
Britain. It was included in the list of fruits in the *Capitulare de Villis* of
Charlemagne in AD 800, but the first record of its cultivation in Britain was
not until after the Norman Conquest. The quince seems to have been popular
with Edward I and his household, as one of the first references to it in
England was an account, in 1275, for four quince trees planted in the royal
gardens of the Tower of London. These cost 6d each, a fairly high price and
the same as peach trees. Their fruits must have been liked by the royal
family as more quince trees were planted in 1292, along with apples and
pears, in the king's gardens at Westminster. For these quince trees, the price
was 41s per 100, slightly cheaper than 17 years earlier, perhaps a reduction
for quantity! In 1372 Chaucer wrote of the 'coyne' or quince, in his *Roman
de la Rose*, indicating that it was being grown in his time.

The quince had a number of uses in Medieval kitchens, for example for
marmalade, jellies and in candied form. The recipe for quince marmalade
required that the peeled and quartered fruits were boiled in red wine,
strained, boiled again in concentrated honey, with the addition of hippocras
(spiced wine) and, after cooling and setting, sliced up into pieces and served
as a sweet in the same way as *membrillo,* quince jelly, is in Spain today.

In the Middle Ages, the quince was usually grown in the gardens of the
wealthy who had probably seen it growing on the Continent and introduced
it into their English gardens, but its popularity must have increased over the
following centuries as it was mentioned by all the authors of books on fruit
culture in the sixteenth century. Mascall in 1575 said that quinces might be
propagated from cuttings or, with great difficulty, might be budded on the
whitethorn. The account given by Heresbachius in 1578 gave advice on their

storage and the making of marmalade very similar to that of earlier centuries:

> To keepe Quinces, they are best coffened betwixt two hollowe Tiles, well closed on every side with claie: some lai them onely in drie places, where no winde cometh: others keepe them in Chaffe and Wheate: many in honie, some in Wine, and maketh the Wine more pleasante. There is made a kinde of Wine of Quinces (beeyng beaten and pressed) and a little Honie and Oile put into it: our countrey men make of them a precious Conserve and Marmelade, beeyng congealed with long seethyng, and boiled with Sugar, Wine and Spices.

Tusser, in 1580, included quinces in his list of fruits to be grown in the garden. Gerard, in 1597, though he said there were a number of different types of quince, did not give names of individual varieties. Like Heresbachius, he emphasized the use of the quince in the kitchen and gave a recipe for quince marmalade. He said many other excellent, dainty and wholesome confections such as jellies, could be made from quince.

THE SEVENTEENTH CENTURY

Gerard's enthusiasm for the quince was echoed by Parkinson. He wrote that no other fruit had so many uses both for meat dishes and for sweet courses. He was the first English writer to name different varieties: the English or Apple, the Portingall Apple, Portingall Pear, the Barberry, Lyons and Brunswicke quinces. The pear-shaped Portingall or Portugal quince had been imported in 1611 by Tradescant and was to become one of the most valuable right up to the present day. In 1665, John Rea said that the Portugal pear quince was ideal for baking and preserving and the Portugal apple quince had a large yellow fruit which was apt to split but was so tender it had to be eaten raw. The Lions had large fruits of a deep yellow colour with ribbed sides and the Brunswick was large and round with a whiter fruit than any other variety.

In spite of the availability of some of the best varieties of quinces and their increasing importance in the seventeenth century, cultivation in Britain was not sufficient to meet the demand as, according to Samuel Hartlib in 1652, this fruit was still imported from Flanders along with fruits from other countries and for this he blamed poor husbandry at home. At this time Austen suggested that quinces could be kept for one or two years, by putting them in a barrel, covering them with perry or ale and then, after 10—12 days, drawing it off and putting in fresh ale, repeating this from time to time.

ROOTSTOCKS

The quince has been used as a rootstock for pears for many centuries, being recommended by Mascall in 1575. It had been used in France even earlier where, in the Angers region, the cultivation of quinces and their propagation has been a major industry for many centuries; many millions of quince rootstocks have been exported from this area to all parts of the world.

The recommendations for quince propagation have always included the use of cuttings and layering. The *French Gardiner* in 1669 described how a quince plant, cleared of all small branches, should be earthed up like a molehill, leaving the ends of the other branches uncovered and these would strike root the same year. These rooted shoots were either transplanted or budded *in situ* with pear. This method of layering the shoots growing from the parent plant is the basis of the stooling system used today.

MODERN QUINCE CULTIVATION

The popularity of quinces continued into the eighteenth century. Switzer wrote that there was not a more delicate fruit for use in the kitchen or for making into conserves. The Portugal apple and pear quinces were still considered among the best. William Forsyth at the beginning of the nineteenth century advised adding some Portugal quinces to apples which had been kept for so long that they had lost their flavour, in order to add piquancy to pies and puddings.

Phillips in 1827 wrote that quinces grew in such abundance in Sussex that private families were able to make up to 200 gallons of quince wine which was of particular benefit to people with asthma but, apart from this, the quince was not so widely cultivated as in the past. The decline of the quince seems to have coincided with the increase in the cultivation of soft fruits, particularly the strawberry. The decline continued throughout the nineteenth century, although quinces were still grown on a limited scale for market and, more generally, in the larger private gardens. In 1826, the Horticultural Society's collection of fruits included six varieties but Robert Hogg, in 1875, only mentioned three: the Apple shaped, Pear shaped and the Portugal, which he considered the best but a poor cropper.

While there was diminishing interest in England, the cultivation of quinces in the United States became more general and most gardens had their quince trees. The enthusiasm for this fruit of the Rev. W. W. Meech resulted in his selection of a seedling, apparently raised in Connecticut before 1850 and which had been distributed under the name of Orange quince, a general name in America for the Apple quince. The superiority of the new quince resulted in a world-wide demand for it under its new name of Meech's Prolific.

In 1925, Edward Bunyard listed the Bereczki variety, larger than the Portugal and which had been grown in the Balkans for a long period, having been named after Bereczki, an eminent Hungarian pomologist. This variety had been imported with two others, Lescovatz and Vranja; of these three, only Vranja from Serbia is still among the few quince varieties recommended for use in gardens. The other two are the Pear shaped and the Portugal.

Lack of general interest in the use of the quince has meant that plant breeders in Britain have paid no attention to improving this fruit, but the quince is still of major importance in some countries of Europe and in Russia numerous varieties are still grown. The major use of the quince in Britain today is as a rootstock for pears. For several centuries these were imported mainly from the Angers area and simply known as the 'Angers' but, as Hatton found out when studying rootstocks at East Malling, the variability of these stocks could affect tree growth and performance. Hatton selected a number of the stocks which he tested, the principal ones distributed by the Research Station being Quince A, B and C. In commercial practice, little difference was found between Quince A and B and the former became the main rootstock for pears in Britain and several other countries. Quince C has a somewhat dwarfing effect on the tree and, since being freed of viruses, has come into more general use. Other quince rootstocks are being tested in Britain and on the Continent.

HAZEL NUTS **25**

The genus *Corylus*, the hazel, includes 15 species distributed throughout the temperate regions of the northern hemisphere. The one native to Europe, including Britain, west Asia and north Africa, is *Corylus avellana*, the common hazel or cob nut. It grows in woods and thickets in all parts of this area and in central and Russian Asia excepting the extreme north. Like many other fruits, *C. avellana* is found extensively in the Caucasus where this species shows exceptional diversity of form.

The other important species, a native of south-east Europe, but not of Britain, is *Corylus maxima*, the parent of the filberts cultivated in England. This species is distinguished from the common hazel and its derivatives, the cob nuts, by the length of its husk or beard which protrudes well beyond the nut and often encloses it.

HAZEL NUTS IN ANTIQUITY

The pollen, wood and fruits of *C. avellana* have been frequently identified among remains from previous ages, especially in post-glacial deposits in Britain. These are probably the most commonly found plant remains in peat and alluvial deposits and it is apparent that this plant was well established in Britain before this country became separated from the Continent.

On many Mesolithic and later human settlements in Europe, such as the Swiss prehistoric lake dwellings, hazel nuts have been found in considerable quantities and were obviously collected for food, as they doubtless were in prehistoric Britain. It has been suggested that they provided a source of food later taken by cereals.

Remains of hazel nuts have been found on many sites of the Neolithic,

Early Bronze and Iron Ages and Roman Britain. Apart from the apparent widespread use of the nuts as food, the branches and shoots of the plants were used in the Late Bronze Age for making roads and track ways, as has been found at Blakeway Farm in Somerset, where faggots consisting of straight hazel branches had been laid side by side to form a track. The hazel bushes on the slopes of the Wedmore Ridge and Mendip Hills were cut back, or coppiced, during the Bronze Age and this provided a plentiful supply of shoots for the many and varied uses to which they were put at this time and in later centuries. These uses included making baskets and containers of all kinds, walking sticks and fishing rods, poles, spars, hoops, forks and cudgels, and the smaller shoots for making withes, bands, springs to catch birds, and springles to fasten down thatch. Where yeast was scarce, hazel twigs might be twisted and steeped in the ale during fermentation, then hung up to dry and later put into the new 'wort' or malt before the next fermentation.

CULTIVATION OF NUTS IN GREECE AND ITALY

The Greek, Theophrastus, was the first to write of hazel nuts:

> *The hazel is naturally a wild tree, in that its fruit is little, if at all, inferior to that of the tree in cultivation, that it can stand winter, it grows commonly in the mountains and it bears abundance of fruit in mountain regions. The cultivated form differs in producing better fruit and larger leaves. There are two kinds of each sort; some have a round, others an oblong nut; that of the cultivated form is paler and it fruits best in damp places.*

The oblong-shaped nuts, known as the Heraclean nuts, had probably been introduced to Greece from ancient Heraclea, now Ponderactie on the Black Sea, Pontus Euxinus. Pliny wrote of the nut:

> *The Hazel is a sort of nut, the previous form of its name having been Abellina after the name of its place of origin (Abella in Campania); but it came into Asia and Greece from Pontus and is consequently also called the Pontic nut. This nut is protected by a soft beard, but the shell and kernel are formed of one solid round piece.*

These nuts, which had reached Italy from Greece or direct from Pontus, were grown on a considerable scale in the valleys in the region of Avellino near Naples and gave their name to the species. In Spain, the name for the hazel nut is also 'avellana'; Miller, in the eighteenth century, said that the nuts growing around Avellino were of the variety he called 'Spanish'.

The Byzantine nut, *Corylus colurna*, which is grown extensively in Turkey, was brought to Italy from Constantinople before Constantine had given the city its name. Pliny said that it had been brought by Vitellius a short time before the death of the Emperor Tiberius and that Flasscu Pompeius, who served in the wars with Vitellius, carried the nuts to Spain. There were later grown in great quantities there and were shipped abroad from Barcelona and so became known as Barcelona nuts. Some botanists have given the name *Corylus barcelonensis* to this type which has large, broad nuts which the husk does not envelop.

The reference by Theophrastus to two kinds of cultivated and two kinds of wild nuts suggests that one of these was the hazel nut and the other, the longer, oblong type, the filbert, *C. maxima*. This latter was probably the type imported from Pontus which Pliny said was protected by a soft beard. The wild hazel was already widespread in Greece and Italy so would not have created any interest if brought in from another country.

Besides saying that the improved nuts had come from Pontus, Pliny wrote that Cato had spoken of a smooth, hard kind of hazel nut, the Palestrina, which he had praised very highly and said could be kept fresh by being put in a pot and buried in the ground.

It was the custom among the Romans for a bridegroom, on his wedding night, to scatter nuts among the boys, indicating that he had dropped boyish amusements and, thenceforth, was to act as a man, doubtless a fertility symbol. Hazel nuts were included in the food of the Roman troops, both in other countries of Europe and in Britain where remains of them have been found at Newstead, near Melrose, at Holt, Slack and Castleshaw and other sites; they had probably been picked locally.

Hazel nuts also featured in Charlemagne's *Capitulare de Villis* in AD 800.

The Hazel Nut in Britain

For many centuries the common hazel nut, wild in the woodlands and coppices of Britain, was harvested by country people and taken to the local markets and in large quantities up to London. Owing to the frequency with which the nuts of the wild plants have been found in excavations of past habitations, it is impossible to say at what time the improved cultivated forms were first introduced. Also, since the hazel grew so freely, it is not surprising that there are virtually no references to the nuts in the accounts of the royal families or in the poems of the early English writers.

One of the earliest references to the filbert nut was in *The Grete Herball* of Peter Treueris in 1526: 'Fylberdes Avelanan. Avelana ben fylberdes / and ben colder than hasyll nottes / theye savour is more pontyke / and hevy / and more tycher than the small nottes be and ben of slower dygestyon and ben later.' Another early reference to the hazel nut was in Turner's list of herbs in 1548 but his remarks were very brief, simply that *Corylus* was called hazel in English and *avellon* in Latin. Tusser, in 1573, included red and white 'filbeardes' in his list of fruits to be grown in the garden, and in 1575 Mascall suggested taking suckers from the roots of the 'hasel' nut for propagation. Heresbachius in 1578 wrote:

> Among Nuttes, is also to bee recounted the Hasell Nuttes, a kinde whereof is the Filberte called in Latine Avellàna; thei are planted after the maner of the Almonde; it delighteth in claie and watrishe groundes, and upon hilles, beeing well able to abide the colde. Thei were first brought into Asia and Greece from Pontus and therefore called Pontice and Heracleotice.

The name filbert seems to have been given to those nuts with long husks covering the fruits, their 'full beards', to separate this type from the common hazel or cob. In the sixteenth century, this was corrupted to 'filberd' or 'Philberte' but though the name 'filbert' was already in use by the end of the seventeenth century, 'Philbeard' was still used by Switzer in 1724. Others have thought that there is a connection between the feast of St Philibert on 22 August and the onset of the nut harvest, but this seems unlikely.

NEW VARIETIES

In 1597, Gerard had more to say about the varieties of nuts:

> Corylus sylvestris *is our hedge Nut or Hasell Nut tree, which is very well knowen, and therefore needeth not any description: whereof there are also sundrie sorts, some great, some little, some rathe ripe, some later, as also one that is manured in our gardens, which is very great, bigger than any Filberd, and yet a kinde of Hedge Nut.*
>
> The Filberd tree is properly that which groweth in gardens and orchards. These Nuts that have their skins red are the garden and planted Nuts and the right Pontike Nuts or Filberds; they are called in English Filberds and red Filberds. The other Nuts which be white are judged to be wilde.

Gerard included illustrations of three kinds of nuts which he named '*Nux Avellana Corylus,* the Filberd Nut, *Corylus sylvestris,* the wilde Hedge Nut and *Avellana pumila Byzantia,* the Filberd nut of Constantinople'. The picture of the first nut shows a typical filbert with the husk covering the whole nut, and the wild hedge nut is also typical of the wild hazel of today. This is also the first reference in an English book to the filbert from

Constantinople, also known as the Byzantine, *Corylus colurna*, unusual for a hazel in growing to a tree, 70−80 ft in height. These records contradict statements made by writers in the past that the first filberts were brought to England in 1759 and show that, by the end of the sixteenth century, gardeners in Britain had all the types of hazel nuts and filberts from which subsequent varieties were developed.

Parkinson said that filberts grown in orchards were very similar to wild hazel nuts but there were in addition a round kind that came from Constantinople and the Virginian hazel that had smaller, rounder and thinner shelled nuts, though he did not know if anyone had yet planted this. The Virginian hazel was *Corylus americana* which had been imported early in the seventeenth century when there was great interest in obtaining new plants from overseas.

John Rea, in 1665, included five varieties, 'the White filbert, the Red filbert of Constantinople, the Great Round, the Great Long and the Soft Shelled'. But, in spite of the availability of more varieties from the Continent, the main ones grown in gardens were still the red- and white-skinned filberts and these were the only ones mentioned by Austen in 1657 and Worlidge in 1697. Switzer, in 1724, wrote in praise of the filbert from Constantinople, saying that the nuts were much larger than most other varieties. The nuts from Barcelona, much sold in London, were valuable as they were available all winter after the home-grown filberts had been finished. In England this variety was sometimes raised from nuts freshly imported from Spain and could produce a fine timber tree.

In 1729, the nurseryman, Batty Langley, only listed three varieties of filberts, the red and white and a large one he called the Cob-nut, while the nurserymen, Luker and Smith of Covent Garden in 1783 still only sold red and white filberts.

COMMERCIAL PRODUCTION OF NUTS

Although there may not have been very much interest in the planting of new varieties of nuts in the eighteenth century, there was considerable extension in their cultivation for market. As early as the mid-seventeenth century, John Evelyn in his *Sylva* wrote of the production of nuts on commercial farms in Kent. He described how the bushes were planted 12 ft apart and limited, by pruning, to 5 ft in height and trained with an open centre in the same way that nuts have been grown on farms in Kent right up to the middle of this century.

In the area of Kent around Maidstone, filberts played a major part in the economy of the district. In Boys' report on the agriculture of the county in 1794, he wrote that it was common practice to plant hops, apples, cherries

Plate LVII.

White Philbert.
July 15. 1727.

Fig: I.

A

Fig: II.

Hazel .nut.
July 20. 1727.

B

Fig: III.

Cob:nut
July 20.
1727.

Black Mulberry
July 10. 1727.

Fig III

D

T. Bowles Sculp

Nuts and mulberries were very popular in the Middle Ages and both fruits were commonly planted in large gardens in the later centuries.

and filberts all together, 800 hop hills, 200 filberts and 40 apple and cherry trees. The hops were grown for about 12 years before being grubbed, and the filberts for 30, by which time the apples and cherries required the whole land.

Boys added that there were several hundred acres of filberts in the Maidstone district. Of the crop, a small part was sold to the higlers who retailed them in different parts of the country, but most of them were conveyed by water up the Thames to London and sent to factors who sold them by the hundred pounds at prices from 16s to 42s per hundred.

Phillips, in 1827, praised the Kent nuts which he said were of excellent quality and which, if quite ripe, would keep for several years in a dry room. In addition to the nuts from Kent, great quantities of Barcelona nuts were imported each year.

VARIETIES IN THE NINETEENTH CENTURY

Although there was much planting of nuts in Kent during the eighteenth century, the varieties used were still the Red- and White-skinned filberts, the Aveline Rouge and the Aveline Blanche Longue, both of which had been leading varieties for several centuries. In 1806, Forsyth listed the varieties most commonly grown in England, as the large Cob-nuts, the large Long nuts, the Barcelona or Spanish, the common wood nuts with red-skinned kernels, the large cluster wood nut and the filbert with red kernels.

The increased interest in the breeding and introduction of new varieties of most fruits at the beginning of the nineteenth century extended to nuts. The thin-shelled Cosford was introduced in 1816 at Ipswich and proved to be of excellent quality and very useful for pollinating other varieties with little pollen. It is still one of the most important varieties today. However, the most outstanding variety to be introduced at this time was Lambert's Filbert, which became known as Kentish Cob, though the name cob was incorrectly applied to the nut as it is an excellent filbert. It is usually said to have been raised by Mr Lambert of Goudhurst, Kent and to have been introduced about 1830, but Robert Hogg in 1875 said he was not sure whether the variety had been raised or only introduced by another Lambert, Aylmer Bourke Lambert of Boynton, Wiltshire, but it was through him that it was first brought to the notice of the Horticultural Society about 1812.

Kentish Cob was soon planted on a large scale in Kent and took the place of the Kent Filbert which was the old white-skinned filbert. It is still regarded as the best all-purpose variety, both for gardens and commercial production. Of the other new nuts introduced during the nineteenth century, although a few came from the Continent, most of the successful ones were raised in England. Richard Webb of Calcot near Reading was an amateur who took a great interest in breeding new nuts which he grew in his old walled garden. Two successful varieties were Daviana and Garibaldi, both good-quality filberts, while Webb's Prize was claimed to be of better flavour than Kentish Cob. The Duke of Edinburgh, raised by Webb but introduced by his successor and son-in-law, T. O. Cooper, was considered the best of his seedlings, especially suited to the garden.

Pearson's Prolific was raised at Newark, Nottinghamshire, and introduced by Messrs Pearson of Chilwell, and Prolific Filbert was a free-cropping variety of unknown origin. Bergeri was introduced by Jacob Mackoy of Liege about 1860–70 and, besides being of good quality, was useful as it opened its catkins early and so could spread the pollination season.

The increase in the number of cob nut and filbert varieties available in the nineteenth century is shown by the fact that by 1875, Lawson's fruit catalogue included 26 distinct varieties as compared with two in Luker and Smith's list about 90 years earlier, though many in Lawson's collection were little planted. It included the ancient varieties Barcelona, Constantinople, Frizzled Filbert and the Red- and White-skinned and the Purple-leaved filberts.

MODERN HAZEL NUT CULTIVATION

Although considerable quantities of cob nuts and filberts were still grown for market in Kent at the beginning of the century, much of the crop being exported to the United States, there was a gradual decline in their acreage from that time. Even in the 1920s some of the farms near Maidstone had as many as 50 acres of nuts, with some plants over 100 years old and still cropping well. Changes in the establishment of apple and cherry orchards and hop gardens and the high cost of the management of nut plantations, involving much hand work, together with the considerable cost of harvesting, made their production increasingly uneconomic. Today, nut culture for market is in the hands of a few specialist growers and the main supplies of nuts on the market still come from Italy and Spain.

Where these nuts are still grown, Kentish Cob, often with Cosford as a pollinator, is still the main variety. Some others have been tried but mostly given up, especially for commercial production. As with the less important fruits, no breeding of new varieties has been undertaken by research stations in Britain. Although cob nuts and filberts are self-fertile, lack of sufficient catkins or poor overlap with the appearance of the female flowers may make it necessary to include a second variety with better pollen production.

In the United States, where some 120 varieties have been tested, few are of commercial importance; of these, Barcelona and Daviana are two grown in Oregon, and in New York varieties suggested include Cosford, Barcelona,

Kentish Cob and White, Red and Purple Aveline. This shows that in America, as in England, there has been little change in the varieties grown for well over a century and these differ less from those which have been popular in the past than is with the case with any other fruit.

WALNUTS

The common walnut, *Juglans regia*, which makes a tree 60—100 ft high, is found growing wild over a wide area of south-east Europe, the Middle East, especially Persia, and grows freely in the forests of Turkestan, in the Caucasus and in Afghanistan. Evidence that the nuts were used as food by prehistoric peoples has come from remains found in Mesolithic middens and among debris from Swiss lake village sites.

Walnuts have been cultivated for several thousand years in Persia, and from there their cultivation spread to Syria and the Lebanon. They became an important article of food throughout the Middle East with the export centres in Persia and Damascus. In pre-Biblical times their cultivation began in Palestine; here they were grown in the coastal region, the hills of Galilee and the Jordan valley. Although constant high temperatures do not suit walnuts, by growing them under the shade of date palms they cropped satisfactorily.

Walnuts were commonly grown in ancient Greece and Italy. Pliny wrote:

> *The Greek name for the walnut proves that it was sent to us from Persia by their kings, the best kind of walnuts being called in Greek, the 'Persian', and the 'Royal', which were their original names. The Romans honoured them with the name of 'Jovis-glans' [Juglans], acorn or mast of Jove.*
>
> *The only difference between the various kinds of walnuts consists in the hardness or brittleness of the shell and in its being thin or thick and full of recesses or uniform. It is generally agreed that the Caryon walnut gets its name from the headache that it causes because of the oppressive scent. The shell of the walnut is used for dyeing wool, and the young nuts, while just forming, supply a red*

hair dye. This was discovered from their staining the hands when handled.

The walnut has won from the service-berry, in point of size, the place that it has yielded to it in popularity, although the walnut also accompanies the Fescennine songs sung at weddings.

Pliny's reference to the use of walnuts at weddings was to the custom of the bridegroom throwing the nuts among the boys carrying the torches as the bride approached. He considered this to be a fertility symbol. The Fescennine songs were scurrilous satires named after Fescennia, a town of Etruria.

Walnuts were regarded as a delicacy in Rome, and remains of them found among the ruins of the Temple of Isis in Pompeii were part of a meal left behind at the time of the volcanic eruption. In Pliny's time the walnut had many medicinal uses, including that, if eaten before meals, of lessening the effects of poisoned food. After Mithridates of Pontus was beaten by the Roman Lucullus in 73 BC, Cnaius Pompeius found, in his secret cabinet, the recipe for a certain antidote against poison: 'Take two dry walnut kernels, as many figs, of rue twenty leaves; stamp all these together into one mass, with a grain or corn of salt. Whoever eats of this confection in a morning, fasting, no poison shall hurt him that day.'

WALNUTS IN BRITAIN

Grains of *Juglans regia* pollen have been excavated from several sites suggesting the introduction of the plant in late post-glacial times, but there is no evidence of remains of any nuts until the time of the Roman occupation. Away from Rome, walnuts were included in the diet of the troops in various parts of Europe, such as Vindonissa and Saalburg. In London, remains of shells have been found on several Roman sites at New Fresh Wharf but, though it has been suggested that walnuts may have been grown in Britain by the Romans, there is no proof of this. It is probable that these nuts were imported.

The general view has been that walnuts were introduced into Britain from France during the fifteenth or sixteenth century, but the evidence is that walnuts were grown here long before then and that the nuts were in common use several centuries earlier. An Anglo-Saxon glossary of the eleventh century includes the name then in current use for the walnut. This, over the following centuries, took various forms of 'walsh nutte', the nut from the Roman lands (Gaul and Italy), as distinct from the native hazel nut.

The accounts for the gardens of the Earl of Lincoln in Holborn, rendered by his sergeant for the year 1295–6, include an item of £9 for pears, apples and 'great nuts' (walnuts) sold from the garden. The Durham Account Rolls for 1358 — 9 include 'walnottes' and those for 1368 — 9 have an item, '2000 de Walsnotes in precio 2s 6d'. Chaucer also mentioned walnuts.

There are other records of walnuts having been grown in the Middle Ages, including their various culinary uses in making fruit pies and sweet and sour meat dishes, some of these being described in *Two Cookery Books* of 1430. Walnut oil was valued both for cooking and in cosmetics, and their shells provided a black hair dye.

The *Holinshed Chronicles* of 1580 included walnuts among the new varieties of fruits imported within the previous 40 years, in comparison with which the old trees were worthless. It therefore seems that walnuts had been grown in Britain for several centuries but that better kinds were imported, together with other new fruits, during the reign of Henry VIII.

THE SIXTEENTH AND SEVENTEENTH CENTURIES

The first references to walnuts in the early printed herbals show that the writers were familiar with them and did not regard the nuts as a recently introduced novelty. Peter Treueris in the *Grete Herball*, 1526, wrote: 'The wal nuttes ben of two meners for some be drye and some be grene. The grene be not so hote as the drye / and have a certayne moysture bycause they be not perfectly rype.' Walnuts were thus already used either green or left to mature. Turner in his Herbal of 1568 said: 'The walnut and walnut trees are so well knowne in all countries / that I nede not to describe / wherefore I entende to leave the description and to go to properties of it. Walnuttes are hard of digestion / not good for the stomake / and ingendre choler / and they make y head ache. They are evell for them that have the coughe.'

By the end of the sixteenth century, walnut trees were planted both in the open country and in orchards, as Gerard in 1597 wrote: 'The Walnut tree groweth in fields neere common high waies in a fat and fruitful ground, and in orchards; it prospereth on high fruitfull banks; it love not to growe in waterie places.' Gerard did not mention any different varieties of the walnut but his remarks show that the trees must have been well established over many years since they are very slow growing. He also accepted the old Roman idea that walnuts gave protection to those who ate them as he wrote that the dried nuts, taken while fasting, with a fig and a little rue, gave protection against poison and also against infection by the plague, while walnuts with onions, salt and honey laid on the wounds, prevented infection from the bite of a mad dog or mad man!

The first reference to the possibility of different varieties of walnuts was made by Parkinson in 1629:

Some doe thinke there are many sorts of them, because some are

greater than others and some longer than others but I am persuaded
that the soyle and climate where they growe, are the whole and only
cause the varieties differeth. Indeed, Virginia hath sent unto us two
sorts of Wallnuts, the one blacke and the other white whereof, as
yet, we have no further knowledge.

All walnuts at this time were propagated from their nuts and so naturally
there would be variations in their progeny. It was the difficulty of vegetative
propagation which delayed the selection of improved forms of walnuts, other
than the few which came relatively true from seed, for several centuries. The
Virginian black walnut was *Juglans nigra.*

Nux Iuglans.
The Walnut tree.

For many centuries walnuts were
grown from seed, so distinct,
named varieties were uncommon
unless imported. The trees
were as important for their
timber as their nuts.

Although walnut trees were being grown for their nuts on a limited scale
in Britain during the first half of the seventeenth century, their cropping was
severely limited by their susceptibility to damage from spring frosts, and the
London markets were largely supplied with nuts from Italy where they were
a much more important and reliable crop. In 1652, Samuel Hartlib
complained about these imports, saying that the production of walnuts in
Britain was neglected.

OTHER USES OF THE WALNUT

The wood of the walnut has always been regarded as of particular value for making the butts of guns and for certain types of furniture, and John Evelyn encouraged the planting of walnut trees for this purpose in his *Sylva* in 1664. Walnut trees were already growing on the chalk hills of Surrey earlier in the seventeenth century but much of the timber had been used up or destroyed during the troubled times of the Commonwealth and Evelyn set an example by planting walnuts on one of his family's estates at Godstone. In his diary he wrote that many of his friends in Surrey were making a great deal of money from their walnuts and thousands of trees were planted around Carshalton, both in avenues and in plantations on their own.

To further his argument, Evelyn wrote that were walnut timber more readily available, it could be used for making better-quality chairs, stools, bedsteads, tables and cabinets, in place of the more vulgar beech which was often counterfeited as walnut by being washed over with a decoction made of green walnut husks. At this time, walnuts were being grown so widely on the Continent in France, Germany and Italy that the timber there was used for panelling and other purposes in the houses of rich and poor alike and was valued for the wheels and bodies of coaches as well as for the butts of guns. In Germany no young farmer was allowed to marry until he had planted a stated number of walnut trees.

Apart from the value of the timber, the fruits also had many uses. Walnut oil was used by painters for mixing white and other delicate colours, for gold size and for varnish. It was used for burning in lamps and as a substitute for butter. Even the husks and leaves, macerated in warm water and poured over grass walks and bowling greens, were used to kill earth worms. The dye made from this mixture could be used to colour wood, hair and wood, while the green husks, if boiled, made a good, dark yellow colouring.

Worlidge, in 1697, was also enthusiastic about planting walnuts and said, as did other writers, that the progeny of thick-shelled walnuts produced the best timber and the thinner-shelled ones, the best nuts. He said that if the markets were over-supplied, the surplus nuts could be used, as in Normandy, for extracting oil to be used by the limners and for burning in lamps. He wrote that Petersfield, his home town in Hampshire, was celebrated for its walnuts, in particular for a thin-shelled variety which had as pleasant a taste as any and was ripe about a fortnight before any other. He had not seen it growing anywhere else.

THE EIGHTEENTH CENTURY

The campaigns for the greater planting of walnuts waged by John Evelyn and others in the seventeenth century seem to have been successful as Switzer in 1724 spoke of those growing about Ewell near Epsom and in many parts of Surrey and his native Hampshire. Writing of different types of walnuts, he said:

> *Of these there are several Kinds, some being larger, others thinner shell'd than the Common, but differ so little from another, that Men have not minded giving them Names; neither is it worth while, since we learn from Experience, that there is no Kind of Fruit so variable as Walnuts are, it being seldom known that one Kind that is sown produces the same Sort, but alters and changes its Nature, which in some Measure is the Case of all Fruits sown. The largest Sort is usually called the French Walnut. The best are those of a tender thin Shell, of a full Kernel, and a Middle size. These are raised by Nuts gathered from the same Tree.*

Switzer's comments emphasize the problem of propagating walnuts which has faced growers at all times in Britain, right up to this century — that is, the difficulty of multiplying them by the time-honoured methods of cuttings, budding or grafting. As growers have always found, buds and grafts made in the normal way fail to take and cuttings do not grow. The result was that in England, where the problem was exaggerated by climatic conditions, propagation was universally achieved by growing seedlings and these, as Switzer said, could differ considerably from their parents. In this way the 'Common' walnut seedlings became the usual ones for planting in Britain and, even in 1929, Witt of East Malling, estimated that 99 per cent of the walnuts grown in this country were seedlings. Seeds were also brought over from France where walnuts were superior to those growing in England and these, as Switzer said, gave the largest nuts.

During the latter part of the eighteenth century there was a falling off in the demand for walnut timber for furniture as a result of the introduction of mahogany from the West Indies, though there was still demand for the timber for coach building and gun stocks. The Napoleonic Wars led to a further reduction in the number of walnut trees as the enormous prices offered by gun and pistol-stock makers for their timber was a great inducement to estate owners to fell their trees, while the high price of all agricultural products at this time dissuaded against replanting. Phillips in 1827 referred to seven walnut trees growing in a small meadow of about three-quarters of an acre at Greenwich. The nuts had been sold every year for £30, while the owner of the trees had refused a thousand guineas for the timber during the Napoleonic Wars.

THE NINETEENTH CENTURY

In 1806, Forsyth listed five different types of walnuts which he said were best raised from seed, so they could not have been very true to type. They were the Double-bearing, the English, the Large French, the Thin-shelled and the Late-ripe. The Black Virginian walnut, *Juglans nigra*, he said was chiefly grown for its timber. Forsyth also spoke of the substitution of walnut wood by mahogany and other foreign timbers, but said that the walnuts still growing on the hills of Surrey yielded a great deal of money in plentiful years when they were thinned for pickling green, both for home consumption and for export. He wrote of the value of the infusion made from walnut leaves, steeped in boiling water and mixed with lime water, soap suds and urine for destroying worms in the ground and insects on trees. This was very similar advice to that given in the seventeenth century.

Although John Evelyn had mentioned the grafting of walnuts, no doubt having seen it done during his extensive travels on the Continent, all attempts at using vegetative propagation in England seem to have failed until Thomas Andrew Knight, in 1807, reported the successful use of grafting by approach. He used two-year-old seedlings growing in pots which he elevated on poles to the level of the branches of the walnut tree to be propagated. A few years later, in 1815, he gave an account of his attempts at budding walnuts.

While vegetative propagation was generally unsuccessful in Btitain, by the early nineteenth century, the grafting of named varieties of walnuts was well established in France in Dauphiny, Anjou, the Lower Limousin, Perigord and in the country bordering Switzerland, and had increased production tenfold. However, the first report of the trials of the fruit varieties at the Horticultural Society's garden at Chiswick said that the difficulty of budding or grafting the walnuts was a great impediment to their multiplication. The walnut collection consisted of the nine principal varieties then known by name in French and English gardens. These were the Common walnut, a Coque Tendre, Dutch nut, Hatif, High flyer, Large-fruited, synonymous with the Double and French walnut, Tardif or St Jean, Thin-shelled and Yorkshire.

Lawsons' nursery catalogue of 1865 included several of the varieties in the original Horticultural Society's collection. The catalogue listed Common walnuts but said they were difficult to propagate apart from seed and they consisted of many diverse types. Other varieties were Highflyer, Yorkshire, Large Fruited, synonymous with Claw nut, said to have nuts of double size but a poor bearer, Late, synonymous with Tardif and St Jean, which escaped spring frosts, Thin shelled, the best of all nuts but a poor bearer and Dwarf Prolific, also called Fertilis, which was a different form of *Juglans, J. praeparturiens.* This only grew 3 — 6 ft high but cropped abundantly and had well-flavoured nuts. It came fairly true from seed and had been found in a bed of seedlings by M. Louis Chatenay about 1830 and introduced in 1837.

All these varieties were also among those listed by Hogg in 1875. He also mentioned that the shells of the Large-fruited or Claw variety were used by jewellers for making jewel cases or for fitting up with ladies embroidery instruments.

THE TWENTIETH CENTURY

In spite of the greater interest in trying to find better varieties of walnuts during the nineteenth century, the numbers of those grown commercially continued to fall, few being planted except in the larger private gardens. Although some green walnuts were sent to market, most of the dry nuts were imported from Europe.

The walnuts which were planted in England were still nearly all seedlings but several of the named, better French varieties had been imported and were offered for sale by a few nurseries during the first quarter of the century. These included Chaberte, an old variety grown especially in the Midi district of France from the end of the eighteenth century, Franquette, a very popular French variety, a seedling found by M. Franquette near Notre Dame de Osier, Isère, and Mayette, known at the beginning of the eighteenth century in the Département of Isère and named after M. Mayet. There were also various types of Common walnut raised from seed, such as the thin-shelled and early and late kinds.

In 1923 the first steps were taken to investigate the possibilities of improving walnut cultivation in England. Some 26 of the best varieties were imported from France, California, Cyprus and Persia and sent to East Malling so that work could be started on their propagation and, in addition, about 300 varieties were collected from farms and gardens all over Britain and, of these, about 100 were also sent to Malling.

On 19 November 1929, the Royal Horticultural Society held a competition for walnuts which attracted 470 separate dishes representing 314 trees. Of these, it was said that a very small percentage was of a satisfactory standard of quality and size. Nearly all were of seedling origin. The competition was of value in showing the urgent need for improvement in the quality of the varieties then grown in Britain.

The investigations into methods of propagation of walnuts at East Malling showed that seedlings of *Juglans regia* or *J. nigra*, the Black walnut, potted in winter and brought into a glasshouse, could be successfully grafted during

July—August, ready for transplanting into the open in September. Subsequent work revealed that some walnut varieties are incompatible with *J. nigra* and so this stock cannot be recommended. During a severe spring frost on 26—27 April 1927, when most of the varieties in the Malling collection were already coming into leaf, they were all badly damaged with the exception of those French varieties which were still dormant. These had been selected in their own country, over a long period, for this and other good characters and were the cream of their varieties. They were nearly all from the famous walnut growing region of Isère near Grenoble, where walnuts had been grown from the time of the Roman Empire. The undamaged varieties were Franquette, Mayette, Meylanaise, Parisienne and Treyve. Vourey also escaped damage.

Following these investigations at East Malling, there was some renewed interest in walnut cultivation in England, and one grower in the eastern counties planted up several acres with the best varieties and equipped the farm with a modern nut-drying tower. Unfortunately, the yield of nuts proved most disappointing and the venture was not a commercial success. Today, it is probable that fewer walnuts are grown in Britain than at any time since the late sixteenth or seventeenth century.

The grape traditionally cultivated in Europe, *Vitis vinifera*, has been known in the Middle East and north Africa for many thousands of years. Although wild plants of this vine are found over a wide area, it is generally thought to have originated in Asia Minor and the Caucasus region. Evidence suggests that Transcaucasia was the principal centre. Great numbers of indigenous forms of grapes in Georgia, Armenia and Azerbaijan show the whole scale of diversity of colour and size of berry. Here grapes have been cultivated for many thousands of years, selected forms being grafted on wild seedling rootstocks found in abundance in the forests. The wild vines found in the forests of Transcaucasia mostly have rather small, sour black grapes but larger and white-berried types do occur. In Asia Media, wild vines are often found with white, sweet berries, sometimes identical to cultivated varieties.

Vines are also found growing wild in many other countries including Greece, in Anatolia, Persia and northern India. In France and Italy, fossil vines dating back to the Quaternary Age have been found, while seeds from middens of lake dwellings in central Europe show that the grape was used as food by early man.

EARLY CULTIVATION OF THE VINE

About 5000 BC or even earlier, the grape vine was spread from Anatolia to Syria and thence to Palestine. There, the first indications of vine growing are from grape seeds found in excavations at Jericho and Lachish, sites of the Early Bronze Age. Records show that vines and figs were cultivated in Canaan about 2400 BC. In both the Old and New Testaments of the Bible, there are frequent references to the culture of vines and the making of wine.

Vineyards existed everywhere, in the mountains of Hebron and Galilee, in the Negev and Edom and at Ein Gedi on the Dead Sea. In Genesis it is said, 'Noah began to be an husbandman, and he planted a vineyard, and he drank of the wine.' This illustrates the importance of the grape in early society.

At this time, the Egyptians bought grain, olive oil and wine from Syria and Palestine. But, later, the cultivation of vines and the production of wine became common in Egypt; Diodorus wrote that Osiris (2200 BC) encouraged the growing of vines and the making of wine. The irrigated land adjoining the Nile yielded abundant wine.

In Egypt, according to Pliny, long before wines were made from grapes grown in Italy, the physician Apollodarus wrote a pamphlet advising Ptolemy which wines to drink; in it, he praised the wine of Nasperence in Pontus, and next to that the Oretic, Oenate, Leucadian, Ambraciote and Peparethian vintages. The last he put before all the rest but said it was less well thought of because it was not fit to drink before it was six years old.

VINE CULTIVATION IN GREECE AND ITALY

The cultivation of the grape and the making of wine began in Greece some time before it did in Italy. Homer wrote in *The Odyssey* of the vineyard in the grounds of the Palace of Alcinous where some of the grapes were dried as raisins and others trodden for wine. Hesiod, the Greek poet of the eighth century BC, also spoke of wine, and Theophrastus wrote of vines and their propagation.

The Roman writers, Cato, Varro, Pliny and Columella, wrote extensively of grape and wine production, generally devoting more attention to this than to any other crop, and going into considerable detail over the selection of the site and soils for the vineyard, planting, methods of training, pruning and other aspects of vine cultivation, and dealing in full with the harvesting, storage of grapes and the making of wine. Much of what they wrote could be used in a modern textbook on the subject.

There was keen appreciation of the value of different varieties for wine making and of the influence of the soil and locality on the quality of the wine. In fact, in the early post-Christian era in Rome, the value attached to the different vintages seems to have been just as great as it is today. Pliny gave first place to the wines of Aminaea, on account both of their body and life which improved with age. There were five types of Aminaean wines. The Romans were great connoisseurs of wines and often paid very high prices for ones they favoured. The Greek, Thasian and Aminaean wines were in such demand that Caesar issued an edict prohibiting their sale at a higher price than 8 asses for 6 gallons. The Greek wine was so esteemed that only one cup could be given to each guest at a banquet. When Caesar was emperor he apportioned a flagon of Falernian and a jar of Chian wine to each table at the banquets in celebration of his victories.

Both Pliny and Columella listed many varieties of grapes and wines. For wines of the highest quality, Columella also recommended the Aminaean varieties, followed by the Eugenians and the Allobrogians. Vines of second quality but recommended for their good growth and fruitfulness were the Bituric, Basilic, the Visula and the smaller Argitis. The varieties were so numerous that Virgil in his *Georgics* wrote:

> *. . . to know their number is of no concern*
> *One who would know of this might also wish to learn*
> *How many grains of Libyan sand by western breeze are stirred.*

As Columella said, all countries and almost all separate regions of those countries had their own particular types of wine which they designated according to their own fashion and some vine stocks changed their names according to the place where they were grown. He added that no kind of vine should be planted except that approved by common report and none should be kept for any length of time unless proved by test.

Cato, Varro and Columella all wrote of the costs involved in grape and wine production and showed a keen appreciation of business methods. When growing fresh grapes for sale, Columella said that it was not profitable to grow them unless the holding was close to a city so that they could be sold to marketers with other fruits. The early ripe and firm-berried varieties, the Purple Bumast, Dactyl, Rhodian, Libyan and Ceraunian were valuable both for their appearance and for their flavour, and the Stephanitan, Tripedanean, Unciarian and Cydonitan especially for their good appearance. Columella gave detailed costings for planting a vineyard of seven iugera which could be managed by one vinedresser who could be some malefactor bought at the auction-block for 6,000−8,000 sesterces. Allowing for a total investment cost, including the price of the land, planting and staking the vines, of 29,000 sesterces, and interest at 6 per cent, and taking no crop until the third year, a useful profit should be made, quite apart from receipts from the sale of rooted cuttings made from the prunings.

Excavations at Pompeii have disclosed the existence of vineyards. On the slopes of Vesuvius a variety Mugentina was grown, sometimes called Pompeianna, from Sicily, which only bore well on rich soils. This produced a wine which was renowned for its quality and was even exported to Britain.

Of the wines imported into Italy from other countries, that from the Balearic Isles challenged comparison with the best vintages of Italy, but wine from the Province of Narbonne was produced in factories where it was coloured by smoke and adulterated by various herbs and drugs to change the colour and flavour of the wine. Many mosaics and murals dating from the early centuries AD found in Italy, Algeria and France show that commercial vineyards existed in these countries when the sale of wine was an important item of international trade.

ROMAN BRITAIN

Before the Roman occupation of Britain, the usual drink of most people was home-brewed beer or ale or mead made from the honey of wild bees. Diodorus, the Greek historian, in the last century BC, wrote that the Egyptians made a drink from barley which he said was little inferior to wine. Beer or ale and mead were also the principal drinks of most countries of northern Europe where there were no vineyards.

However, even in these early times, wine exports from the southern countries were reaching those of the north, including Gaul and Britain. Contrary to common belief, agriculture and trade were well developed in Britain before the first invasion of Caesar in 54 BC, especially in the southern coastal areas. There was an established export trade with the Continent, principally with Gaul but even with Rome, where hunting dogs from Britain were much appreciated. Other exports from Britain were corn, cattle, hides, tin, copper and other metals. Wine was imported by those who could afford it, both in Britain and Gaul, where Diodorus said some people were willing to give a slave in exchange for a jar of Italian wine.

The Roman writer, Tacitus, in the first century BC, specifically noted that the climate of Britain was not suited to the growing of vines owing to excessive rain and the general moistness; Diodorus, in the previous century, had written that vines were not grown in Gaul. Apart from this discouragement to grape production, there was also the edict of the Emperor Domitian, AD 81 – 96, limiting the planting of new vineyards in Italy and the occupied provinces. Whether the edict prevented the planting of vineyards in Britain is uncertain, but grape seeds of cultivated types have been found at a number of Roman sites in this country including Silchester, Gloucester, York, Doncaster and London. In London, many seeds have been found at the New Fresh Wharf and St Thomas Street sites. The origin of these seeds is not known, but they could have come from imported fruits.

Although the diet of Roman soldiers included vegetables, fruits and nuts and their rations included wine, there is still no definite evidence of grape growing or wine production in Britain at this time but large quantities of wine were imported for the military. Their basic diet when on active service included a daily allowance of sour wine which was normally diluted with water. In the wine cellars of the army stores depot at Richborough, an important Roman port in Kent, wine amphorae found there bore a note saying that the wine had come from Mount Vesuvius before the eruption in AD 79.

The First Experimental Vineyard?

About the year AD 280, the Emperor Probus issued an edict permitting the cultivation of grapes in Gaul, Spain and Britain, and it is believed that this was an encouragement to the planting of vineyards in Britain. Excavation of a series of trenches or ditches on a 12-acre Roman site at North Thoresby in Lincolnshire has suggested that these may have been made for an unsuccessful experimental vineyard, established soon after the edict of Probus. Pottery remains on the site suggest a date of perhaps five to ten years after AD 275. This attempt to grow vines, if this was the object, did not apparently last long, perhaps because of the unsuitable site or climate. This area of Lincolnshire would not be considered suitable for vine culture today, but it is likely that at this period the climate was more favourable. The Roman writer Saserna, in the last century BC, wrote that the cultivation of the olive and vines was spreading further north in Italy where, in previous years, the winters were too cold for transplants to survive. This milder weather seems to have continued for several centuries, although Tacitus had not considered Britain suited to vine cultivation.

It is more likely that any successful vineyards were developed by some of the more wealthy villa owners in the south of the country, but definite evidence of their existence is still scanty, apart from the finding of grape seeds at various sites and the discovery of remains of vine plants near a villa at Boxmoor. Any vineyards which were planted during the 150 years following the edict of Probus and before the end of the Roman occupation are likely to have been destroyed during the troubled times of the fifth and sixth centuries.

Influence of the Monasteries

The first written evidence that vines were being cultivated in England appears in Bede's *A History of the English Church and People* (AD 731) when he said that vines were grown in some places in England and probably to a greater extent in Ireland. It is likely that Bede was referring to vines grown by the monasteries. In the second half of the seventh century a number of monasteries were established in various parts of the country including Ely, which was later to become famous for its vineyards. The slopes around the cloisters of the abbey, and the cathedral which replaced the monastery, were so thickly planted with vines that the Normans gave Ely the name, 'Isle des Vignes'. However, probably most of the wine consumed in the early monasteries was imported, supplemented by their own production where conditions were favourable. Aelfric, the English Benedictine Abbot (AD 955—1020), said that the diet of the novices included beer, or failing beer, water as 'wine is not for the young, but for the old and wise'.

THE NORMAN CONQUEST

In *Domesday Book* (AD 1086) 38 vineyards were recorded in Kent, Middlesex, Hampshire, Wiltshire, Dorset, Berkshire, Gloucestershire, Worcestershire, Hertfordshire, Essex, Norfolk and Suffolk. The largest was at Bitesham in Berkshire, on the land of Henry de Ferrieres, which extended to about 12 acres. The quantity of wine yielded by a vineyard of about six acres in Essex amounted, if the season was favourable, to about 40 gallons. As some of the vineyards in *Domesday Book* were described as not bearing grapes, it does not appear that a great amount of wine could have been made from the grapes grown at this time in England, at any rate from the vineyards of sufficient importance to be recorded.

Following the Norman Conquest, many new varieties of fruits were brought over from the Continent and, with the interest stimulated by the newcomers from Normandy, there was increased planting of vineyards in many parts of the country. At the long-established monastery at Canterbury, in the eleventh century, it is recorded that although beer was the staple drink of the monks, the best French wines were also drunk, imported through the port of Sandwich. However, by 1165, a plan of the monastery grounds included a

Saxon vine-dressers pruning their vines, from an eleventh-century MS.

vineyard and so it seems the monastery was trying to become more self-sufficient.

During the next two centuries, the vineyards belonging to the Archbishopric of Canterbury became some of the most successful and famous in the country. One of the most renowned was at Teynham near Sittingbourne, the village which was later the site of the famous orchard planted by Harris, the fruiterer to Henry VIII. By the fourteenth century the Archbishopric had vineyards widely scattered throughout Kent, including ones at North Fleet, Chartham, Brookland, Wingham and Hollingbourne. The Bishops of Rochester also had a famous vineyard at Halling, of which Lambard wrote that when, in the nineteenth year of his reign, Edward II was at Bockinfold, Bishop Hamiliton sent him thither 'a present of his drinkes, and withal both wine and grapes of his own growth in his vineyards at Halling'.

Gloucestershire was also noted for its vineyards about which William of Malmesbury wrote in 1125: 'This county is planted more thickly with vineyards than any other in England, more plentiful in crops and more pleasant in flavour. For the wines do not offend the mouth with sharpness since they do not yield to the French in sweetness.' Vines were also of importance in Worcestershire in the twelfth and thirteenth centuries, and vineyards were planted even as far north as Derbyshire and Northamptonshire. In the time of King Stephen (1135−54), Martin, Abbot of Peterborough, planted a very large vineyard in Northamptonshire; and there were many vineyards attached to the monasteries of East Anglia.

The vineyards of the royal family were prominent throughout the Middle Ages. During the reign of Henry II (1154−89) allowances were made to the officer who was responsible for the production of wine, perry and cider at Windsor. During the reign of Richard II (1377−99) the Little Park at Windsor was still being used as a vineyard. According to Lambard this vineyard was so productive that it not only provided the king's household with wine but left a surplus which was sold at a profit.

The famous vineyard at Ely continued to be of importance for several centuries. The accounts for the priory for 1298 show that 27 gallons of verjuice were sold in that year. In the following year, 21 gallons were sold in addition to the production of 9½ butts of wine. In 1372, the accounts of the 'Manor of Holbourne' for the vineyard attached to the garden of Ely Place, part of the estate of the Bishops of Ely, record the sale of 30 gallons of verjuice. Verjuice was an acid liquor or vinegar made from sour grapes or sometimes from crab apples, which played an important part in Medieval kitchens. Although their vineyards might not often produce very satisfactory crops for wine, they were of use for verjuice, though the high costs of maintaining the vineyards rarely made the enterprises economic.

There is no record of the grape varieties used in Medieval vineyards, but they must have come from Europe, perhaps from Rome and, although successful in their countries of origin, seem to have given very variable results in Britain under a less favourable climate. But this did not deter many people from starting vineyards in London and elsewhere as the occurrence of the word 'vine' in numerous street names suggests.

DECLINE IN ENGLISH VINEYARDS

The century 1225 to 1325 saw the manorial and monastic farming systems, established after the Norman Conquest, at their most prosperous. Trade with the Continent increased and it was found more advantageous to import wines than to depend on the product of the English grape crop which, in any case, was an uncertain one.

In spite of the imposition of the first duty in 1272, when customs officers were appointed in London and at other principal ports to deal with wine imports, the price of imported wines was relatively cheap. The first duty was only 1d per tun and seems to have been mainly on French and Rhenish wines; by 1409, the duty had risen to 3s a tun.

Although wine was still produced in England, many vineyards began to be neglected as early as the reign of Henry III (1216—72), owing to the fondness of people for French wine. In 1260, a dolium (36 gallons) of the best imported wine could be bought for 20—40s. By the reign of Edward III (1327—77), after the capture of Calais in 1347, the English commanded a great part of France and wine imports increased still further.

However, quite apart from competition from imported wines, other factors contributed to the decline of English vineyards. The period of agricultural prosperity suffered a sudden reversal after the early part of the fourteenth century. A succession of droughts and disease seriously devastated both crops and livestock, while the Black Death (1348—9) probably killed about a third of the population. Many rural areas became deserted and everywhere there was general unrest. Following the Black Death, there was a shortage of labour in the country and a decline in the prosperity both of the monasteries and their farms. More of the latter were let to tenants who lacked the efficiency of the monks. With such shortage of labour, the landowners and tenants turned to cereals and other crops which would give a reasonable and reliable livelihood rather than the uncertain income of the labour-intensive vines.

Although the vineyards attached to the monasteries and on lands belonging to the royal household might still be kept under cultivation, even these suffered after the Black Death. The famous vineyard belonging to the Archbishop of Canterbury at Teynham in Kent showed a marked reduction in wages paid for labour 'on account of the pestilence', while there was an increased cost of feed for oxen and cows 'as there was no hay'. Possibly no one was left to cut it.

INFLUENCE OF THE CLIMATE ON VINEYARDS

A major factor which contributed to the success or failure of English vineyards and is still of over-riding importance today, is the variable climate.

In the first century AD, Tacitus had considered the climate of Britain too cool and wet for vines. In the seventh century, Bede, while saying that vines were grown in England, considered that the climate of Ireland was far better and more grapes were grown there. However, during late Saxon and Viking times a more Continental type of weather prevailed which may well have encouraged further planting of vineyards in Britain.

The greater planting of vineyards after the Norman Conquest coincided with a prolonged period of weather, from about the middle of the eleventh century until the early years of the fourteenth, which was better suited to vine culture, the peak of the warmer climate being in the twelfth and thirteenth centuries. As a result of the instability of the polar ice, summer temperatures were rather higher than today and there was greater freedom from damaging spring frosts.

However, following this warmer phase, during the fourteenth and fifteenth centuries the weather in Europe deteriorated with frequent severe winters and cold springs. This change in the weather initiated a period of generally lower average temperatures which continued until the middle of the seventeenth century, culminating in the Little Ice Age.

Although there were years when the winters were less severe and the summers relatively warmer, the harder weather, coming on top of the general decline in agriculture and horticulture in the fourteenth and fifteenth centuries, probably meant the end of commercial vineyards in England. They may have persisted in the monastery gardens but the monasteries had lost their previous prosperity so that, by the time of their dissolution by Henry VIII in 1536, they no longer occupied their former position of influence. It is also likely that those to whom the lands of the old religious houses were sold or granted had not the same horticultural skills as the monks.

Evidence illustrating the dramatic effect of the colder weather on vineyards in Europe, in the first half of the fifteenth century is given in *A Parisian Journal* (1405—49), written by an unknown Frenchman living in Paris. In this he included an account of the weather and its effect on the yields of fruits and vegetables, together with their availability and prices in the shops and markets of the city.

The journal gives a detailed description of how the weather influenced production from the vineyards and the effect on the supply and price of wine. Since there has always been considerable argument as to the reasons for the decline of English vineyards at this time, and it is frequently said that this was mainly the result of increasing competition from imported wines, especially from France, it is worth examining the account given by this unknown Frenchman to see how the disastrous weather affected the vineyards in his country. The following is a summary of his observations for the period 1421 — 43:

1421. Winter very long and bitter. Severe cold till end May. Vines had not flowered by end of June.

1422. This year vines all over France looked more promising than ever before but, on the 25th and 26th April, severe frost cut down all vines as if by fire. Wine very short. 2 acres gave one cask at most.

1423. Jan. 12th severest frost anyone could remember. Heaviest snow-fall for thirty years. Vines frozen, very few grapes and wine very dear.

1424. Finest vintage within living memory. Wine very cheap.

1425. Very bad season for caterpillars. All fruits spoiled as were many vines.

1427. Very hard winter, freezing for 36 days from 1st Jan. Frost continued from February until end of May. Not more than one month of summer. Constant rain and hailstorms. Vines did badly, only one cask per acre. Wine very thin and dear.

1428. Weather in June very cold with constant rain and thunder storms. No vine blossoms. Wine so dear people made and drank beer.

1429. Weather in April very cold after early spring. Wine thin and worthless. Best of it like verjuice and yet very expensive.

1430. Frost on 12th and 14th May froze vines which had most promise for 30 years, but August fine and grapes which escaped frost gave excellent vintage.

1432. Froze hard for 17 days from 13th Jan. Seine frozen over. From then until 20th April constant hail and frost. All buds and flowers blackened by frost. Severe frosts in May and very wet July. Vines severely damaged.

1433. Winter hard and Seine frozen over. Exceedingly cold with frost nearly every day until Easter. Very cold with snow and hail on 25th April and cold continued until end of May.

1434. Frost began a week or two after Christmas and continued for 30 days. March very, very hot with no rain and dry weather continued until 28th April when severe frost froze all vines. Wine very dear.

1435. Very severe frost from mid-winter until end March. Then frosts began again and continued until 17th April. All low-lying vines frozen.

1436. Excellent wine and very cheap.

1437. Hard frosts from end previous Nov. until 12th Feb. All fruit crops failed with exception of medlars and crab apples.

1440. Good fruit crops.

1442. Vintage best for 50 years.

1443. Winter hardest in living memory. Frost began in previous Dec. and continued until 15th April. Froze again for two weeks from beginning of May. Much damage to vines and wine very poor quality.

Records in England show that in 1434 there was frost for ten weeks and the Thames was frozen over as far as Gravesend. Even if in the other years reported in this French journal the weather in England may have been less severe, it was obviously not conducive to the good cropping of vines or the production of quality wines, and was no encouragement to the planting of new vineyards in a country which was already suffering from many other problems.

THE DEBATE ON VINEYARDS

In the printed literature which appeared in the sixteenth century there were regrets that vineyards had almost disappeared in Britain. In the *Holinshed Chronicles* in 1580, the author of the description of England, William Harrison, wrote:

> *I will touch in this place on one benefit which our nation wanteth, and that is wine, the fault whereof is not in our soil, but the negligence of our countriemen (especially of the south parts) who do not inure the same to this commoditie, and which by reason of long discontinuance, is now become unapt to beare onie grapes almost for pleasure and shadow, much less then the plaine fields or several vineyards for advantage and commoditie.*
>
> *Yet of late times some have assaied to deale for wine. But sith that liquor, when it cometh to the drinking, hath been found more hard than that which is brought from beyond the sea, and the cost of planting and keeping thereof so chargeable, that they may buie it far better cheape from other countries; they have given over their enterprises without onie consideration, that in all other things, so neither the ground itselfe in the beginning, nor successe of their travell can anser their expectations at the first, until such time as the soil be brought, as it were, into acquaintenance with this commoditie.*

Sir Hugh Platt, however, was not deterred from trying to sell his ideas about making English wine. At this time and during the following centuries, wine was often made from soft fruits, such as gooseberries and currants, and from cider apples and perry pears, the products of the latter frequently being sold in London taverns as imported wines including Rhenish. These wines were sometimes distilled to produce brandies. Sir Hugh Platt was a noted writer in the early seventeenth century who had apparently developed his own method of making wines and was prepared to sell his ideas to others. This would have been one way of using the juice from poorly ripened grapes. He also suggested that growers in Worcestershire and the west country shires should convert their considerable surplus of cider and perry into white wines or claret which, as he said, were already being sold as Rhenish wines in London. Sir Hugh claimed that his wines had been praised by the French ambassador who said they were as good as any new French wines but had been condemned by others without even bothering to taste them!

From the publication of the first books on fruit growing in the sixteenth century to the present day, the arguments for or against the establishment of vineyards in Britain have continued. It has been characteristic of most writers in favour of planting vineyards to base their arguments on the supposed success of those in the past; while those against their planting, though agreeing that there were numerous apparently successful vineyards in the past, consider that our variable climate weighs against the commercial viability of wine production in Britain.

John Parkinson, in his important book *Paradisi in Sole* in 1629, considered that it would be pointless to try to establish a vineyard since the weather was not so hot as it had been in the past, and though various noblemen and others endeavoured to plant vineyards, bringing over Frenchmen to do the work, they had been unable to produce any wine worth drinking and so soon gave up their efforts. Parkinson was correct in saying that the climate in his time was not so warm as it had been. By 1650, average temperatures were probably at their lowest for the previous two millennia. Glaciers in Europe reached their most advanced line since the Ice Age. This affected vine growing in parts of Europe, just as it did in England. This Little Ice Age continued until the early part of the nineteenth century.

However, in spite of the problems of the climate, there were advocates of wine making in England who wrote enthusiastically about successful vineyards they knew. Samuel Hartlib quoted the success of Sir Peter Richard of Great Chart in Kent who made 6—8 hogsheads of wine each year, and the Surrey woman who found her verjuice made from unripe grapes fermented and produced a very brisk wine. Since the French wines were subject to excise and customs duty, the British wines could be sold far cheaper.

Ralph Austen in 1657 thought that it might be possible, using early ripening varieties of grapes planted on a south-east facing slope on a light sandy soil, trained so that they did not grow over a yard in height and with the vineyard soil kept bare and free of weeds and grass, to grow grapes which would ripen satisfactorily and produce a good-quality wine — even in England. But on other sites and soils the grape juice would only be suitable for vinegar or verjuice. He added that, since England had such a store of good-quality apple varieties for making cider, there was not the same need to try to make wine from grapes.

The emphasis placed by Austen on the careful choice of site for a vineyard was also considered of prime importance by both Roman writers and others throughout history, and was underlined by John Rose in his book *The English Vineyard Vindicated*, published in 1666. Rose was gardener to Charles II at the Palace of St James, and was a friend of John Evelyn. In his dedication to the king, Rose said that he knew that the king had no great opinion of English wines but, if the varieties he recommended and their method of cultivation were used, the wines could once again be highly esteemed.

Rose advised planting vineyards on the lighter soils with gravelly or chalky subsoils, avoiding the highly fertile soild which can produce excessive growth. He also recommended sites on a hillside where the risk of damage from frosts and low-lying mists would be lessened. Sites facing south and taking full advantage of the sunshine were also considered essential. This need for special care in the choice of site for a vineyard has often been overlooked by potential vine growers and has accounted for many failures both in the past and in more recent years.

Vineyards in the Eighteenth Century

In spite of the arguments of writers such as John Rose, there does not seem to have been any general enthusiasm for the planting of vineyards and the production of wine from English grapes. This was a time when there was, however, some demand for a wine made from distilled cider, sometimes known as Cyder-royal.

However, such vineyards as were planted still created some interest. Professor R. Bradley, Professor of Botany at Cambridge, described one such in 1726:

> I shall begin with particulars of the celebrated vineyard near Bath, which has made so much noise in the World; it lies upon the side of a steep hill, facing the south, the ground very rocky or stony. The vines are planted in lines 6 ft asunder, and are treated much after the manner that Vines are managed in Germany.
>
> The sorts of grapes are the White Muscadine and the Black-cluster and though they are not proper Wine-making grapes, nor the most early in ripening, yet there were made 66 Hogsheads of Wine

*four years ago, from this vineyard which contains 6 acres of Ground;
But in the Year 1721, there was made not above 3 Hogsheads, and
the last year, 1722, when I was there July 26th, the Vines were then
hardly in blossom, so that little could be expected from them that
year; but as there was upon them a great deal of bearing wood, I
suppose this year they may produce a good crop; especially
considering the extraordinary Summer we have had.*

This 'celebrated' vineyard was probably at Bitton, half-way between Bath
and Bristol where, even today, the hillside is stepped; it is thought there may
have been a vineyard there in the time of the Romans. However, to have one
good crop of grapes in three years would hardly make it an economic
success.

Bradley also described two successful vineyards owned by Fairchild at
Hoxton and Warner at Rotherhithe and, from their experience, calculated
that, provided there were no frosts or 'blight', the grapes should yield 2,832
gallons per acre, equal to 44 hogsheads of 66 gallons each, worth £10 a
hogshead or £440 per acre. Bradley's calculation seems rather optimistic and
the relatively cheap prices at which good-quality wines could be imported
from the Continent was still a major factor counting against extended
planting of vineyards in England.

Miller's *Gardener's Dictionary* of 1731 included a description of the
vineyard planted by the Hon. Charles Hamilton at Pain's Hill. This vineyard
was planted on the south side of a gentle hill on a gravelly, sandy soil, with
two sorts of Burgundy Grape, the Auernat and the Black Cluster. The first
year that he attempted to make wine it was harsh and austere but the second
year he made a white wine, nearly resembling Champagne in flavour. This
improved in subsequent years when it was sold to wine merchants for 50
guineas a hogshead. One wine merchant to whom he sold wine worth £500
at one time assured him that in turn he sold some of the best of it from 7s 6d
to 10s 6d a bottle! On this experience, Charles Hamilton was convinced that
much good wine might be made in many parts of the south of England, but
he agreed that the uncertainty of the climate was much against vineyards
and many fine crops were spoiled by May frosts and wet summers, though
one good year might balance many disappointments.

PROTECTION FROM FROST

Loss of the grape crop as the result of spring frosts or wet summers was
frequently referred to by writers, and a number of suggestions were made to
reduce the risk of loss by careful choice of site. In 1786, Francoise Vispre
wrote his *Dissertation on the Growth of Wine in England, in a Country from*

which they seem at Present Entirely Eradicated. To protect the vines from frost damage, he suggested training them along the ground so that when there was risk of frost they could be covered with hay, straw or fern. In a favourable season, he claimed, the grapes from vines trained near the ground were considerably larger than those grown on a south wall. For giving publicity to this idea of training vines, Vispre was threatened with prosecution by the Rev. Le Brocq who had been granted the king's patent for his method of training fruit trees and vines along the banks at the sides of trenches cut into the ground. His idea was that the plants could be protected from frost by lattice work, covered with glass or oiled paper. However, neither of these ideas seems to have been widely adopted.

The suggestions of Vispre and Le Brocq for protecting vines indicate that the weather was still a dominating factor in the cultivation of vineyards. In 1790, William Speechly wrote his famous *Treatise of the Culture of the Vines*, and described the cultivation of grapes in glasshouses. In his preface he wrote: 'From the situation of this island and from the nature of the vine, it may seem doubtful whether wine can be made in this country to any National advantage. But still, we find by experience that by artificial means, even the latest kinds of grapes may be brought to a high degree of perfection.'

VARIETIES OF GRAPE

There never seems to have been any shortage of grape varieties suited to growing under different conditions. The Roman writer, Cato the Elder, described ones suited to particular soils:

> *In soil which is thought to be best adapted for grapes and which is exposed to the sun, plant the Small Aminnian (almost the only variety known to the ancients) the Double Eugeneum and the small Parti-coloured; in soil that is heavy or more subject to fogs, plant the Large Aminnian, the Murgentian, the Apician and the Lucanian. The other varieties and especially the hybrids grow well anywhere.*

The varieties first grown in England probably came from Rome or countries of the Continent where grape culture had been long established, but there is no record of the names of those grown here until the sixteenth and seventeenth centuries. Parkinson in 1629 listed 23 varieties. Austen writing in 1657 said that the Parsley Vine was the best for growing in this country and the Fox Grape had large berries and was a heavy cropper. The Franiniack was excellent when it ripened satisfactorily which it rarely did except on a south wall. The Red and White Muskadine also needed the protection of a wall. There were many other varieties, including the Curran and the Cluster grapes which varied very much according to where they were grown.

Samuel Hartlib in 1652 also gave the Parsley Vine as the best variety. He said it was also called Canada as it had come from that country where it grew naturally and was able to endure considerable cold. His other three best varieties were Rhenish-grape, Paris grape and Small Muscadell, though the last was tender and subject to frost damage. John Rose in 1666, after considerable experience, recommended the Small Black or Cluster Grape, the White Muscadine, Parsley grape, Muscadella, Frontiniaq and a new white grape, 'ripe before Muscadins which I found growing in His Majesties garden at St James'.

Professor R. Bradley, who was anxious to further the planting of vineyards in England, included a chapter on vines in his book published in 1726, describing the 49 varieties most valued in France. He also recounted a visit he made to France where he selected a number of varieties which were early ripening and grew well in the north of France and which he thought might do well on some of the poorer, more rocky soils of the west country in England where cider apples would not thrive. Having obtained plants of the kinds he wanted, Bradley wrote of the problems he experienced trying to bring them to England, which must strike a familiar note with anyone who has imported new plants:

> *The sorts of Grapes which I chose for this End were the kinds of Melie Grapes, some kinds call'd Morinon or Morilon, and some of the Muniers; I bought several hundred of these to be transplanted to England, with a Design at once to plant two or three Vineyards in divers Soils; but first the Carriage of them from Paris to Roan was tedious, and from Roan to England near two months elapsed before a Ship could be found to bring 'em to London, and then, which was worse, the Difficulties they met at the Custom-house, detain'd them so long, that hardly one in fourscore had living Juices left in them, as I found to my Sorrow after they had been planted a Year: However there are some yet alive and prosperous; but 'tis from thence alone we must expect Increase; for 'tis not worth our while to be at the Expence and Trouble I have been at in bringing over such things, without they could be readily brought on Shore. The same Year I had likewise, with a great deal of Trouble, collected several new Plants from other Place which, in my Judgement, would have been in a few Years as serviceable to England, as any thing has appeared in the Way of Gardening and Husbandry; but they were detained so long at Dover by the Custom-house Officers, that when they came to London they were all destroy'd and my Time and Expence lost. Now unless there can be some Way found out, which may allow free Passage for things of this Nature which cannot bear Delays, I fear we shall make few Additions to our Plants in England, whether useful or curious.*

Although Bradley thought that 'few if any of the English Catalogues of Grapes are right', the principal varieties included by Thomas Hitt in his book in 1757 were also correctly described by Robert Hogg in his *Fruit Manual* in 1875. Hitt's list included the following sorts, most of which are still available today: Sweetwater, Currant Cluster or Burgundy, White Muscadine, Royal Muscadine, Black Frontiniac, Claret Grape, Black Spanish or Alicant, Red Hamburgh, Black Hamburgh, White Frontiniac, Tokay, Lombardy and St Peters.

In 1790, William Speechley described 50 varieties of grapes but these were nearly all for growing under glass for dessert use as were nearly all the varieties recommended during the nineteenth century for growing outside on south-facing walls. William Speechley made the point that as good wines were made in Germany as far north as 51° latitude, he considered that this should be taken also to apply to vineyards in England and that these should be limited to the south of the country. It is interesting that the same point has recently been advanced concerning the planting of vineyards in England, though the latitude figure usually quoted is 52°.

NINETEENTH-CENTURY GRAPES AND VINEYARDS

Although there continued to be occasional planting of vineyards in England during the nineteenth century, few of these proved really successful financially. Loudon, in his *Encyclopaedia* of 1834, while agreeing that some English vineyards could produce wine equal to some of that imported from France, added 'But in a national point of view, we may conclude with equal safety, that the culture of the vine, as a branch of rural economy, would not be a profitable concern here on the broad general principle, that it cannot be long worth growing anything at home which we can get cheaper from abroad.' Exactly the same point had been made as early as 1580 when William Harrison wrote in the *Holinshed Chronicles*, with reference to the declining prosperity of the fourteenth and fifteenth centuries and increasing reliance on imports, 'For having all things at reasonable prices as we supposed, by such means from them, we thought it meare madness to spend time or cost about the same here at home.'

In the nineteenth century, the main interest of gardeners and professional horticulturists was in the production of grapes under glass or on south-facing walls outside to be used for dessert. William Forsyth, gardener to the king at Kensington and St James, in his book on fruit growing published in 1824, included a list of 50 grape varieties which he considered suitable for growing in hot houses or on outside walls, but did not mention any as useful for wine. Peter Lawson's nursery catalogue of 1865 listed 108 distinct varieties of grapes for dessert, while Robert Hogg in 1875 described 143 varieties.

Towards the end of the century another attempt was made to produce wine from a vineyard in Britain, this time in Wales. In 1875, the Marquis of Bute planted his first vineyard at Castle Coch, Glamorganshire and, a few years later, a second one at Swanbridge near Cardiff. The variety used was Gamay Noir and, with the exception of a few bad seasons, useful crops of grapes were harvested and made into wine which sold well commercially, but like many earlier vineyards these disappeared and it was nearly 50 years before any further serious efforts were made to grow grapes in the open.

MODERN VINE CULTIVATION

During the past 20 years interest in establishing vineyards in Britain has been renewed. A pioneer in the culture of grapes in the open and under cloches was Barrington Brock who planted his first vineyard on the North Downs at Oxted in Surrey in 1946. Here he tested a wide range of varieties and drew up lists of ones he considered likely to succeed in Britain. The writer, Edward Hyams, also became interested in grape growing and in 1949 published *The Grape Vine in England.*

The first of the new commercial vineyards was that of Sir Guy Salisbury Jones at Hambledon in Hampshire, planted in 1951, followed by one at Beaulieu planted by Mrs Gore Brown in 1960. In 1967, the English Vineyards Association was formed with 15 members who had between them ten acres of vineyards. In 1975, at the time of the first Ministry of Agriculture's census of vineyards, there were nearly 500 acres, and by 1981 the acreage is thought to have risen to 865. Long Ashton Research Station and the Ministry of Agriculture Efford Experimental Horticulture Station both established experimental vineyards but these suffered seriously from adverse weather in some seasons.

Much more care has recently been taken in the selection of varieties suitable for wine making. For some time many vineyards included Muller Thurgau but this is now losing favour and increasing attention is given to varieties which have some resistance to disease and can ripen their berries and wood in less favourable seasons.

Although the economic viability of some of the vineyards recently planted in England is questionable, and there are years when late flowering and wet sunless weather have ruined many potential crops, factors contributing to greater success than in the past have been increased knowledge both of varieties and vineyard management and greater expertise in the making of wine. Above all, the ability to produce wines of really acceptable quality has enabled their producers to sell them at a price often well above that of the majority of imported wines. Public interest in home-produced wines and successful publicity, including visits to vineyards, have aided the English grower.

However, English vineyards are still at the mercy of the weather, late spring frosts and cold wet summers. It is true that the climate has become warmer than it was in the Little Ice Age, but complete failure of the crop of a very high investment vineyard can spell disaster. Writers in the past sometimes said that one good year could balance many disappointments but, in an increasingly competitive world, when the prices obtained for the greater quantities of English wines may show relative decline, only the best and most favourably situated vineyards are likely to survive.

RASPBERRIES

The red raspberry native to Britain is *Rubus idaeus*, a member of the genus *Rubus* which is widely distributed in many parts of the world. *R. idaeus*, which gave rise to our first garden varieties of raspberries, occurs naturally in woods throughout Europe and the temperate parts of Asia. It is a very variable plant with several distinct geographical types, often considered as distinct species or subspecies. The American species, *R. strigosus*, is found throughout North America and during recent years this, with other species, has been used in the breeding of new varieties in Britain.

Evidence that the wild raspberry was very widely distributed in Great Britain in the past has been obtained from the discovery of seeds in late glacial deposits, especially in Scotland. Seeds from this period have been found at Gayfield near Edinburgh and in other parts of the Scottish Lowlands and, in the south, near Southampton. Seeds from the pre-Bronze Age were excavated at Peacocks Farm, Shippea Hill, Cambridgeshire, from the Early Bronze Age near Stonehenge and from the Late Bronze Age at Minnis Bay in Kent.

Seeds of the wild raspberry have also been found on a number of sites of Roman settlements, including Silchester. Although these finds have not been so frequent as the finding of blackberry seeds, this does indicate that the berries were collected as food at this time.

Although the raspberry was known to the ancient Greeks and Romans, it seems to have been regarded as of more use medicinally than as food. Pliny the Elder, after writing about brambles added, 'A third kind the Greeks call the Ida bramble from the place where it grows, a more slender variety than the others, with smaller and less hooked thorns; its blossom is used to make an ointment for sore eyes, and also, dipped in honey, for St Anthony's fire [erysipelas] and also, soaked in water, it makes a draught to cure stomach troubles.'

That *R. idaeus* originally only came from Mount Ida in Greece, as some early botanists thought, is of course incorrect since it is indigenous to many countries in Europe, but it may well have been taken from there to Rome as Palladius, the Roman agricultural author, writing in the fourth century, mentions the raspberry as one of the cultivated fruits in his time. It is therefore likely that it was cultivated before the strawberry, though both had been collected for food from the wild for many centuries before this. Nevertheless, the raspberry did not seem to show any improvement over the wild type for many hundreds of years.

EARLY RECORDS OF RASPBERRY CULTIVATION

At the beginning of the ninth century, Charlemagne's list of plants did not include the raspberry, nor did the *Forme of Cury* of 1391, listing English fruits and vegetables. During the Middle Ages in Britain raspberries, like strawberries, many cherries, plums and other fruits, were still gathered from the countryside and no attempt was made to cultivate them in gardens. Their fruits were already being used for making drinks as they were in later centuries. In 1241, Henry III's clerk paid 6s 8d for raspberry and mulberry drinks for the king.

Turner's herbal of 1568 was the first to mention the raspberry:

> *The bushe that I take for the ryght Rubo ideo / groweth in the greate hughe / hilles a little above Bone / and in East Fresland in a wood besyde Anrik / and in many gardines of England. It hath much shorter stalkes then the bramble / and no great howky prickles at all / the berries are rede.*
>
> *The Raspis hath the same vertues as that of the common bramble hath / and besydes also the floure of it brused with honey / and layed to / is good for inflammationes and hote humores gathered together to the eyes / and it quencheth the hote burnings / called the erisypelata it is good to be given with water unto them that have weyk stomaches. It were good to kepe some of the juyce of the berries / and to put it into some pretty wooden vessel / and to make of it as it were raspis wine / which doubtless should be good for many purposes / both for a weyke stomack / and also for the fire and divers diseases of the goumes / teth uvula tong / and pallet and other places there about.*

This account of the uses of the raspberry is practically identical to that written by Pliny, but it was common practice for writers on horticultural subjects in the sixteenth and seventeenth centuries to quote the works of the classical writers. The early use of the name 'raspis', later developed into raspberry, referred to the spines or thorns of the plant, which is also shown by the name 'Kratsberre' or 'Scratchberry' given to it in Germany at this time.

Thomas Tusser in his *Five Hundred Pointes of Good Husbandrie*, in 1573, included raspberries in his hints for September:

> *The Barbery, Respis and Gooseberry too*
> *Look now to be planted as other things doo*
> *The Gooseberry, Respis, and Roses, al three*
> *With strawberries under them trimley agree.*

He also included 'Respis' in his list of fruits to be planted or removed in January. John Gerard in 1597 included brambles and raspberries, together with illustrations of both, in his herbal. He headed the raspberry as, 'Rubus Idaeus, The Raspis or Hindberries' and wrote:

> *The Raspis is planted in gardens; it groweth not wilde that I know of, except in the fielde by a village in Lancashire called Harwood, not farre from Blackbushe. I have found it among the bushes of a*

2 *Rubus Idæus*.
The Raſpis buſh, or Hindberrie.

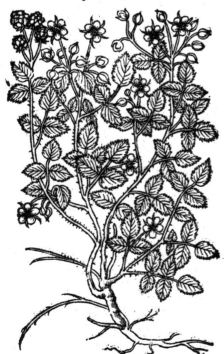

⁑Tʰᵉ

The only raspberry or hindberry known in the sixteenth century.

> *cawsey, neere unto a village called Wisterton, where I went to
> schoole, two miles from the Nantwich in Cheshire. The Raspis is
> thought to be like the Bramble, in temperature and vertues; the fruit
> is good to be given to those that have weake and queasie stomackes.*

It seems that Gerard did not know the British flora so well as he might — for
the wild raspberry must have had a wider distribution than he suggested.

RASPBERRIES IN THE SEVENTEENTH CENTURY

The early references to the raspberry do not indicate very great interest in the
fruit or show that there had been any improvement in the plants grown over
the wild types. The first writer to give details of different varieties was
Parkinson in 1629:

> *The Raspis berrie is of two sorts, white and red, not differing in the
> forme either of bush, leafe or berry, but onely in the colour and taste
> of the fruit . . . small berries, somewhat bigger than Strawberries,
> and longer, either red or white, made of many graines, more eminent
> than in the Strawberry, with a kinde of downiness cast over them,
> of a pleasant taste, yet somewhat soure, and nothing so pleasant as
> the Strawberries. The white Raspis is a little more pleasant then the
> red, wherein there is a small seede inclosed: the rootes creepe under
> ground verie farre, and shoote up againe in many places, much
> encreasing thereby.*
>
> *There is another whose stemme and branches are wholly without
> prickles: the fruit is red and somewhat longer, and a little more
> shape.*
>
> *The berries are eaten in the Summer time, as an afternoon dish,
> to please the taste of the sicke as well as the sound. The juyce and
> the distilled water of the berries are verie comfortable and cordiall.*

In Evelyn's translation of the *French Gardiner* in 1669, and the *Compleat
Gard'ner* in 1693, the red and white types of raspberries were still the only
ones mentioned, but Worlidge, in his *Vinetum Britannicum*, 1678, wrote of
three varieties: the Common Wild, the Large Red Garden, which he said was
useful in the conservatory and for its delicate juice, and the White. This is
the first reference to a larger form of the red raspberry, though where it came
from is uncertain. It does not seem to have been known in France at this
time. Subsequent history showed the importance of Hungary as a source of
new raspberries, so possibly this larger-fruited variety arose in the Balkans
and was brought over to England from Holland.

In a later book, 1697, Worlidge waxed enthusiastic about raspberries, saying they ought not to be omitted from the garden as they yield one of the most pleasant juices of any fruit and make an excellent wine, invaluable for adding colour and flavour to other drinks.

THE EIGHTEENTH CENTURY

In the early part of the eighteenth century, the number of varieties was still limited to the wild type, the Large Red and a white form but, by 1757, Thomas Hitt spoke of additional varieties, saying he knew of four kinds — the common small red, the white and two others with much larger fruits, called rombullions. Hitt was the first to describe a method of training the canes so that they remained upright. He said that if there were two, three or four canes on one root, the tops should be slightly shortened and then the canes plaited together so as to make them stand up. The second summer after planting, six canes could be so treated.

A study of the floras and nursery catalogues issued during the last quarter of the eighteenth century reveals the first changes. In the *Flora Anglicana* of Richard Weston, 1775—80, only three raspberries are listed, the red, white and twice-bearing, although at this time the numbers of different sorts of other fruits being offered was considerable. Again, the 1783 catalogue of Luker and Smith of Covent Garden listed the same varieties. However, in 1788 the first of the new raspberry varieties was recorded in the *Pomona Britannica*, produced by William Driver, nurseryman of Kent Road, London. Among the coloured illustrations of a limited number of different fruits was Golden Antwerp or Lord Middleton's raspberry. The description accompanying the illustration stated: 'Large size, golden. Lord Middleton first cultivated it in England; his son received it from the Governor of Antwerp who procured it from Hungary. Ripe early July, 8—12 ft high, best shortened to 4—5 ft in Oct.—Nov. Leave 3 shoots per plant. Next year cut back one to renew growth leaving two shoots to fruit.' This new variety was obviously a strong, vigorous grower if the cane could reach 8—12 ft in height, very different from the old varieties which were usually fairly short, and though they might be cut back, did not generally require any form of support.

Yellow Antwerp was introduced into cultivation by the end of the century, two nurserymen being credited with this, North of Lambeth and Maddock of Walworth, but William Driver's account in his *Pomona* clearly anticipated this by some years.

THE NINETEENTH CENTURY

The new variety doubtless served as a parent for the many new kinds of raspberries which were introduced throughout the nineteenth century. This was the time when there was very great interest in raising new varieties of many garden fruits from seed. Up till the end of the eighteenth century, most of the limited number of new varieties of the soft fruits, including strawberries and raspberries, had been naturally occurring mutations or selections from the wild species, with little attempt at deliberate hybridization. Great impetus to efforts to breed new fruits from seed was given by the success of the market grower Keens of Isleworth in raising new large-fruited strawberries and the work of Thomas Andrew Knight in his hybridization of a wide range of fruits. His work, and that of the newly formed Horticultural Society, stimulated interest in new fruits.

Brookshaw, in his *Pomona Britannica* of 1812, illustrated three raspberry varieties: White Autumn, the common Red and a new variety Red Antwerp which he said had been raised by Cornwall of Barnet, who gave it its name since it grew as large as the 'White Antwerp', the yellow type. Cornwall also introduced another variety of historic importance which he named Barnet, after his own district. Hogg, in 1866, described Barnet as larger than Red Antwerp and, though not equal to this variety in flavour, it was an excellent sort and an abundant cropper. This variety and Red and Yellow Antwerp all had a prolonged period of popularity and were still in cultivation during the first half of the twentieth century.

Thomas Haynes of Oundle, Northamptonshire, in his *Treatise of the Improved Culture of the Strawberry, Raspberry and Gooseberry* also published in 1812, mentioned by name only three varieties: the Red and Yellow Antwerp and a 'dwarf red early Premier'. This does not seem to have been recorded by any other writer.

William Forsyth, gardener to George III and George IV at Kensington and St James's palaces, gave the following as the best raspberries in 1806:

Early White	Large Red Antwerp
Double-bearing White	Large White Antwerp
Large Common White	Smooth Cane Double-bearing
Large Red	Woodward's new raspberry

Forsyth's book is significant as he was one of the first to mention the use of any support for the canes. This was following the introduction of Yellow Antwerp which had such strong-growing canes. As he said, with this and other strong-growing varieties, it is necessary to support the canes with stakes and run a couple of small rails along the top to which the canes are tied.

Forsyth advised planting the dwarf-growing Early White in rows 3 ft apart with 2 ft between the plants and shortening their canes to 2½ — 3 ft. Other, more vigorous varieties, such as Smooth Cane Double-bearing which generally bore a second crop in autumn but in good years would continue bearing from June to November, should be cut to 3 — 4 ft and Red Antwerp to 5 — 6 ft. These suggestions about training indicate a further step towards present-day practice.

Phillips in 1827 wrote that the Yellow or White Antwerp was most admired for dessert and that all white-berried fruits were sweeter than the coloured forms but with other fruits the reverse was true. He considered red raspberries the finest for flavouring ice creams, making jams etc. The October fruits picked from the double-bearing kinds seldom had much flavour.

A contemporary of Phillips, Dr Short, was a keen advocate of raspberry and strawberry wines which he said were not only delicious to taste but strongly recommended in scorbutic disorders. Mixed with water, they made a good reviving draught in severe fevers. Thus, for a period of 1800 years, from the time of Pliny, the raspberry had been especially advised for its medicinal virtues, while the fruits had been considered of great value for making wines. Raspberry wines are still made on a limited scale and the juice of the berries is extracted for making cordials and flavourings.

The Horticultural Society's collection of raspberries in 1826 included 23 varieties and 25 synonyms. By 1834, those recommended for planting by Loudon were:

Early Prolific	Red Antwerp	Bromley Hill	Cornish	Superb
Barnet's	Yellow Antwerp	Woodwards Red Globe		Double-bearing

This shows that since the beginning of the century the varieties grown had changed markedly since the first introduction of the Antwerp raspberries. Of the successful varieties, one of the earliest was Fastolff, discovered about 1820 by Colonel Lucas of Yarmouth, growing in a garden attached to an old castle, formerly the residence of Sir John Fastolff. It was probably a seedling of Red Antwerp. It was widely distributed both in England and America.

Fillbasket was another English raspberry, popular over a long period from the first half of the nineteenth century, which was sent to the United States before 1856. This was a time when there was considerable exchange of new plant varieties between the two countries. Some of the raspberries sent from this country were not sufficiently hardy in the eastern states though they grew successfully on parts of the west coast, as near San Francisco.

About 1865, John Baumforth of Pontefract raised a batch of seedlings from berries of Fillbasket. He selected one, Baumforth's Seedling, which was still one of the leading commercial varieties for late picking during the first half of this century. This proved too tender for the States. Norwich Wonder was another very successful variety which was grown in Kent for the fresh-fruit market for over 60 years.

Messrs Carters of Keighley, Yorkshire, raised two very valuable raspberries, Carter's Prolific and Semper Fidelis, introduced in 1885. The latter
was used especially for 'boiling' or jam making. These two varieties, together
with Baumforth's Seedling, all raised within 30 miles of each other in
Yorkshire, made up a large proportion of the commercial acreage of
raspberries up to the end of the nineteenth century. Another heavy-cropping
dessert variety of major importance was Superlative, raised about 1877 by
Merryfield of Waldersham Gardens, Dover, and introduced by George
Bunyard in 1888. The latter said Superlative took first place for market sale,
either in punnets or tubs, made the highest price and yielded three times as
much as any other sort.

In 1882, D. T. Fish included Carter's Prolific, Northumberland, Fillbasket,
Barnet, Fastolff, Hornet, Red Antwerp, Yellow Antwerp and Prince of Wales
as the most valuable varieties, but by 1899 George Bunyard recommended
only four, Superlative, Norwich Wonder, Carter's Prolific and Semper Fidelis.
In 1904, for the garden, he added Red Antwerp, Hornet and Baumforth's
Seedling. By this time Red Antwerp was about 100 years old.

THE TWENTIETH CENTURY

During the early years of this century the leading breeder of raspberries was
George Pyne of Topsham, near Exeter in Devon. The first of these varieties
was Pyne's Royal, raised in 1907 and introduced in 1913. This, though
rather a weak grower, produced fruits of excellent quality and on this
account was later used by Norman Grubb of East Malling Research Station
as one of the parents in his breeding of raspberries. Other varieties of Pyne's
were Red Cross, introduced in 1917 and Imperial in 1928. Messrs Laxton of
Bedford introduced several new raspberries, including Rival in 1907 and
Reward in 1905, but neither had a very long life.

As with other fruits, a number of new varieties of raspberries arose as
chance seedlings. Lloyd George, which enjoyed a period of great popularity,
was found by J. J. Kettle as a seedling growing in a wood in Kent. He took the
variety with him when he settled at Corfe Mullen in Dorset and introduced it
for distribution in 1919. Norfolk Giant, important over a very long life as one
of the few late varieties, was found as a seedling in Norfolk and introduced
by a horticultural adviser, H. Goude, in 1926.

In 1921, C. H. Hooper of Wye College and a member of the Royal
Horticultural Society Scientific Committee said that the most popular
raspberries for field culture were Superlative, Hornet introduced by Rivers,
Bath's Perfection for jam, and Baumforth's Seedling. He added Pyne's
Devon and Red Cross as newer varieties good for bottling. These varieties
had replaced Carter's Prolific and Norwich Wonder which had been

favourites 20 years earlier, as raspberry, like potato, varieties gradually deteriorate in yield and vigour.

The same point about the deterioration of the older varieties of raspberries was made by A. N. Rawes, Fruit Trials Officer at Wisley, on the occasion of the RHS Cherries and Soft Fruit Conference in 1935. He spoke of the difficulty of maintaining the growth of Lloyd George, the poor behaviour of Pyne's Royal and the almost complete failure of many of the varieties at one time widely grown for market.

The history of raspberry varieties, from the beginning of the nineteenth century when the first of the new large-fruited sorts were being planted, has frequently been the introduction of new varieties, many of which were acclaimed as being outstanding in their own way which, after a brief period of popularity, disappeared from use. The reason in some cases was their replacement by better sorts, but the cause of their short life was often deterioration through virus disease infection. Until the past 50 years, when more has been known about these diseases and their control, many excellent varieties disappeared from cultivation.

The studies of the workers at East Malling Research Station, particularly Dr Harris, and Dr Cadman in Scotland during the late 1940s and throughout the 1950s, resulted in greater understanding of the virus diseases involved, their mode of transmission and possible methods of control. The latter depended on growing stocks of known health in isolated cane nurseries, free from risk of new infection, either air-borne by aphids or soil-transmitted by eelworms. By making use at first of a virus-free stock of Lloyd George which was found growing in New Zealand and later, where virus-free material did not already exist, using the heat treatment method for eliminating virus infection, nurseries and growers have been continuously supplied, through the Nuclear Stock Association and certification schemes, with healthy planting material. In this way, the health of old valuable varieties has been improved and maintained and that of the new varieties safeguarded.

The continued existence of raspberry varieties over a long period in the past was often because they were tolerant of common viruses, while other virus-sensitive varieties quickly succumbed and disappeared from cultivation. Even though virus-free stocks of Lloyd George were introduced, this variety proved so sensitive to virus infection that it quickly became useless and was abandoned. On the other hand, a more recent variety, Malling Jewel, is largely virus tolerant and so can continue to yield reasonable crops even when infected.

MODERN RASPBERRY VARIETIES

As with the breeding of new varieties of many other fruits, the raising of new raspberries during recent years has been mainly undertaken by scientifically trained workers at one of the research stations. The first plant breeder whose varieties proved to be outstanding was Norman Grubb at East Malling. Grubb began breeding raspberries in the 1920s and continued for over 30 years. As well as making use of English varieties, including Lloyd George and Pyne's Royal, he crossed these in turn with the German, Preussen and the American, Newburgh. From these parents, he bred and introduced into commercial production a number of varieties of which Malling Promise and Malling Jewel were outstanding. Malling Promise occupied an important place as an early sort both for market and garden use, and Malling Jewel quickly rose to be the most important variety grown in Scotland and elsewhere, being especially suited to processing. It filled a serious gap left by the decline of older varieties, including Lloyd George, and has been most useful for garden use, to be eaten fresh or for freezing.

The work of Grubb at East Malling was carried on by Dr Knight and Dr Keep, who have been responsible for the introduction of a number of new varieties of merit. These workers painstakingly studied various characters in their parent material, including disease resistance, heavy cropping and good quality, and subsequently brought these desirable characters together by inter-crossing. Among varieties bred were Malling Admiral, Malling Orion, Malling Delight, Malling Joy and Malling Leo. The work at East Malling, which was later transferred to the Scottish Crop Research Institute, included the use of several *Rubus* species, *R. crataegifolius, R. occidentalis* and *R. spectabilis* in addition to *R. idaeus.*

The work in Scotland has resulted in the introduction of a number of varieties of which the heavy-cropping Glen Clova was one of the first to be used commercially and in gardens and which replaced much of the Malling Jewel grown for processing. Seeds of wild raspberries from late glacial deposits were found in Scotland and today the cooler, moister climate has been found particularly suited to raspberry growing where most of the crop is used for freezing and other forms of processing. To meet the needs of the commercial growers, the Scottish Institute undertook breeding of varieties which might prove suitable for mechanical harvesting. Other work has involved hybridization between raspberries and blackberries, especially some of the American self-supporting kinds. In this way new types of fruits have been introduced.

In England most raspberries have always been grown for the fresh-fruit market, and with the increasing costs of labour for picking, much of the crop is now grown for 'pick-your-own' sales.

DEVELOPMENT OF RED RASPBERRIES IN THE UNITED STATES

In the early days, settlers in America collected fruits of the wild, red raspberry, *Rubus strigosus*, for food. This grew freely in the forests and soon established itself on any wasteland cleared of trees. Even when the cultivation of the raspberry began during the latter part of the eighteenth century, Common Red, thought to have come from the wild species, was still the principal variety grown.

It was not until the end of the eighteenth and early years of the nineteenth centuries, when gardens were developed around the new settlements, that new raspberry varieties were imported from Europe. These included the celebrated Red Antwerp, Yellow Antwerp and Barnet and, though some imported varieties proved to lack hardiness, the comparative large size of their berries was much appreciated. These and other varieties certainly had their influence in the development of the present-day varieties of red raspberries in America. Lloyd George, though itself not suited to production in America, has, as in England, been a very useful parent in breeding new varieties, while *Rubus strigosus* and varieties from the United States have been used by British plant breeders.

AUTUMN-FRUITING VARIETIES

Some varieties of raspberries produce late summer or early autumn berries on trusses formed near the tips of the new, current season's canes. This late cropping is encouraged by cutting down the canes formed in the previous season. The earliest recorded variety which bore a late crop, was twice or double bearing, sold by nurseries in the latter part of the eighteenth century and grown in the nineteenth century until replaced by improved varieties. One of the most important was Belle de Fontenay, raised by a nurseryman Gartier, at Fontenay-aux-Roses, prior to 1850 and introduced to England in 1863. Another French variety, was the yellow-fruited Surprise d'Automne introduced in 1865.

In the early years of the twentieth century, autumn-fruiting varieties included November Abundance, raised by Messrs Veitch from Catawissa crossed with Superlative, and Queen Alexandra, raised by Allan in 1902 at Gunton Park Gardens. September, bred at Geneva, New York, in 1934, from Marcy crossed with Ranere, and introduced in 1947, has been popular in both America and Britain. Zeva Herbsternte from Switzerland and Heritage and Fall Crop from America, have all been planted to a limited extent.

Following increased interest in autumn-fruiting raspberries, plant breeders at East Malling raised a number of varieties, using as parents *Rubus idaeus vulgatus* varieties such as Lloyd George, *R. idaeus strigosus, R. odoratus,* the herbaceous *R. articus* and *R. spectabilis.* The first named seedling from this work was Malling Autumn Bliss, issued in 1984.

Strawberries all originate from the genus *Fragaria*. When the physician, William Butler (1535—1618) said, 'Doubtless God could have made a better berry but doubtless God never did', he was referring to the fruit of the wood strawberry, *Fragaria vesca*. This is the common strawberry of woodlands and banks in the British Isles and it is also widely distributed throughout Europe, while forms of it occur in eastern regions of North America. It is also found as far north as Lapland and Iceland.

The fruit of the wood strawberry, though variable in size, is small and while the berries are often of good flavour and are still sometimes picked for making good-quality jam, the species is not considered to have been of importance in the development of our present-day, large-fruited berries. For many hundreds of years, however, it was of great importance to our ancestors since it was the only kind available to them.

Evidence of the existence of this species in England in the post-glacial period has been found in the discovery of fossilized fruits at Cross Fell in Cumberland. The period of their growth was during the Climatic Optimum when trees grew at this altitude of 2,350 ft in the Pennines, before the climate became cooler. Excavations of Iron Age lake sites in Switzerland have disclosed seeds of berried fruits, including the strawberry, though these were the rarest. At Rockbarton in County Limerick remains of strawberry fruits have been found associated with the Beaker Folk, and seeds of *F. vesca* were found in 1901 on the Roman site at Silchester. There is also evidence that Roman soldiers were in the habit of eating the fruits of wild strawberries and blackberries as remains of both were found on the site of the fort at Newstead near Melrose.

These discoveries indicate that fruits of the wood strawberry were collected for food for many years before any attempt was made to bring the plants into cultivation.

EARLY HISTORY OF STRAWBERRIES

In view of the popularity of the strawberry, it is perhaps surprising that its recorded history of cultivation in the gardens of Europe does not go back nearly as far as that of many other fruits, for example apples, pears, plums, figs and grapes which have been grown for several thousand years.

Although the plant was known to the ancient Greeks and Romans, the strawberry was not cultivated by them. There is, however, evidence from the works of Virgil, Ovid, and Pliny the Elder that the berries were picked for food. In Virgil's *Eclogues 3*, Damoetas the shepherd warns:

> *Ye boys gathering flowers and the ground loving strawberry picking,*
> *Run away quickly, hid within the grass an adder lies.*

Ovid, in his *Metamorphoses*, refers twice to strawberries. In his description of the Golden Age he wrote: 'They gathered Arbutus berries and mountain strawberries, wild cherries and blackberries that cling to thorny bramble bushes.' Pliny, in his *Natural History* also referred to the strawberry tree: 'The tree is termed the Strawberry tree; and there is not any other tree that gives fruit which resembles the fruit of a herb growing on the ground. The flesh of the ground strawberry is different from that of the Strawberry tree.'

All these references were to *Fragaria vesca* which was first referred to in Britain in the *Glastonbury Herbal*, early in the tenth century: 'The strawberry is produced in secret places and in clean ones and also on the downs', presumably referring to plants growing in woodlands and hedges and on the open downs. The fact that strawberry seeds dating from the Iron Age were also found at Glastonbury indicates a very long period of their growth in Somerset.

In his Anglo-Saxon Latin glossary, published in AD 995, the Benedictine monk Aelfric, the most important writer of the late West-Saxon period, included *Fragaria* as 'streabariye'. This name referred to the fact that the runners allow the plants to 'stray', and this doubtless gave rise to the name of the strawberry. However, other writers have considered the name refers to the use of straw placed around the fruiting plants. This view was held by Sir Joseph Banks but was questioned by Henry Phillips in 1827 who pointed out that the name had been used long before strawberries were cultivated in gardens. Phillips suggested that: 'The name originated from the old practice of threading these berries on straws of grass, in which shape they were brought from the woods. It is still practised by children in many country places where the wild strawberry abounds, who offer you the fruit, so many straws of berries for a penny.'

EARLY STRAWBERRY CULTIVATION

The earliest reference to the purchase of strawberries in England is found in the Rolls of Edward III for the year 1328—9: 'furcam de argento pro straubertis' (payment of silver for strawberries). The first record of strawberries having been brought into cultivation in Europe is of 1200 plants grown in the royal gardens of King Charles V of France (1364—80) at the Louvre in Paris.

An early reference to the wood strawberry being sold in England occurs in the poem 'London Lickpenny', written by John Lydgate (1330—1400), a Benedictine monk of Bury St Edmunds. Lydgate wrote of the London street cries used by the market women who hawked fruits and flowers in the streets of the city:

> *Then unto London I dyd me hye*
> *Of all the land it beareth the pryse:*
> *Hot pescodes, one began to cry,*
> *Strabery rype, and cherrys in the ryse.*

In Europe, Ruellius spoke of the wood strawberry in 1536 as growing wild in shady places but, when grown in gardens, the fruit was larger and that there was a white variety. This white variety, like others selected for their berries, was grown in gardens for many years. Fuchsius in 1542 mentioned such a larger-berried garden variety. In 1545, Estinne said strawberries were used as delicacies at table, with sugar and cream or wine, and that they were the size of a hazel nut. He also noted that some wild strawberries grew in the mountains and others in woods, but that nothing could be more fragrant than some of the cultivated ones which were larger, with white or red fruits or fruits of both colours.

In England, during the latter part of the sixteenth century, writers frequently referred to the wood strawberry, and it seems that at this time it was still the practice to collect wild plants from the woods for use in gardens. Thomas Tusser, in his *Five Hundred Pointes of Good Husbandrie*, 1580, wrote:

> *Set strawberries wife*
> *I love them for life.*
>
> *Wife into the garden and set me a plot*
> *With strawberry roots of the best to be got.*
> *Such growing abroade, among thorns in the wood*
> *Wel chosen and picked prove excellent good.*

> *The Gooseberry, Respis and Roses al three*
> *With Strawberries under them trimley agree.*

In his advice for the month of January, Tusser recommended:

> *If frost doe continue take this for a lawe*
> *The strawberries looke to be covered with straw,*
> *Laid overly trim, upon crotchis and bows,*
> *And after uncovered, as weather allows.*

The covering of strawberry plants with straw or other material during the coldest months of winter is still practised in some countries, such as parts of North America where the soil remains frozen for a long period and there are persistent cold, drying winds. In Tusser's time, during the Little Ice Age, the winters were often much colder than they are today.

It was not only the country folk who collected wild strawberry plants for growing in their gardens. There is reference in the Hampton Court accounts for 1533 to the purchase of strawberry runners for planting in the garden of Henry VIII: 'Emptions of strawberry roots violettes and primerose roots for the new garden — also paid to Ales Brewer and Margaret Rogers for gathering of 34 bushels of strawberry roots, primerose and violettes at 3d the bushel, 8s 6d. Item by Mathew Garrett of Kyngston for setting of the said rootes and flowers by the space of 20 days at 3d the day, 5s.'

STRAWBERRIES IN EARLY GARDENING BOOKS

In 1578 Heresbachius wrote that the wild plants of the wood strawberry brought in from the woods prospered for two or three years before they were renewed or moved to another place. Normally they gave two crops a year, in the spring and towards the end of the summer. Thomas Hill also wrote, in 1577, of cultivating wood strawberries and of their use:

> *The Berries eaten with white Wine and a little sugar doth marvellously amende the hardness and swelling of the spleene, these same doth the juyce of the berrie, taken with honye, and the leaves sundry tymes used in a bath, is said to be the most profitable against the stone.*
>
> *If any shall be mightily molested with grievous ache and paynes of the hyppes lette him take three or four handfulles of the Strawberry leaves, and boylyng them tender, sitte in the bath and rubbe the legges well (with the licour and leaves) from the nether part upwards. Which done, and thoroughly dryed with a warm cloathe, applye thys Oyntment following prepared after thys manner.*

*Take of the oyntment of the Marche Mallowes one ounce, unto
whiche myxt halfe an ounce of stone honey, and a dramme weight of
ware, makyng thereof an oyntment by a softe syse; this on suche
wyse handeled amendeth the griefs of the hippes, and softeneth the
matter hardened in them.*

*The Berries in the Summer tyme, eaten with Creame and Sugar,
is accompted by a greate refreshing to Man, but more commended
beyng eaten with Wine and Sugar, for on suche use these
marvellously coole and moisten Chollericke stomaches or such
beyng of a cholericke complexion.*

*Among other commodities whiche the Berries yield, the Juice or
wine pressed forth of them is a soveraigne remedie for the removing
of the great redness, spots and red pimples, which happen on the
face, through the heate of the Lyver: the selfe same assuageth and
putteth away the rednesse of the eyes, the spots and hot distillings
fro the hed, by dropping of it sundry times into the eyes.*

In the first edition of his famous herbal in 1597, John Gerard included two
illustrations of the wood strawberry, a red and white variety. Referring to
these he wrote:

*There be divers sorts of Strawberries, one red, another white, a
thirde sort greene, and likewise a Strawberrie, which is altogether
barren of fruite. The leaves boiled and applied in maner of a pultis,
taketh away the burning heate in wounds: the decoction thereof
strengthneth the gums, fasteneth the teeth, and is good to be helde
in the mouth against the inflamation or burning heate thereof, and
also of the almonds of the throat.*

*The berries quench thirst — the distilled water drunke with white
wine, is good against the passion of the hart, reviving the spirits,
and maketh the hart merrie.*

The popularity of strawberries in the sixteenth century is also shown by
reference to this fruit in some of Shakespeare's plays. In *Richard III*, Richard,
speaking to the Bishop of Ely, says:

> *My Lord of Ely, when I was last in Holborn,*
> *I saw good strawberries in your garden there:*
> *I do beseech you send for some of them.*

The account of the cultivation of strawberries in the garden of the Bishop of
Ely's palace in the time of Richard III (1483—5) was copied by Shakespeare
from information in Stow's *Annals*. At this time the Bishops of Ely had a
noted garden adjoining their palace at Holborn, renowned for its vineyard as
well as for its strawberries.

Sir Francis Bacon (1561—1626), in his essay *Of Gardens*, inspired by his own extensive gardens which he had developed on his Gorhambury estate in Hertfordshire, described his plan for planting up a heath: 'Ground set with violets, strawberries and primroses: for these are sweet and prosper in the shade. Standards of roses, juniper, holly, barberies (but here and there, because of the smell of their blossoms) red currants, gooseberries, rosemary and bays.'

DIFFERENT TYPES OF STRAWBERRY

After 300 years of cultivation in the gardens of Europe, *F. vesca* varied comparatively little from the wild type, though some forms had rather larger or white or green berries and others produced no runners. Even when other species of strawberries were cultivated, the runners of the wood strawberry were still collected from the wild as described in *The French Gardiner* in 1669:

> *Strawberries are of four kinds, the white, the large red, the Capron and the small wild red. Concerning these last which are the small kind, you need not put yourself to the trouble of cultivating them if you dwell near the Woods, where they abound; for the Children will bring them to you for a small reward; And in case you be far from these pretty Sweets, you may furnish small carpets of them on the sides of some of your Alleys with out other care or pains then to plant them, sending for such as are in little sods from the places which naturally produce them, or else you may sowe them by casting the water wherein you wash the Strawberries before you eat them, upon the foresaid Beds.*

Wood strawberries were picked for sale throughout the eighteenth century. Gilbert White in his *Journal* (1768—93) recorded that these were regularly collected in the woods by children and sold to the householders in his village of Selborne in Hampshire. He described how, when old beech trees were cleared, within a year or two the bare ground became covered with strawberry plants the seeds of which must have lain in the ground for an age.

The fruits of *F. vesca* were still popular in the markets of Holland in 1817 where they were known as Boskoeper as the plants were obtained from the woods near Boskoop. By varying the planting time, the fruit at Haarlem was sometimes gathered over a period of nine months, from March until November.

Alpine Strawberry

An important type of *F. vesca*, still grown today, is the Alpine, *F. vesca semperflorens*. Though this was known to the Swiss naturalist Conrad Gesner (1516—56) as occurring in mountain regions, it did not come to the notice of gardeners in northern Europe until the eighteenth century.

According to the French botanist Duchesne, writing in 1766, a M. de Fougeron saw the Alpine strawberry growing on Mount Conis in Italy and brought back seed for his uncle, M. du Hamel, who raised plants from the seed on his farm at Nain Villiers. He grew these for three to four years and it is said that George III received the first seed which at first sold for a guinea a pinch. From England plants were sent to nurseries in Holland and sold for £5 a hundred.

The plants of Alpine varieties are somewhat larger than the wild form of *F. vesca*; they fruit over a long season and produce an autumn crop. From its everbearing habit, it was sometimes called the Monthly or Perpetual. Many of the Alpines breed true from seed. In 1825 a variety, Galleon, was introduced in France; this produced no runners and was known there as 'buisson'; it had red and white forms. Later, many larger-fruited forms of the Alpine appeared. In 1855, Reine des Quatre Saisons was introduced by M. Gautier who grew strawberries for the Paris market where the delicate flavour was much appreciated.

The Alpines were not quite so popular in England as in France but in the early years of the nineteenth century they were still cried in the London streets as late as November. Today, Baron Solemacher is considered one of the best varieties.

The Hautbois

This species of *Fragaria* (*Fragaria elatior* syn *F. moschata*) was cultivated to some extent in the past and is still grown in a few places in Europe. It is not a native of Britain but is found in woods in central Europe whence it was brought into cultivation in the sixteenth century. It produces a more vigorous and larger plant than *F. vesca*; the berries are small, oval and tapered and are sweet with an aromatic, slightly musky flavour. The fruits stand up stiffly above the foliage. In general it is not very productive as the sexes are often separate.

In England, the Hautbois was grown from the seventeenth century but never equalled the Alpine in popularity, probably owing to its poor production. Initially it was known by the French name of Capron but was also called the Polonian and Hauboy. Several distinct varieties were introduced including Prolific or Royal, Apricot and Framboise in France and

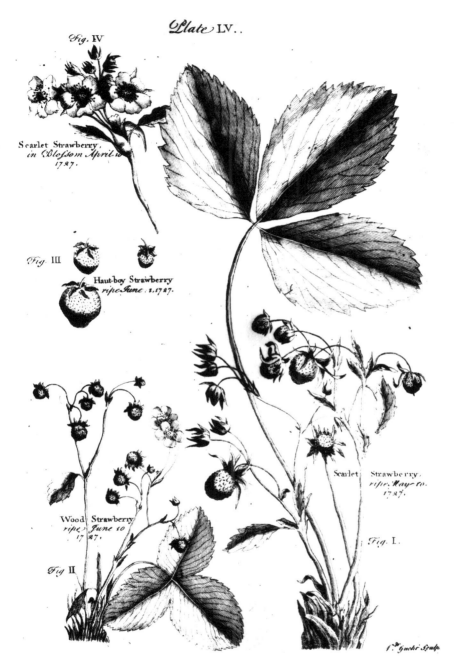

The four types of strawberries grown in British gardens in the early eighteenth century. The large fruited varieties were not introduced until 100 year later.

Globe and Prolific in England. Later, in the early nineteenth century, the Black Hautbois was introduced. In Germany, near Hamburg, a variety of Hautbois was grown for many years and liked for its flavour and musky odour but was of small size and cropped poorly.

One person who did appreciate the Hautbois was Mr Knightley, together with his guests at his strawberry party in Jane Austen's, *Emma*. Comments made by them were: 'These are the finest beds and finest sorts — Hautboy infinitely superior — no comparison — the other hardly eatable — Hautboys very scarce — Chili preferred — white wood finest of all.'

To improve cropping of the Hautbois, Duchesne in France in 1766 had discussed the need to include male flower bearing plants and this was referred to by Michael Keens in 1809 who said he included one male to ten female plants in beds of this strawberry.

Virginian Strawberry

The Virginian strawberry (*Fragaria virginiana*) played a very important part in the development of the large-berried varieties grown today. This species is a native of the eastern part of North America where it is common in woodlands and hedgerows, just as *F. vesca* is in Europe. Before the arrival of the first settlers in New England, the Indians used the berries for food. They called this 'wattahimneah'. They bruised the strawberries with Indian corn meal in a mortar and made bread with the product.

It was reported that settlers on the ship *Arabella* who went ashore on 12 June 1630, regaled themselves with the wild strawberries. In 1643, a naturalist, Roger Williams wrote: 'This berry is the wonder of all the fruits growing naturally in these parts. It is of itself excellent. In some parts where the Indians have planted, I have many times seen as many strawberries as would fill a good ship, within a few miles compass.'

This strawberry had been recorded in 1624 by Jean Robin, botanist to Louis XIII, and it is probable that the first plants were brought from France to England. Later, seeds and plants were imported direct from America. Parkinson mentioned it in 1629, saying it carried more leaf than other varieties but cropped poorly, probably because they lacked sufficient skill in managing it. However, by 1687, Worlidge was full of praise for it, saying that it was the earliest type grown in England being ready the first week in May.

Compared with modern varieties, the Virginian berries are relatively small, rather necked and pointed and have a pronounced sweet scent. The plants form runners freely and readily show symptoms when infected with virus diseases. Although this species shows a greater capacity for variation than *F. vesca* or *F. elatior*, and many different forms exist in its native country, the cultivated forms showed relatively little improvement over the wild species and it was probably about 100 years or more before any named varieties appeared. In 1766 Duchesne wrote of a variety, Strasburg, with longer fruits, and a variety, Oblong Scarlet, raised by Gibbs, a nurseryman of Old Brompton, was in cultivation some time after 1820. During the early part of the nineteenth century, some 20 to 30 different varieties of the Virginian were introduced. Among these were Grove End Scarlet, raised by William Atkinson of Grove End, Marylebone, Duke of Kent's Scarlet and Knight's Large Scarlet.

Many seedlings were raised from seeds imported from Canada and North America, but the fruit size was still limited and it was generally agreed that the flavour of the original Virginian Scarlet was still unsurpassed. In the United States, several cultivated varieties, such as Earl Hudson and Large Early Scarlet, appeared in about 1820, and were important commercially until the middle of the century when they were replaced by the new improved hybrid types. Today, only one or two of the Virginian varieties remain in cultivation in Britain. Of these, Little Scarlet is grown for high-quality preserves and is much esteemed for its delicious flavour, fine scent and its retention of shape and colour when made into jam.

During the eighteenth and nineteenth centuries, the Virginian Scarlet was much used for forcing for marketing early. Bradley in 1726 suggested including one or two rows in any heated structure which should provide ripe fruits by the end of February or early March.

Chilean Strawberry

Following the introduction of the Virginian strawberry to Europe, it was the importation of another species, the Chilean strawberry (*Fragaria chiloensis*), which eventually led to the development of our present-day, large-fruited varieties.

In hybridization between different species, the chromosome number is of paramount importance as normally only species with similar chromosome numbers are able to cross freely with each other. Exceptionally, species with different numbers may be crossed if, for example, the numbers of one of them become doubled so as to match those of the other species. Of the two species which had been grown for many years, the wood strawberry, *F. vesca*, is a diploid with 14 chromosomes, and the Hautbois, *F. elatior*, is a hexaploid with 42. The introduction of the Virginian strawberry, *F. virginiana*, an octoploid with 56 chromosomes, followed by *F. chiloensis* with a similar number, meant that two species were being grown which were capable of hybridization.

Fragaria chiloensis is a common wild species growing from Alaska to California and from Peru, in the mountain ranges near the coast, to Patagonia in South America. It is the South American form which played the more important part. The Chilean strawberry has larger fruit than any other species of *Fragaria*. The berries are large and rounded, somewhat conical in shape, and often rather hollow. The flavour is sweet without being pronounced. The flowers are usually dioecious, with separate male and female forms. The flower stalks are usually shorter than the leaf stalks so that the flowers are rather hidden by the foliage. The plants appear to be very resistant to virus degeneration and symptoms of virus infection are often masked.

It was the large fruit of the Chilean strawberry which appealed to a French naval officer, Capt. A. F. Frézier (1682—1773) who, in 1712, found it growing on the Isle de la Conception in Chile. Capt. Frézier who was a spy, was a member of the crew of a ship operating under the orders of the French king which paid visits to the coasts of Chile, Peru and Brazil during the period 1712—14. He subsequently wrote an account of these voyages which was published in 1716 in which he described the countries he had visited and some of the plants he had seen.

Writing of the Isle of Conception he said:

> They cultivate in the open country a species of strawberry differing from ours, with more rounded leaves and with more fleshy fruits of better quality. The fruits are normally as large as a nut and sometimes as large as a hen's egg; they are of a red whitish colour and of a little less delicate taste than our wood strawberry. I have given several roots to M. de Jussieu for the Royal Gardens where it is hoped they will be made to fruit.

This simple statement concealed the problem that Frézier experienced in bringing plants back to his native country and keeping them alive during the six months' voyage. However, by using part of his own limited water ration, he did manage to get five plants back to France. Unfortunately, all the plants were apparently females, but two were given to M. de Jussieu, who cultivated them with fair success in the royal gardens in Paris. One of the runners was planted at Brest where the new variety was grown interplanted with other varieties, principally with forms of the Hautbois and Virginian Scarlet which served to fertilize the flowers of the Chilean plants. These strawberries formed the basis of the industry at Brest which still flourishes in that area today.

From France, plants of *F. chiloensis* were taken to Holland where some were grown by a Mr George Clifford at Amsterdam who grew large beds of it in his garden. In 1727 Phillip Miller, who was in charge of the Apothecaries Garden at Chelsea, brought some of these plants from Amsterdam to England. It was reported as flowering in an Eltham garden in 1730, but it had not then produced ripe fruit.

Although the Chilean strawberry attracted attention when it was first brought to Europe, it did not at first find much favour since the need for cross-pollination was not appreciated. In England in the eighteenth century cultivated varieties of the wood strawberry, *F. vesca*, were considered better than all others. Apart from its poor cropping, the Chilean strawberry was thought to be too pale and have a bland, sweet taste lacking quality. In addition, it was not very hardy.

The Pine Strawberry

The first important derivative of *F. chiloensis*, which appeared in France during the middle of the eighteenth century, was the Pine, also described as *F. grandiflora* and *F. ananassa*. An account of this was given by the French botanist, Duchesne, in his *Historie Naturelle des Fraisiers* in 1766. By this time, the strawberry industry based on *F. chiloensis* and the Hautbois and Virginian Scarlet had been developed in the north-west of France and Duchesne said that seed of one variety, Fruitilles, was sent, in 1764, from Cherbourg to the garden at the Trianon and that of the king. The resulting plants he described as true Pine strawberries which had perfect flowers. Fruitilla was the name under which *F. chiloensis* had long been cultivated in Chile, Peru and Ecuador.

The Pine usually varied little when raised from seed and was noteworthy for both its size and its distinctive pine flavour. Other varieties of this type, which appeared during the latter part of the eighteenth century, were Bath, Quoimio and Carolina. Evidence that the Pine strawberry became popular in England is given in Gilbert White's *Journal* for 1 July 1791, when he wrote that large American strawberries were hawked about which the sellers called Pine. These strawberries, which had a delicate flavour, had largely replaced the old Scarlet and Hautbois.

PRODUCTION OF LARGE-FRUITED VARIETIES

Although Sir Francis Bacon (1561 – 1626) in his natural history, *Sylva Sylvarum* published in 1627 after his death, had seen the possibilities of cross-fertilization for producing new varieties of plants, this had not been followed up, although Richard Bradley, Professor of Botany at Cambridge University, in 1739 described in detail the fertilization process in flowers and the possibilities of producing new varieties by cross-pollination. He wrote that anyone with this knowledge, by choosing as parents two plants which were nearly alike in their flowers and seed vessels, might produce rare kinds of plants not yet heard of. As an example, he suggested the carnation and sweet william, and said that, by using this method, new varieties of flowers and fruits might be created.

It was really the work of Duchesne which initiated the first serious examination of cross-fertilization in strawberries. However, although some improved, larger types of Pine strawberries were introduced in France, the Revolution there hindered much further development in the latter part of the eighteenth century, and it was work in England which resulted in a major breakthrough leading to the eventual introduction of our present-day, large-fruited varieties.

The initiative of the market gardener at Isleworth, Michael Keens, who supplied strawberries to the London markets, led the way with the new varieties. In 1817 he described how he came to raise the first of these, Keens' Imperial. He found that, when propagated by runners or other vegetative methods, his strawberry stocks deteriorated (probably the result of virus infection). He therefore began raising his new plants from seed. In 1806 he sowed seed of the large white Chilean. Most of the progeny were white and poorly flavoured, but one, a red variety, stood out by its superiority. The growth of the plant was free and vigorous, the flower stalks erect, the berries round, like its parent, with a deep crimson colour, and altogether more attractive than any existing variety. As Keens was in the habit of including pollen-bearing male plants along with strawberries such as the Hautbois which were deficient in pollen, it is probable that he had included plants of *F. virginiana* with the imperfectly fertile *F. chiloensis*.

Although the new variety was received with somewhat muted enthusiasm by the committee of the newly formed Horticultural Society, it was his second introduction, Keens' Seedling, which he bred from seed of his Imperial, which really created a sensation and was a variety of major importance both in its own right and as a parent of many other important varieties. The large size and excellent flavour of the new variety was universally acknowledged and, in 1821, the Horticultural Society presented Keens with a Silver Cup to show their approval.

OTHER NEW VARIETIES

The successful introduction of Keens' Imperial and Seedling gave a marked impetus to the breeding of strawberries by others both in Europe and the United States. In 1822, John Wilmot, who like Keens was a market gardener at Isleworth, raised Black Prince from seed of Keens' Imperial and, in the following year, Wilmot's Superb, by crossing the Chilean with a scarlet strawberry. In 1824, he brought out Wilmot's Coxcombe Scarlet, also a seedling from Keens' Imperial. This variety had larger fruit than the old Scarlet but the colour and flavour were as rich. A particular feature was its

Keens' Imperial strawberry raised in 1806 by Michael Keens,
one of the first large fruited varieties.

Keens' Seedling strawberry bred from Keens' Imperial. Introduced in 1821,
a most important new variety and parent of many other varieties of note.

unusual 'cockscomb' shape, previously unknown in other varieties. The similarity in colour and flavour of this variety to the Virginian Scarlet lends strength to the idea that the Virginian strawberry contributed to the success of Keens' varieties.

About 1824, Keens' Imperial was taken to the United States, and from 1830 to 1840 was a standard variety in the gardens of amateurs. The plants proved to be rather tender but its introduction was of great importance as it is thought to have been one of the parents of Hovey, a variety which had a major impact on the development of the strawberry industry in America. Hovey was bred by Charles Hovey, a nurseryman of Cambridge, Mass., and first fruited in 1836. It was important as the first fruit of any kind in the United States to result from a deliberate cross. Hovey proved a sensation. Its large, handsome, good-flavoured berries resulted in it being distributed to all parts of North America, and the interest it stimulated made the strawberry industry of major importance before the middle of the century.

In France, the introduction of Keens' varieties was welcomed as the greatest advance so far in strawberry culture, and for many years these large-fruited varieties were known as 'Les Fraises Anglaises'. The impetus given to strawberry breeding in France resulted in 1844 in the introduction of Princess Royale which became a leading variety in France for 50 years.

Apart from Keens, the other major contributor to the development of large-fruited strawberries in the early nineteenth century was Thomas Andrew Knight. His work extended from breeding tree fruits to other crops including strawberries. The success of Keens was the result of his practical observations and ability as a good plantsman, while Knight was a pioneer in knowing the source of his parent material and controlling the cross-pollination. His success in breeding strawberries was only moderate but his Elton Pine remained in commercial use for many years. He had about 400 new varieties growing in his garden and gave details of 18 he was ready to supply to the Horticultural Society for trial. Apart from Elton, introduced in 1827, another seedling of note was Downton, probably *F. chiloensis* crossed with *F. virginiana*.

It is generally recognized that the three varieties, Keens' Seedling, Downton and Elton were the forerunners of most of our large-fruited strawberries. The Pine flavour they introduced was of particular value.

Other new varieties of particular note in the first half of the nineteenth century were British Queen (1840) and Eleanor (1847), raised by Mr Myatt of Deptford. British Queen was grown commercially in England for many years and was still grown 100 years after its introduction in areas of Hampshire and Somerset. It was still a recommended variety for gardens in 1940, as was Black Prince which had an even longer history, having been raised in 1822. Another famous variety, raised by Samuel Bradley of Elton

Manor, Nottingham, was Sir Joseph Paxton and the highly flavoured Dr Hogg in 1866.

One of the most successful of English strawberry breeders was the nurseryman Thomas Laxton of Bedford, who raised outstanding new varieties of many tree and soft fruits. He bred Traveller strawberry in 1872, and Noble and King of the Earlies in 1884, the merits of both of which were recognized by RHS First Class Certificates. It was the result of a cross between these two varieties, Royal Sovereign, introduced in 1892, for which Laxton is chiefly remembered and it is a worthy tribute to the memory of this great plant breeder that Sovereign is still regarded by many as our best-flavoured variety still in use.

During the early years of this century, apart from Royal Sovereign, a number of continental varieties, including Tardive de Leopold, Madame Lefebvre and Oberschlesien, enjoyed some popularity, but it was Huxley, raised in California and brought to this country in 1912, which had the longest period of commercial use, extending for more than 50 years. Huxley showed characters typical of *Fragaria chiloensis*, with dark green glossy foliage, and cropped well with firm berries but these lacked good flavour, being sweet but insipid. It was grown especially in the Wisbech area for processing.

By the beginning of this century the old types of strawberries, including the wood strawberry and the Hautbois, had virtually disappeared from commercial use, though they were occasionally grown in gardens, and had been replaced by the large-fruited, hybrid varieties. Types of the Alpine strawberry, *F. vesca semperflorens* are still grown and Little Scarlet, a form of *F. virginiana*, continues to be grown on a limited scale for high-quality preserves.

MODERN STRAWBERRY BREEDING

Until this century, the breeding of new varieties of strawberries was largely done by nurserymen. Today, however, the production of new varieties of strawberries and other fruits has become more and more the work of the scientifically trained plant breeder, working at one of the research stations.

The modern strawberry breeder usually has several objectives in view, such as extending the picking season, producing heavier cropping varieties of improved colour, size and texture, suited for the fresh-fruit market or for processing, and breeding varieties resistant to disease.

Improvement of flavour in strawberry breeding often seems to take second place to breeding for a character such as ability to travel well during transport to market though, during the nineteenth century when the first large-fruited varieties were being developed, the importance of flavour usually came first. Today, the general appearance of the berries is the overriding factor in deciding the popularity of a variety with the buyer — a sad reflection on modern tastes.

In Great Britain during this century the breeding of strawberries has been mainly the work of D. Boyes at the now defunct Horticultural Research Station of Cambridge University, Robert Reid who worked at Auchincruive, Ayr in Scotland and whose work was later carried on by plant breeders at the Scottish Horticultural Research Institute, John Innes Horticultural Institution in Norfolk and, more recently, Long Ashton Research Station.

At Cambridge during the 1930s and 1940s, Boyes carried out an extensive breeding programme, using as parents a wide range of existing varieties, including Huxley, Royal Sovereign and Early Cambridge and species of *Fragaria*, especially *chiloensis*. Of the many new varieties he raised, which were tested and distributed by Howard Jones of Kingsley Fruit Farm in Hampshire, Cambridge Favourite, a derivative of *F. chiloensis*, soon established itself in the post-war years as a valuable, heavy-cropping second early variety for both protected and open-air production. Its firm texture and suitability for both processing and the fresh-fruit market meant that it rapidly became popular with growers in most parts of the country, in the early production areas under cloches, the main fresh-fruit areas of Kent and other counties and the processing region of Wisbech. In many trials, carried out at the National Fruit Station at Brogdale, Faversham and at the Ministry of Agriculture's Horticultural Stations, Cambridge Favourite consistently out-cropped other varieties and quickly became the leading commercial variety, over 70 per cent of the total strawberry acreage being devoted to this type. Although other varieties challenged its position, even after 25 years, Cambridge Favourite maintained its place as the most planted strawberry.

Of the many other varieties bred by Boyes, the early Cambridge Prizewinner, and the red core resistant Cambridge Rival, enjoyed some popularity but the other variety of leading importance has been Cambridge Vigour, valued for its earliness under protected cultivation and for growing in the early areas of the south-west and Ireland.

At Auchincruive, Robert Reid worked for many years breeding strawberries resistant to the soil-borne disease, red core, caused by the fungus *Phytophthora fragariae*. This disease attacks the roots of the plants and can cause very severe losses, while the fungus can exist in the soil for many years ready to attack anew any strawberries which may be planted there.

The first result of Reid's patient work was seen in the issue of Auchincruive Climax in 1946−7. This had a complex parentage including an American sort, Blakemore, showing red core resistance, and proved itself to be a very heavy-cropping variety of excellent quality, valuable for the fresh-fruit grower as well as being ideal for canning and freezing. Unfortunately, after a few years of great popularity, Climax developed a physiological fault, a mutation of the chloroplasts, called June yellows, inherited from its Blakemore parentage, which led to its rapid breakdown and virtual disappearance from cultivation.

Another good-quality variety bred by Reid was Talisman, released in 1955. Lack of good berry size was its main drawback. Redgauntlet, introduced in 1956−7, though lacking the good flavour of Reid's other varieties — a fact which at first made him reluctant to release it — proved to be heavy cropping with berries of good size and especially suited for early production under cloches and tunnels. It also has the ability, especially in early districts, if the first crop has been protected in the spring, to produce a second crop from flowers which were differentiated during the shorter days in spring and yield their fruit from the latter part of August.

Several other varieties, either bred by Reid or by his successors, have been introduced, including Saladin, Silver Jubilee and Tantallon, but none has so far gained the popularity of the earlier ones. Resistance to red core disease is still a main objective with these varieties, but they have not usually had the good flavour of Climax or Talisman.

For a time the breeding of strawberries was carried on by Wilson at Long Ashton Research Station but was ended by the closing of the plant breeding section in 1983. That being done at John Innes, by Hedley Williams, who was originally an assistant to Boyes at Cambridge, came to an end with Williams' untimely death. One aspect of his work had been to breed varieties for cropping in late summer and early autumn but this was unfinished at the time of his death. All strawberry breeding work is now centred on East Malling Research Station.

Outside the research stations, the only breeder of strawberries who has met with any success in recent years in England has been Richard Cumberland. Working in Hampshire and making use of parent varieties with autumn-cropping tendencies, he raised Aromel, a cross between Redgauntlet and one of his earlier seedlings. This variety, having good-sized though somewhat soft berries, is outstanding for its flavour and produces a useful second crop in late summer.

In addition to those raised in Britain, many new varieties bred on the Continent and in the United States have been introduced since the 1950s. One of the most successful has been Gorella, raised at Wageningen in Holland. Tamella is another variety from the same source. Domanil from Belgium has also been popular. Few of the varieties bred in the United States have proved of general use in Great Britain.

Of recent years, there has been interest in breeding varieties with upright growing flower trusses which might prove suitable for mechanical harvesting and in varieties suited to freezing and other processing outlets. Future breeding will make use of day neutral parent varieties from California which will allow strawberry plants to crop continuously, limited only by temperature.

AUTUMN-FRUITING AND EVERBEARING STRAWBERRIES

Although since the introduction of large-fruited berries plant breeders in Britain have mostly concentrated on the production of strawberries which give a single crop in the summer, in some countries, in particular France and the United States, attention has been given to breeding varieties which will crop over a long period and give both summer and autumn fruit. However, some attention has been given to this aspect of breeding in recent years in England.

Some of the autumn-fruiting Alpine strawberries were grown for many years before the use of *Fragaria chiloensis*. Attempts to obtain any size in the berries of the Alpines met with little success until the Abbé Thivolet, at Chenoves in France, introduced St Joseph in 1893. The exact origin of this variety is a little obscure, but the fruit showed distinct improvement in size over existing sorts and the plants yield two crops a year, one in early summer and the second in early autumn. St Joseph, crossed with Royal Sovereign, gave St Antoine de Padoue. Other French varieties of this type were Louis Gauthier and St Fiacre, the latter a cross between Louis Gauthier and St Antoine de Padoue raised by M. Vilmorin in 1903.

In 1929 a further step forward in the development of everbearing or autumn-fruiting varieties (the remontants of France) was the introduction of Mme Raymond Poincare by M. Roland Chapron at Caen. The same breeder, in 1937, introduced Sans Rivale, one of the best of this class of strawberry which was grown to a very limited extent in Great Britain. Other varieties of this type were Triomphe and St Claude.

These autumn-fruiting French varieties normally carry a light crop at the usual time in early summer, and then grew rapidly and come into flower again in July and early August and continue to blossom and fruit, often on the newly formed runners, until stopped by the cold weather in autumn. When grown in Britain, the berries of the French varieties formed in late summer are often rather acid and rotting of the berries, through attacks by the *Botrytis fungus*, can be troublesome.

While the autumn-fruiting strawberries were being developed in France, the first large-fruited varieties of this type were also introduced in the United States. There, in 1898, Samuel Cooper of Delevan, New York, found a plant carrying an autumn crop in a field of Bismarck, a summer-fruiting variety introduced in 1895. This new variety, named Pan-American, was presumably a mutation of Bismarck, and was used as one of the parents for several other varieties bred during the early years of this century. Red Rich which was distributed in 1951 was grown on a limited scale in England but, apart from this, the American varieties are not generally suited to the British climate.

Apart from the French, American and some other autumn-fruiting strawberries, many varieties normally regarded as summer cropping also bear a crop in autumn; for example, Redgauntlet. The tendency to produce a crop in autumn is bound up with the conditions which influence flower differentiation in the strawberry and the reaction of different varieties to variations in these conditions. Normally, flower differentiation takes place during the period of shortened day length and lower temperature in the autumn, and the flower buds so initiated produce the flowers in the following spring. Such is the way in which flower differentiation takes place in Royal Sovereign, a typical single-crop variety.

With other varieties, including Redgauntlet, the relationship between temperature and day length is delicately balanced, and moderately low temperatures in spring and early autumn can induce flower differentiation and result in autumn cropping. Where Redgauntlet is grown in an area with comparatively late springs, such as Scotland, secondary flowering is unusual.

In the United States, in California, this relationship between temperature and hours of day length is the reason for the long fruiting periods of varieties such as Tioga and Fresno. In the northern states, these varieties behave like Redgauntlet, producing a summer and sometimes an autumn crop but, depending on the region of California in which they are grown, there they flower and fruit from late winter until the following autumn. This is the result of the short day length allowing continuous flower differentiation.

The California varieties similarly crop over a long period in other parts of the world with latitudes similar or less than California where day length is limited and temperatures are suitable. Nearer the tropics, these strawberries can be grown at relatively high altitudes where the temperatures are lower. Even a variety such as Cambridge Favourite, when grown in the Canary Isles, will continue in crop over several months, starting in mid-winter. The day neutral California varieties will completely change the cropping pattern of strawberries in the future.

RED AND WHITE CURRANTS　　　30

All types of currants and gooseberries belong to the genus *Ribes*, of which there are many species distributed in various parts of the northern hemisphere. The three fruits, red and white currants, black currants and gooseberries, have originated from different species, although several have been involved in the development of the red and white currants. The cultivated varieties of the latter have evolved from at least three wild species, *Ribes rubrum, R. vulgare* and *R. petraeum*, and there is a likelihood that additional species may have influenced the production of some of the garden varieties.

Ribes rubrum is a native of central and northern Europe and Asia, eastwards into Siberia and Manchuria and extending to the Arctic circle. It is found in Scotland and parts of the north of England and, though found occasionally in the south, it is difficult to say how far the plants are indigenous as long cultivation has resulted in seedling currants arising as escapes from gardens. *Ribes petraeum* occurs in a wild state further south than *R. rubrum* in the high mountain areas of central and southern Europe, north Africa, the Caucasus and parts of Asia. *Ribes vulgare* is a native of western Europe, found growing wild in parts of Great Britain, France and Belgium. It occurs more in the cold and temperate regions of western Europe than in southern areas.

The nomenclature of the red and white currants is very complex but it has been possible to relate certain varieties to a particular species. For example, Raby Castle and Houghton Castle belong to the *Ribes rubrum* group, the Dutch types belong to *R. vulgare* and Prince Albert to *R. petraeum*. However, many varieties are hybrids between these different groups.

EARLY HISTORY

Unlike many other fruits, currants have a comparatively short history of use whether collected from the wild or cultivated in gardens. There are few records of seeds or other remains having been found during excavations of prehistoric sites. One of the few gives evidence of currants, along with other fruits, at a Mesolithic site of the Mullerup culture. A probable reason why currant remains are not more common is because the fruits of the wild species of *Ribes* are generally small and unattractive, so would not demand attention from early seekers of food.

These species mostly grow in more mountainous or northern countries where temperatures are lower than in the Mediterranean and Middle East where so many of the other cultivated fruits evolved by selection and were brought into cultivation. There is no reference to currants in the literature of the Greeks and Romans who had a wide range of more attractive fruits, and no seeds of any of these fruits have been found on Roman sites in Britain.

FIRST DESCRIPTIONS

The first drawing of a red currant, when the plant was probably grown as a herb, appears in the *Mainz Herbarius* in 1484, but nothing is known as to how far its berries were used as a food at that time. However, by the next century, there were a number of references, both on the Continent and in England, to its value in the garden. In 1536, Ruellius, a French writer, praised it as a border plant and its fruit as an appetizer. In 1539, Ammonius wrote 'we cherish it in our gardens'; in 1542 Fuchsius included a drawing of what was probably the Common Red and, in 1552, a German writer, Tragus, had an illustration of the same 'garden' currant. In 1558, Mathiolus referred to it as being common in gardens.

The earliest reference to red currants in English literature is in William Turner's *Names of Herbs* of 1548. Turner was a friend of Conrad Gesner, a famous German-Swiss naturalist, whom he met during his travels in Europe. Later, in 1561, Gesner found *Ribes petraeum* growing wild in woods near Berne and grew this in his own garden where its large berries attracted much attention. This species, from which the variety Prince Albert was evolved, was imported into England about 1620.

Though the red currant had become well known in Europe by the sixteenth century, it seems to have been first grown as a common garden plant in Holland and the adjoining region where it was, and still is, a favourite fruit. The names of some of the earliest varieties of both red and white currants indicate a Dutch origin. On the other hand, the old French name for currants was 'groseillier d'outre mer' (currant from over the sea), suggesting that they had been imported.

In the 1568 edition of his herbal, Turner wrote:

> *The bushe and fruite called Ribes*
> *Ribes is a little bushe and hath leaves lyke a vyne / and in the toppes of the bushe are red berries in clusters / in taste at the first somethinge sower / but pleasant enough when they are fully ripe. I have seene them growynge in gardins in Englande / and also by a water side at Clouer in Somersetshyre in the possession of maister Horner.*

This last remark is of particular interest in view of the discovery of currant seeds at the lake village site in the Glastonbury area, as Turner's 'Clouer' is probably the village of Clewer, near Wedmore, in the same area. Turner himself lived in Somerset. His account continued:

> *The vertues of the Common Ribes.*
> *The juyce and syrope of Ribes / are good for hote agues and agaynst hote fires and vomitinge of choler. They stoppe lares provoke appetite / and quenche thyrste. Ye maye two wayes kepe Ribes / ether in there owne juyce and verges / or ellis dried in the sunne and so kept. Ribes in al pyntes hath vertue of Barberies.*

At this time the fruits of berberis were commonly used for flavouring meat and fish dishes.

The next reference to currants came in 1578 in Heresbachius' *Foure Bookes of Husbandry*, originally published in Germany. The text took the form of different characters speaking. One of them, Thrasybulus asks:

> *'What say you to small Reazyns, called in Latine, Ribes? doe you thinke the olde writers knewe this bushe?' Marius replied —*
> *'That whiche we call at this day Ribes, and the Dutchmen, Saint Johns pearle, because about Midsommer it is garnished with redde and ritch berries, having a tarte, quenchyng thirst, cheefley, the ragyng and extreame thirst of fevers, and coolyng the Stomache, whiche the Apothecaries in Suger or Honie kepe all the yere, is thought was unowen to the olde wryters: but nowe a common bushe used for encloasyng of Gardens, and makyng of Borders and Herbes: it will easely growe, but that it is something troublesome, by reason of his sharpe prickles to be bent aboute sommer houses.'*

In the sixteenth century fruit bushes were commonly used for borders around the vegetable or herb garden, and vines and other plants were trained around bowers and seats. The reference to 'prickles' suggests that there was some confusion between currants and gooseberries. St John's pearle was certainly the name given to red and white currants in Holland. John Gerard, in 1597, also classified currants with gooseberries under the same heading as gooseberries or feaberries. After writing of gooseberries Gerard continued, 'We have also in our London gardens another sort altogether without prickles, whose fruit is verie small, lesser by much than the common kinde but of a perfect red colour, wherein it differeth from the rest of his kinde.' In his *Five Hundred Pointes of Good Husbandrie*, 1580, Thomas Tusser included gooseberries and 'reisons', or currants, separately, the currants being the red and white types.

ORIGIN OF THE NAME 'CURRANT'

The name 'currant' was derived from the ancient Greek city of Corinth, and was the word used to describe a small grape exported from the area as a dried fruit. The similarity of the berries of the cultivated species of *Ribes* to this dried grape accounted for the name, which in many early English books had several forms — corinthes, corans, currans and bastard corinthes. The name most commonly used was corans, attributed to Francis Bacon.

In 1629, John Parkinson began his account of currants by explaining that those grown in gardens were not the same as ones sold in grocers which came from vines. The red were usually eaten fresh when ripe and especially appreciated in hot weather but were also preserved. The white variety was less common and had a more pleasant winey taste. He said currants would grow to the height of a man but a gardener at Hoxton, in 1732, wrote that those growing in the garden of a house at Petty Cury, Cambridge, reached 20 ft high and that gooseberries could be 12 ft. These were obviously trained on the walls of houses.

Parkinson spoke of a type of red currant twice as large as the Common Red, which showed little improvement over the wild fruit. The larger kind was doubtless the Great Red currant brought to England from Holland in 1611 by John Tradescant Senior and included in the accounts at Hatfield House for 3 January 1611 'for the great red currants 6 plants 1s'. This was referred to in the 1633 edition of Gerard's *Herball*. Its introduction led to a great extension in currant planting and increased their popularity, both as fresh fruit and for making wines and jellies, so that when Worlidge wrote in 1687 he said that the small English Red currant had been cast out of all gardens, as had black currants, and though white currants were more esteemed, they too had been replaced by the Red Dutch.

Following its introduction to England, this currant had been improved even further and replaced by the Greatest Red Dutch. This, said Worlidge,

1 *Rubus Idæus*. The Rafpis. 2 *Ribes fructu rubro vel albo*. White or red Currans. 3 *Groffularia vulgaris*. The ordinary Goofeberry. 4 *Groffulária fructu rubro*. The great red Goofeberry. 5 *Groffularia aculeata*. The prickly Goofeberry. 6 *Oxyacantha
feu Berberis*. The Barbary bufh. 7 *Auellana Byzantina*. The Filberd of Conftantinople. 8 *Auellana rubra noftras*. The beft red
Filberd.

The most important bush fruits grown in the early seventeenth century.
The Berberis was used at this time for adding flavour to meat and fish dishes.

was the only currant fit to be planted and propagated, both for wine and preserving. The juice was much used, mixed with an equal quantity of water, to make vinegar. During the seventeenth century considerable use was made of soft fruits for wines, both at home and commercially. Currants seem to have been the most popular for wine, but gooseberries, raspberries and strawberries were also used.

THE EIGHTEENTH CENTURY

The popularity of currants continued into the eighteenth century and such was the liking for this fruit that gardeners adopted all sorts of devices to extend the season of picking, both by forcing for early production and by covering up the plants to delay ripening. At the beginning of the century they were especially expert in forwarding fruits by structures built of brick and equipped with sloping glass frames and heated by flues and hot beds. For late crops, the bushes were covered up for the latter part of the year or planted against a north wall to delay ripening. By these means Switzer said currants could be available for use raw, for sweetmeats or tarts from March to the end of November.

Switzer recommended the Great White and Great Red Dutch as the largest and best varieties, while the Great Yellow Dutch only differed in colour. All others, he said, were worthless. These varieties maintained their position for the rest of the century, as shown by the lists of varieties of fruits approved and available in nurseries published in *The British Fruit-gardener* by John Abercrombie, in 1779. The list of currants still only included Common Red, Large Red Dutch, White and Large White Dutch, the only new variety being Champagne Large Pale-red. Champagne was in fact an old variety thought to be a cross between Common Red and Common White. The catalogue of Luker and Smith, nurserymen of Covent Garden, in 1783, only offered Large Red Dutch and Large White.

THE NINETEENTH CENTURY

Even in 1812, George Brookshaw's *Pomona Britannica*, which had hand-coloured plates of all fruit varieties of importance at the time, simply illustrated the Large Red and White Dutch, and W. Hooker's *Pomona Londoniensis* in 1818, comprising the most esteemed varieties then cultivated in British gardens, only included the White Dutch.

However, among the fruits to which Thomas Andrew Knight turned his attention in 1810, were red and white currants. As reported in the

Transactions of the Horticultural Society, in that year he planted cuttings of the best varieties of both fruits and, after three years, cross-pollinated the two kinds. Out of the 200 seedlings resulting, only three red and two white showed any improvement over their parents. These were Knight's Sweet Red, Knight's Early Red, Knight's Large Red and two white. Although these were not particularly successful and have long since disappeared from British nurseries, some were still included in Hedrick's *The Small Fruits of New York* in 1925.

In 1826, the Horticultural Society reported that there was probably no class of fruit about which there was so much ignorance as to the merits and differences of varieties as red and white currants, and it was impossible to obtain them true to type. Of the nine red and four white currants in the collection at Chsiwick, the best were considered Red Dutch, Knight's Large Red, Knight's Sweet Red, Knight's Early Red and of the whites, White Dutch. Champagne, with pale red or flesh-coloured fruits, was valued by some for its appearance for dessert.

Two other varieties introduced at this time were Houghton Castle, from Houghton Castle near Hexham, Northumberland and introduced about 1820, and Raby Castle. Both of these were widely planted during the next hundred years and are still grown today.

The mixing of varieties mentioned by the Horticultural Society was aggravated by the ease with which they were propagated so that, as Phillips said in 1827, every cottage gardener could grow them. Forsyth was so keen on producing currants for wine that he suggested planting out the seedlings found growing under the bushes or sowing the seed left after the juice had been squeezed from the berries in the same way that cider pomace is used.

Phillips, like others before him, spoke of the medicinal value of currants and the fact that they would keep for years, in corked bottles, for making tarts, if they were gathered perfectly dry but not too ripe, and as long as they were stored away from air in a dry situation. If the bottles were packed, corks downwards, in a chest, and the space around them filled with sand, this would ensure their longest keeping. Phillips also wrote of the use of red currants for making jelly and white currants for making wines which, if matured, were similar to Graves and Rhenish wines. Even in London, these wines could be made more cheaply than even moderate ciders. Distilled, they provided excellent English brandy.

Apart from the English varieties, Houghton Castle, Raby Castle and Knight's new seedlings, the currants introduced in the nineteenth century included several from abroad. The most important was Cherry. This was found by M. Adrienne Seneclause, a distinguished French horticulturist, in a batch of plants he received from Italy. He was impressed by the large size of the berries. In 1843 it fruited in the nursery of the Museum of Natural History and quickly spread to other countries, including England and the

United States, where it enjoyed a long period of popularity as a large-berried, early variety.

Fay's Prolific was another variety of importance. It was the first of the American red currants to be brought to Europe, having been bred by Lincoln Fay of Portland, New York, about 1868, from Cherry crossed with Victoria. These American varieties were forerunners of another variety from the United States, Red Lake, which had a major impact in Britain during this century. It was raised, from unknown parents, at the Minnesota Fruit Breeding Farm about 1920.

Other important varieties were Versailles, raised about 1835 by M. Bertin of Versailles, Wilson's Long Bunch, often considered a synonym of Victoria of unknown parentage and Prince Albert, known in Germany in the early eighteenth century and described as *Ribes pallidum*, thought to be a hybrid between *R. patraeum* and *R. vulgare*.

MODERN CURRANT CULTIVATION

During the early part of this century, two varieties of red currants of major importance were introduced by the famous firm of Laxton Brothers. The first of these was Laxton's Perfection in 1910, and the second Laxton's No. 1. The latter has occupied a leading position for many years as one of the heaviest cropping early varieties, and Laxton's Perfection is still liked by many gardeners on account of its very large berries.

These two Laxtons' currants are about the only remaining English varieties which are still recommended for planting. All the others have come from Holland, where red currants are still of importance, or from the United States. During this century, as black currants have become more important commercially in Britain, interest in red currants has declined. A very small acreage is grown for making into wine but very few are grown for market, this in spite of the fact that they are usually heavier cropping than black currants and are more resistant to frost damage. They do, however, present greater difficulties in picking and marketing in good condition.

Lack of commercial demand has meant that British plant breeders have not paid much attention to this fruit in the past, but East Malling Research Station has now introduced Malling Redstart, the first red currant to be released by the station. This was bred in 1963 from a cross between Red Lake and a selection B 156/34 (*R. sativum* × *R. multiflorum* × Red Lake). Red currants have also been bred in Holland, an outstanding variety being Jonkheer van Tets, raised by J. Maarse, as a seedling from Fay's Prolific. Another is Rondom, bred by Dr J. Rietsema in 1935 by crossing *R. multiflorum* with Versailles and then back-crossing to an old sweet Dutch variety. Rondom is considered best used as fresh fruit.

In America, breeding of red currants has been continued at the University of Minnesota, which introduced the well-established Red Lake. Of the old varieties, one of the few still grown on a limited scale is Earliest of Fourlands, an early variety of Prince Albert type introduced from the Continent. White Versailles, raised by M. Bertin of Versailles in 1843, is one of the few white currants in use today.

Although little attention has been paid in the past to the virus diseases of red and white as of black currants, they are subject to some of these. Many varieties, however, have continued to crop, though at a reduced level, when infected, which probably accounts for the very long life, extending over several hundreds of years, of a number of the old varieties, such as Red Dutch, which was responsible for the great popularity of red currants during the seventeenth and eighteenth centuries.

In the past, most of the cultivated black currants were developed from *Ribes nigrum* but, of recent years, in order to introduce new characters, this species or derivatives from it, has been hybridized with other species of *Ribes. Ribes nigrum* is a native of Europe, north and central Asia, and is found as far north as Scandinavia and Siberia. Although it is found growing wild in parts of Britain, like red currants, it is likely that the plants originated as escapes from cultivation and are not indigenous.

As with red and white currants, there are no records of black currants having been known or used by the ancient Greeks and Romans, and although it is likely that they had a very long history of use in northern Europe and Siberia, the first mention of the black currant in Britain was in Medieval times for adding colour and flavour to wines. Although there were references to black currants in the sixteenth century, they did not attract the same attention from the herbalists as red currants which were illustrated by several Continental writers at that time.

It is likely that the strong scent of the black currant bush and the strong flavour of the berries, which were often referred to by later writers as unpleasant and repugnant, made herbalists reluctant to use the plant or its fruit though, once the black currant was accepted in gardens, it was highly thought of for its medicinal qualities.

Although both Turner, in his *Names of Herbes*, 1548, and Heresbachius, in 1578 mentioned the red currant, neither included any direct reference to the black currant. This may well have been the result of confusion concerning the whole family of currants and gooseberries. The French at this time used the name 'Grosseilles d'outre mer' (currants beyond the sea) to apply to plants which had been imported into their country. Even today, there is often misinterpretation of the French name for currants and gooseberries, 'groseille à grappes' and 'groseille à maquereau', the word 'groseille' often mistakenly being taken to refer only to gooseberries. The addition of the word 'maquereau' indicates the use of gooseberries for making a sauce used especially with mackerel. This means that Lyte, in his 1578 translation of Dodoens' *Historie of Plantes*, writing of the 'Black and Red beyond the Sea Gooseberry', may well have meant red and black currants.

Gerard, in the first edition of his *Herball* in 1597, dealt with both gooseberries and red currants but made no reference to black currants. However, in the 1633 edition of the herbal, revised and edited by Thomas Johnson, the black currant is included after red currants: 'Besides these there is another, which differs little from the former in shape, yet grows somewhat higher, and hath lesser leaves: the floures are of a purplish green colour and are succeeded by fruit as big againe as the ordinary red, but of a stinking and somewhat loathing savour, the leaves also are not without the stinking smell.' This black currant was doubtless the one which had been imported by John Tradescant in 1611, after the publication of the first edition of Gerard's *Herball*. An account, dated 5 January 1611, for plants imported from Holland for the garden of the newly built Hatfield House, belonging to Tradescant's patron, the Earl of Salisbury, included the item 'for on dussin of great blacke currants 1s'. The importation of the dozen black currants, as with so many other plants brought in by John Tradescant, marked the first record of the fruit being grown in English gardens.

In 1629, before the reference to black currants in the 1633 edition of Gerard's herball, the first English writer to mention this fruit specifically was Parkinson:

> *The black Curran bush riseth higher than the white — black berries of the bigness of the smaller red Currans — both branches, leaves and fruit have a kind of stinking sent with them, yet they are not unwholesome but the berries are eaten of many, without offending either taste or smell. Some use both the leaves and berries in sauces and other meates, and are well pleased both with the savour and taste although many mislike it.*

As these berries were only the size of the smaller red currants, they must have been little removed, if at all, from the wild species, *Ribes nigrum*. They still did not receive approval from other writers. Rea, in 1665, said neither the black nor the small red currant were worth planting, and Worlidge, in 1687, and Switzer, in 1724, expressed the same view.

It was not until Bradley wrote in 1739 that the black variety of currant, both for the sake of variety and its value as medicine, should be planted in the garden, that anyone since Parkinson, had a good word to say about it, though Bradley did add that scarce one in twenty likes its flavour. By 1768,

Gibson, a Scottish writer said they had four kinds of currants, the large white, the red, the yellow and the black. The last was preferred by some as they believed they were more healthsome, their juice sweeter and less acid.

This change in attitude to the black currant and reference to its medicinal value has been evident in the writings of all authors from this time right up to the present day. John Abercrombie, in 1779, in his lists of approved fruit varieties, under currants, said that the black was more for medical use but very wholesome and a few should be included in all gardens. Luker and Smith's nursery catalogue in 1783 included black currants but did not mention separate varieties. In Gilbert White's *Journal* of his garden at Selborne in Hampshire, on 16 July 1784, he wrote that he had made currant and raspberry jam, the fruit hardly ripe but would soon be eaten by the small birds. On 30 July 1791, he reported he had made black currant jelly.

THE NINETEENTH CENTURY

The 1807 edition of Miller's *The Gardener's Dictionary* included a description of the uses of black currants which showed that the fruit was then valued by many people although others still disliked its distinctive flavour. The currants were commonly eaten in puddings and, in some parts of the country, black currant tarts were considered little inferior to cranberry ones. The juice was frequently boiled down to concentrate it and then, with the addition of a small amoung of sugar, made 'Rob', used for the treatment of sore throats, especially as a gargle. As a result of this, the fruit acquired the name of 'Squinancy Berries' owing to its use in quinsies.

In Russia, where black currants have long been an important crop, the berries were also valued for their medicinal uses and were made into wine, either alone or fermented with honey. In England, currants were pickled in brandy in the same way as black cherries, while in Ireland they steeped the currants in whisky and used this to make a punch recommended as a good medicine for coughs. William Forsyth, gardener to George III and George IV, wrote that he once had two gallons of this punch sent to him and he gave some to a friend who had a very severe cough and was thought to be in a decline: he was perfectly cured in three to four nights.

Phillips, in 1827, wrote that in some parts of Siberia the black currants were said to grow to the size of hazel nuts, but the twentieth-century Russian breeder of fruits, Michurin, made no such claim. Phillips also wrote of a new variety of black currant, recently cultivated in Cambridgeshire, whose berries were so large that a single one weighed 61 grains and measured 2½ in in circumference. Extreme as these claims seem to be, it is interesting that in 1866, Robert Hogg, who was a most painstakingly reliable writer, said that Black Naples currants had berries larger than any other variety, frequently measuring about ¾ in in diameter. These figures are much greater than for any currants of today but more like the dimensions of the gooseberries shown in the gooseberry clubs, but Hogg is unlikely to have confused the two fruits!

Although Brookshaw's *Pomona Britannica* of 1812 only illustrated one variety of black currant, without any name, when the Horticultural Society published its list in 1826, it included five. Three of these, Wild Black, Common Black and Russian Grape, were native types, with inferior-sized berries and of little importance at the time, but two, Black Naples and Black Grape, were leading varieties for many years. Loudon, in 1834, referring to the Chiswick trials, said that Black Naples was the largest and best and Black Grape came second.

The origins of Black Naples and Black Grape are not known but the former occupied a position of first importance for about 100 years. William Paul, when he spoke at the 1888 Royal Horticultural Society's National Fruit Congress, said it was still one of the best two varieties.

George Bunyard in 1890 gave Black Naples as the best currant for general use and, in 1925, Edward Bunyard in his *Handbook of Hardy Fruits*, said he considered that it and Baldwin were synonyms. In support of this idea, he said that some old growers in Kent remembered Baldwin coming to notice late in the nineteenth century and then averred that it was the old Naples under a new name. This however, seems doubtful, as Hedrick in *The Small Fruits of New York*, in 1925, said Naples was the most widely grown black currant in America, having been imported from England early in the nineteenth century. His description of Baldwin, which had been noted in an American government report of 1891, was quite different from that of Naples and similar to Baldwin as grown in England today.

The other variety, Black Grape, had a synonym, Ogden's Black, and though having smaller berries than Black Naples, was hardier. It was popular for over 50 years.

Although Black Naples and Black Grape maintained their positions as the leading currants for most of the nineteenth century, during the second half, several new sorts of importance were introduced. Of these, Lee's Prolific, raised in 1860 by George Lee, a market gardener of Clevedon, Somerset, and introduced in 1863, was awarded a RHS First Class Certificate in 1869, rapidly gained popularity and was regarded by Hogg as 'the best of all black currants'.

Carter's Champion, a chance seedling in the garden of a Mr Dunnett of Dedham, Essex in 1880, was introduced in 1888 by Messrs Carter and Sons, of which Mr Dunnett was a partner. Another important variety was French Black, which was identical to Merveille de la Gironde, thought to have been imported from Bordeaux where black currants have been in use for many years for the production of the liqueur Cassis. Both at Bordeaux and Burgundy, black currant growing has long been associated with the vineyards. French Black is also classified with Seabrook's Black, introduced by Seabrook's nurseries in 1913.

A variety still grown today and well liked for its sweet berries is Boskoop Giant, raised by Mr Hoogendyk of Boskoop, Holland in 1880 and introduced in England by Bunyard in 1895. Goliath was another imported variety of unknown origin which was grown for many years. Goliath with French Black, Boskoop and Baldwin formed distinct groups which could be separated by their vegetative characters but today, with modern hybrids, these have largely disappeared. By the end of the century, black currants were a very popular crop for market and were planted on a large scale.

TWENTIETH-CENTURY VARIETIES

During this century, as with other fruits, more attention has been given to breeding new varieties using controlled fertilization rather than relying on haphazard pollination or chance seedlings. Messrs Laxton Brothers of Bedford raised several valuable black currants during the early years of this century. These included Raven (Boskoop crossed with Baldwin) bred in 1905 but not released until 1925, Blacksmith introduced in 1916, and Laxton's Giant, a very large-berried variety, introduced in 1946.

Laxton Brothers were the last of the commercial nurserymen in Britain to breed new black currants and now virtually all breeding of soft fruits is done by the official research stations. The first new black currant from the latter was Wellington XXX, bred by R. Wellington, first Director of East Malling, in 1913 and introduced in 1927. This, a cross between Boskoop Giant and Baldwin, has had a long period of popularity, especially with commercial growers, coming second to Baldwin as the most widely planted currant for both market and juice production.

The introduction of Wellington XXX was followed by several varieties bred by G. T. Spinks of Long Ashton Research Station: Mendip Cross (Baldwin × Boskoop Giant) and Cotswold Cross (Baldwin × Victoria), both bred in 1920 and released in 1932, Malvern Cross (Baldwin × Victoria) bred in the same year but not released until 1946, and finally Tor Cross, bred in 1924 and released in 1962.

During the Second World War, considerable emphasis was given to the value of black currants as a soure of vitamin C, at the same time that rose hips, also high in vitamin C were being collected by school children for processing as a juice. The growing of black currants commercially was encouraged and the fruit sent to factories for production as a purée which was distributed throughout the country for babies and young children. Following further work by Dr Charley at Long Ashton, black currant juice, with a high vitamin C content, was produced commercially.

This development was carried on and extended after the war and resulted in an industry of great value to British growers, giving stability to their currant production by contract price-fixing arrangements. The increasing importance of the crop also led to new developments in breeding currants at East Malling, the Scottish Horticultural Research Institute and Long Ashton and also to the successful mechanical harvesting of the crop.

Modern breeding has involved the use of species of *Ribes* other than *R. nigrum* in an attempt to introduce new characters which could not be induced by relying on varieties already existing in Britain as parent material. Desirable characters include disease and frost resistance, late flowering, lengthening of the cropping season, improved berry size and good cropping capacity, coupled with satisfactory processing qualities and suitability for mechanical harvesting.

Some of the many *Ribes* species used by plant breeders include *R. bracteosum,* to give increased strig length and even berry size, *R. cereum, R. glutinosum* and *R. sanguineum* to give aphid resistance, and the introduction of resistance to the black currant gall mite by making use of the natural resistance of the gooseberry. Frost hardiness has been brought in by using the Finnish variety Brodtorp which, though frost resistant, has a tendency to prostrate branches, an undesirable character for mechanical harvesting. This has been corrected by using upright growing varieties, including the Canadian Consort and Magnus, as one parent.

The first of the new varieties using Brodtorp as one parent was Blackdown, bred by D. Wilson at Long Ashton in 1960, from Baldwin crossed with Brodtorp, and introduced in 1971. Jet, introduced by East Malling in 1974, was the first to have *R. bracteosum* in its parentage. It was raised in 1963 from a cross of *Ribes fuscescens* (a hybrid of *R. bracteosum* × black currant) with Brodtorp. This variety is noteworthy for the changes in flower truss shape and time of flowering and harvesting which it exhibits. These characters of long truss, even berry size, later flowering and harvesting will be seen in many varieties to be introduced in the future.

From the Scottish Horticultural Research Institute a new race of valuable black currants, bred by M. Anderson, has already been distributed. Ben Lomond, raised in 1961 and introduced in 1975, is a heavy-cropping variety which usually escapes damage from spring frosts. This and its sister seedling, Ben Nevis, inherited the large berries and high-cropping capacity, together with considerable frost resistance from their parents (Consort × Magnus) × (Brodtorp × Janslunda). Another variety released at the same time, Ben More, was bred using similar parents and is also heavy cropping and frost resistant.

While black currant growing and the breeding of new varieties have developed in recent years on a scale never previously seen in Britain, there has also been increasing interest in this fruit on the Continent. Two new varieties from Holland were Tenah and Tsema, both introduced by H. J. A. Slits in 1974. As in the breeding of black currants in Britain at this time, Brodtorp was used as one parent, the other principal one being Boskoop.

Having begun as a plant held in little esteem in the sixteenth century, the black currant was generally reviled for about 100 years at a time when the red currant was at the height of its popularity. Though used to some extent for adding to wines and particularly popular in France for making Cassis, it was not until its medicinal values were appreciated that the black currant was more generally planted in gardens. It was the recognition of its high vitamin C content that led to the very considerable extension in commercial planting in Britain during this century, its economic production for juice being made possible by the extensive use of machanical harvesting. As the black currant increased in popularity, so that of the red currant declined.

Britain has been the principal country where the black currant has attained such popularity but it has long been grown in Russia and other countries of the north. Its cultivation has extended in Poland and it is still used for making wine in France and on a more limited scale in other countries. In the United States black currants have been little grown. Few Americans have tasted them and few like their flavour. Although the climate in some of the northern states would be suitable for their cultivation, the law in many states prohibits the culture of the fruit because the bush is an alternative host for the fungus which causes pine blister-rust, causing great damage to certain forest pines. For these reasons, although the black currant was introduced into the States as soon as the red variety, it never attained the popularity of the latter. On the other hand, black currants have been quite popular in parts of Canada where the breeding of new varieties has been of value during recent years to the plant breeders in Scotland seeking new characters to include in their seedlings.

GOOSEBERRIES

The original parent of most of the gooseberries cultivated in the past in Europe was *Ribes grossularia*, although some modern varieties are the result of hybridization with other species of *Ribes* introduced to impart some special character such as disease resistance. *R. grossularia* occurs wild in many parts of Europe including the Caucasus and north Africa but the plants found growing wild in Britain are considered to be escapes from cultivation.

As with red currants, improved forms of gooseberries were selected and brought into cultivation much earlier in some countries on the Continent than in Britain. The earliest record of their use in Britain was in the Middle Ages when gooseberries were included among trees and bushes supplied by the fruiterer to Edward I in 1275 for planting in the royal gardens at the Tower of London. These bushes were obtained from France and cost 3d each but no details of varieties were given.

The name 'gooseberry' is generally considered to have arisen from the use of the berries for making a sauce to go with young or green geese, though one writer, Soke, thought it was derived from the fact that the bush bore a resemblance to gorse, hence 'gorseberry'. For many centuries, however, it had other names in different parts of the country. The most common was 'Feaberrie' which Gerard, in 1597, said was the name used in Cheshire, his native county. It had the same name in Lancashire and Yorkshire. In Norfolk, according to Miller, it was abbreviated to 'Feabes', pronounced 'Fapes'. In Scotland, it was sometimes called 'grozer' or 'grozet', probably a corruption of the French 'groseille'.

GOOSEBERRIES IN THE SIXTEENTH CENTURY

It was reported that the 'pale' gooseberry was brought over from Flanders in the first year of the reign of Henry VIII in 1509. Between the reigns of Edward I and Henry VIII, Britain had suffered a period of great stress during which many plants went out of cultivation and it is possible that this was merely a reintroduction of a variety previously grown in England, although it is more likely that it was a representative of the 'white' or pale green group of gooseberries, so adding to the range of types which, within 100 years, comprised all those grown today.

Turner, in his *Names of Herbes*, 1548, was the first English writer to mention the gooseberry, saying 'It groweth only that I have sene in England, in gardines, but I have sene it in Germany abrode in the fields among other bushes.' This supports the idea that gooseberry cultivation was already fairly widespread on the Continent.

However, although gooseberry growing was well established in the sixteenth century, there was often some confusion between the various members of the *Ribes* family. For example, in the English translation of Heresbachius, the German writer in 1578, after an account of red and white currants it is stated '. . . is thought was unknowne to the olde wryters; but nowe a common bushe used for encloasying of Gardens, and makyng of Borders and Herbes: it will easely growe, but that is something troublesome, by reason of his sharpe prickles to be bent about sommer houses.' This can only have referred to the gooseberry which, with other fruit bushes, was commonly planted alongside paths and walks and between the dwarf trees of apples and pears; gooseberries were also like vines and currants, trained around summer houses and arbours.

Thomas Tusser in his *Five Hundred Pointes of Good Husbandrie* in 1580, giving instructions for the planting of various soft fruits, said:

> *The Barbery, Respis and Gooseberry too*
> *Looke now to be planted as other things doo,*
> *The Gooseberry, Respis and Roses al three*
> *With Strawberries under them trimley agree.*

John Gerard was the first author to give any details of different gooseberry varieties. His description included an illustration of a bush in crop under the heading:

> *Of Gooseberries or Feaberrie bush.*
> *There be divers sorte of the Gooseberries, some greater, others lesse, some rounde, others long and some of red colour. . . . the fruit*

is round growing scateringly upon the branches, greene at the first but waxing a little yellow through maturities; ful of winie juice; something sweete in taste when they be ripe, in which is conteined hard seed, of a whitish colour; the roote is woodie and not without strings aunexed thereto.

There is another whose fruite is almost as bigge as a small cherrie, and verie rounde in forme: as also another of the like bignes of an inch in length; in taste and substance agreeing with the common sort.

These plants do grow in London gardens and else where in great abundance. This shrub had no name among old writers, who as we deeme knew it not or else esteemed it not.

Among the many uses of the gooseberry, Gerard included:

The fruit is used in divers sawces for meate, as those that are skilfull in Cookerie can better tell then my selfe.

They are used in brothes in steede of Verjuice; which maketh the broth not onely pleasant to the taste, but is greatly profitable to such as are troubled with an hot burning ague.

The ripe berries as they are sweeter, so do they also little or nothing binde, and are something hot, and yeeld a little more nourishment then those that be not ripe, and the same not crude or rawe, but these are seldome eaten or used as sauce.

The juice of the greene Gooseberries, cooleth all inflamations, Erysipelas, and Saint Anthonies fire.

The young and tender leaves eaten rawe in a sallade.

Gerard's account shows that the cultivation of gooseberries had developed to a considerable extent since the beginning of the sixteenth century. The reign of Elizabeth I was a time when there was keen interest in gardens, and the introduction of new plants of value would have soon attracted attention. Gooseberries were by now commonly grown in gardens and their fruits were widely used in the kitchen and for dessert, as well as for treating certain ailments. The substitution of gooseberries for verjuice is of especial interest. Verjuice was originally made from unfermented juice from unripe, sour grapes or from crab apples, but as by this time the vineyards of England had virtually disappeared, the gooseberry would be welcomed to make up for this shortage. In Gerard's day, gooseberries were not only grown for their fruits, but their young leaves were used for a salad. Until the immigration of the Walloon refugees from the Low Countries between 1560 and 1570, who settled at Sandwich in Kent and established a market gardening industry, Britain had largely depended on imports from the Continent for the supply of lettuces and other salads. Even in this century, children have been in the habit of picking the young leaves of hawthorn, which are very similar to those of gooseberries, to eat as 'bread and cheese'.

THE SEVENTEENTH CENTURY

An unusual use for gooseberry and currant bushes was suggested by Francis Bacon in his essay *On Gardens*, published in 1625. Writing of the laying out of a decorative garden he said, 'The standards to be of roses, juniper, holly, berberies, but here and there, because of the smell of their blossom, red currants, gooseberries, rosemary, bays, sweet briar, and such like. But these standards, to be kept with cutting, that they grow not out of course.'

By the time Parkinson wrote in 1629, he was able to add much to what had already been written about this fruit. Like Gerard, he described it as the 'gooseberrie or feaberrie' and wrote of the different types then available. These were the common, pale green, almost transparent when ripe, which existed in three varieties, the small and round, a similar but larger form and a third, much larger and longer than the others. All of them when ripe had a pleasant winy taste.

There were three kinds of red gooseberries. The first was rather similar to the common green but somewhat longer and of a dark, brownish red colour, almost black when ripe, but a poor cropper and so not popular. The second red gooseberry was of a fine red colour which became dark when ripe, of fairly small size and tart in taste. The third type was then little known, similar in size to the greater green but of reddish colour, some of them paler with red stripes.

Another kind was the 'blew' gooseberry which developed the colour of a damson, and which was similar to the small red in size. A final type was the green, prickly gooseberry, of medium size, green when ripe but mellowing in colour and with a few short prickles or hairs. Seedlings grown from this variety might have few or no prickles.

The 1633 edition of Gerard's *Herball* included most of the types of gooseberries described by Parkinson and shows that this fruit, at the beginning of the seventeenth century, represented a more advanced state of development than the other members of the *Ribes* family, that is red, white and especially black currants, or strawberries or raspberries, all of which had to evolve much further before their fruits approached our present-day varieties. This early development was carried even further by subsequent generations by the common practice of using seed for raising new varieties. This resulted in many new gooseberries which established England as the leading country for the culture of this fruit.

The same basic characters shown by these early varieties can be traced over succeeding centuries in the many hundreds of varieties bred and brought into use to the present day. Three hundred years after Parkinson, Edward Bunyard, in his *Handbook of Hardy Fruits*, included a classification of gooseberry varieties which he grouped as red, green and yellow, each colour having round and oval—oblong forms and also a 'white' or pale green group — very similar to Parkinson's grouping.

Although Parkinson described the different varieties by their colours and other characters, John Rea in 1665 was one of the first to refer to gooseberries by individual names, of which two, Amber and Hedge-hog, are both still in existence 300 years later.

On the uses of gooseberries, Parkinson said the common ones, while green and hard, were boiled or scalded to make sauce, both for fish and meat and, before they were ripe, were used in tarts and many other ways. Other sorts were not used in cooking but, when ripe, were eaten raw. Worlidge, in 1687, wrote that gooseberries could be used for making wine. His list of gooseberries consisted of three forms of Early Red, the Blue, the Hedgehog, the English Yellow, the Great Yellow Dutch and the Great White Dutch. This last was the White Holland of Rea and Worlidge considered it 'the fairest and best, the fittest for our vineyard and a very great bearer'. At this period, plantations of gooseberries and red currants were grown commercially especially for making into wine. Writing later, in 1697, Worlidge again emphasized the value of gooseberries both for market and for fermenting. When ripe, he said, they tasted most like grapes of any English fruit, and yielded a delicate summer wine. When pressed with a little water and well fermented, they could be distilled to yield an excellent brandy, little inferior to the best French. The two Dutch varieties seem to have been imported in the early seventeenth century, probably by Tradescant.

THE EIGHTEENTH CENTURY

Switzer in 1724 praised the gooseberry for being the first ready to pick and said the best sorts were the Large Dutch, the Large Amber, the early Red and Green, both hairy varieties, together with Early Green and Walnut, raised by Mr Lowe at Battersea. Bradley, in 1727, discussed methods of forcing gooseberries so that, in this way, green berries for tarts could be ready in January and February and ripe fruits by the end of March. In 1722, green gooseberries were sold in Covent Garden on 3 April for 8s a quart but if they had been given heat for forcing, he said, they would have been ready in February. In 1721, green gooseberries from the open were sold at the beginning of May for 2s a quart; by the end of the month they were down to 1½d.

During the eighteenth century there was considerable development in the cultivation of horticultural crops and a great extension in the area of market gardens around London. According to Bradley, the art of gardening had been so much developed since the Restoration of the Monarchy in 1660, that the

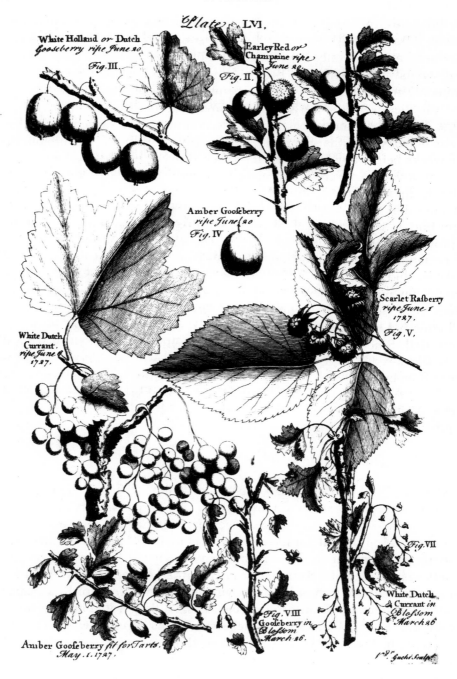

Plate LVI.

White Holland *or* Dutch
Gooseberry ripe June 20
Fig. III.

Earley Red *or*
Champaine *ripe*
June 20
Fig. II.

Amber Gooseberry
ripe June 20
Fig. IV

Scarlet Rasberry
ripe June 1
1727.
Fig. V.

White Dutch
Currant.
ripe June 1
1727.

Fig. VII

White Dutch
Currant *in*
Blossom
March 26

Fig. VIII
Gooseberry *in*
Blossom
March 26

Amber Gooseberry *fit for Tarts.*
May 1 1727.

I.P. Guchi Sculp.

*Some of the gooseberry and currant varieties introduced in the seventeenth
century are still in existence today. The include the Champagne and Amber
gooseberries and the white Dutch currant.*

10,000 acres then used for market gardens around London had been increased to 110,000 acres. This is an enormous area even by today's standards, and illustrates the considerable demand there must have been for fresh fruits and vegetables. Bradley also said that gooseberries were so commonly grown that hardly any garden was without them. He said that the best varieties were the Large White Dutch, excellent for eating fresh, the Large Amber, best for cooking green, the Walnut, which exceeded all others in size of berry and was soonest ready for picking green, the Champion, ripe two weeks before any other, and the Black Hairy. He added that every year many new varieties were being raised from seed.

By the middle of the century, Hitt in 1757 wrote that gooseberries were so common that most people would not think it worth improving the soil for them but, as they were generally grown on borders with strawberries, any improvement would benefit both crops. The cultivation of gooseberries had also extended in Scotland where seeds were also being used for raising new varieties and Abercrombie and Mawe, in 1778, described 24 varieties, saying that many of these were new seedlings. Some had round berries, others oval; some were hairy, others smooth and of different colours, including red, green, yellow and white. Of the red kinds, Mawe mentioned Hairy Red, Smooth Red, Deep Red-Crimson, Blueish, Red Raspberry and Early Black-red. Of green, Hairy and Smooth types, Green Gascoigne and Green Raspberry. Of yellow, Great Oval Yellow, Great Amber, Hairy Amber and Early Amber and of white, Large White Crystals, Common White and White Veined. Other varieties were Champaigne, Rumbullion, Large Ironmonger, Smooth Ironmonger, Hairy Globe and Large Tawny or Great Mogul.

THE GOOSEBERRY CLUBS

The observations of all these eighteenth-century writers show that gooseberries were very widely grown in their time, that the separate groups of varieties had widely differing characters and that gardeners and others were being encouraged to try raising their own new varieties from seed. This point is of particular significance when considering the further history of the gooseberry. Such advice was not usually given to the growers of the other soft fruits. It was against this background that the gooseberry clubs were started.

The cultivation of gooseberries in Britain during the latter part of the eighteenth century was far more widely distributed than in any country in Europe and Britain gained the reputation as the home of this fruit. While gooseberries were of some importance in Holland and parts of northern

Germany, in the southern countries of Spain and Italy they were scarcely known and, in France, neglected and little esteemed.

There has always been a spirit of keen competition among industrial workers in the north of England and this has been shown by their rivalry in whippet, greyhound and pigeon breeding and racing, and competitions for the largest onions and leeks. The popularity of gooseberry growing in the gardens of the handloom weavers and other workers in Lancashire led to the beginning of the annual gooseberry shows where prizes were given for the heaviest berries. The first of these shows is believed to have been held about 1740 and quickly led to the starting of gooseberry clubs throughout Lancashire; the fashion soon spread to adjoining counties.

So important did these shows become, that an annual register, the *Gooseberry Grower's Register*, was published in Manchester, beginning in 1786. This gave the list of prizewinners in each club, the varieties exhibited and the individual weights of the berries. All the energy of the competitors was directed to obtaining the heaviest berries. Every competitor had his own method of breeding and growing large, heavy berries; these methods, like the gooseberries themselves were closely guarded. The bushes were severely pruned and the number of flowers and fruits on each strictly limited so that only three or four of the best berries were retained. The bushes were carefully protected by mats to prevent damage by frosts or wind; they were planted in specially prepared composts and regularly fed with the grower's own special stimulants.

The continuous records of the weights of the gooseberries given in the registers proved of interest to Charles Darwin and he included reference to these in his book *The Variation of Plants and Animals under Domestication* in 1868. He noted the way in which breeding and selection had improved the size of the berries since, as he said, the fruits of the wild plants weighed about a ¼ oz or 5 dwts (Troy system), i.e. 120 grains. By 1786 gooseberries weighing 10 dwts were exhibited, and by 1817, 26 dwts or 17 grains. The size of the heaviest berry increased steadily until, in 1844, the variety London, weighed 35 dwts or 12 grains. London, which had been raised by J. Banks of Acton, Northwich and introduced in 1831, maintained its position as champion berry for 36 seasons and gained 333 prizes but never attained a greater weight than in 1852, 37 dwts or 7 grains, nearly 2 oz.

Although Darwin thought that much of the increase in weight of the berries was the result of the management of the bushes, the size of the leading varieties, Highwayman, Roaring Lion and London, was doubtless the effect of continued selection. All of these had been bred by competitors, but although a few of the new varieties entered into commercial production, most were confined to use in competitions. In 1775, Richard Weston, in his *Flora Anglicana*, listed 21 gooseberries and, in 1783, the nursery catalogue of Luker and Smith of Covent Garden had 34. Of these, a number, including

Amber, Golden Drop, Rumbullion and Warrington, still exist today, over 200 years later.

HORTICULTURAL SOCIETY'S COLLECTION OF GOOSEBERRIES

When in 1826 the Horticultural Society published its first catalogue of plants grown at the Chiswick gardens, 185 gooseberries were included. At the time, Mr Thompson, who was in charge of the trials, was reported as saying that less confusion had been found in the nomenclature of varieties of gooseberries than in any other fruit in the collection, which could only be accounted for by the great interest which the prize growers had taken in detecting sorts which came before them wrongly named.

The first list included Amber, Golden Drop, Ironmonger, Warrington Red, Crown Bob and Roaring Lion. By 1831, the Society had 360 gooseberry varieties which had been increased by many more of the Lancashire ones but, by 1842, the number had been reduced to 149 as it had been decided to eliminate many of the latter varieties which were considered to be of poor quality and had only been selected by their raiser for the large size of the berries.

However, some of the Lancashire varieties have persisted on their own merits. Of these, Lancashire Lad, raised by Mr Hartshorn in 1824, is still recommended. Wonderful, introduced in 1841, was popular for over 100 years. Even as late as 1865, Peter Lawson's catalogue of fruits, listed 227 distinct varieties of gooseberries. Included in this were Amber, Careless, Crown Bob, Dan's Mistake, Ironmonger, Lancashire Lad, King of Trumps, Early Sulphur, Warrington and Whitesmith which are still grown, Careless, Lancashire Lad and Whitesmith being three of the comparatively few varieties grown commercially.

GOOSEBERRY CULTIVATION IN THE NINETEENTH CENTURY

Phillips, in 1827, wrote of methods to preserve fresh gooseberries hanging on the bushes so that they could be picked right up to Christmas. For this purpose, the Warrington variety was considered the best. The technique described could also be used with red and white currants, and involved covering the bushes. The bushes to be covered were to be kept pruned to a size suitable for the cases intended for them, which could be made similar in shape to a beehive, and made of straw, rushes or any other material which would effectively keep off heat and light. These covers were to be placed over the bushes just as the fruit began to turn towards ripening, but not before it had reached full size. By protecting the fruit from the dew, rain, the heat of the sun and light, complete maturity would be retarded and the berries could be gathered fresh and ripe until December. The same bushes were not to be covered in succeeding years as the covering weakened the plants, and some ventilation was needed at the base of the bush.

Phillips was a keen advocate of gooseberry wine. Green gooseberries, he said, made a wine little inferior to Champagne and the black gooseberry, when ripe, also produced a luscious wine. In Phillips' opinion, if people could discard their prejudices against all English wines, gooseberries could cover the fields of England as profitably as the vineyards of the south. Taking into account the ease of propagation and how seldom the crop fails, he thought gooseberry wine could be made more cheaply than cider.

COMMERCIAL PRODUCTION

For several centuries, gooseberries were a useful crop grown by the market gardeners around London and in Kent for the London markets. The abolition of the sugar tax in 1874, however, led to a dramatic increase in the importance of the fruit. There was now an enormous demand for jam, and gooseberries, being relatively cheap and easily grown, were together with strawberries and plums, the principal fruits required. The Wisbech region became the centre for much of this increased production. Here, gooseberry bushes were interplanted between trees of Bramley's Seedling apples. Careless was introduced into this area in 1897, the first cutting having been obtained from Lancashire where some Lincolnshire growers had seen this variety at a fruit show in 1887. Although Careless has always been the principal variety in the Wisbech area, Crown Bob, Whinham's Industry and Lancashire Lad have also been grown. In Kent, besides Careless, Keepsake, synonymous with Berry's Early Kent, has been important for picking green for the early market.

Early gooseberries were also produced in the west country in the Tamar Valley, in Devon and Cornwall, and at Cheddar in Somerset. Here, for many years, the main variety was May Duke, raised by George Pyne of Topsham near Exeter, and introduced in 1900, at a time when the Tamar Valley smallholdings were being extended. Another area of specialized gooseberry production has been, and still is, the Chailey—Newick district of Sussex, where the cultivation of large-sized Leveller berries for the dessert trade has reached a very high degree of perfection.

MODERN VARIETIES AND CULTIVATION

Although gooseberries are still of commercial importance in Britain, the area devoted to the crop has declined dramatically since the nineteenth century, especially during the past 50 years. The public demand for all jams, and especially for gooseberry and plum jam, is now a small fraction of that in the past, while the use of gooseberries as a source of pectin by the confectionery and jam industries ended when better sources of pectin became available. Gooseberries are still of some importance for canning and freezing and for picking green for the early market; there is still a limited demand for berries for dessert. However, the biggest increase has been in gooseberries for the 'pick-your-own' outlet.

The declining demand for gooseberries and the adequacy of the varieties already in existence has meant that there has been little interest in or call for the breeding of new varieties. The age of the leading varieties included in the Ministry of Agriculture's bulletin as being of commercial importance in 1977 indicates the reliability of those raised at a time when the cultivation of gooseberries was of major significance:

Lancashire Lad, raised by Mr Hartshorn, recorded in 1824.
Whitesmith raised by Mr Woodward before 1824.
Howard's Lancer raised by T. Howard of Blackley, introduced in 1831.
Keepsake, raised by Mr Banks, recorded in 1841.
Whinham's Industry raised by R. Whinham of Morpeth, before 1850.
Leveller, raised by J. Greenhalgh of Ashton-under-Lyne, introduced in 1851.
Careless, raised by Mr Crompton and known before 1860.
May Duke, raised by Pyne of Topsham, introduced in 1900.

All of these varieties, with the exception of May Duke now of little importance, were raised before or shortly after the middle of the nineteenth century, nearly all by private individuals, members of the many gooseberry clubs then flourishing. Some of these clubs are still in existence and members have their own particular favourite varieties, but no longer have they the same incentive to try to breed new ones.

One reason why it has been possible to continue so long with the old varieties is that, although gooseberries are subject to infection with virus diseases, the effect of these is not so marked or so devastating as it is with many other fruits. In fact, there has never been any call for the introduction of a certification scheme to ensure the production and distribution of healthy, virus-tested bushes of this fruit.

Workers at East Malling Research Station have been able to eliminate certain viruses from gooseberries but, unfortunately, such virus-free plants can become reinfected in the field by aphids which transmit these diseases. Other workers have been breeding new varieties using different species of *Ribes* in an attempt to breed spine-free plants, resistant to aphids and resistant to American gooseberry mildew and leaf spot. Species used include

M

R. oxyacanthoides for the character of spinelessness, and the flowering currant, *R. sanguineum, R. leptanthum* and *R. watsonianum* for disease resistance. The first of the new gooseberries to be released as a result of this work was Invicta, bred by crossing the mildew-resistant German variety, Resistenta, with Whinham's Industry, followed by a further cross of a mildew-resistant selection of this origin with Keepsake.

The genus *Rubus* includes many hundreds of species and, apart from their importance as parents of our modern raspberries, several species have been involved in the development of brambles or blackberries and the various hybrid berries many of which have been bred in the United States.

Species of *Rubus* exist in a wild state in many parts of the world, but it is those native to Great Britain and other parts of Europe and those growing in North America which have been responsible for the types grown today. Until this century, all the British blackberries were included under one species, *Rubus fruticosus*, but today they are separated into several different ones.

In Britain, native species include *Rubus thrysiger*, a species with fruits of excellent flavour, ripening over a period of several weeks and *R. nitidiodes*, having large berries ripening early in the season. Merton Early is a form of the latter. *R. laciniatus*, the so-called 'Cut-leaved' or 'Parsley-leaved' blackberry, is considered to be indigenous to Europe but was taken to the USA where several varieties, such as Oregon Evergreen, were introduced. *R. rusticanus* is one of the most common blackberries wild in the hedgerows in the south of England. Its fruits ripen late in the season. There is a thornless form, *R. rusticanus inermis*, and also one with amber-coloured berries, the White Blackberry. John Innes Blackberry was obtained from a cross between the thornless form and *R. thrysiger* and, in turn, gave rise to Merton Thornless. *R. procerus*, of which the Himalaya berry is a selection, is a native of western Europe.

BLACKBERRIES IN ANTIQUITY

The discovery of seeds of blackberries in inter-glacial and post-glacial deposits in various parts of Great Britain indicates that the plant must have grown freely at these times. Post-glacial sites include Penzance and Mount's Bay in Cornwall. Seeds were also found on a Neolithic site at Westward Ho!

The excavation of early habitations on an Iron Age Glastonbury lake site has revealed, with those of other berries, blackberry seeds which suggests that the berries were collected for food. Blackberry seeds, dating back to the Late Bronze Age, have also been excavated at Minnis Bay in Kent.

The discovery of blackberry seeds, along with those of wild strawberries, near the Roman fort at Newstead, Melrose, in the Borders, and also of blackberry seeds at the fort at Caersws in Wales, show a fondness of the Roman troops for this fruit. Other Roman sites where blackberry seeds have been found are Silchester near Reading, Selsey, West Wittering and Pevensey on the south coast and a number of sites in London including Finsbury Circus.

There are several references to wild blackberries in the writings of Greek and Roman authors. Theophrastus in his *Enquiry into Plants*, writing of plants found near rivers and lakes said, 'And in some such places are found brambles, Christ's Thorn and other trees.' Ovid in the first book of his *Metamorphoses* gives two references. Of the Golden Age, he said: 'Men were content with foods that grew without cultivation. They gathered arbutus berries and mountain strawberries, wild cherries and blackberries that cling to thorny bramble bushes.' In a later poem, he said:

> *Or to a Hare,*
> *Which under a bramble closely lies,*
> *And hence of dogs a number*
> *The hostile mouths espies.*

Pliny the Elder, in his *Natural History*, made several mentions of the blackberry. In one he suggested that this plant had shown the ancients how to propagate plants by layering:

> *Nature has likewise also taught the art of producing from layers. Brambles, curving over with their slender and also excessively long shoots, plant their ends in the earth again and sprout afresh out of themselves, in a manner that would fill up the whole place if resistance were not offered by cultivation, so that it would be positively possible to imagine that mankind was created for this service of the earth. Thus a most evil and execrable circumstance has nevertheless taught the use of the layer and the quickset.*
>
> *Brambles bear blackberries. . . . The berries have a desiccative and astringent virtue, and are most appropriate remedy for the gums and inflamations of the tonsils.*

Roman physicians, like herbalists later in England, considered blackberries and their juice especially valuable for infections of the mouth and eyes.

THE BLACKBERRY IN BRITAIN

The blackberry was a common wild fruit in many parts of Europe, whose berries were more acceptable, without any improvement by selection or cultivation, than those of other wild fruits, for example currants, gooseberries or raspberries. Moreover, the blackberry is generally a vicious, thorny plant and not of the kind readily accepted into the garden. As Pliny had said, the plants would soon take over the whole of the land 'if resistance were not offered by cultivation'.

This probably explains why, although the early references to the blackberry in the ancient world and later show that its fruits were greatly valued, there was no suggestion, either at this time or for many centuries, that it was taken into cultivation. Blackberries were probably picked by succeeding generations from earliest times until the first records of their use in the Middle Ages, but though there were descriptions of the plant and its fruits in the early herbals, it was very rarely mentioned by horticultural writers during the sixteenth to eighteenth centuries.

Aelfric, in his Anglo-Saxon Latin glossary, in AD 995, included the blackberry as 'blaceberian'. In the Middle Ages blackberry juice was added to that of mulberries, elderberries and bilberries to make a blue dye, and the juice and wine made from it were added to grape wines to sweeten them. This was the practice in Kent at the vineyards of the Archbishop of Canterbury at Teynham and North Fleet in the thirteenth century.

William Turner, in the 1568 edition of his herbal wrote:

> *There are two kindes of this bramble / one that groweth commonlye in hedges and with other bushes / and one other kinde that groweth in small lendes of freshe waters / and about rivers sydes / and also in corne fieldes. This is called of some Chamebatos. As the great kinde hath alwayes black berries when they are rype / and full of sedes so the lesser / kind hath somtyme rede berries / with as they are rype but a few sedes. But that they are much pleasanter to eat then the greater berries be.*
>
> *The bramble bindeth, drieth and dieth heyre. The juyce of the berry of a bramble bushe / if it be full rype / is fit for y medicine of the mouth.*

Thomas Tusser did not mention the blackberry in his *Five Hundred Pointes of Good Husbandry* of 1573, but John Gerard, in 1597, had much to say about the common blackberry and two other species of *Rubus, R. saxatilis*, the Stone berry, and *R. chamaemorus*, the Knot berry. He did not suggest growing blackberries in gardens but wrote of their medicinal virtues:

> *The young buds or tender tops of the Bramble Bush, the flowers, the leaves, and the unripe fruit, do very much dry and binde withall: being chewed they take away the heate and inflamations of the mouth, and almonds of the throte. They heale the eyes that hang out. The leaves of the Bramble boiled in water with honie, allum and a little white wine added thereto, maketh a most excellent lotion or washing water, to heale the sores of the mouth and fastneth the teeth.*

During the two centuries following the publication of Gerard's *Herball*, none of the leading contemporary horticultural writers — Parkinson, Austen, Worlidge, Switzer, Bradley and others — mentioned the blackberry. Though the wild fruits were picked and appreciated for their domestic and medicinal uses, the plant had not yet been taken into cultivation in private or market

1 *Rubus.*
   The Bramble Bush.

The wild blackberry in the sixteenth century. Only when less unruly forms were introduced early in the nineteenth century was it considered suitable for planting in gardens.

gardens. This is confirmed by the fact that the blackberry was not included in any of the pomonas or nursery catalogues published up to the end of the eighteenth century.

It was not till the beginning of the nineteenth century, when there was increasing interest in growing many of the soft fruits, that blackberries were gradually accepted into gardens. The account of blackberries given in the 1807 edition of Miller's *The Gardener's Dictionary*, revised by Thomas Martyn, Professor of Botany at Cambridge, is important for the description it gives of those then available. The common blackberries were then known in some counties as Bumblekites, in others as Scald-berries, from their supposed quality of giving 'scald-heads', a disease of the scalp, to children who ate too many. The green shoots were of great use in dyeing woollens, silk and mohair black. Silk-worms sometimes fed on the leaves in the absence of mulberries. The types of brambles then recognized were:

(1) That with white berries, found in a hedge not far from Oxford by Bobart.
(2) The form with a double flower, introduced into shrubberies.
(3) The bramble without thorns.
(4) With cut leaves.
(5) With variegated leaves.

This list shows that the Cut-leaved, *R. laciniatus,* the Thornless, *R. rusticanus inermis* and the white-berried mutation of the blackberry were already in existence. In 1826, the Horticultural Society listed 21 types of *Rubus.*

DEVELOPMENTS IN THE UNITED STATES

Although the development of many fruits in the United States depended, in the first place, on pioneer growers using plants or seeds brought over from Europe, with blackberries and similar fruits the reverse was true. The attention given to the cultivation of the blackberry in America encouraged their planting in Britain.

Hedrick described how, in the early part of the nineteenth century, the culture of this fruit began in the United States. Its domestication had been delayed for two centuries by prejudice on the part of pioneers from Europe who regarded the bramble or briar as a pestiferous weed difficult to rid from their land and not worth cultivating when the wild fruits were so plentiful. The main reference to blackberries in the farming press was how to get rid of them with, occasionally, a recipe for blackberry wine, popular as a medicine and a cordial.

The earliest reference to the cultivation of the blackberry in American gardens was in a magazine, *The New York Gardener*, in 1829, when it was suggested that one of their native shrubs, the blackberry, was worthy of a place in the farmer's garden and would liberally repay the expense of cultivation. In 1833, William Kendrick, in his *New American Orchardist*, recommended the blackberry for garden use where it could be much improved in size and cropped abundantly. The first large-scale plantations of blackberries were grown by a Captain J. Lovett of Beverley, Massachusetts who, in 1835, tried growing the high bush blackberry of the woods without much success, but a few years later he obtained plants of a new variety, Dorchester, first seen at the Horticultural Society's Show in Boston in 1841.

Also, in 1835, Lewis A. Seacor of New Rochelle, New York, saw a plant of a blackberry with fruits larger than normal growing by the roadside and from there it was taken into neighbouring gardens. This variety, named first Lawton and later New Rochelle, did much to make the blackberry popular in gardens in America, though it proved subject to winter killing and was later replaced by other varieties.

BLACKBERRY CULTIVATION IN BRITAIN

In 1865, Lawson's catalogue of fruits, published in Edinburgh, included a long list of blackberries, nearly all of which were of American origin. The catalogue described Lawton as synonymous with New Rochelle and Seacor's Mammoth, and 'Esteemed in the Northern United States and Canada as one of the best native Blackberries, very profitable for market.'

Apart from the American blackberries and most of the *Rubus* species, considered of value for their fruits, Lawson's catalogue included an improved Common Bramble, cropping in October and introduced by Rivers Nursery as Rivers' Autumn Blackberry. Another variety, named Rivers' Blackberry or River's Summer Blackberry, was listed as 'supposed to be a hybrid between one of the native Brambles and the Raspberry, found at Westerfield, in Essex, upwards of forty years ago', i.e. about 1825.

The catalogue also listed the Common Bramble which was described as 'The most common native Bramble, seldom cultivated except for game cover. Fruit is in all respects inferior to the other nearly equal common sort, the Hazel-leaved Bramble, but frequently used for preserves, tarts etc.'

The Hazel-leaved blackberry, *Rubus coryfolius*, was described as 'One of the most common Brambles; select sub-varieties of which yield the largest, most juicy-fruited, and the finest of native Blackberries.'

In spite of the beginnings of interest in blackberry culture in Britain in the second half of the nineteenth century, Robert Hogg, whose celebrated *Fruit Manual* went into several editions, failed to include this fruit even in the fourth edition of 1875. On the other hand, there was increasing interest in the cultivation of blackberries in the United States. With the extension of the urban areas and the destruction of hedges and woodlands, there were fewer wild berries and an increase in the planting of the blackberry in gardens and on commercial holdings.

One of the varieties which became popular in the United States during this time was the Oregon Evergreen Black, also known as Cut-leaved and Everbearing. This is a form of the European species, *Rubus laciniatus*, which probably came from England where it had been found growing wild on Walton Heath in Surrey. It was apparently taken by a settler to the South Sea Islands where it now grows wild. From there, a Frenchman took some plants to Oregon where it was propagated and distributed to the other coastal states and eventually to the rest of the country. Plants were also brought back to England where it had already been described in Miller's *Dictionary* in 1807 and was included in Lawson's nursery catalogue in 1865 as the Cut-leaved Bramble, *Rubus laciniatus*. It is still known as the Cut-leaved or Parsley-leaved blackberry.

Another important blackberry is the Himalaya or Himalaya Giant. Early in the 1890s the American nurseryman, Luther Burbank, introduced a blackberry under the name of Himalaya Giant. His stock was said to have originated from seed sent him from 'high up in the Himalayan Mountains' in 1889 or 1890. In 1893 he listed it as an improved variety of *Rubus himalaya*. However, it was shown to be a form of *Rubus procerus*, a well-known species, indigenous to Europe, of which Theodor Reimens, a Hamburg nurseryman, in 1889 had introduced a garden form identical, or almost identical, to the American Himalaya Giant. This variety is still cultivated today, both commercially and in gardens. It is a very strong grower, somewhat difficult to manage in a restricted area though, unlike many other blackberries, it will crop on canes older than one year.

HYBRID BERRIES

A number of hybrids between raspberries and blackberries have been bred, both in America and England. One of the latter, of rather poor quality though given an Award of Merit by the RHS in 1901, was Mahdi, raised by Messrs James Veitch and Sons from a cross between the raspberry, Superlative, and a blackberry. The Veitchberry was another hybrid bred by the same firm, from the raspberry, November Abundance, and a large-fruited blackberry.

The Veitchberry was important as the parent of Bedford Giant, bred by Messrs Laxton, and one of the few blackberry types still grown to any extent today in Britain. Bedford Giant is earlier than Himalaya and, being less vigorous, is more easily managed in a garden.

Although many hybrid berries have been raised, especially in America, few have had general appeal in Britain, where they have often been rather poor croppers. However, one of them, the loganberry, now over 100 years old, has met with widespread success. The loganberry was raised by Judge J. H. Logan of Santa Cruz, California, in 1881. In his own account of its origin, Judge Logan said he planted seeds of the common wild blackberry or dewberry of California, *Rubus ursinus*, gathered from plants in his garden, on one side of which was growing a kind of evergreen blackberry, Texas Early. On the other side there was an old red raspberry which had been growing there for 40 years. This was of a type similar, but not identical, to the Red Antwerp. From the seed, about a hundred plants were grown, and when these fruited in 1883 the loganberry stood out as an apparent cross between a raspberry and *Rubus ursinus*. This parentage has since been confirmed.

The loganberry was brought to England about 1897. A thornless form is now in use and has been found to crop equally as well as the thorned type. The introduction of virus-tested stocks of loganberries by East Malling Research Station has done much to maintain their good cropping.

Messrs Laxton introduced the Laxtonberry which was a cross between the loganberry and the Superlative raspberry. Kings Acre berry is thought to be an American blackberry, and Phenomenal berry, introduced by Burbank, was a cross between the Western Dewberry and the Cuthbert raspberry. It has fruits very similar to the loganberry and was introduced into Britain at the beginning of the century.

Youngberry was a cross between Phenomenal and Mayes (an American dewberry) raised about 1905 by B. M. Young of Morgan City, Louisiana. The Boysenberry was introduced in 1935 by R. Boysen of California, a hybrid with the Himalaya blackberry as the female parent, pollinated by an unknown male. It is very similar to the Youngberry.

The Wineberry is not a hybrid berry, but is *Rubus phoenicolasius*, a native of China and Japan. It is not of commercial importance but is often grown in gardens for its decorative value.

DEVELOPMENTS IN BRITAIN

In 1890, George Bunyard, writing of blackberries, said that although some, especially the cut-leaved, were grown commercially in Kent, it would be well worth while growing wild blackberries on stony banks, the heaps of refuse from quarries, chalk works and similar places and using the berries for jam. On Lord Sudeley's estate the brambles were allowed to grow in the hedges and their fruits made into jellies and jam which sold very well.

From Bunyard's account, it is obvious that the cultivation of blackberries had still not proceeded very far in Britain by the end of the nineteenth century. However, the introduction of the loganberry to Britain about 1897 resulted in more interest being taken in the hybrid berries. Hooper of Pershore, in 1921, said the loganberry had only been cultivated commercially on any scale during the previous 15 years. It was being grown by some farmers in old hop gardens, the poles and wires being adapted for training the plants.

During this century the two research stations, John Innes Horticultural Institution and Long Ashton Research Station, have bred new varieties of blackberries. John Innes was obtained from a cross between the thornless *R. rusticanus inermis* and *R. thrysiger*. John Innes blackberry in turn gave rise to Merton Thornless. Long Ashton Cross is an early variety having berries of good flavour.

From the beginning of the century to 1939, the commercial acreage of blackberries and loganberries, with some fluctuations, showed a general increase. The acreage fell during the war period and, though it showed some increase up to 1960, it has shown a general fall to the present. However, the introduction of a virus-tested stock of loganberries in 1959, with its improved cropping capacity, did encourage its planting for a time. The high costs of training and picking these berries has, however, reduced the incentive to plant them, especially in view of the wide fluctuation in demand from processors for canning, freezing and jam production.

During recent years, plant breeders at the Scottish Horticultural Research Institute have been concentrating on raising erect growing blackberries, raspberries and hybrid berries. Attention has also been given to breeding for freedom from spines and resistance to disease. Use has been made as parents of *R. ursinus*, the American Early Harvest blackberry, Darrow Thornfree and Comanche. In addition, the species *R. glaucus*, the Andean blackberry, *R. parviflorus* and others have been used to introduce special characters.

This use of widely differing species of the same genus has been a feature of much of the breeding work with soft fruits carried out in recent years and promises the introduction of hybrid berries which may well replace existing varieties. The first of the new hybrid berries to be released was the Tayberry, a hybrid having the same genetic parentage as the loganberry, a hexaploid raspberry—blackberry cross, which has large berries of good quality and is a heavy cropper. It was introduced in 1977.

BIBLIOGRAPHY

ANCIENT SOURCES

Pytheas of Marseilles. *La Geographie de son temps.* Lelewel, Joachim. Paris, 1836.
Stubbs, W. *Gesta Regnum Anglorum* and *Historia Nouvella* of Malmesbury. London, 1887.
The Anglo-Saxon Chronicles (ed. Garmonsay, G. N.) London, 1953.
The Holy Bible.

Loeb Classical Library (Harvard University Press and William Heinemann)
Cato and Varro. *De Re Rustica* (trans. Hooper, W. D.) London, 1967.
Columella. *De Re Rustica, I–XII* (trans. Forster, L. E. S. and Heffner, E. H.) London, 1979.
Diodorus Siculus. *Library of History, I, II, IV, VIII* (trans. Oldfather, C. H.) London, 1968–79.
Herodotus. *Books, V–IX* (trans. Godley, A. D.) London, 1969, 1971.
Hesiod. *The Homeric Hymns and Homerica* (trans. Evelyn-White, H. G.) London, 1977.
Pliny. *Natural History, VIII–XIX* (trans. Rackham, H.) London, 1967.
Strabo. *Geography, II* (trans. Jones, H. L.) London, 1969.
Theophrastus. *De Causis Plantarum I* (trans. Einarson, B. and Link, G. K. K.) London, 1976.
Theophrastus. *Enquiry into Plants, I and II* (trans. Hort, L. A.) London, 1968.
Xenophon. *Memorabilia, Oeconomicus IV* (trans. Marchant, E. C.) London, 1979.

Penguin Classics
Bede. *A History of the English Church and People* (trans. Sherley-Price, L.) London, 1955.
Caesar, Gaius Julius. *The Conquest of Gaul* (trans. Handford, S. A.) London, 1979.
Suetonius, Gaius. *The Twelve Caesars* (trans. Graves, R.) London, 1957.

Tacitus. *The Agricola and the Germania* (trans. Mattingly, H. and Handford, S. A.) London, 1977.

Everyman's Library
Virgil. *Eclogues and Georgics* (trans. Royds, T. F.) London, 1965.
Virgil. *The Georgics of Vergil* (trans. Wilkinson, L. P.) Cambridge, 1969.

GENERAL

Amherst, Alicia. *A History of Gardening in England.* London, 1896.
Bean, W. J. *Trees and Shrubs Hardy in the British Isles.* London, 1970.
Bentham, George. *Handbook of the British Flora* (revised J. D. Hooker and A. B. Rendle). London, 1924.
Brettschneider, E. *History of European Discoveries in China.* London, 1898.
Brothwell, D. and Brothwell, P. *Food in Antiquity.* London, 1969.
Crane, M. B. and Lawrence, W. J. C. *The Genetics of Garden Plants.* London, 1938.
Davies, R. W. The Roman Military Diet. *Britannia* II (1971), pp. 122–42.
De Candolle, A. L. P. *Origin of Cultivated Plants.* London, 1883.
Finberg, H. P. R. *The Agrarian History of England and Wales, I and II.* Cambridge, 1964.
Funk and Wagnall's *Standard Dictionary of Folklore.* New York, 1949.
Godwin, H. *The History of the British Flora.* Cambridge, 1970.
Goor, Asaph and Nurock, Max. *The Fruits of the Holy Land.* Jerusalem, 1968.
Graves, Robert. *The Twelve Caesars.* London, 1979.
Grun, Bernard. *The Timetables of History.* London, 1975.
Harvey, John. *Medieval Gardens.* London, 1981.
Hershall, S. and Wilkinson, J. *Domesday.* London, 1799.
Jessup, Frank W. *A History of Kent.* London, 1958.
John, G. W. *History of English Gardening.* London, 1829.
Lamb, H. H. *Climate of England.* London, 1964.
Melling, Elizabeth. *Kentish Sources. Aspects of Agriculture and Industry.* Maidstone, 1961.
Moody, H. *Domesday Book: Hampshire.* London, 1862.
Oxford Dictionary of English Proverbs. Compiled Smith, W. G. revised Harvey, P. Oxford, 1963.
Parish, W. D. *Domesday Book: Sussex.* London, 1885.
Roberts, J. M. *History of the World.* London, 1976.
Royal Horticultural Society *Dictionary of Gardening.* Oxford, 1956.
Scullard, H. H. *Roman Britain.* London, 1979.
Vavilov, N. J. *Wild Progenitors of the Fruit Trees of Turkestan and the Caucasus and the Problem of the Origin of Fruit Trees.* International Horticultural Congress, 1930.
Wacher, J. S. *Roman Britain.* London, 1978.
Webster, D., Webster, H. and Petch, D. F. A possible vineyard of the Romano-British period at North Thoresby, Lincolnshire. *Lincolnshire History and Archaeology* no. 2, pp. 55–61. 1967.

Whistlecraft, Orlando. *The Climate of England.* London, 1840.

White, K. D. *Roman Farming.* London, 1970.

Willcox, G. H. Exotic Plants from Roman waterlogged sites in London. *Journal of Archaeological Science*, 4. pp. 269–82, 1977.

Fourteenth, Fifteenth and Sixteenth Centuries

Camden, William. *Britannia.* London, 1586.

Chaucer, Geoffrey. *Complete Works* (ed. Walter Skeat). Oxford, 1894.

Condus, Valerius. *Historia Plantarum.* Strasbourg, 1561.

Didymus Mountain (Thomas Hill). *The Gardener's Labyrinth.* London, 1577.

Dodoens–Lyte. *A Niewe Herball or Historie of Plantes.* Antwerp, 1578.

Fitzherbert, Sir Anthony. *Boke of Husbandry.* London, 1523, 1525.

Gardener, Mayster Jon. 'The Feate of Gardeninge', 1440–1450.

Gerard, John. *Catalogue of Plantes.* London, 1596.

Gerard, John. *The Herball.* London, 1597.

Hentzner, Paul. *A Journey into England in 1598* (ed. Horace Walpole) London, 1757.

Heresbach-Googe. *Foure Bookes of Husbandry, collected by M. Conradus Heresbachius.* London, 1577, 1578.

Holinshed, Ralph. *Chronicles of England, Scotland and Ireland.* London, c.1580.

Hill, Thomas. *The Profitable Arte of Gardeninge.* London, 1574, 1579.

Lambard, William. *A Perambulation of Kent.* London, 1576.

Langland, William. *Piers Plowman.* London, 1981.

Lyte, H. *English Herball.* London, 1578.

Mascall, Leonard. *The Booke of Arte and Maner, howe to plant and graffe all Sortes of Trees.* London, 1572, 1575.

Ruellius, Jean. *De Natura Stirpium libri tress.* Paris, 1536.

Shakespeare, William. *Plays.* Oxford, 1921.

Shirley, Janet. *A Parisian Journal, 1405–1449.* Oxford, 1968.

Treueris, Peter. *The Grete Herball.* London, 1526.

Turner, W. *Names of Herbes.* London, 1548.

Turner, W. *A New Herball.* London, 1551, 1568.

Tusser. T. *A Hundreth Good Pointes of Husbandrie.* London, 1557.

Tusser, T. *Five Hundred Pointes of Good Husbandrie.* London, 1573, 1580.

Seventeenth Century

Austen, Ralph. *A Treatise of Fruit Trees.* Oxford, 1635, 1657, 1665.

Austen, Ralph. *A Dialogue, or Familiar Discourse, and Conference betwene the Husbandman, and Fruit-trees.* Oxford, 1676.

Bacon, Francis. *The Works of Lord Bacon.* London, 1856.

Beale, John. *Aphorisms Concerning Cider.* London, 1664.

Beale, John. *Herefordshire Orchards: a pattern for all England.* London, 1657.

Beale, John. *Nurseries, Orchards, Profitable Gardens.* London, 1677.

Beale, John. *A Treatise of Fruit Trees.* Oxford, 1653.

Blith, Walter. *The English Improver Improved.* London, 1652.

Cook, Moses. *Manner of Raising, Ordering and Improving Forest trees.* London, 1676.

Drope, Francis. *A Short and sure Guid in the practice of raising and ordering Fruit Trees.* Oxford, 1672.

Evelyn, John. *Diaries, 1659 – 1669.* London, 1906.

Evelyn, John. *The French Gardiner.* London, 1658, 1669.

Evelyn, John. *Sylva, to which is annexed the Pomona.* London, 1664.

Gerard, John. *Herball* (revised by Thomas Johnson). London, 1633.

Haines, Richard. *Aphorisms upon the new way of improving Cyder, or making Cyder Royal.* London, 1684.

Hanmer, Sir Thomas. *Garden Book*, unpublished 1659; published London, 1933.

Hartlib, Samuel. *Cornucopia.* London, 1652.

Hartlib, Samuel. *A Designe for Plentie, by an Universal Planting of Fruit-trees.* London, 1652.

Hartlib, Samuel. *Discourse of Husbandrie used in Brabant and Flanders.* London, 1645, 1650.

Langford, T. *Plain and Full Instructions to raise all sorts of Fruit Trees.* London, 1681.

Lawson, William. *A New Orchard and Garden.* London, 1618.

Le Gendre. *The Manner of Ordering Fruit Trees* (trans. John Evelyn). London, 1660.

Markham, Gervase. *The English Husbandman.* London, 1613.

Markham, Gervase. *A Way to Get Wealth.* London, 1648.

Meager, Leonard. *The English Gardener.* London, 1670, 1688.

N. F. *The Fruiterer's Secrets.* London, 1604.

Parkinson, John. *Paradisi in Sole.* London, 1629.

Platt, Sir Hugh. *Floraes Paradise.* London, 1608.

de la Quintinye. *The Compleat Gard'ner* (trans. John Evelyn). London, 1693.

Ray, John. *Historia Plantarum generalis.* London, 1686, 1688, 1704.

Rea, John. *Flora, seu de Florum cultura.* London, 1665.

Rea, John. *Flore, Ceres et Pomona.* London, 1676.

Rose, John. *The English Vineyard Vindicated.* London, 1666, 1669.

Taverner, John. *Certaine Experiments concerning Fish and Fruit.* London, 1600.

Temple, W. *The Compleat Planter and Cyderist.* London, 1685.

Williams, Edward. *Virginias discovery of Silk-wormes.* London, 1649.

Worlidge, John. *Systema Agriculturae.* London, 1669, 1675, 1681, 1697.

Worlidge, John. *Vinetum Britannicum.* London, 1676, 1678, 1691.

EIGHTEENTH CENTURY

Abercrombie, John. *The British Fruit-gardener.* London, 1779.

Abercrombie, John and Mawe, Thomas. *Every Man his own Gardener.* London, 1767, 1839.

Barnes, Thomas. *Flora Anglicana. A New Method of Propagating Fruit Trees.* London, 1758.

Boys, John. *General View of the Agriculture of the County of Kent.* Board of Agriculture, 1794.

Bradley, Richard. *A General Treatise of Husbandry and Gardening.* London, 1726.

Bradley, Richard. *The Gentleman and Gardener's Kalendar.* London, 1718.

Bradley, Richard. *A Survey of Ancient Husbandry and Gardening.* London, 1725.

Bucknall, Thomas Skip Dyot. *The Orchardist.* London, 1797, 1805.

Bradley, Richard. *New Improvements of Planting and Gardening.* London, 1739.

Clark, John. *General View of the Agriculture of the County of Hereford.* Board of Agriculture, 1794.

Collins, Samuel. *Paradise Retrieved.* London, 1717.

Cowell, John. *The Curious Fruit Gardener.* London, 1732.

Driver, Abraham and Driver, William. *General View of the Agriculture of the County of Hampshire.* Board of Agriculture, 1794.

Driver, William. *Pomona Britannica.* London, 1788.

Duchesne, A. N. *Histoire Naturelle des Fraisiers.* Paris, 1766.

Ellis, William. *The Compleat Cyderman.* London, 1754.

Fiennes, Celia. *Journeys, 1685–1703.* London, 1947.

Frézier, Capt. A. F. *Relation du Voyage de la Mer du Sud aux Côtes du Chily et du Perou, fait pendant les années 1712, 1713 et 1714.* Paris, 1716.

Furber, Robert. *Twelve Months of Fruits.* London, 1732.

Gibson, John. *The Fruit Gardener.* London, 1768.

Hitt, T. A. *A Treatise of Fruit-trees.* London, 1755, 1757.

Knight, Thomas Andrew. *A Treatise on the culture of the Apple and Pear and on the manufacture of Cyder and Perry.* London, 1797, 1809.

Kyle, Thomas. *Catalogue of Plants sold by Luker and Smith.* London, 1777.

Langley, Batty. *Pomona or the Fruit Garden Illustrated.* London, 1729.

Le Brocq. *A description with notes — of planting fruit trees.* London, 1786.

Locke, John. *Observations upon the growth and culture of vines.* London, 1766.

Loddige, Conrad. *Catalogue of Plants and Seeds sold by C. L. at Hackney.* London, 1777.

Marshall, William. *Rural Economy of the West of England,* vols 1 and 2. London, 1796.

Miller, Philip. *The Gardener's Dictionary.* London, 1731.

Miller, Philip. *The Gardener's Kalendar.* London, 1732.

Speechly, William. *Treatise on the Culture of Vines.* London, 1790.

Stafford, Hugh. *A Treatise of Cyder Making.* London, 1755.

Switzer, Stephen. *The Nobleman, Gentleman and Gardener's Recreation.* London, 1715.

Switzer, Stephen. *The Practical Fruit Gardener.* London, 1724.

Trowel, Samuel. *Farmer's Instructor.* London, 1747.

Vispre, Francois. *Dissertation on the Growth of Wine in England.* London, 1786.

Walpole, Horace. *Journey into England.* London, 1757.

Weston, Richard. *Flora Anglicana.* London, 1775–89.

White, Gilbert. *Journals, 1768–1793.* London, 1970.

White, Gilbert. *The Natural History of Selborne.* London, 1971.

Wilson, William. *A Treatise on Forcing Early Fruits.* London, 1777.

Woodforde, James. *The Diary of a Country Parson, 1758—1802.* Oxford, 1978.
Young, Arthur. *A six weeks tour through Southern counties.* London, 1767.

Nineteenth Century

Bliss, G. *The Fruit Grower's Instructor.* London, 1825.
Brehaut, Rev. Collings T, and Rivers, Thomas. *The Modern Peach Pruner and Variations from Seed.* London, 1866.
Brookshaw, George. *Pomona Britannica.* London, 1812.
Bunyard, George. *Fruit Farming for Profit.* Maidstone, 1881, 1890.
Caledonian Horticultural Society. *Journal of a Horticultural Tour through Flanders, Holland and North France in 1817.* Edinburgh, 1823.
Cobbet, William. *The English Gardener.* London, 1829.
Cooke, C. W. Radcliffe. *A Book about Cider and Perry.* London, 1898.
Downing, A. J. *The Fruits and Fruit Trees of America.* New York, 1857.
Fish, D. T. *The Gooseberry and Currant. Their History, Varieties and Cultivation.* London, 1882.
Fish, D. T. *The Raspberry and Strawberry. Their History, Varieties and Cultivation.* London, 1882.
Forsyth, William. *Culture and Management of Fruit Trees.* London, 1802, 1806, 1824.
Fuller, Andrew. *Woodward's Record of Horticulture.* London, 1867.
Haynes, Thomas. *Improved Culture of Strawberries etc.* London, 1812.
Haynes, T. *Treatise of the Improved Culture of the Strawberry, Raspberry and Gooseberry.* London, 1812.
Hayward, Joseph. *The Science of Horticulture.* London, 1818.
Hogg, Robert. *The Apples and Pears as Vintage Fruits.* London, 1886.
Hogg, Robert. *British Pomology.* London, 1851.
Hogg, Robert. *The Fruit Manual.* London, 1860, 1866, 1874, 1875.
Hogg, Robert. *Herefordshire Pomona.* London, 1876—85.
Hooker, Sir William. *Outlines of a General History of Gardening.* London, 1821.
Hooker, William. *Pomona Londoniensis.* London, 1818.
Horticultural Society. Notice of new or remarkable varieties of fruits. *Transactions V,* pp. 260—2. London, 1824.
Horticultural Society. *Catalogue of Fruit in the Society's Garden at Chiswick.* London, 1826, 1827 and 1832.
House of Commons. *Report of a Committee on the Fresh Fruit Trade.* London, 1839.
Johnson, George William and Reid, R. *The Strawberry, its Culture and History.* London, 1847.
Keens, Michael. An account of a new strawberry. *Horticultural Society Transactions II* pp. 101—2. London, 1817.
Knight, Thomas Andrew. Letter respecting his strawberry breeding. *Horticultural Society Transactions III* pp. 207—10. London, 1820.
Lindley, John. *A Guide to the Orchard and Kitchen Garden.* London, 1831.

Lindley, John. *The Pomological Magazine, varieties of fruits grown in England.* London, 1828.

Loudon, John Claudius. *The Encyclopaedia of Gardening.* London, 1822, 1834.

Marshall, William. *Review and Abstract of the County Reports of the Board of Agriculture Southern and Peninsular Departments.* York, 1818.

Marshall, William. *Review and Abstract of the County Reports of the Board of Agriculture Western Department.* York, 1818.

Miller, Philip. *The Gardener's Dictionary* (revised by Martyn, Thomas). London, 1807.

Phillips, Henry. *Pomarium Britannicum.* London, 1820, 1827.

Phillips, Leonard. *A Catalogue of Fruit Trees for sale.* London, 1814.

Pitt, W. *General View of the Agriculture of the County of Worcester.* London, 1813.

Rivers, Thomas. *The Minature Fruit Garden.* London, 1865.

Robinson, W. *The Parks, Promenades and Gardens of Paris.* London, 1869.

Royal Horticultural Society. *Report of the Great Apple Exhibition.* London, 1883.

Royal Horticultural Society. *Report of National Apple and Pear Conference.* London, 1888.

Salisbury, William. *Hints to the Proprietors of Orchards.* London, 1816.

Scott, J. *The Orchardists.* London, 1868.

Speechley, W. *Practical Hints in Domestic Rural Economy.* London, 1820.

Vancouver, Charles. *General View of the Agriculture of the County of Devon.* London, 1808.

Walpole, Horace. *Observations on Modern Gardening.* London, 1801.

Wright, John. *Profitable Fruit-growing.* London, 1896.

Young, Arthur. *General View of the Agriculture of the County of Hertfordshire.* London, 1804.

TWENTIETH CENTURY

Allan, Mea. *The Tradescants (1570– 1662).* London, 1964.

Bagenal, N. B. *Fruit Growing.* London, 1939.

Bedford, Duke of and Pickering, S. *Science and Fruitgrowing.* London, 1919.

Brooke, Justin. *Peach Orchards in England.* London, 1947.

Brooke, Justin. *Peaches, Apricots and other Stone Fruits.* London, 1951.

Bunyard, Edward A. *A Handbook of Hardy Fruits. Apples and Pears.* London, 1920.

Bunyard, Edward A. *A Handbook of Hardy Fruits. Stone and Bush Fruits, Nuts etc.* London, 1925.

Bunyard, Edward A. History and development of strawberries. *Journal of the Royal Horticultural Society* 39 (1913), pp. 541–52.

Bunyard, G. and Thomas, O. *The Fruit Garden.* London, 1904.

Childers, Norman Franklin. *Modern Fruit Science.* New Jersey, 1961.

East Malling Research Station Reports.

Fleming, Lawrence and Gore, Alan. *The English Garden.* London, 1979.

Grubb, Norman H. *Cherries.* London, 1949.

Hall, Sir A. Daniel and Crane, M. B. *The Apple*. London, 1933.

Hatton, R. G. Results of Researches on Fruit Tree Stocks. *Journal of Pomology*, **II** No. 1. November 1920.

Hatton, R. G. Suggestions for the Right Selection of Apple Stocks. *Journal of the Royal Horticultural Society*, XLV Parts II and III, 1920.

Hedrick, U. P. *Cyclopedia of Hardy Fruits*. New York, 1922.

Hedrick, U. P. *The Peaches of New York*. New York, 1917.

Hedrick, U. P. *The Pears of New York*. New York, 1921.

Hedrick, U. P. *The Small Fruits of New York*. New York, 1925.

Hooper, Cecil H. *Fruit Farming*. London, 1921.

Hyams, Edward. *The Grape Vine in England*. London, 1949.

Hyams, Edward and Jackson, A. A. *The Orchard and Fruit Garden*. London, 1961.

John Innes Institute of Horticulture Reports.

Long Ashton Research Station Reports.

Luckwill, L. C. and Pollard, A. *Perry Pears*. University of Bristol, 1963.

Ministry of Agriculture, Fisheries and Food. *Bulletins of Fruit, Reports of National Fruit Trials*, Brogdale, Faversham, Kent.

Oldham, Charles H. *The Cultivation of Berried Fruits in Great Britain*. London, 1946.

Royal Horticultural Society. *Apples and Pears. Report of the Conference held in 1934*. London, 1935.

Royal Horticultural Society. *Cherries and Soft Fruits. Report of the Conference held in 1935*. London, 1935.

Royal Horticultural Society. *Dictionary of Gardening*. Oxford, 1956.

Scottish Horticultural Research Institute Reports.

Seabrook, W. P. *Modern Fruit Growing*. London, 1918.

Shoemaker, James Sheldon. *Small-fruit Culture*. New York, 1955.

Smith, Muriel W. G. *National Apple Register of the United Kingdom*. London, 1971.

Sturtevant, E. L. *Notes on Edible Plants*. Edited by V. P. Hedrick. New York, 1919.

Taylor, H. V. *The Apples of England*. London, 1948.

Taylor, H. V. *The Plums of England*. London, 1949.

Wallace, T. and Marsh, R. W. *Science and Fruit*. Bristol, 1953.

Williams, R. R. and Child, R. D. *Cider Apples and their Characters*. Report of the Long Ashton Research Station for 1961, 1962, 1963, 1964, Bristol.

INDEX